CASE CLOSED

VOLUME 7

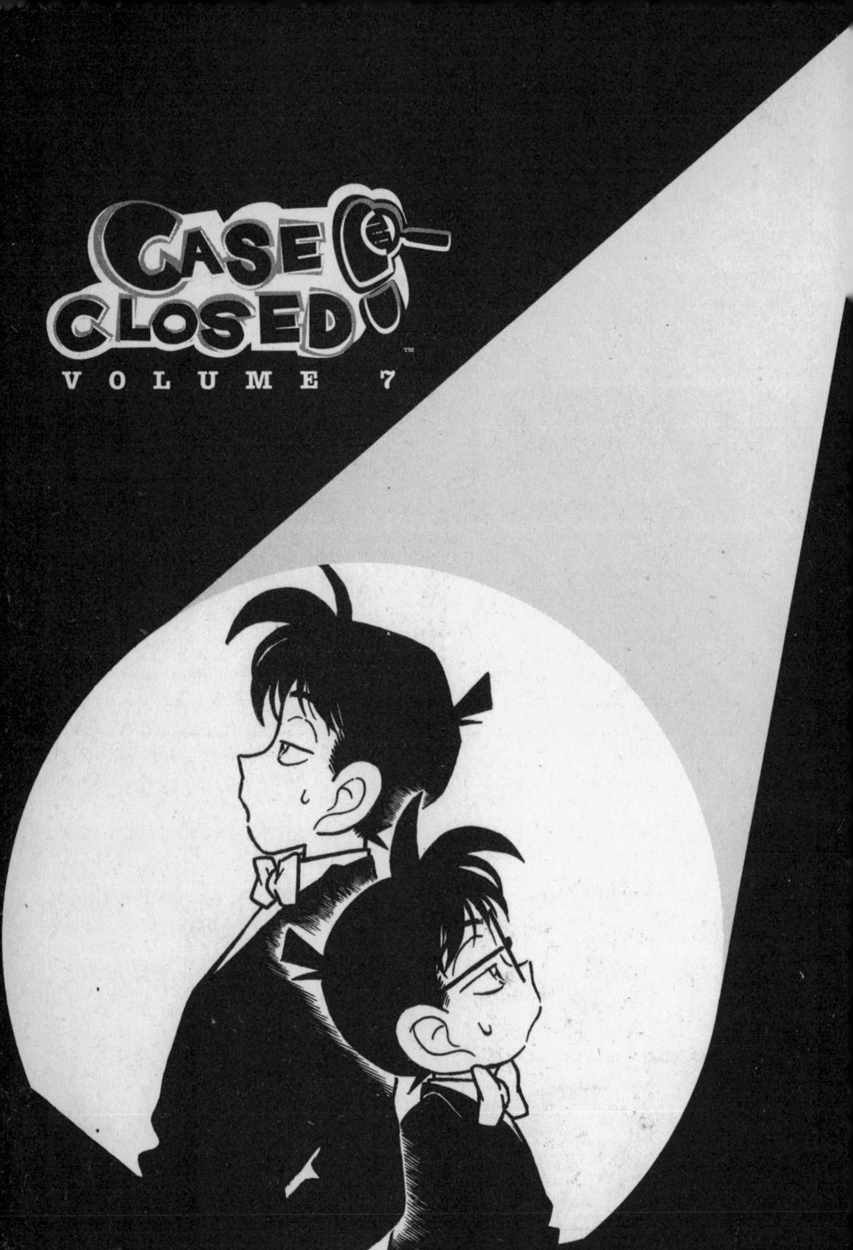

Gosho Aoyama

Case Briefing:

Subject:
Occupation:
Special Skills:
Equipment:

Jimmy Kudo, a.k.a. Conan Edogawa
High School Student/Detective
Analytical thinking and deductive reasoning, Soccer
Bow Tie Voice Transmitter, Super Sneakers,
Homing Glasses, Stretchy Suspenders

The subject is hot on the trail of a pair of suspicious men in black when he is attacked from behind and is administered a strange substance which physically transforms him into a first grader. When the subject confides in the eccentric inventor Dr. Agasa, they decide to keep the subject's true identity a secret for the safety of everyone around him. Assuming the new identity of first-grader Conan Edogawa, the subject continues to assist the police force on their most baffling cases. The only problem is that most crime-solving professionals don't want to listen to a little kid.

Conan, Rachel, and Richard go to the Tenkaichi Festival where they take a picture of a man who turns out to be the prime suspect for a murder! The only problem is that the suspect uses this photograph for a perfect alibi! Will Conan be able to disprove what appears to be irrefutable photographic evidence?

Table of Contents

CASE CLOSED

CONFIDEN

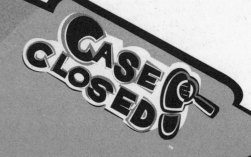

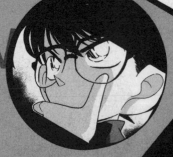

CASE CLOSED

Volume 7 • Action Edition

GOSHO AOYAMA

English Adaptation
Naoko Amemiya

Translation
Joe Yamazaki

Touch-up & Lettering
Walden Wong

Cover & Interior Design
Andrea Rice

Editor
Andy Nakatani

Managing Editor **Annette Roman**
Director of Production **Noboru Watanabe**
Vice President of Publishing **Alvin Lu**
Sr. Director of Acquisitions **Rika Inouye**
Vice President of Sales & Marketing **Liza Coppola**
Publisher **Hyoe Narita**

Printed in the U.S.A.
Published by VIZ Media, LLC
P.O. Box 77010
San Francisco, CA 94107

Action Edition
10 9 8 7 6 5 4 3 2 1
First printing, August 2005

RATED T+ FOR OLDER TEEN

PARENTAL ADVISORY
CASE CLOSED is rated T+ for Older Teen.
Contains realistic and graphic violence.
Recommended for older teens (16 and up).

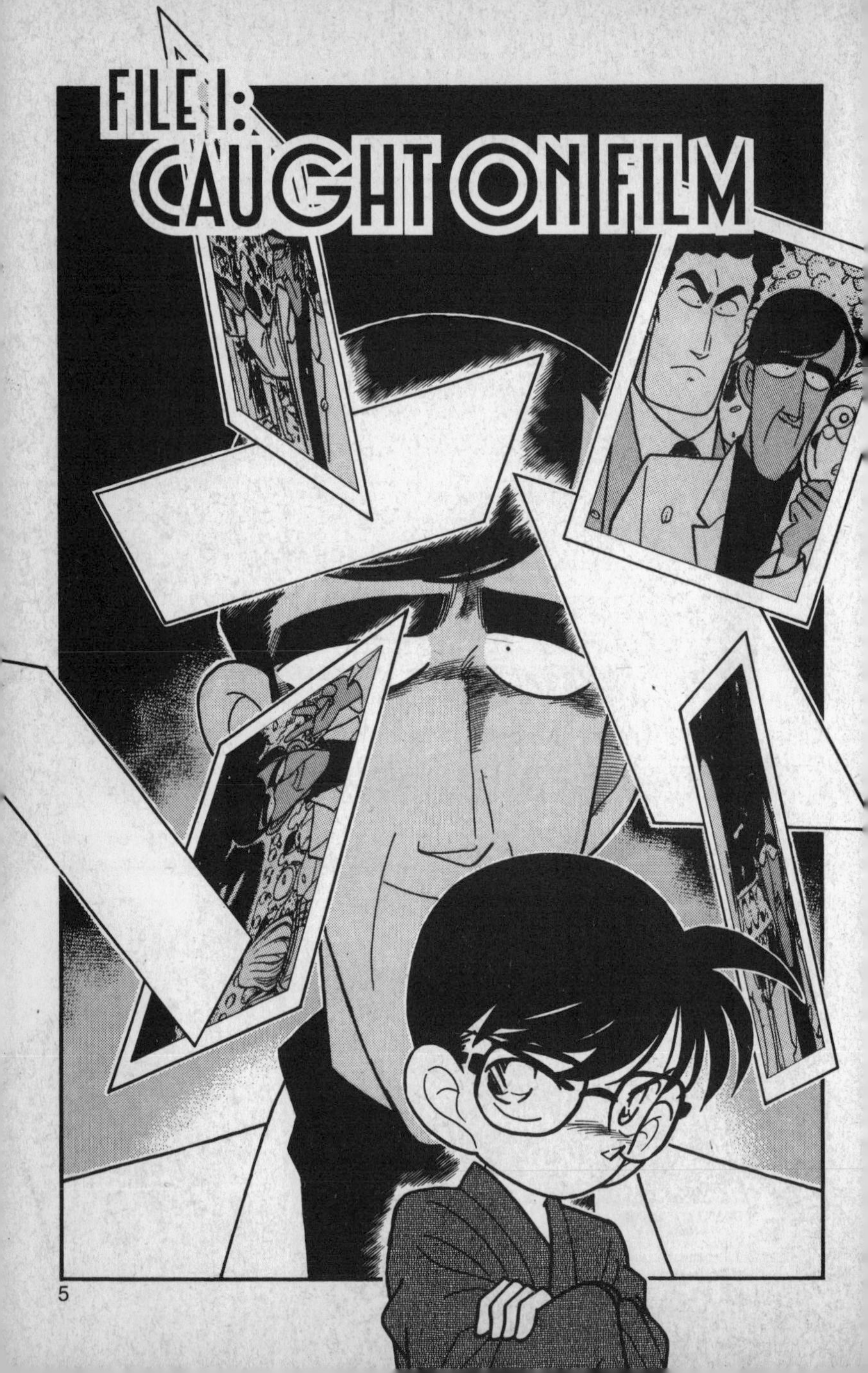
FILE 1:
CAUGHT ON FILM

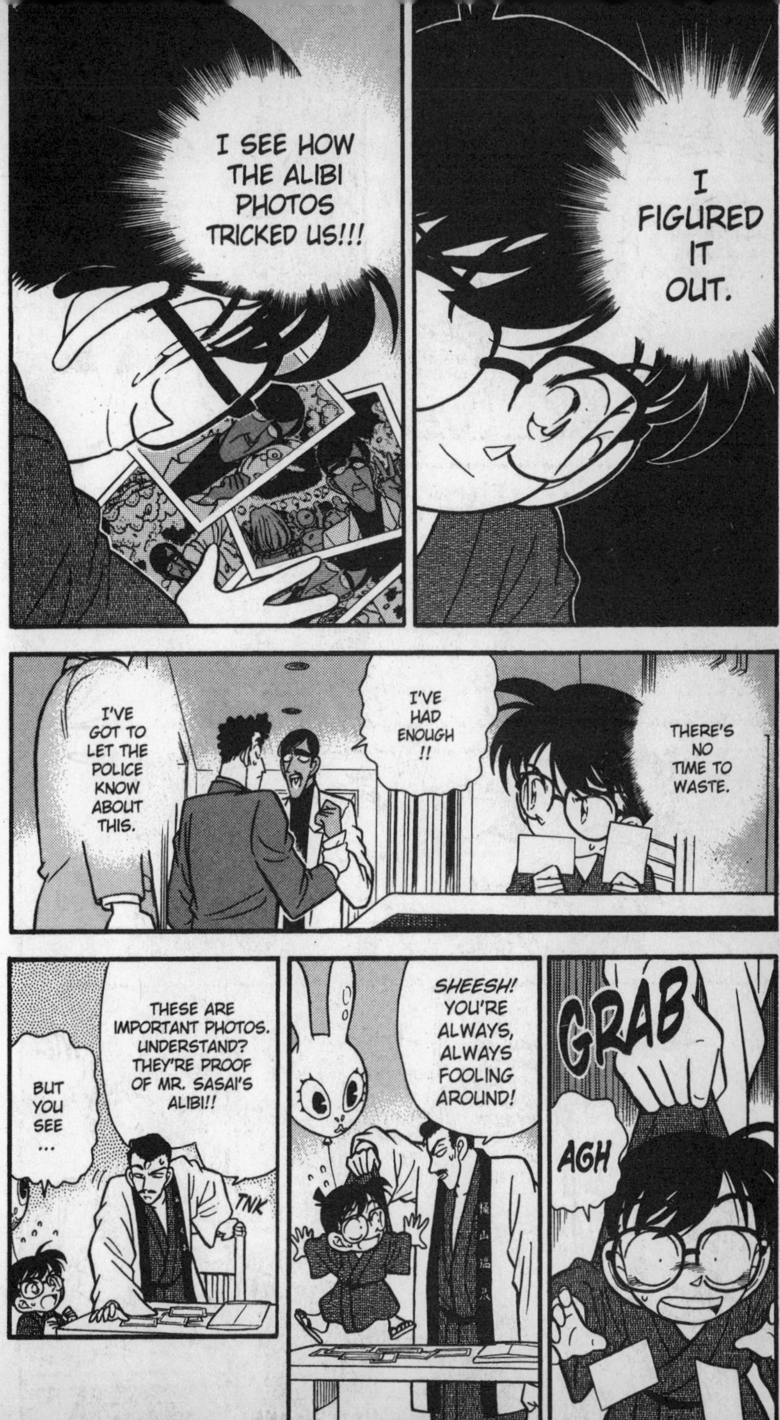
I FIGURED IT OUT.
I SEE HOW THE ALIBI PHOTOS TRICKED US!!!
THERE'S NO TIME TO WASTE.
I'VE HAD ENOUGH !!
I'VE GOT TO LET THE POLICE KNOW ABOUT THIS.
GRAB
AGH
SHEESH! YOU'RE ALWAYS, ALWAYS FOOLING AROUND!
THESE ARE IMPORTANT PHOTOS. UNDERSTAND? THEY'RE PROOF OF MR. SASAI'S ALIBI!!
BUT YOU SEE ...
TNK

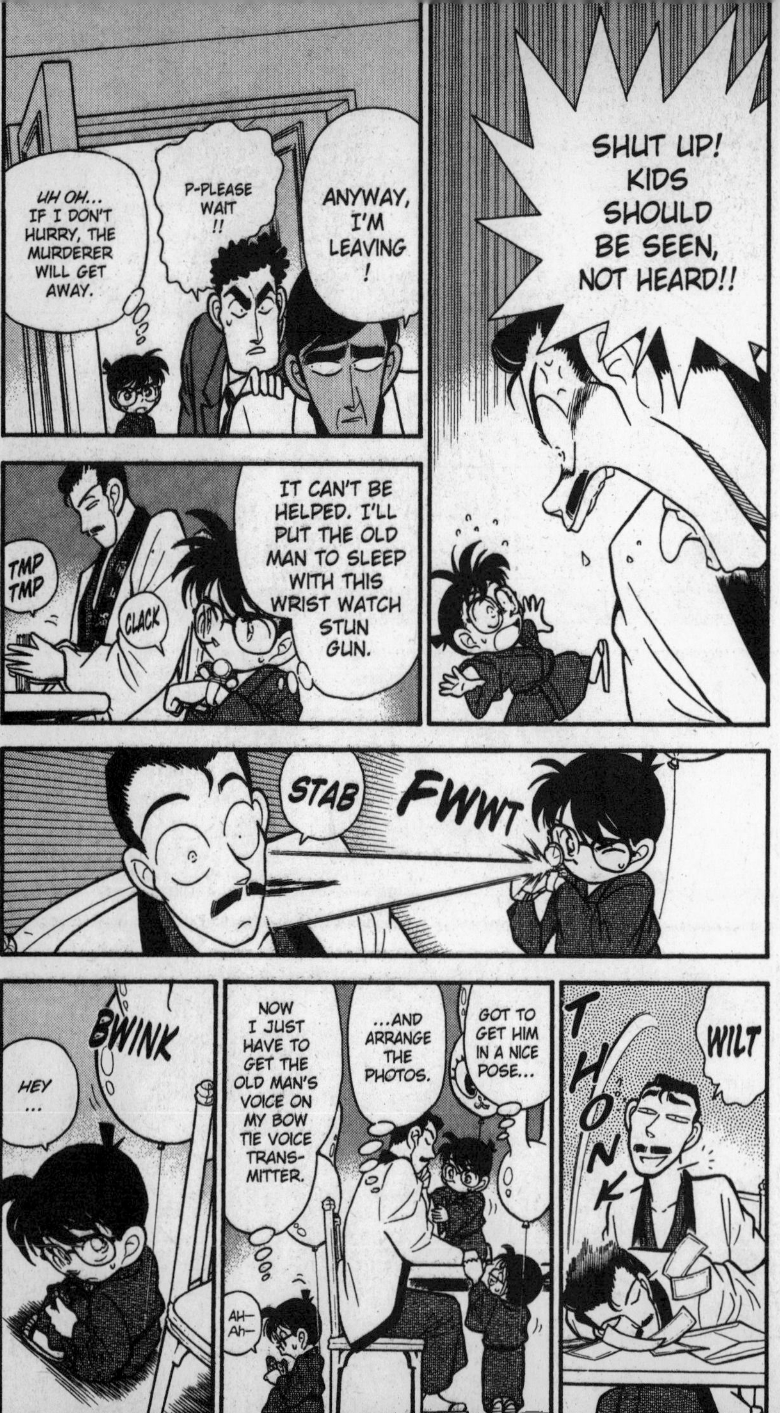
SHUT UP! KIDS SHOULD BE SEEN, NOT HEARD!!
ANYWAY, I'M LEAVING!
P-PLEASE WAIT!!
UH OH... IF I DON'T HURRY, THE MURDERER WILL GET AWAY.
IT CAN'T BE HELPED. I'LL PUT THE OLD MAN TO SLEEP WITH THIS WRIST WATCH STUN GUN.
CLACK
TMP TMP
FWWT
STAB
WILT
THONK
GOT TO GET HIM IN A NICE POSE...
...AND ARRANGE THE PHOTOS.
NOW I JUST HAVE TO GET THE OLD MAN'S VOICE ON MY BOW TIE VOICE TRANS-MITTER.
AH-Ah-
BWINK
HEY...

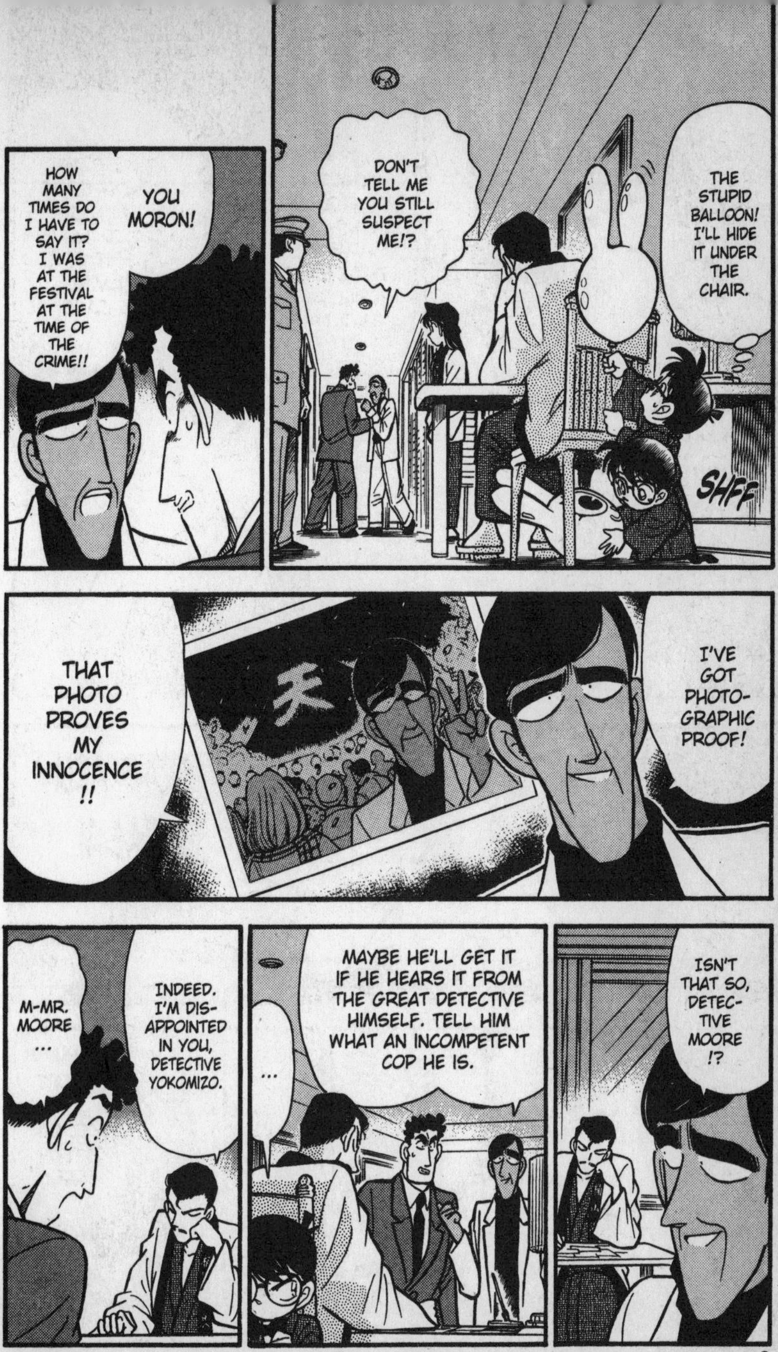
THE STUPID BALLOON! I'LL HIDE IT UNDER THE CHAIR.
DON'T TELL ME YOU STILL SUSPECT ME!?
SHFF
YOU MORON!
HOW MANY TIMES DO I HAVE TO SAY IT? I WAS AT THE FESTIVAL AT THE TIME OF THE CRIME!!
I'VE GOT PHOTO-GRAPHIC PROOF!
THAT PHOTO PROVES MY INNOCENCE!!
ISN'T THAT SO, DETEC-TIVE MOORE!?
MAYBE HE'LL GET IT IF HE HEARS IT FROM THE GREAT DETECTIVE HIMSELF. TELL HIM WHAT AN INCOMPETENT COP HE IS.
...
INDEED. I'M DIS-APPOINTED IN YOU, DETECTIVE YOKOMIZO.
M-MR. MOORE ...

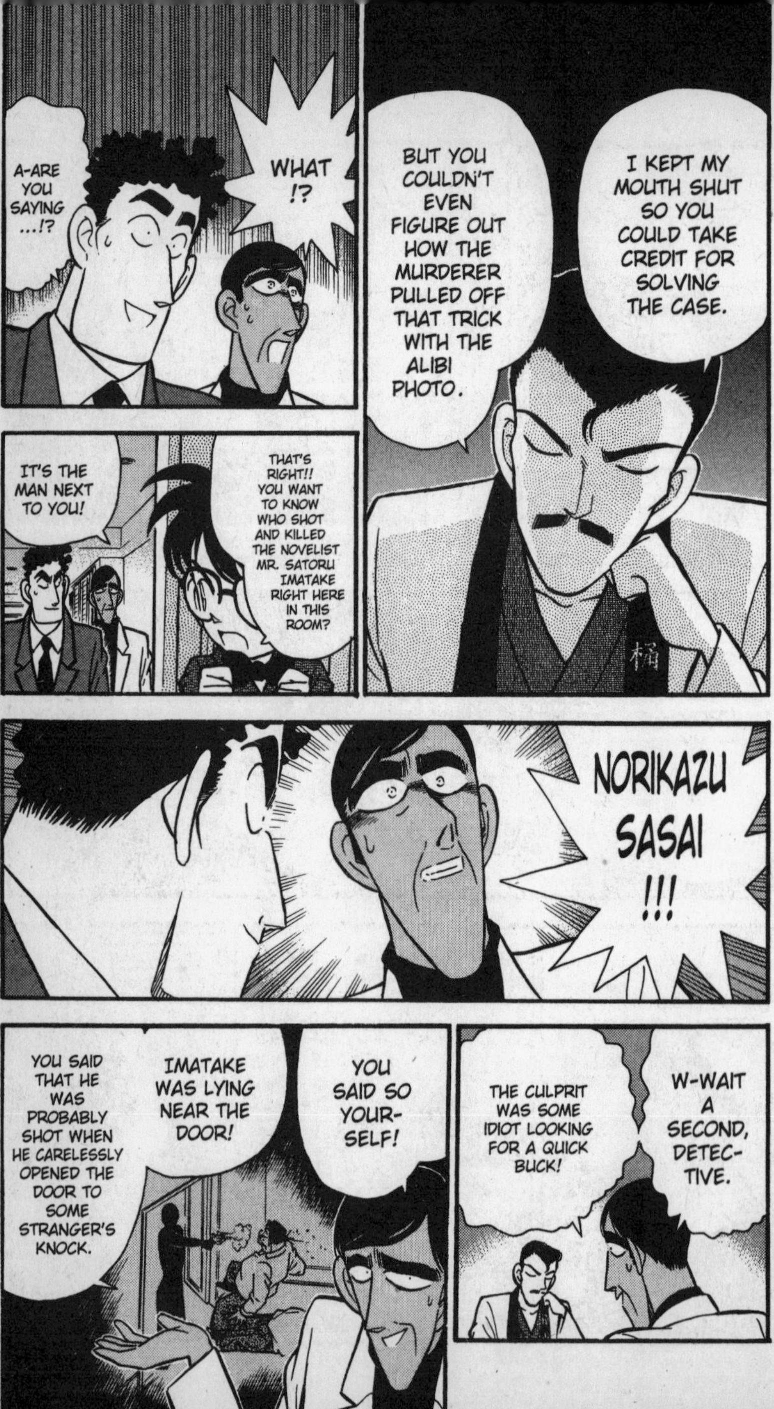
I KEPT MY MOUTH SHUT SO YOU COULD TAKE CREDIT FOR SOLVING THE CASE.
BUT YOU COULDN'T EVEN FIGURE OUT HOW THE MURDERER PULLED OFF THAT TRICK WITH THE ALIBI PHOTO.
WHAT!?
A-ARE YOU SAYING...!?
THAT'S RIGHT!! YOU WANT TO KNOW WHO SHOT AND KILLED THE NOVELIST MR. SATORU IMATAKE RIGHT HERE IN THIS ROOM?
IT'S THE MAN NEXT TO YOU!
NORIKAZU SASAI!!!
W-WAIT A SECOND, DETECTIVE.
THE CULPRIT WAS SOME IDIOT LOOKING FOR A QUICK BUCK!
YOU SAID SO YOURSELF!
IMATAKE WAS LYING NEAR THE DOOR!
YOU SAID THAT HE WAS PROBABLY SHOT WHEN HE CARELESSLY OPENED THE DOOR TO SOME STRANGER'S KNOCK.

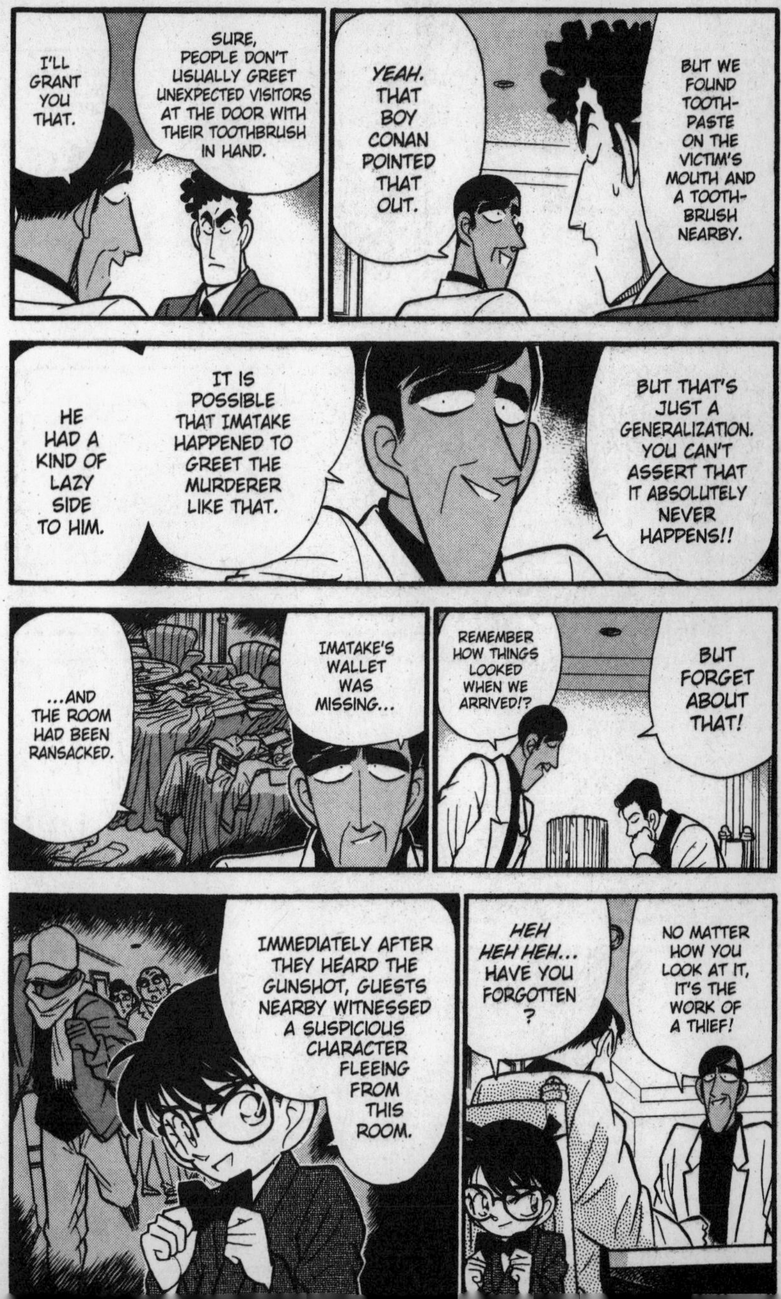
BUT WE FOUND TOOTH-PASTE ON THE VICTIM'S MOUTH AND A TOOTH-BRUSH NEARBY.
YEAH. THAT BOY CONAN POINTED THAT OUT.
SURE, PEOPLE DON'T USUALLY GREET UNEXPECTED VISITORS AT THE DOOR WITH THEIR TOOTHBRUSH IN HAND.
I'LL GRANT YOU THAT.
BUT THAT'S JUST A GENERALIZATION. YOU CAN'T ASSERT THAT IT ABSOLUTELY NEVER HAPPENS!!
IT IS POSSIBLE THAT IMATAKE HAPPENED TO GREET THE MURDERER LIKE THAT.
HE HAD A KIND OF LAZY SIDE TO HIM.
BUT FORGET ABOUT THAT!
REMEMBER HOW THINGS LOOKED WHEN WE ARRIVED!?
IMATAKE'S WALLET WAS MISSING...
...AND THE ROOM HAD BEEN RANSACKED.
NO MATTER HOW YOU LOOK AT IT, IT'S THE WORK OF A THIEF!
HEH HEH HEH... HAVE YOU FORGOTTEN ?
IMMEDIATELY AFTER THEY HEARD THE GUNSHOT, GUESTS NEARBY WITNESSED A SUSPICIOUS CHARACTER FLEEING FROM THIS ROOM.

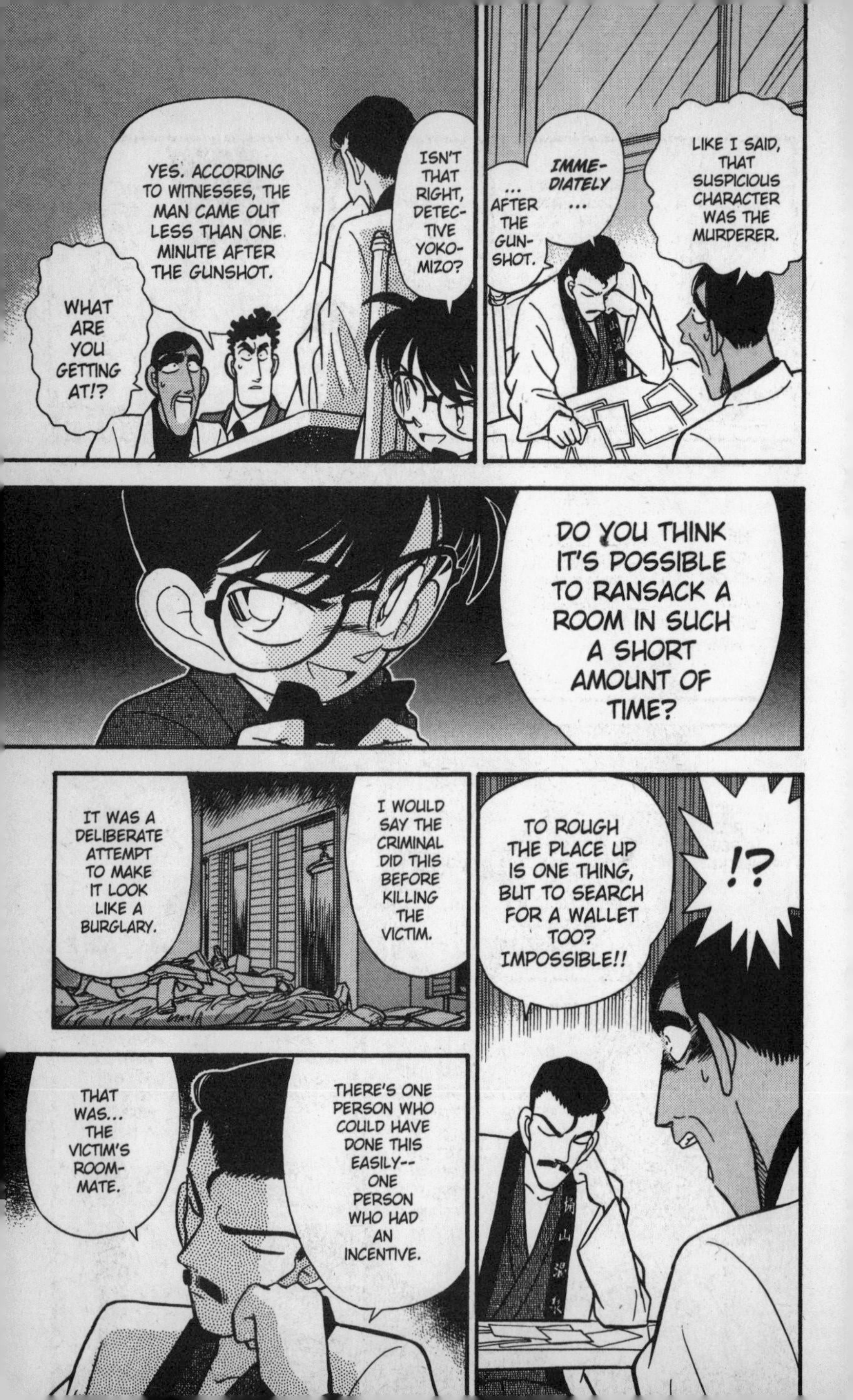
LIKE I SAID, THAT SUSPICIOUS CHARACTER WAS THE MURDERER.
IMMEDIATELY...
...AFTER THE GUNSHOT.
ISN'T THAT RIGHT, DETECTIVE YOKOMIZO?
YES. ACCORDING TO WITNESSES, THE MAN CAME OUT LESS THAN ONE MINUTE AFTER THE GUNSHOT.
WHAT ARE YOU GETTING AT!?
DO YOU THINK IT'S POSSIBLE TO RANSACK A ROOM IN SUCH A SHORT AMOUNT OF TIME?
!?
TO ROUGH THE PLACE UP IS ONE THING, BUT TO SEARCH FOR A WALLET TOO? IMPOSSIBLE!!
I WOULD SAY THE CRIMINAL DID THIS BEFORE KILLING THE VICTIM.
IT WAS A DELIBERATE ATTEMPT TO MAKE IT LOOK LIKE A BURGLARY.
THERE'S ONE PERSON WHO COULD HAVE DONE THIS EASILY-- ONE PERSON WHO HAD AN INCENTIVE.
THAT WAS... THE VICTIM'S ROOMMATE.

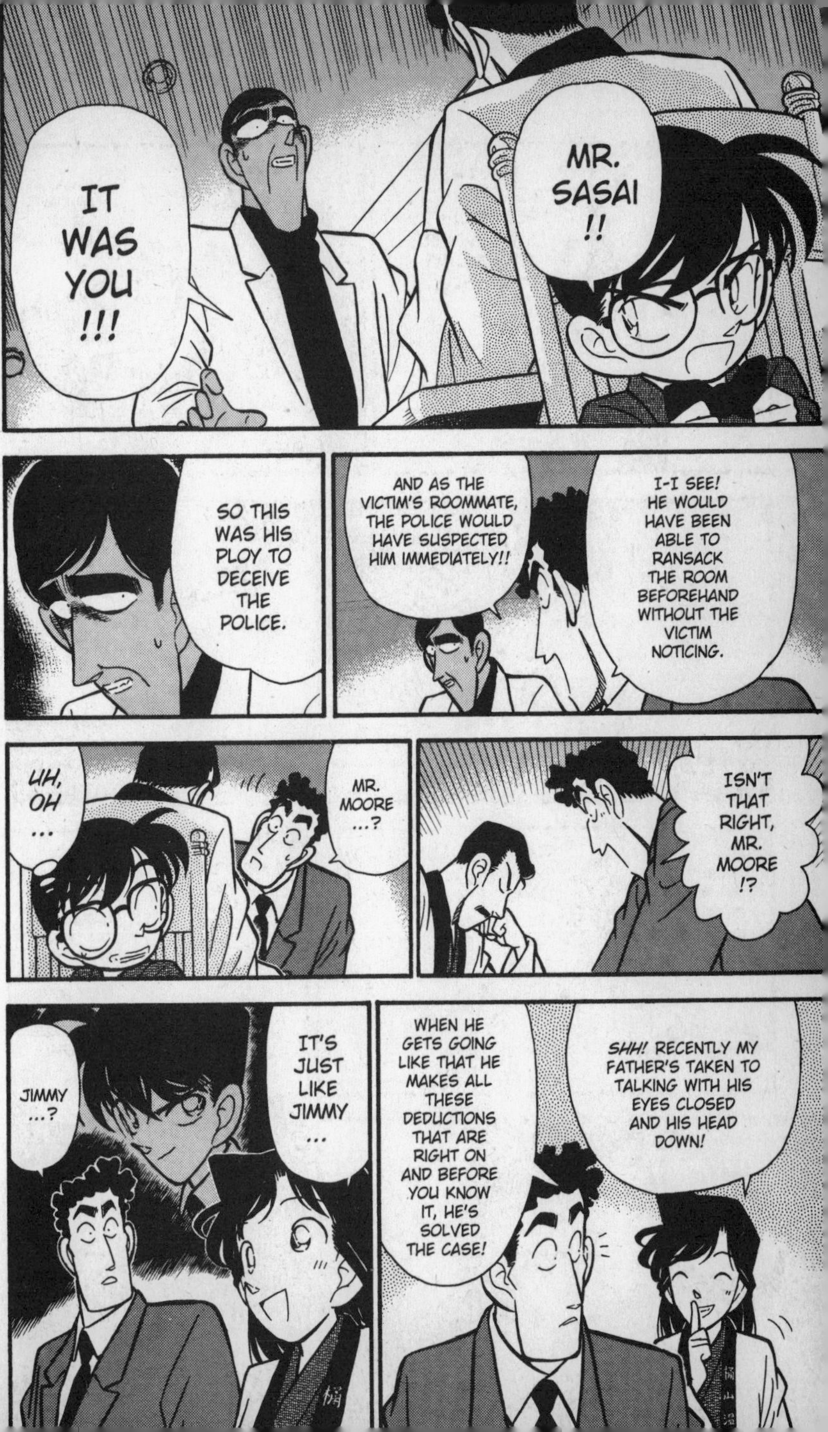
MR. SASAI !!
IT WAS YOU !!!
I-I SEE! HE WOULD HAVE BEEN ABLE TO RANSACK THE ROOM BEFOREHAND WITHOUT THE VICTIM NOTICING.
AND AS THE VICTIM'S ROOMMATE, THE POLICE WOULD HAVE SUSPECTED HIM IMMEDIATELY!!
SO THIS WAS HIS PLOY TO DECEIVE THE POLICE.
ISN'T THAT RIGHT, MR. MOORE !?
MR. MOORE ...?
UH, OH ...
SHH! RECENTLY MY FATHER'S TAKEN TO TALKING WITH HIS EYES CLOSED AND HIS HEAD DOWN!
WHEN HE GETS GOING LIKE THAT HE MAKES ALL THESE DEDUCTIONS THAT ARE RIGHT ON AND BEFORE YOU KNOW IT, HE'S SOLVED THE CASE!
IT'S JUST LIKE JIMMY ...
JIMMY ...?

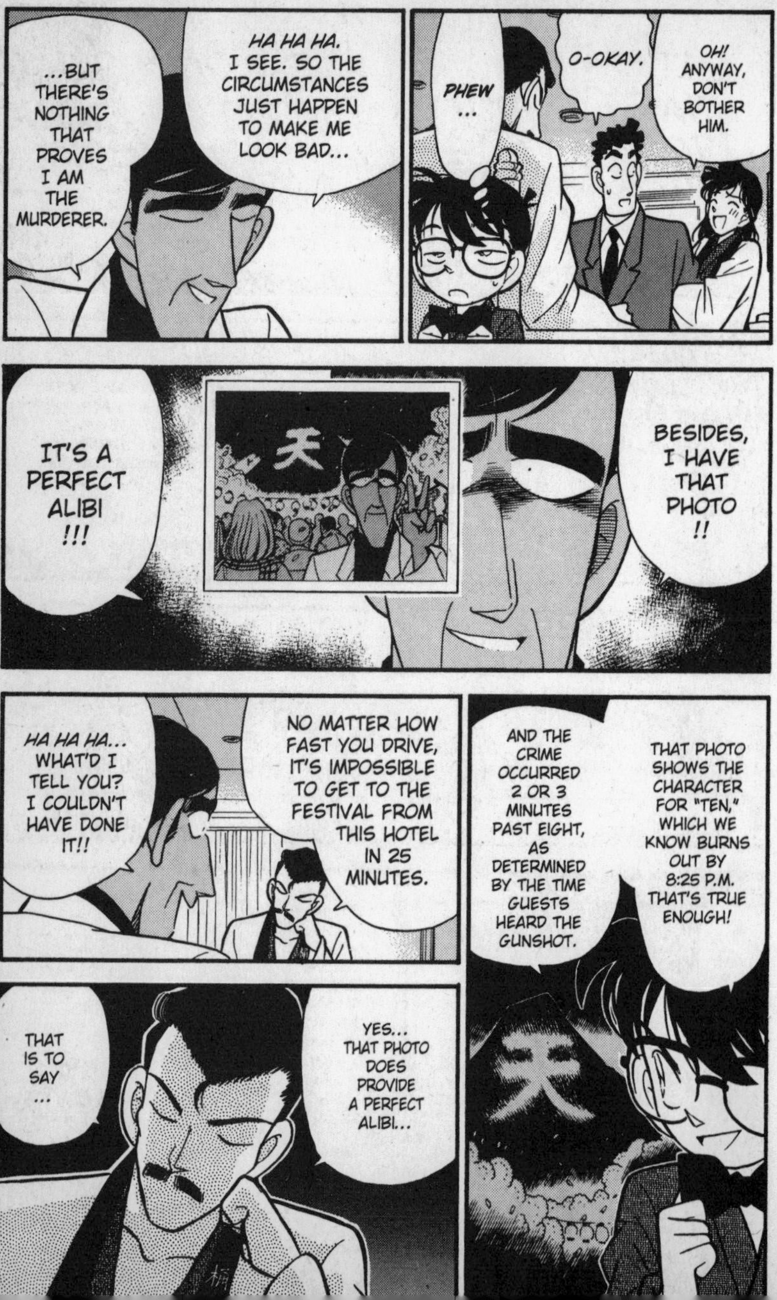
OH! ANYWAY, DON'T BOTHER HIM.
O-OKAY.
PHEW ...
HA HA HA. I SEE. SO THE CIRCUMSTANCES JUST HAPPEN TO MAKE ME LOOK BAD...
...BUT THERE'S NOTHING THAT PROVES I AM THE MURDERER.
BESIDES, I HAVE THAT PHOTO !!
IT'S A PERFECT ALIBI !!!
THAT PHOTO SHOWS THE CHARACTER FOR "TEN," WHICH WE KNOW BURNS OUT BY 8:25 P.M. THAT'S TRUE ENOUGH!
AND THE CRIME OCCURRED 2 OR 3 MINUTES PAST EIGHT, AS DETERMINED BY THE TIME GUESTS HEARD THE GUNSHOT.
NO MATTER HOW FAST YOU DRIVE, IT'S IMPOSSIBLE TO GET TO THE FESTIVAL FROM THIS HOTEL IN 25 MINUTES.
HA HA HA... WHAT'D I TELL YOU? I COULDN'T HAVE DONE IT!!
YES... THAT PHOTO DOES PROVIDE A PERFECT ALIBI...
THAT IS TO SAY ...

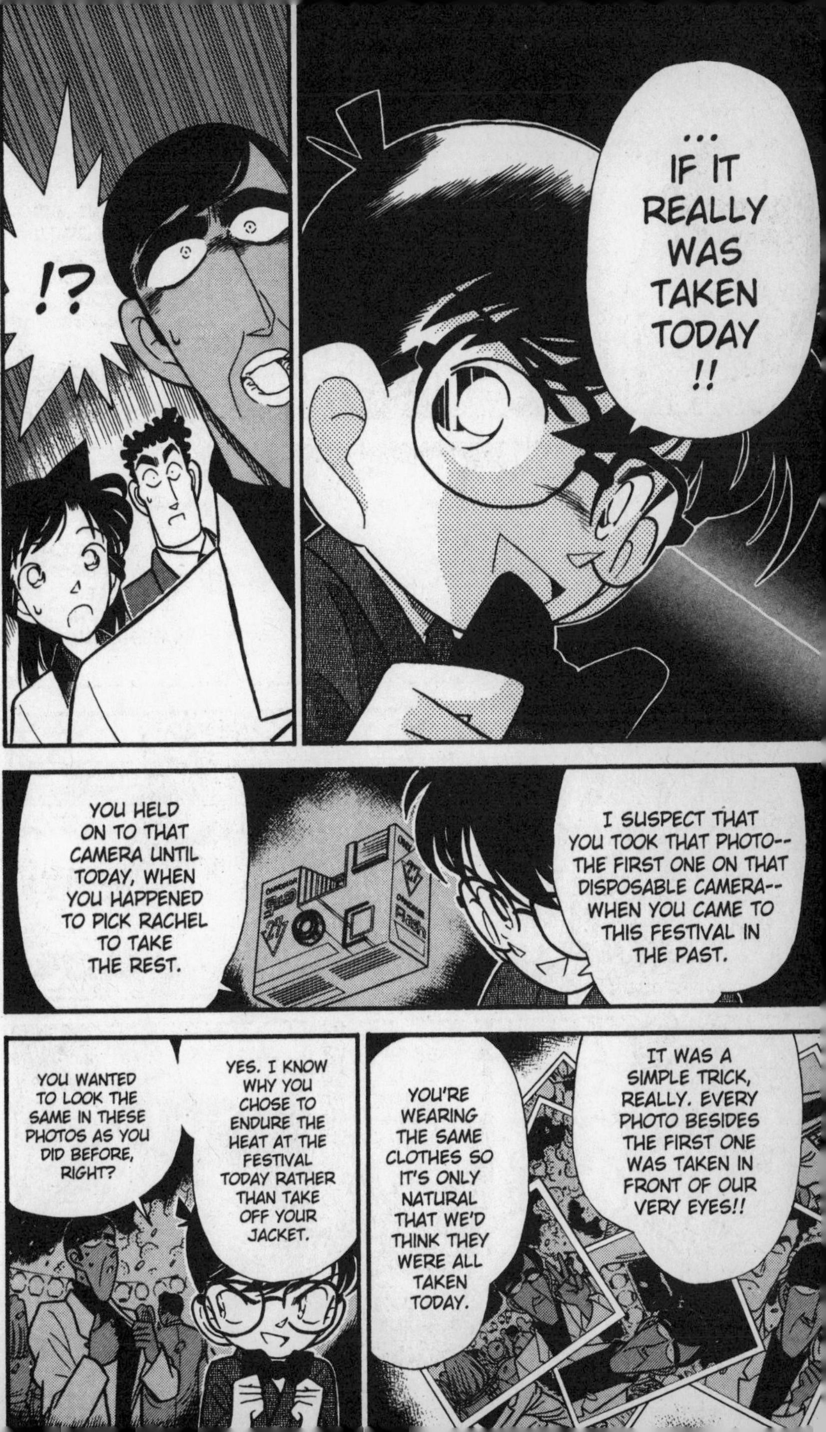
... IF IT REALLY WAS TAKEN TODAY !!
!?
I SUSPECT THAT YOU TOOK THAT PHOTO-- THE FIRST ONE ON THAT DISPOSABLE CAMERA-- WHEN YOU CAME TO THIS FESTIVAL IN THE PAST.
YOU HELD ON TO THAT CAMERA UNTIL TODAY, WHEN YOU HAPPENED TO PICK RACHEL TO TAKE THE REST.
IT WAS A SIMPLE TRICK, REALLY. EVERY PHOTO BESIDES THE FIRST ONE WAS TAKEN IN FRONT OF OUR VERY EYES!!
YOU'RE WEARING THE SAME CLOTHES SO IT'S ONLY NATURAL THAT WE'D THINK THEY WERE ALL TAKEN TODAY.
YES. I KNOW WHY YOU CHOSE TO ENDURE THE HEAT AT THE FESTIVAL TODAY RATHER THAN TAKE OFF YOUR JACKET.
YOU WANTED TO LOOK THE SAME IN THESE PHOTOS AS YOU DID BEFORE, RIGHT?

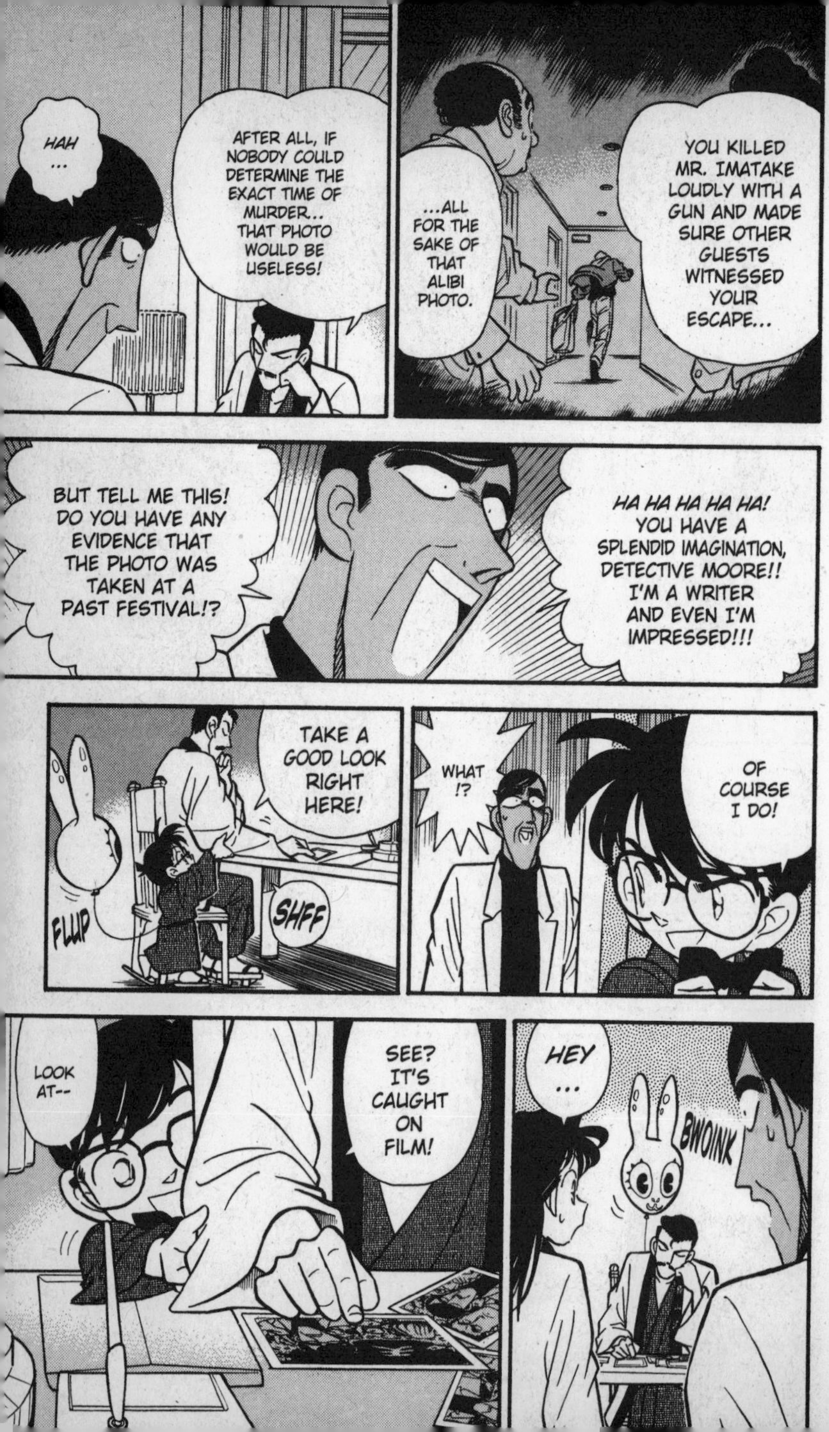
YOU KILLED MR. IMATAKE LOUDLY WITH A GUN AND MADE SURE OTHER GUESTS WITNESSED YOUR ESCAPE...
...ALL FOR THE SAKE OF THAT ALIBI PHOTO.
AFTER ALL, IF NOBODY COULD DETERMINE THE EXACT TIME OF MURDER... THAT PHOTO WOULD BE USELESS!
HAH ...
HA HA HA HA HA! YOU HAVE A SPLENDID IMAGINATION, DETECTIVE MOORE!! I'M A WRITER AND EVEN I'M IMPRESSED!!!
BUT TELL ME THIS! DO YOU HAVE ANY EVIDENCE THAT THE PHOTO WAS TAKEN AT A PAST FESTIVAL!?
OF COURSE I DO!
WHAT !?
TAKE A GOOD LOOK RIGHT HERE!
SHFF
FLUP
HEY ...
BWOINK
SEE? IT'S CAUGHT ON FILM!
LOOK AT--

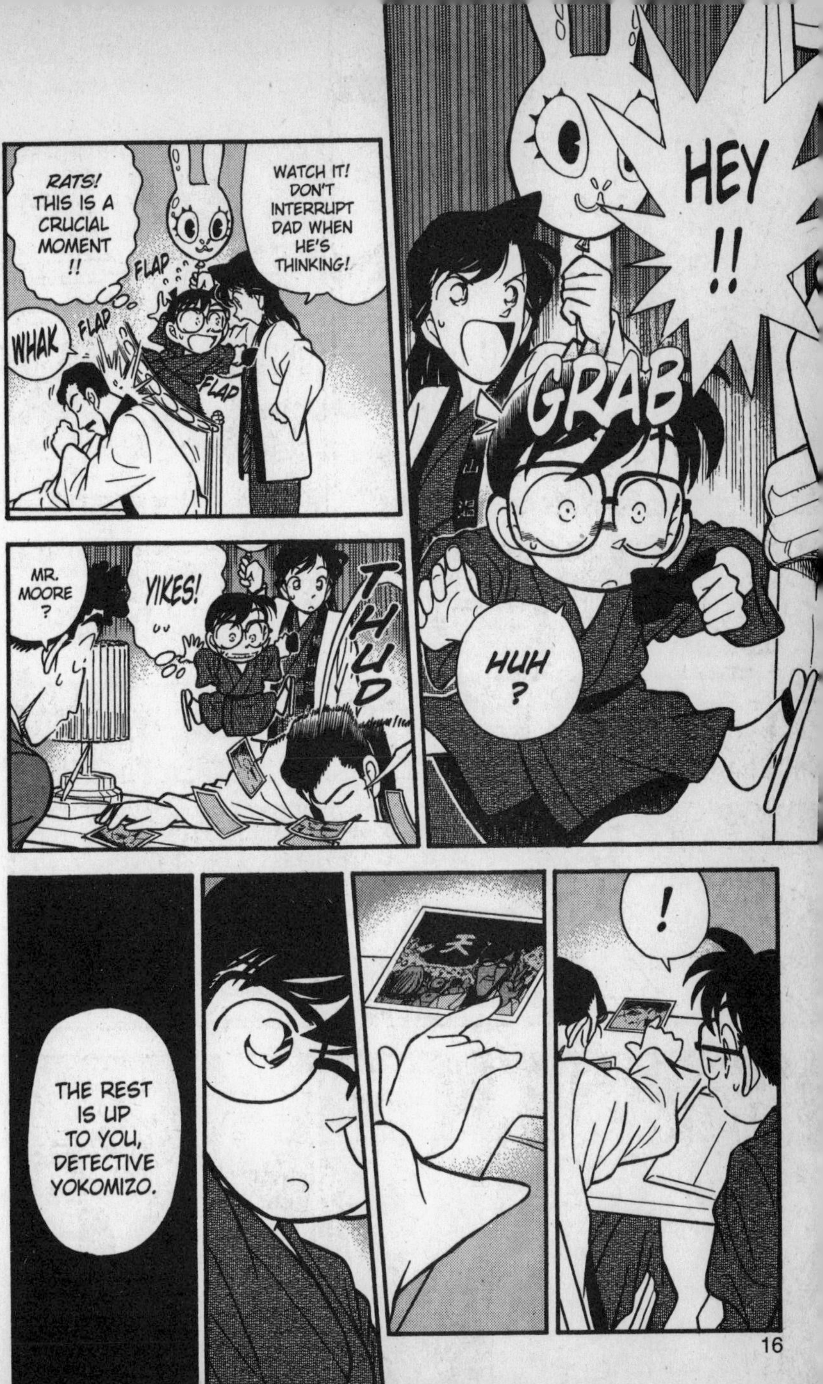
HEY !!
GRAB
HUH ?
WATCH IT! DON'T INTERRUPT DAD WHEN HE'S THINKING!
RATS! THIS IS A CRUCIAL MOMENT !!
FLAP
WHAK
FLAP
FLAP
THUD
YIKES!
MR. MOORE ?
!
THE REST IS UP TO YOU, DETECTIVE YOKOMIZO.

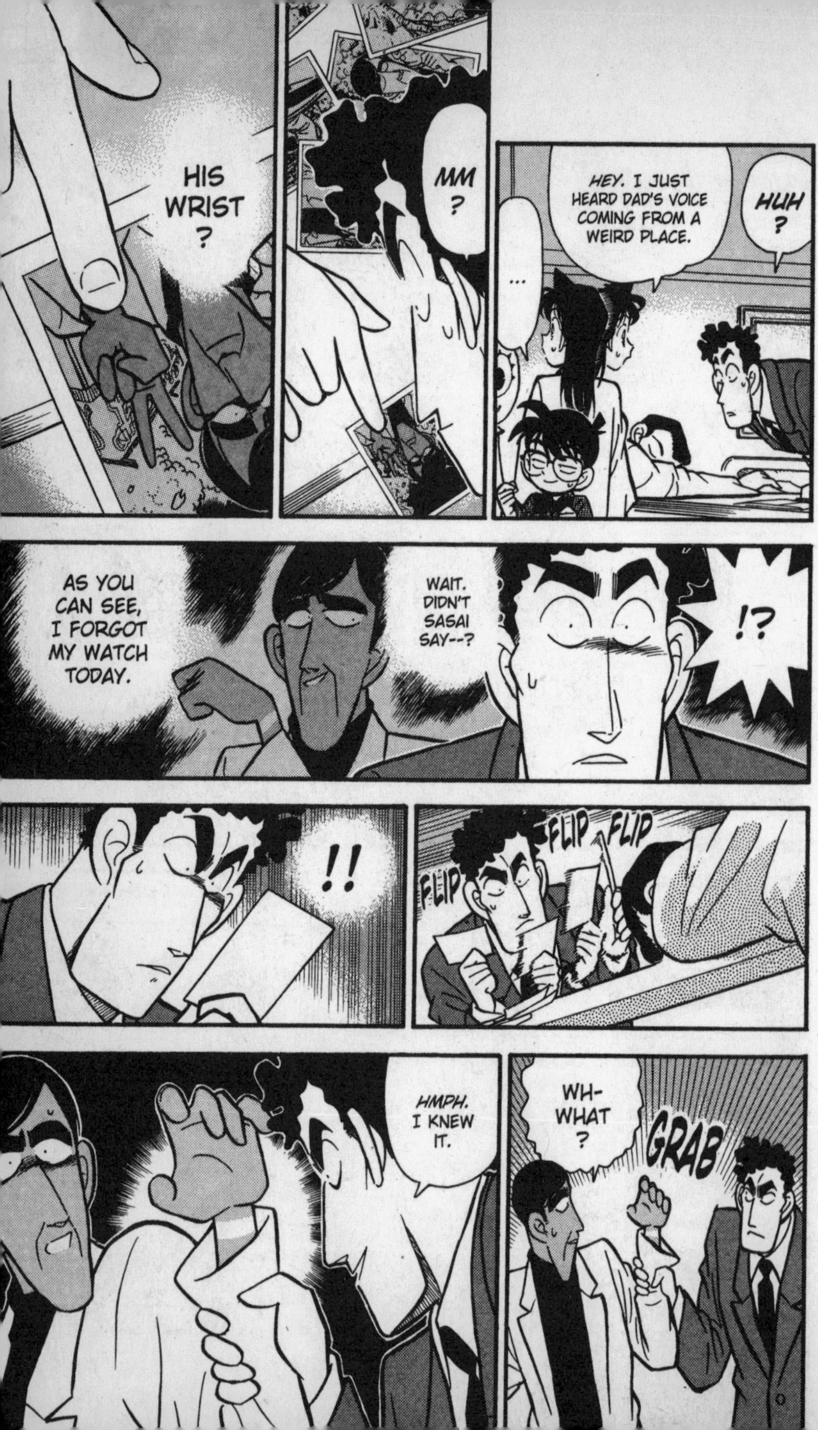

HUH ?
HEY. I JUST HEARD DAD'S VOICE COMING FROM A WEIRD PLACE.
...
MM ?
HIS WRIST ?
!?
WAIT. DIDN'T SASAI SAY--?
AS YOU CAN SEE, I FORGOT MY WATCH TODAY.
FLIP FLIP
FLIP
!!
WH-WHAT ?
GRAB
HMPH. I KNEW IT.

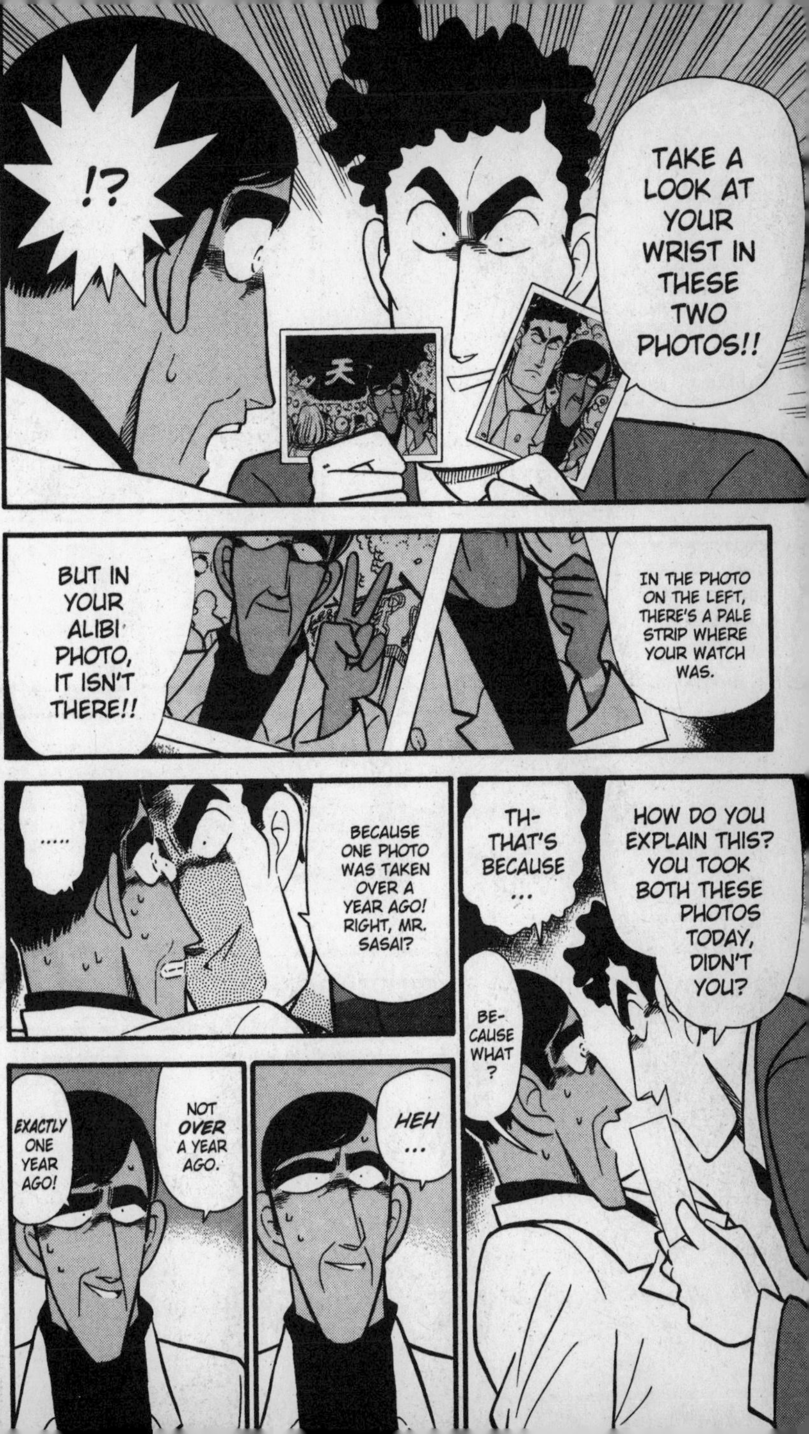
TAKE A LOOK AT YOUR WRIST IN THESE TWO PHOTOS!!
!?
天
IN THE PHOTO ON THE LEFT, THERE'S A PALE STRIP WHERE YOUR WATCH WAS.
BUT IN YOUR ALIBI PHOTO, IT ISN'T THERE!!
HOW DO YOU EXPLAIN THIS? YOU TOOK BOTH THESE PHOTOS TODAY, DIDN'T YOU?
TH-THAT'S BECAUSE ...
BE-CAUSE WHAT ?
BECAUSE ONE PHOTO WAS TAKEN OVER A YEAR AGO! RIGHT, MR. SASAI?
.....
HEH ...
NOT OVER A YEAR AGO.
EXACTLY ONE YEAR AGO!

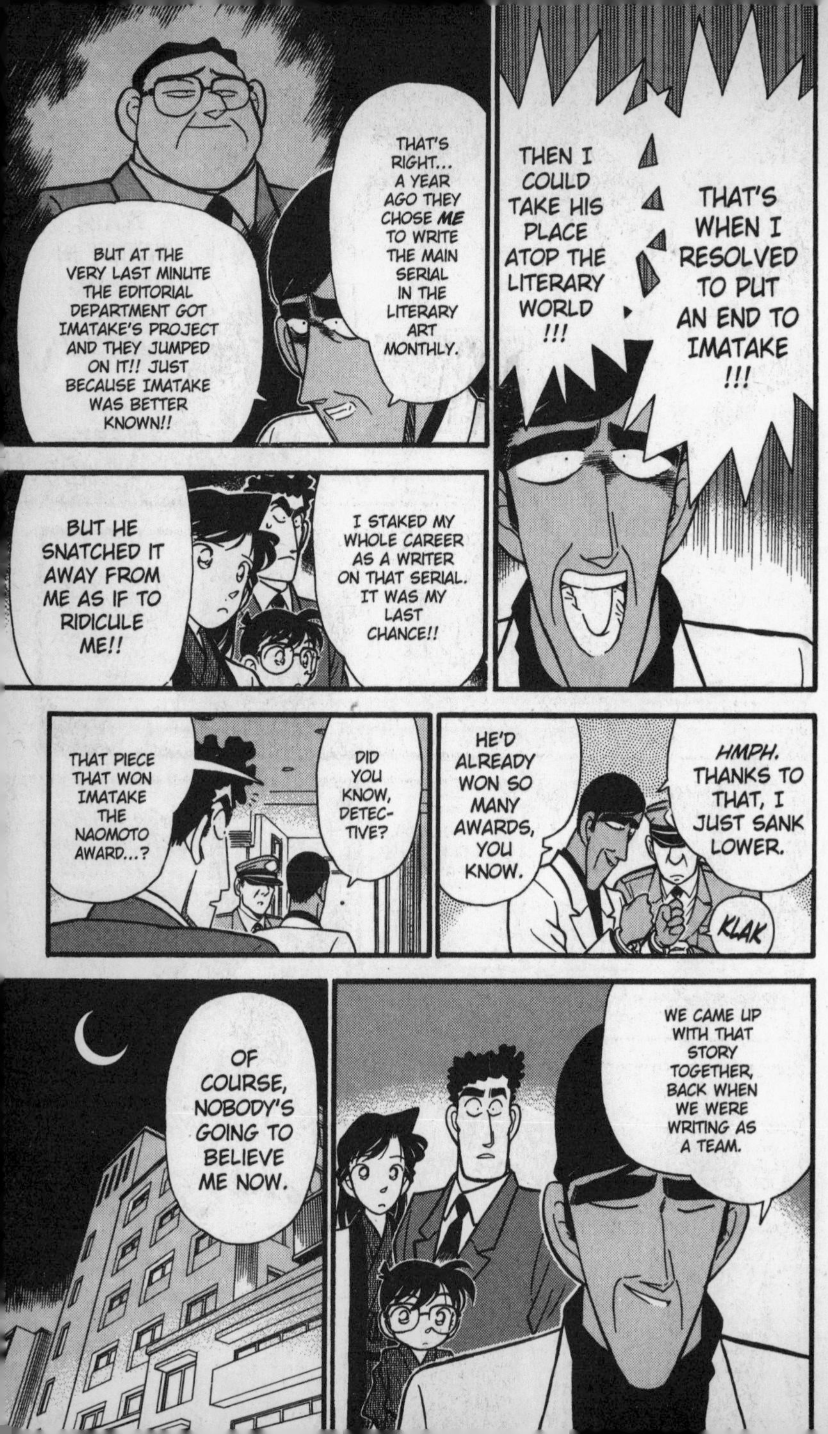
THAT'S WHEN I RESOLVED TO PUT AN END TO IMATAKE !!!
THEN I COULD TAKE HIS PLACE ATOP THE LITERARY WORLD !!!
THAT'S RIGHT... A YEAR AGO THEY CHOSE *ME* TO WRITE THE MAIN SERIAL IN THE LITERARY ART MONTHLY.
BUT AT THE VERY LAST MINUTE THE EDITORIAL DEPARTMENT GOT IMATAKE'S PROJECT AND THEY JUMPED ON IT!! JUST BECAUSE IMATAKE WAS BETTER KNOWN!!
I STAKED MY WHOLE CAREER AS A WRITER ON THAT SERIAL. IT WAS MY LAST CHANCE!!
BUT HE SNATCHED IT AWAY FROM ME AS IF TO RIDICULE ME!!
HMPH. THANKS TO THAT, I JUST SANK LOWER.
HE'D ALREADY WON SO MANY AWARDS, YOU KNOW.
KLAK
DID YOU KNOW, DETECTIVE?
THAT PIECE THAT WON IMATAKE THE NAOMOTO AWARD...?
WE CAME UP WITH THAT STORY TOGETHER, BACK WHEN WE WERE WRITING AS A TEAM.
OF COURSE, NOBODY'S GOING TO BELIEVE ME NOW.

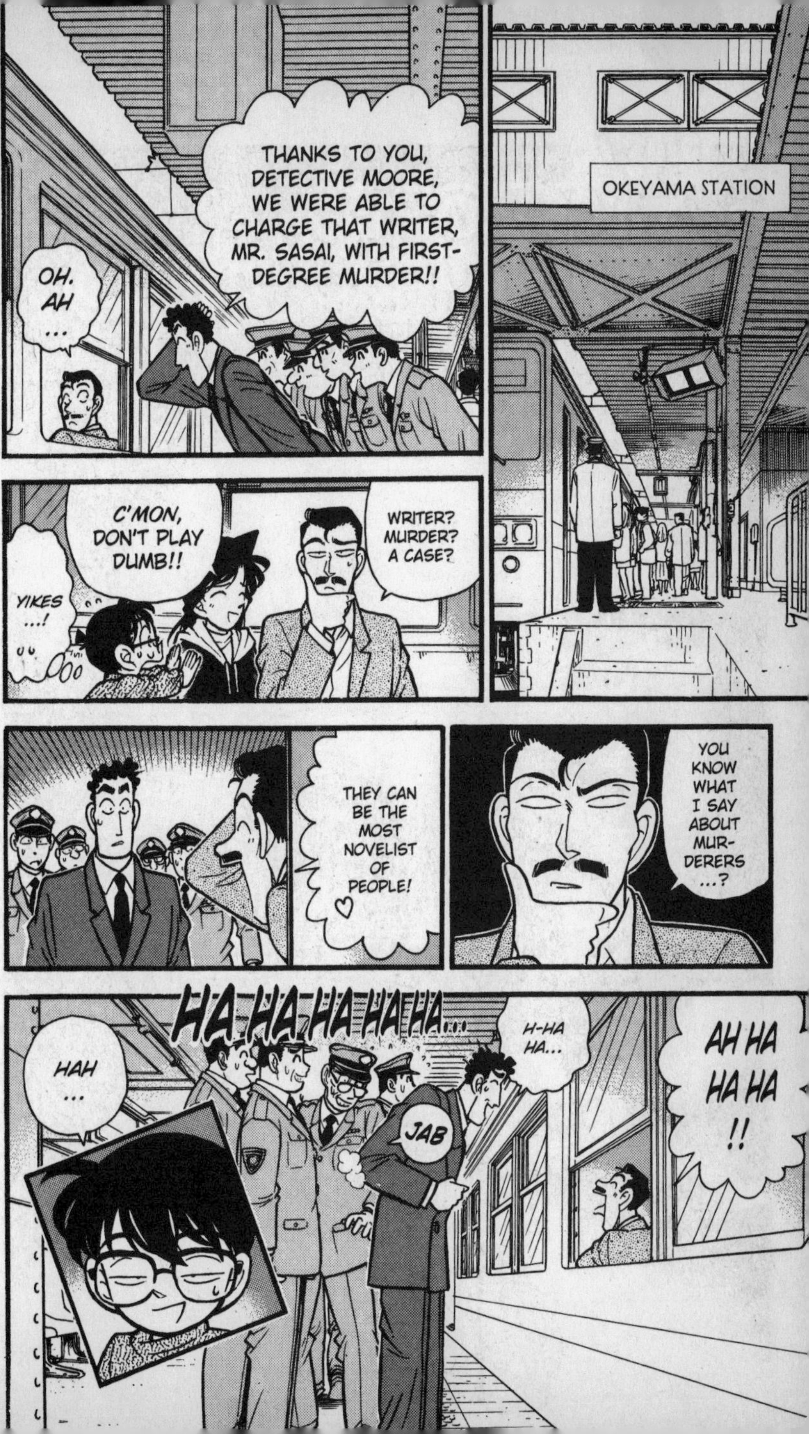
OKEYAMA STATION
THANKS TO YOU, DETECTIVE MOORE, WE WERE ABLE TO CHARGE THAT WRITER, MR. SASAI, WITH FIRST-DEGREE MURDER!!
OH. AH ...
WRITER? MURDER? A CASE?
C'MON, DON'T PLAY DUMB!!
YIKES ...!
YOU KNOW WHAT I SAY ABOUT MUR-DERERS ...?
THEY CAN BE THE MOST NOVELIST OF PEOPLE! ♡
AH HA HA HA !!
H-HA HA...
HA HA HA HA HA HA...
JAB
HAH ...

FILE 2: INVITATION TO MOONSHADOW ISLAND

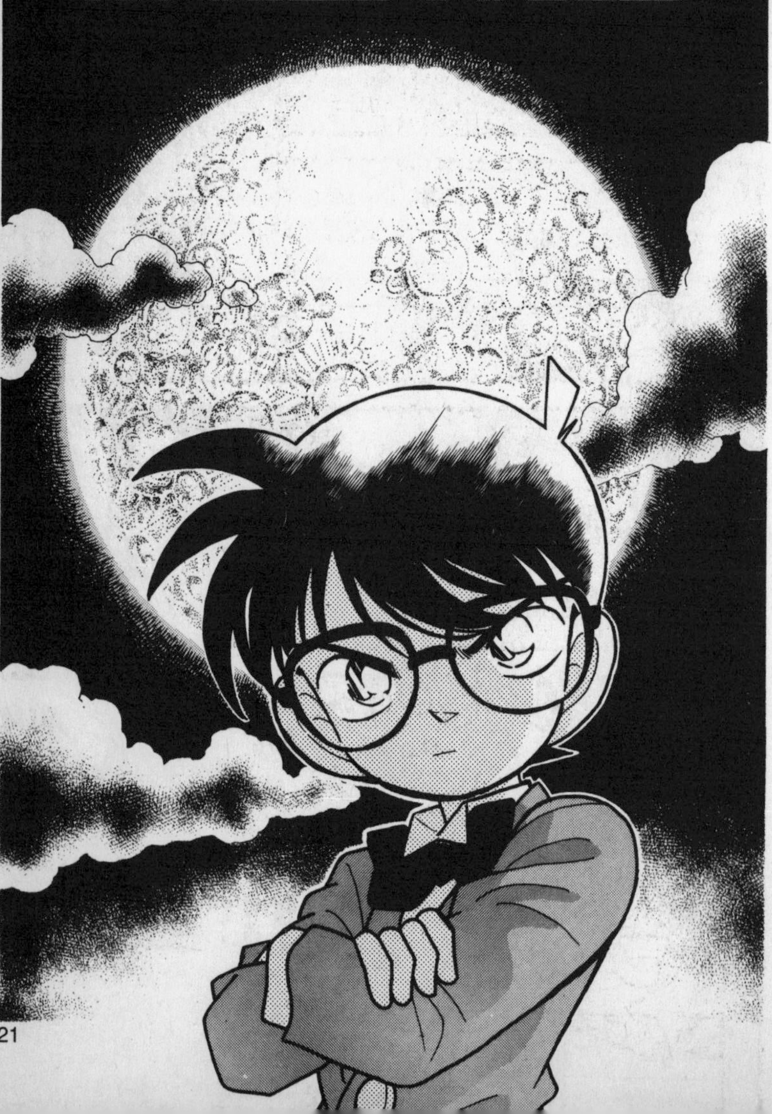

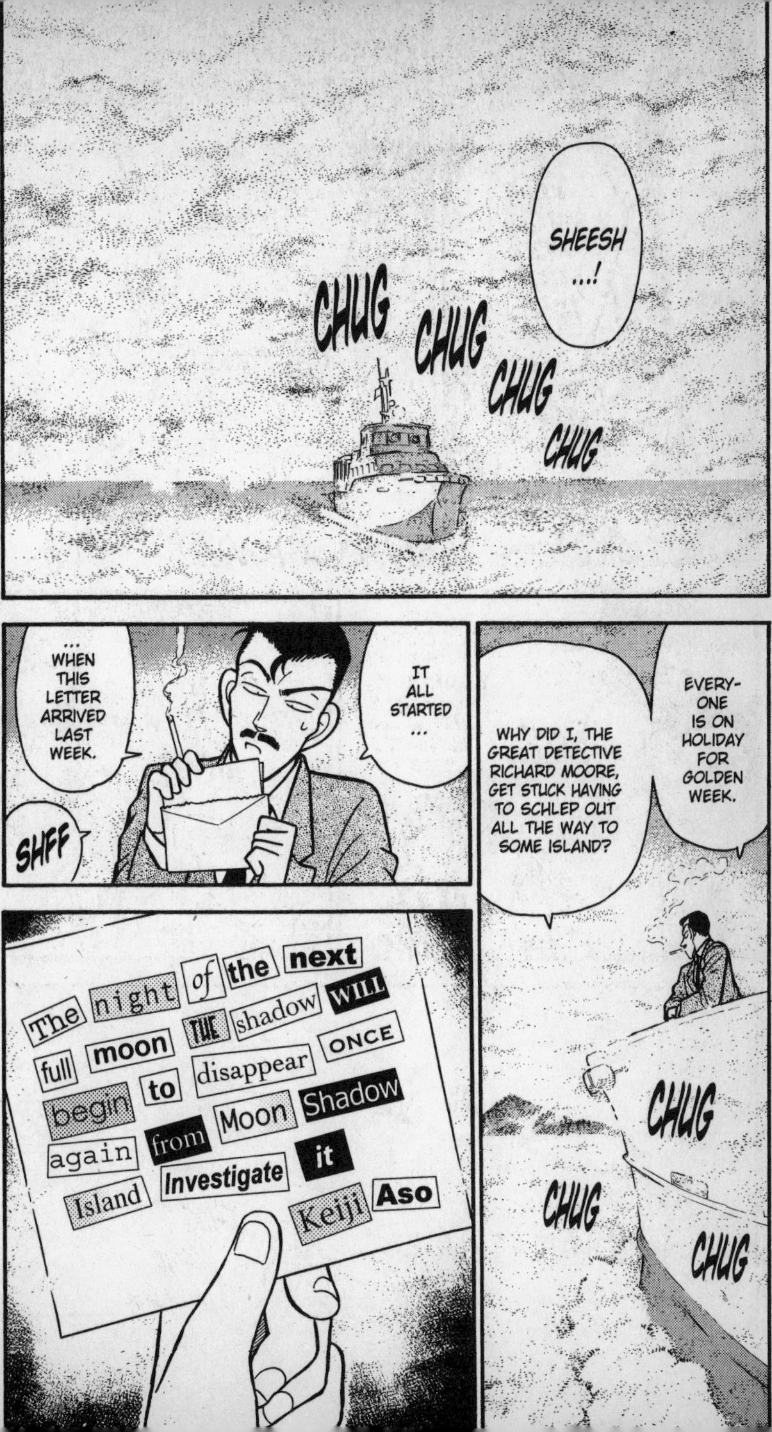
SHEESH ...!
CHUG
CHUG
CHUG
CHUG
EVERY-ONE IS ON HOLIDAY FOR GOLDEN WEEK.
WHY DID I, THE GREAT DETECTIVE RICHARD MOORE, GET STUCK HAVING TO SCHLEP OUT ALL THE WAY TO SOME ISLAND?
CHUG
CHUG
CHUG
IT ALL STARTED ...
... WHEN THIS LETTER ARRIVED LAST WEEK.
SHFF
The night of the next
full moon THE shadow WILL
begin to disappear ONCE
again from Moon Shadow
Island Investigate it
Keiji Aso

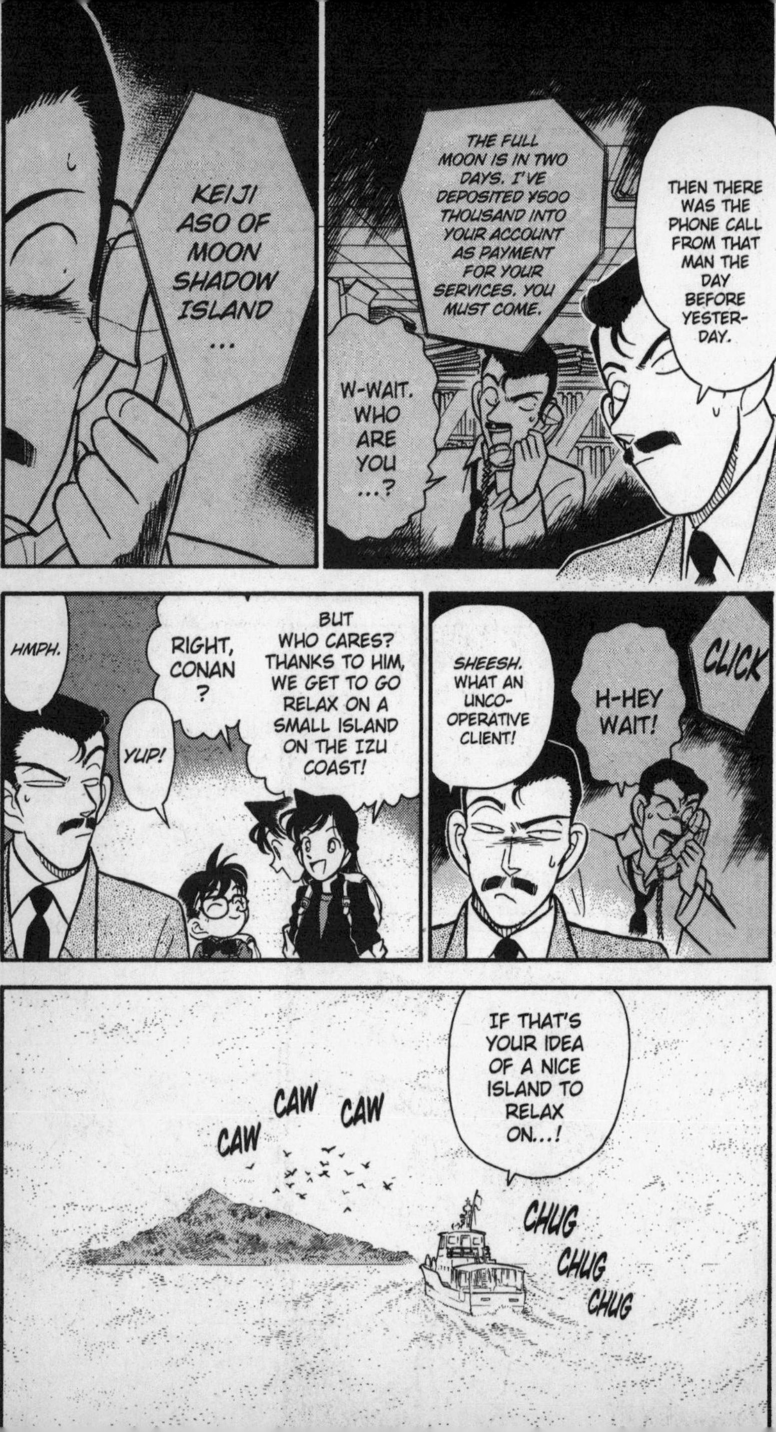
THEN THERE WAS THE PHONE CALL FROM THAT MAN THE DAY BEFORE YESTER-DAY.
THE FULL MOON IS IN TWO DAYS. I'VE DEPOSITED ¥500 THOUSAND INTO YOUR ACCOUNT AS PAYMENT FOR YOUR SERVICES. YOU MUST COME.
W-WAIT. WHO ARE YOU ...?
KEIJI ASO OF MOON SHADOW ISLAND ...
CLICK
H-HEY WAIT!
SHEESH. WHAT AN UNCO-OPERATIVE CLIENT!
BUT WHO CARES? THANKS TO HIM, WE GET TO GO RELAX ON A SMALL ISLAND ON THE IZU COAST!
RIGHT, CONAN ?
YUP!
HMPH.
IF THAT'S YOUR IDEA OF A NICE ISLAND TO RELAX ON...!
CHUG
CHUG
CHUG
CAW
CAW
CAW

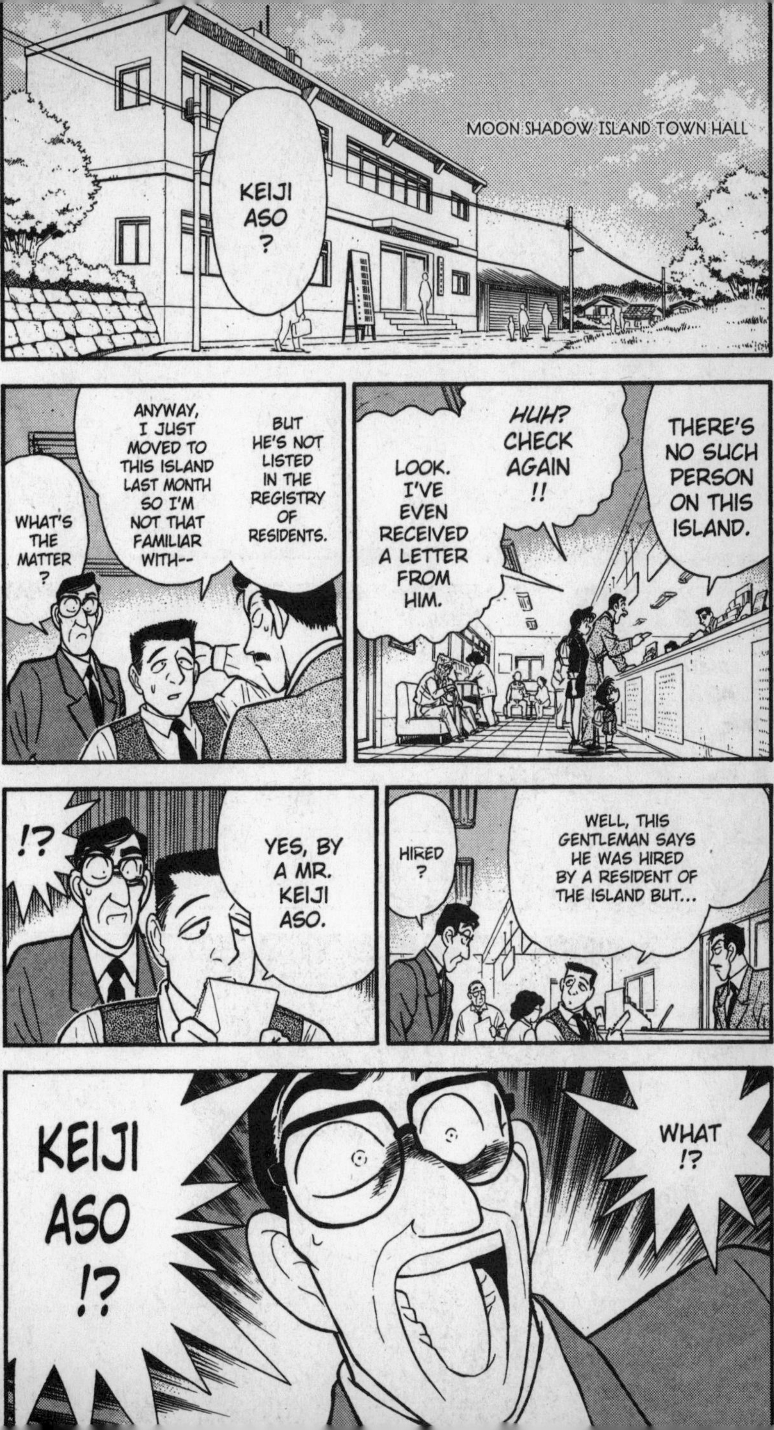
MOON SHADOW ISLAND TOWN HALL
KEIJI ASO ?
THERE'S NO SUCH PERSON ON THIS ISLAND.
HUH? CHECK AGAIN !!
LOOK. I'VE EVEN RECEIVED A LETTER FROM HIM.
BUT HE'S NOT LISTED IN THE REGISTRY OF RESIDENTS.
ANYWAY, I JUST MOVED TO THIS ISLAND LAST MONTH SO I'M NOT THAT FAMILIAR WITH--
WHAT'S THE MATTER ?
WELL, THIS GENTLEMAN SAYS HE WAS HIRED BY A RESIDENT OF THE ISLAND BUT...
HIRED ?
YES, BY A MR. KEIJI ASO.
!?
WHAT !?
KEIJI ASO !?

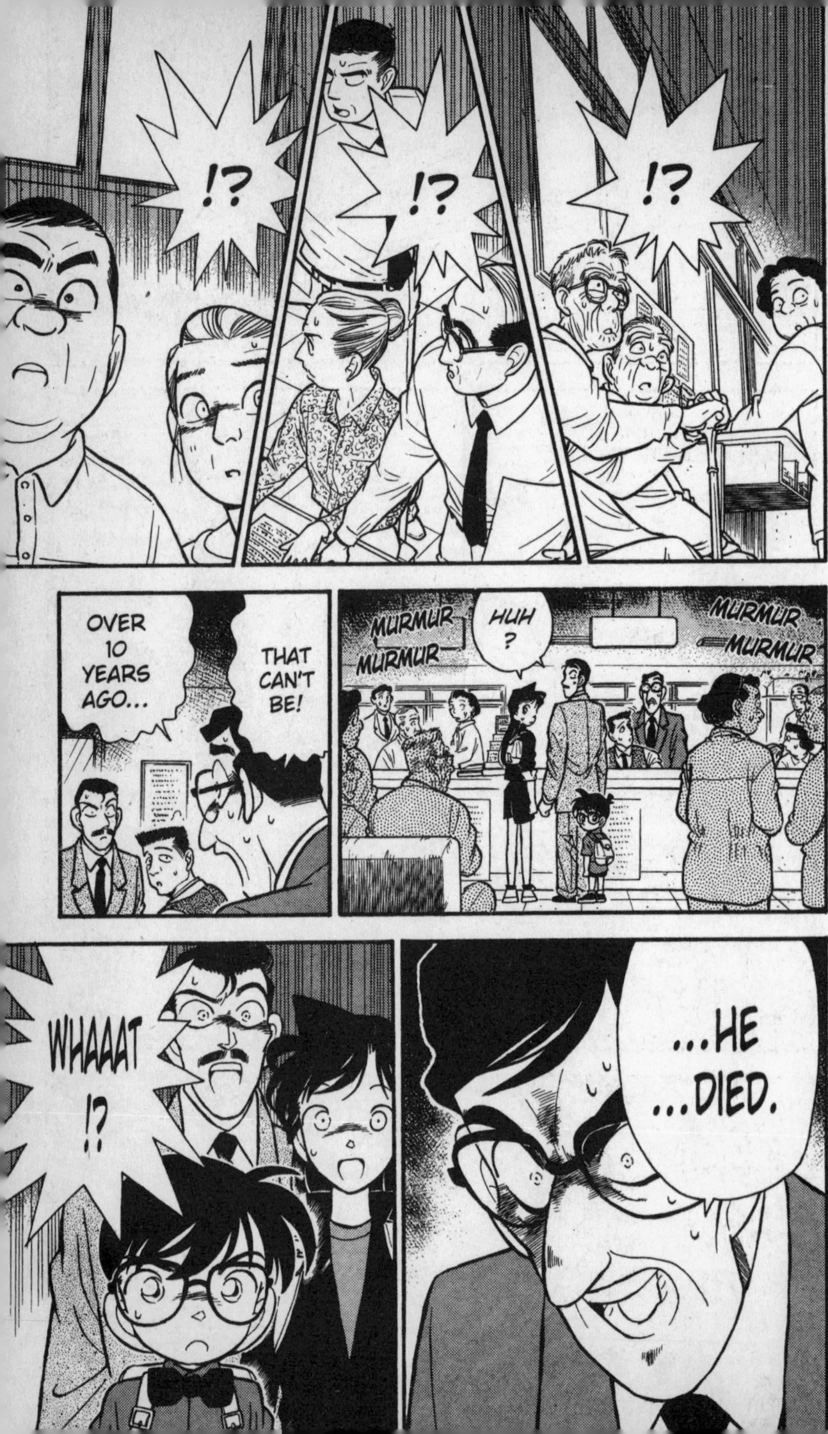
!?
!?
!?
MURMUR MURMUR
HUH ?
MURMUR MURMUR
THAT CAN'T BE!
OVER 10 YEARS AGO...
...HE ...DIED.
WHAAAT !?

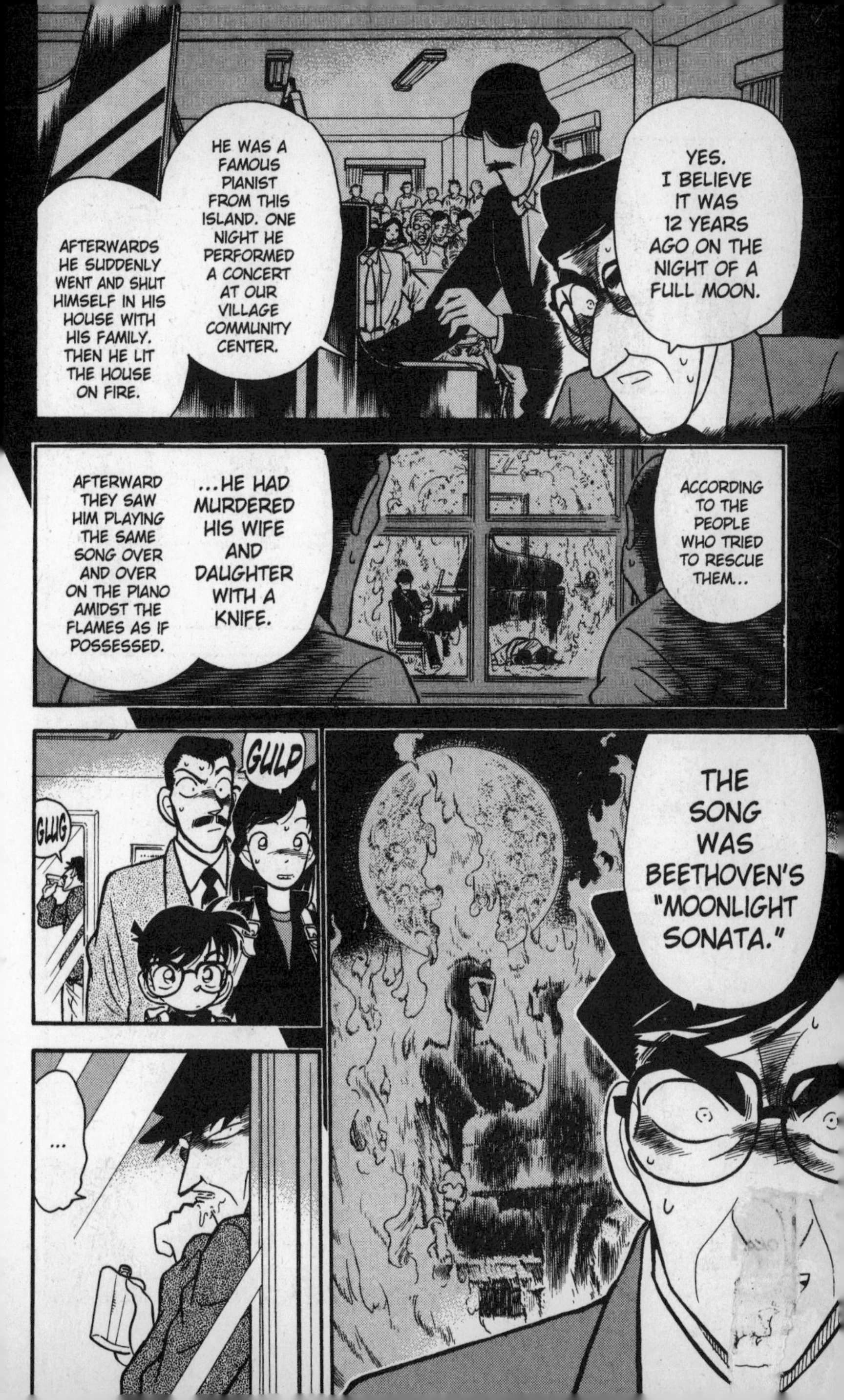
YES. I BELIEVE IT WAS 12 YEARS AGO ON THE NIGHT OF A FULL MOON.
HE WAS A FAMOUS PIANIST FROM THIS ISLAND. ONE NIGHT HE PERFORMED A CONCERT AT OUR VILLAGE COMMUNITY CENTER.
AFTERWARDS HE SUDDENLY WENT AND SHUT HIMSELF IN HIS HOUSE WITH HIS FAMILY. THEN HE LIT THE HOUSE ON FIRE.
ACCORDING TO THE PEOPLE WHO TRIED TO RESCUE THEM...
...HE HAD MURDERED HIS WIFE AND DAUGHTER WITH A KNIFE.
AFTERWARD THEY SAW HIM PLAYING THE SAME SONG OVER AND OVER ON THE PIANO AMIDST THE FLAMES AS IF POSSESSED.
THE SONG WAS BEETHOVEN'S "MOONLIGHT SONATA."
GULP
GLUG
...

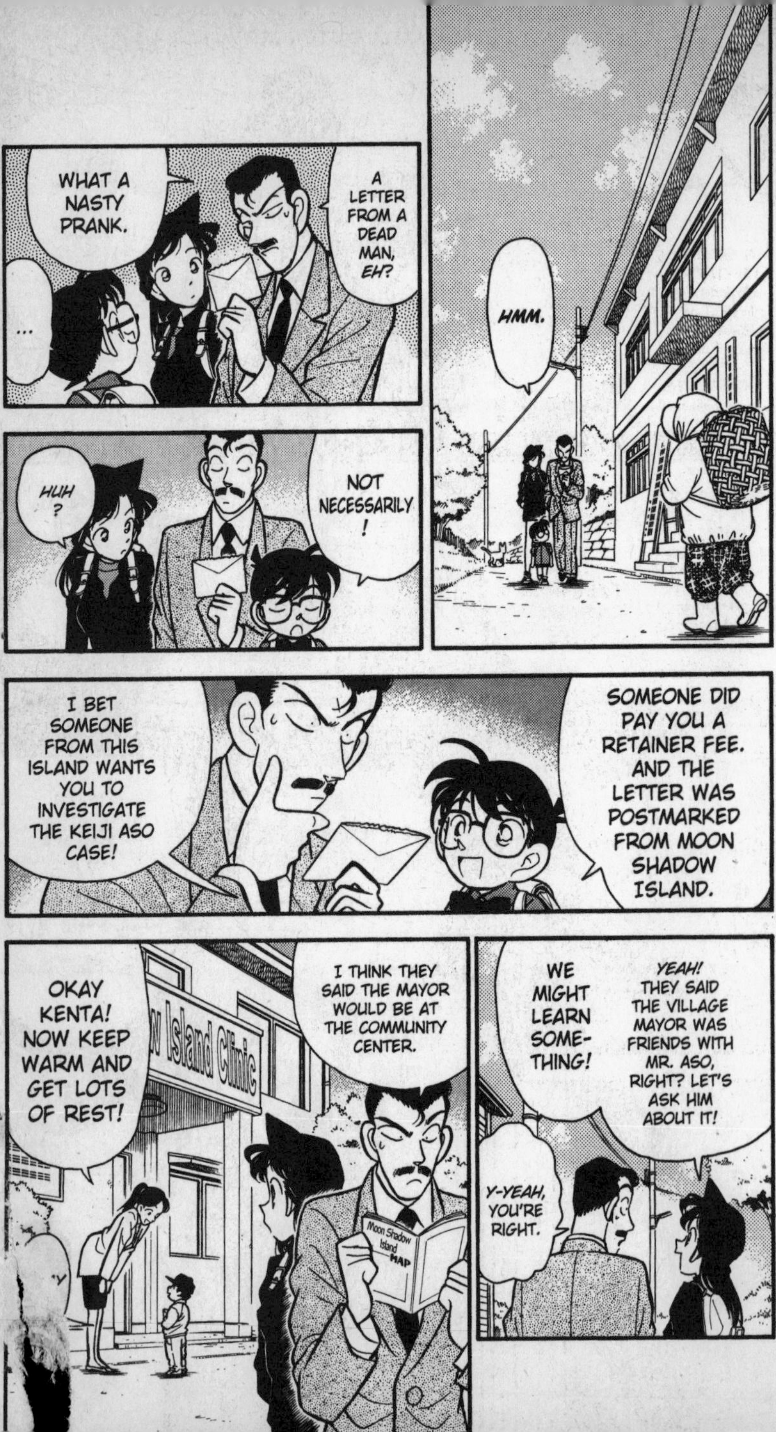
HMM.
A LETTER FROM A DEAD MAN, EH?
WHAT A NASTY PRANK.
...
NOT NECESSARILY!
HUH?
SOMEONE DID PAY YOU A RETAINER FEE. AND THE LETTER WAS POSTMARKED FROM MOON SHADOW ISLAND.
I BET SOMEONE FROM THIS ISLAND WANTS YOU TO INVESTIGATE THE KEIJI ASO CASE!
YEAH! THEY SAID THE VILLAGE MAYOR WAS FRIENDS WITH MR. ASO, RIGHT? LET'S ASK HIM ABOUT IT!
WE MIGHT LEARN SOME-THING!
Y-YEAH, YOU'RE RIGHT.
I THINK THEY SAID THE MAYOR WOULD BE AT THE COMMUNITY CENTER.
Island Clinic
OKAY KENTA! NOW KEEP WARM AND GET LOTS OF REST!
Moon Shadow Island MAP

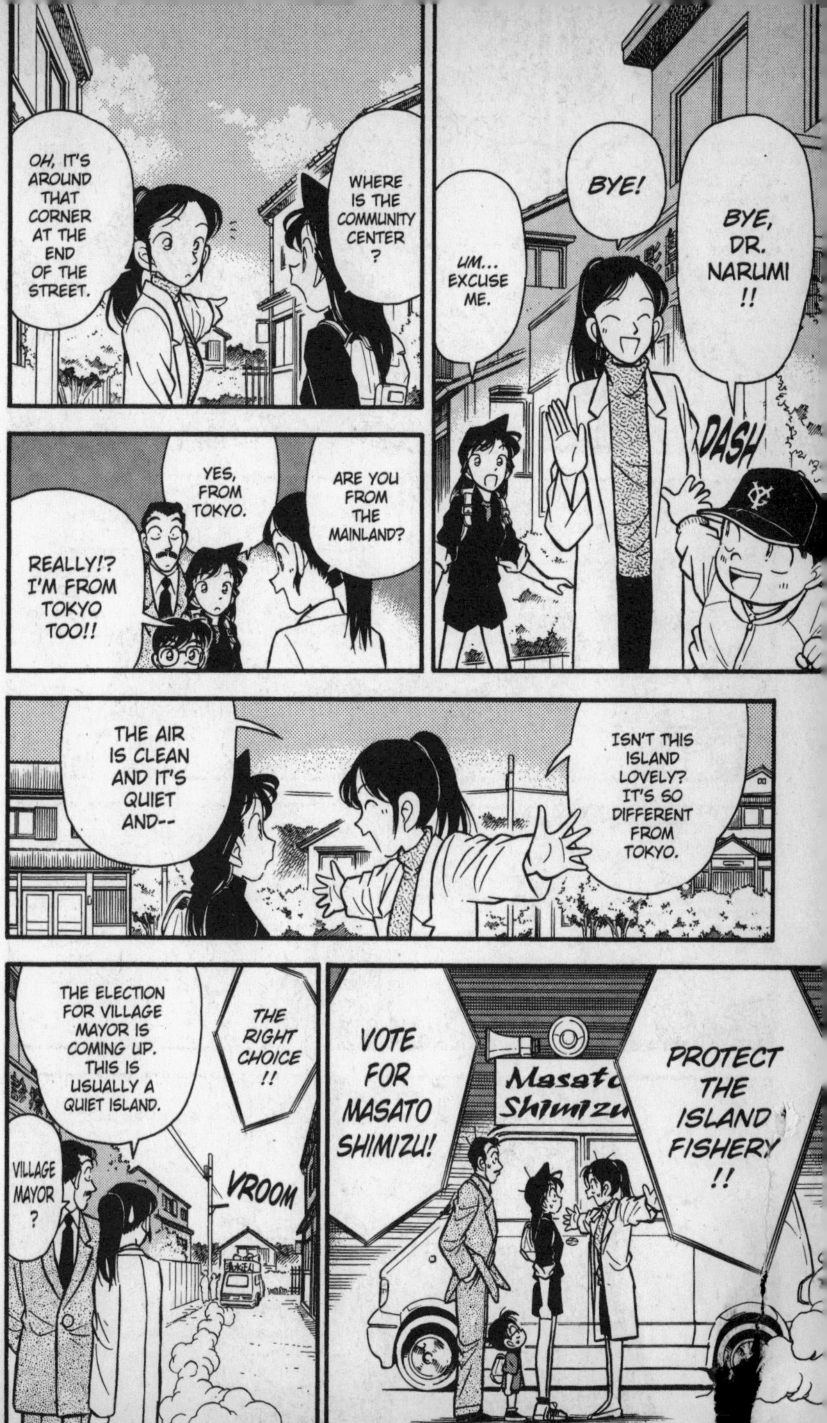
BYE, DR. NARUMI!!
BYE!
UM... EXCUSE ME.
DASH
WHERE IS THE COMMUNITY CENTER?
OH, IT'S AROUND THAT CORNER AT THE END OF THE STREET.
ARE YOU FROM THE MAINLAND?
YES, FROM TOKYO.
REALLY!? I'M FROM TOKYO TOO!!
ISN'T THIS ISLAND LOVELY? IT'S SO DIFFERENT FROM TOKYO.
THE AIR IS CLEAN AND IT'S QUIET AND--
PROTECT THE ISLAND FISHERY!!
Masato Shimizu
VOTE FOR MASATO SHIMIZU!
THE RIGHT CHOICE!!
THE ELECTION FOR VILLAGE MAYOR IS COMING UP. THIS IS USUALLY A QUIET ISLAND.
VROOM
VILLAGE MAYOR?

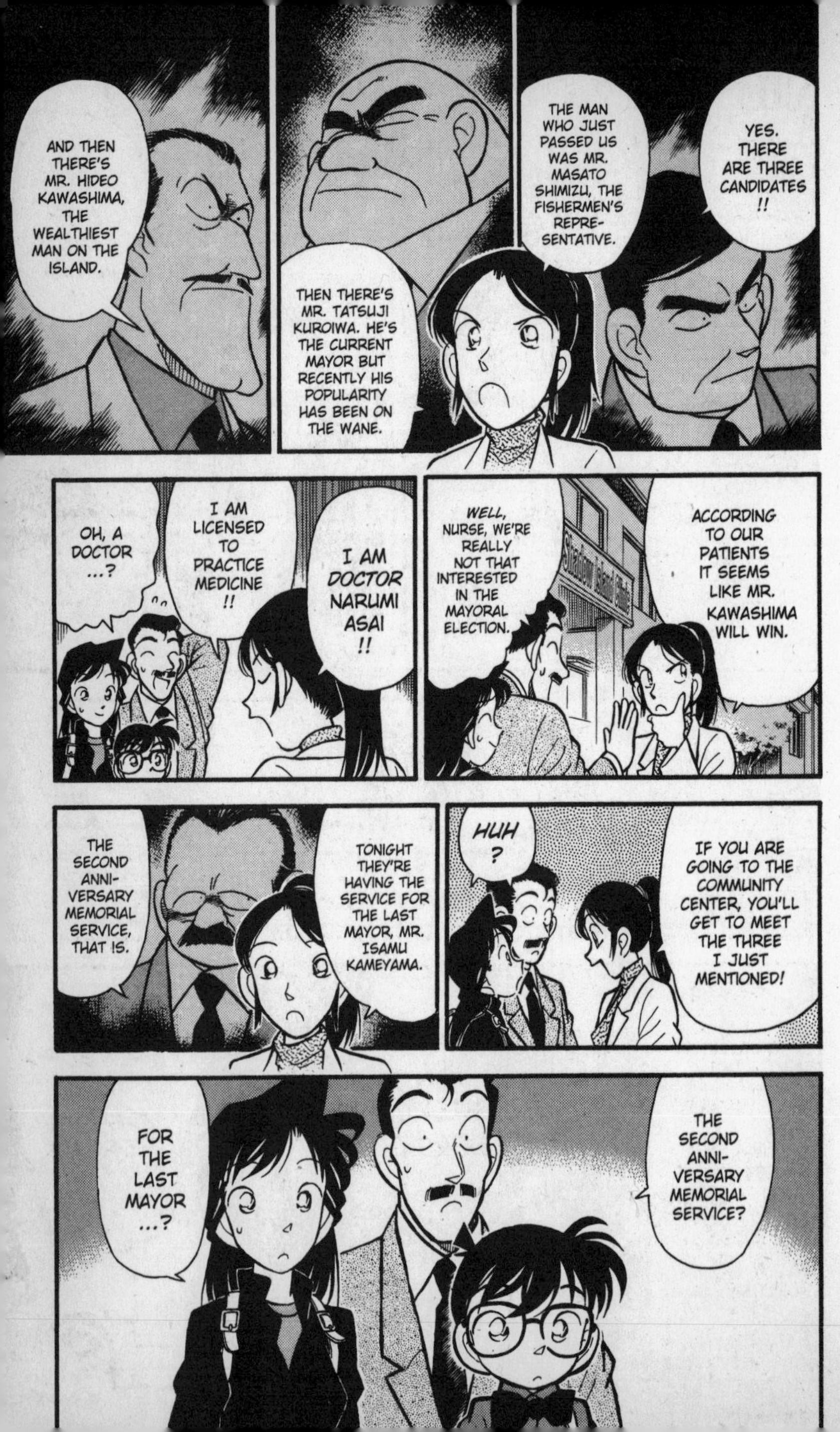
YES. THERE ARE THREE CANDIDATES !!
THE MAN WHO JUST PASSED US WAS MR. MASATO SHIMIZU, THE FISHERMEN'S REPRE-SENTATIVE.
THEN THERE'S MR. TATSUJI KUROIWA. HE'S THE CURRENT MAYOR BUT RECENTLY HIS POPULARITY HAS BEEN ON THE WANE.
AND THEN THERE'S MR. HIDEO KAWASHIMA, THE WEALTHIEST MAN ON THE ISLAND.
ACCORDING TO OUR PATIENTS IT SEEMS LIKE MR. KAWASHIMA WILL WIN.
WELL, NURSE, WE'RE REALLY NOT THAT INTERESTED IN THE MAYORAL ELECTION.
I AM DOCTOR NARUMI ASAI !!
I AM LICENSED TO PRACTICE MEDICINE !!
OH, A DOCTOR ...?
IF YOU ARE GOING TO THE COMMUNITY CENTER, YOU'LL GET TO MEET THE THREE I JUST MENTIONED!
HUH ?
TONIGHT THEY'RE HAVING THE SERVICE FOR THE LAST MAYOR, MR. ISAMU KAMEYAMA.
THE SECOND ANNI-VERSARY MEMORIAL SERVICE, THAT IS.
THE SECOND ANNI-VERSARY MEMORIAL SERVICE?
FOR THE LAST MAYOR ...?

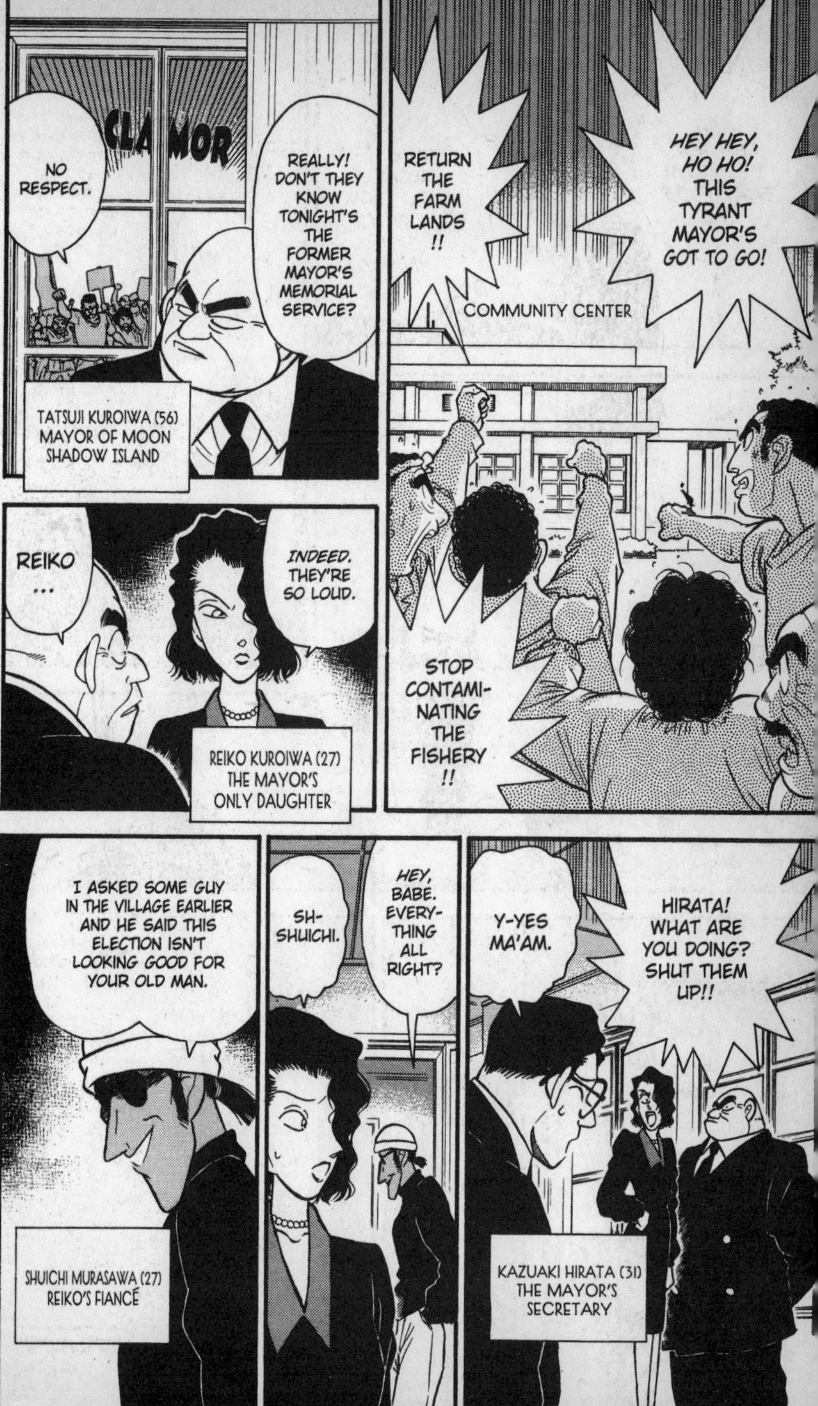
HEY HEY, HO HO! THIS TYRANT MAYOR'S GOT TO GO!
RETURN THE FARM LANDS !!
COMMUNITY CENTER
STOP CONTAMI- NATING THE FISHERY !!
REALLY! DON'T THEY KNOW TONIGHT'S THE FORMER MAYOR'S MEMORIAL SERVICE?
CLAMOR
NO RESPECT.
TATSUJI KUROIWA (56) MAYOR OF MOON SHADOW ISLAND
INDEED. THEY'RE SO LOUD.
REIKO ...
REIKO KUROIWA (27) THE MAYOR'S ONLY DAUGHTER
HIRATA! WHAT ARE YOU DOING? SHUT THEM UP!!
Y-YES MA'AM.
KAZUAKI HIRATA (31) THE MAYOR'S SECRETARY
HEY, BABE. EVERY- THING ALL RIGHT?
SH- SHUICHI.
I ASKED SOME GUY IN THE VILLAGE EARLIER AND HE SAID THIS ELECTION ISN'T LOOKING GOOD FOR YOUR OLD MAN.
SHUICHI MURASAWA (27) REIKO'S FIANCÉ

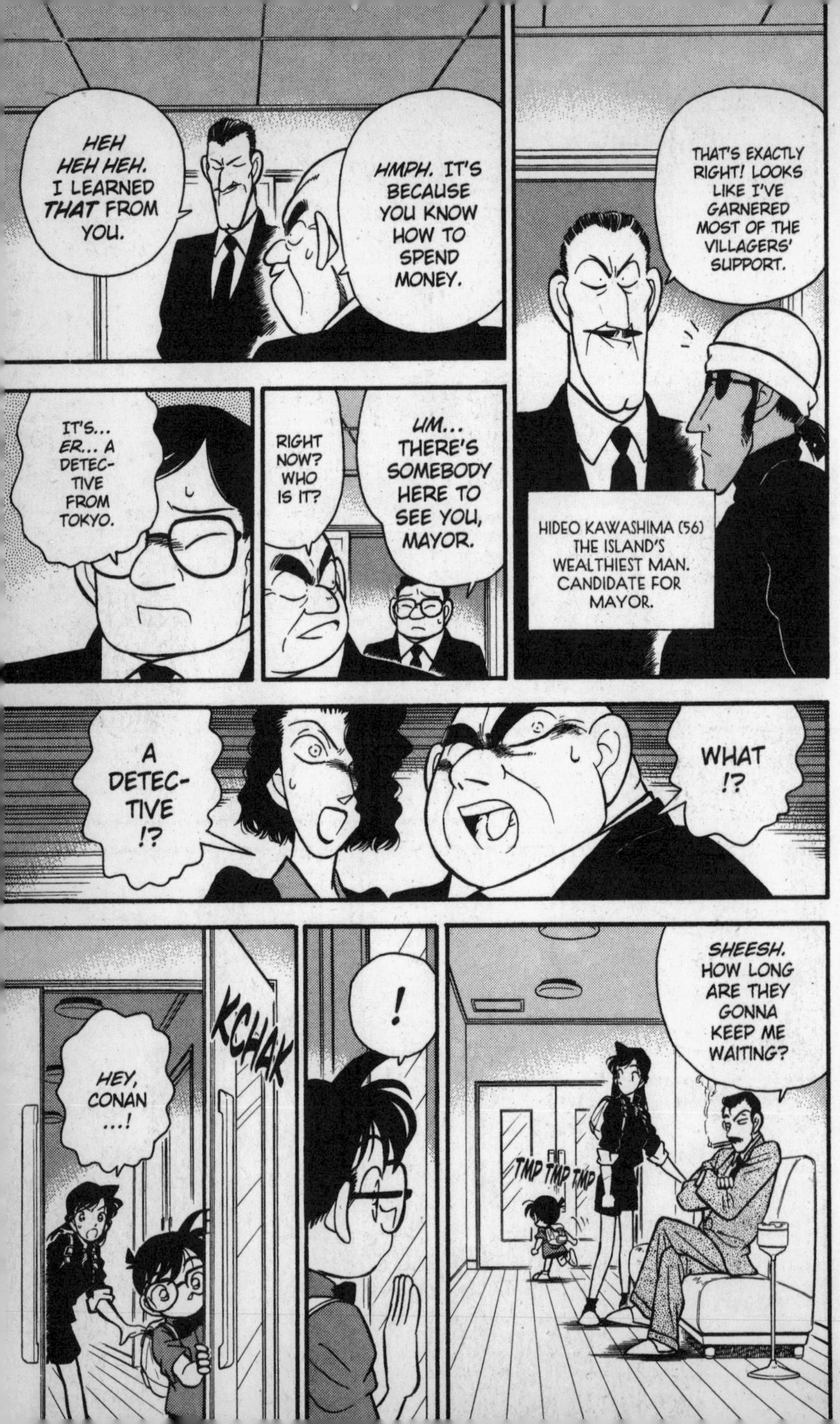
THAT'S EXACTLY RIGHT! LOOKS LIKE I'VE GARNERED MOST OF THE VILLAGERS' SUPPORT.
HIDEO KAWASHIMA (56) THE ISLAND'S WEALTHIEST MAN. CANDIDATE FOR MAYOR.
HMPH. IT'S BECAUSE YOU KNOW HOW TO SPEND MONEY.
HEH HEH HEH. I LEARNED THAT FROM YOU.
UM... THERE'S SOMEBODY HERE TO SEE YOU, MAYOR.
RIGHT NOW? WHO IS IT?
IT'S... ER... A DETECTIVE FROM TOKYO.
WHAT!?
A DETECTIVE!?
SHEESH. HOW LONG ARE THEY GONNA KEEP ME WAITING?
TMP TMP TMP
!
K'CHAK
HEY, CONAN...!

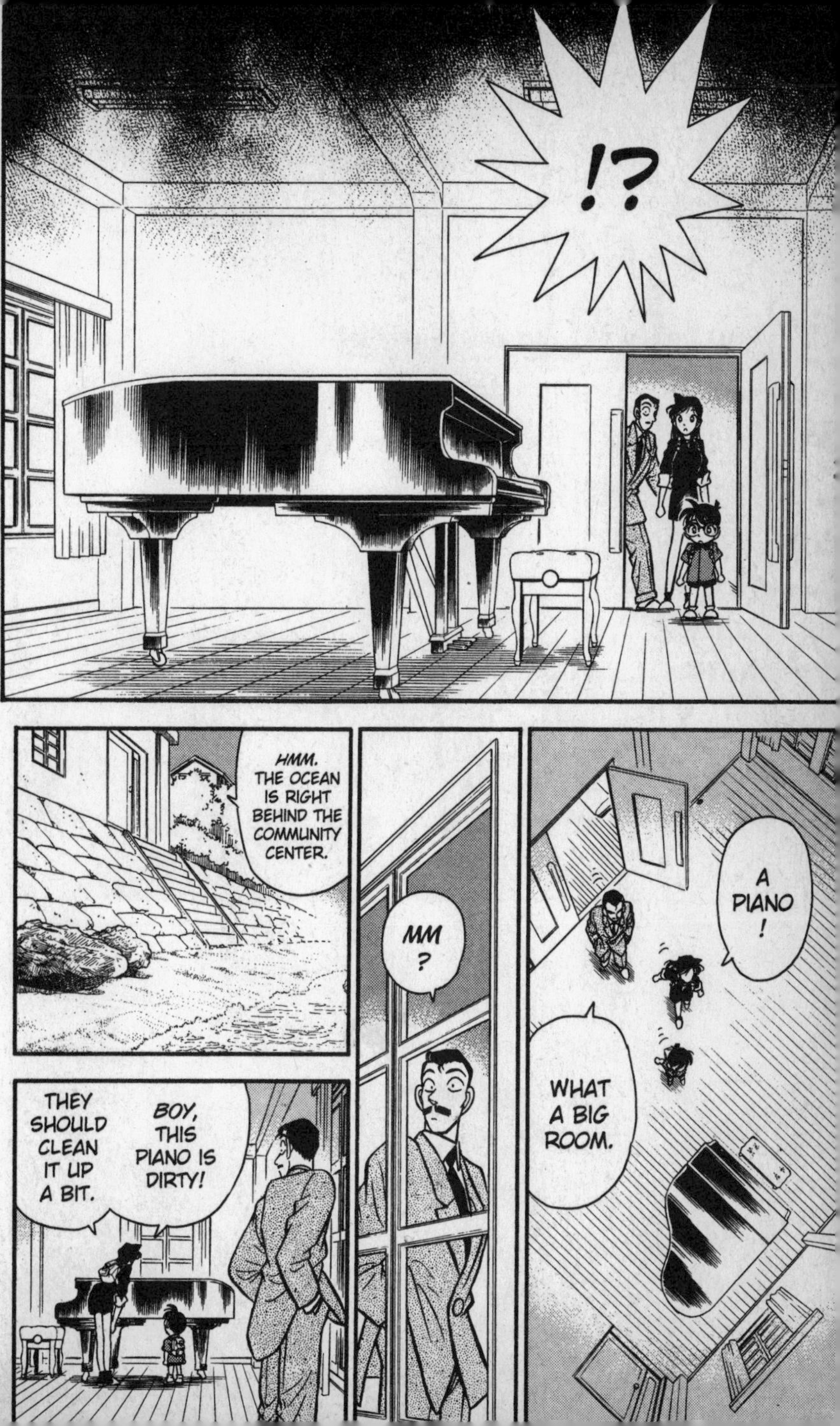
!?
A PIANO!
WHAT A BIG ROOM.
MM?
HMM. THE OCEAN IS RIGHT BEHIND THE COMMUNITY CENTER.
BOY, THIS PIANO IS DIRTY!
THEY SHOULD CLEAN IT UP A BIT.

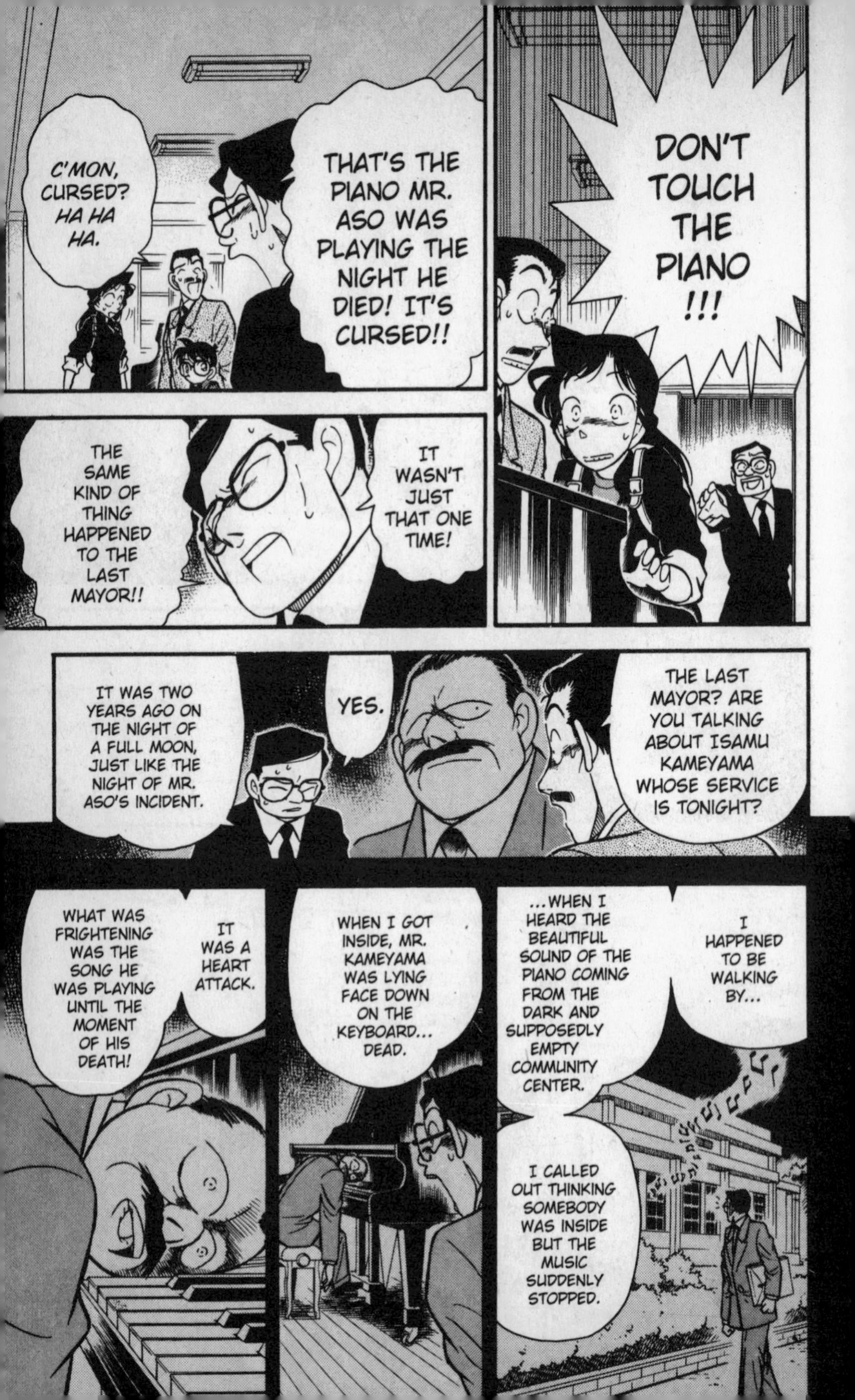
DON'T TOUCH THE PIANO!!!
THAT'S THE PIANO MR. ASO WAS PLAYING THE NIGHT HE DIED! IT'S CURSED!!
C'MON, CURSED? HA HA HA.
IT WASN'T JUST THAT ONE TIME!
THE SAME KIND OF THING HAPPENED TO THE LAST MAYOR!!
THE LAST MAYOR? ARE YOU TALKING ABOUT ISAMU KAMEYAMA WHOSE SERVICE IS TONIGHT?
YES.
IT WAS TWO YEARS AGO ON THE NIGHT OF A FULL MOON, JUST LIKE THE NIGHT OF MR. ASO'S INCIDENT.
I HAPPENED TO BE WALKING BY...
...WHEN I HEARD THE BEAUTIFUL SOUND OF THE PIANO COMING FROM THE DARK AND SUPPOSEDLY EMPTY COMMUNITY CENTER.
I CALLED OUT THINKING SOMEBODY WAS INSIDE BUT THE MUSIC SUDDENLY STOPPED.
WHEN I GOT INSIDE, MR. KAMEYAMA WAS LYING FACE DOWN ON THE KEYBOARD... DEAD.
IT WAS A HEART ATTACK.
WHAT WAS FRIGHTENING WAS THE SONG HE WAS PLAYING UNTIL THE MOMENT OF HIS DEATH!

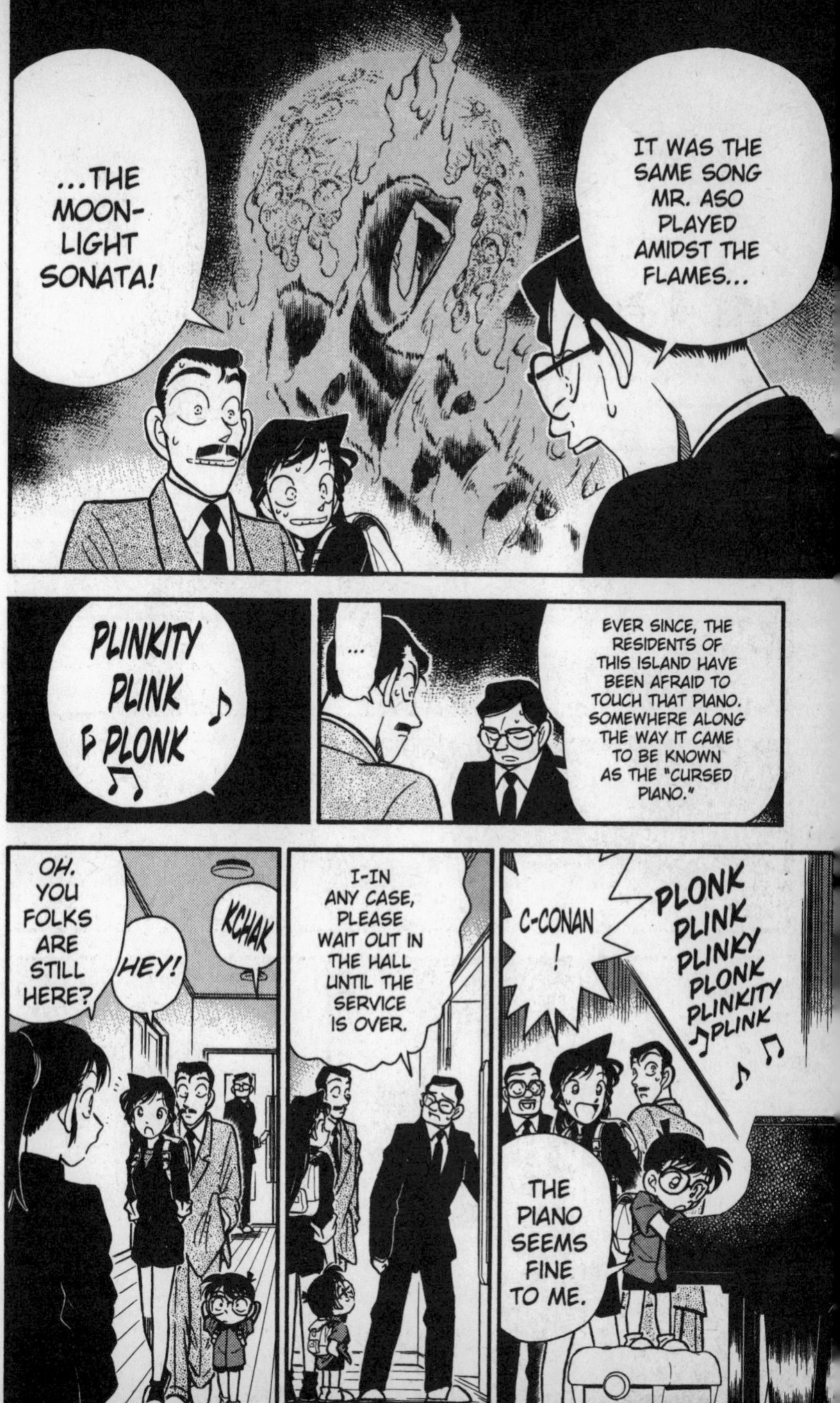
IT WAS THE SAME SONG MR. ASO PLAYED AMIDST THE FLAMES...
...THE MOONLIGHT SONATA!
EVER SINCE, THE RESIDENTS OF THIS ISLAND HAVE BEEN AFRAID TO TOUCH THAT PIANO. SOMEWHERE ALONG THE WAY IT CAME TO BE KNOWN AS THE "CURSED PIANO."
...
PLINKITY PLINK PLONK
PLONK PLINK PLINKY PLONK PLINKITY PLINK
C-CONAN!
THE PIANO SEEMS FINE TO ME.
I-IN ANY CASE, PLEASE WAIT OUT IN THE HALL UNTIL THE SERVICE IS OVER.
KCHAK
HEY!
OH. YOU FOLKS ARE STILL HERE?

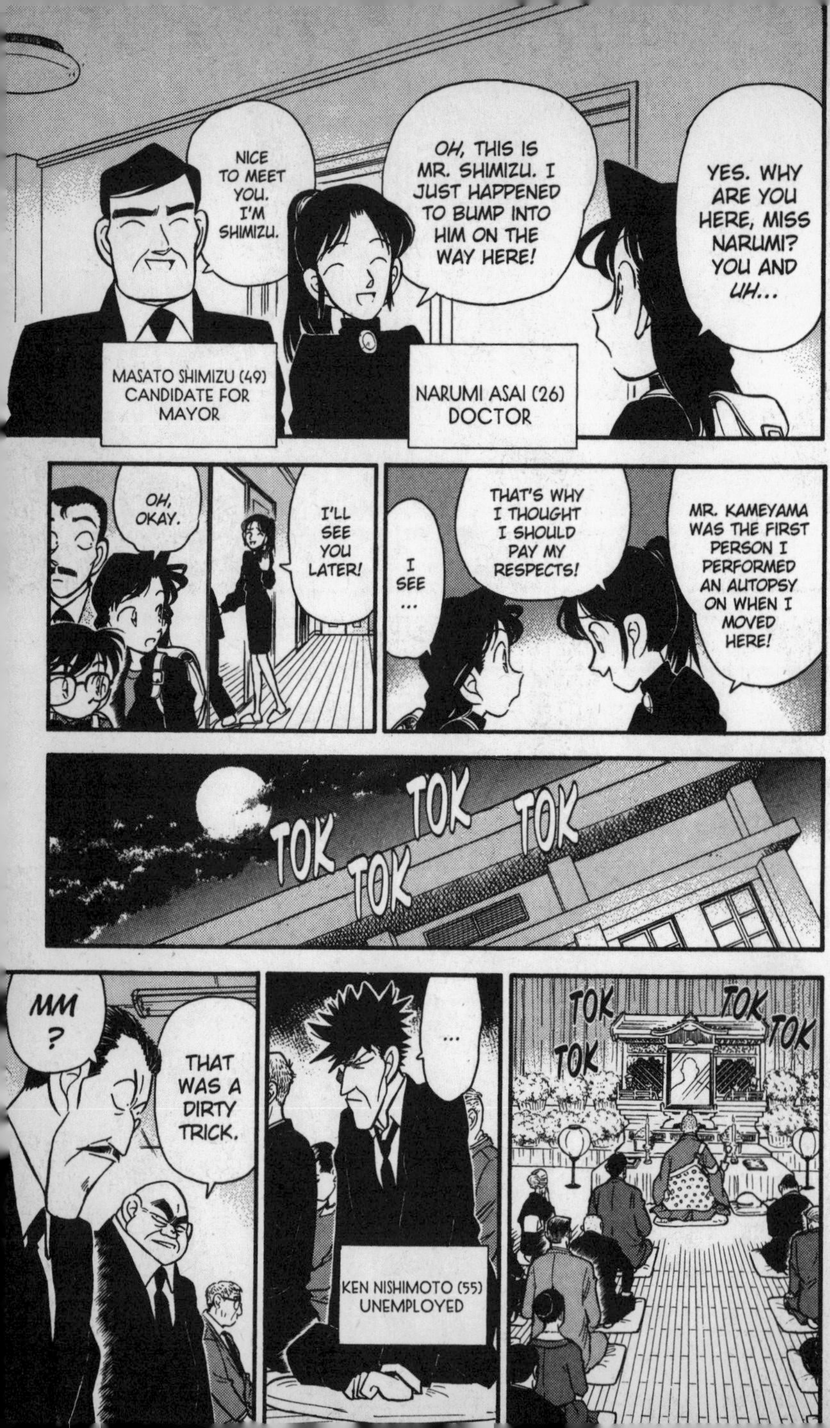
YES. WHY ARE YOU HERE, MISS NARUMI? YOU AND UH...
OH, THIS IS MR. SHIMIZU. I JUST HAPPENED TO BUMP INTO HIM ON THE WAY HERE!
NICE TO MEET YOU. I'M SHIMIZU.
NARUMI ASAI (26) DOCTOR
MASATO SHIMIZU (49) CANDIDATE FOR MAYOR
MR. KAMEYAMA WAS THE FIRST PERSON I PERFORMED AN AUTOPSY ON WHEN I MOVED HERE!
THAT'S WHY I THOUGHT I SHOULD PAY MY RESPECTS!
I SEE ...
I'LL SEE YOU LATER!
OH, OKAY.
TOK
TOK
TOK
TOK
TOK
TOK
TOK
TOK
...
KEN NISHIMOTO (55) UNEMPLOYED
MM ?
THAT WAS A DIRTY TRICK.

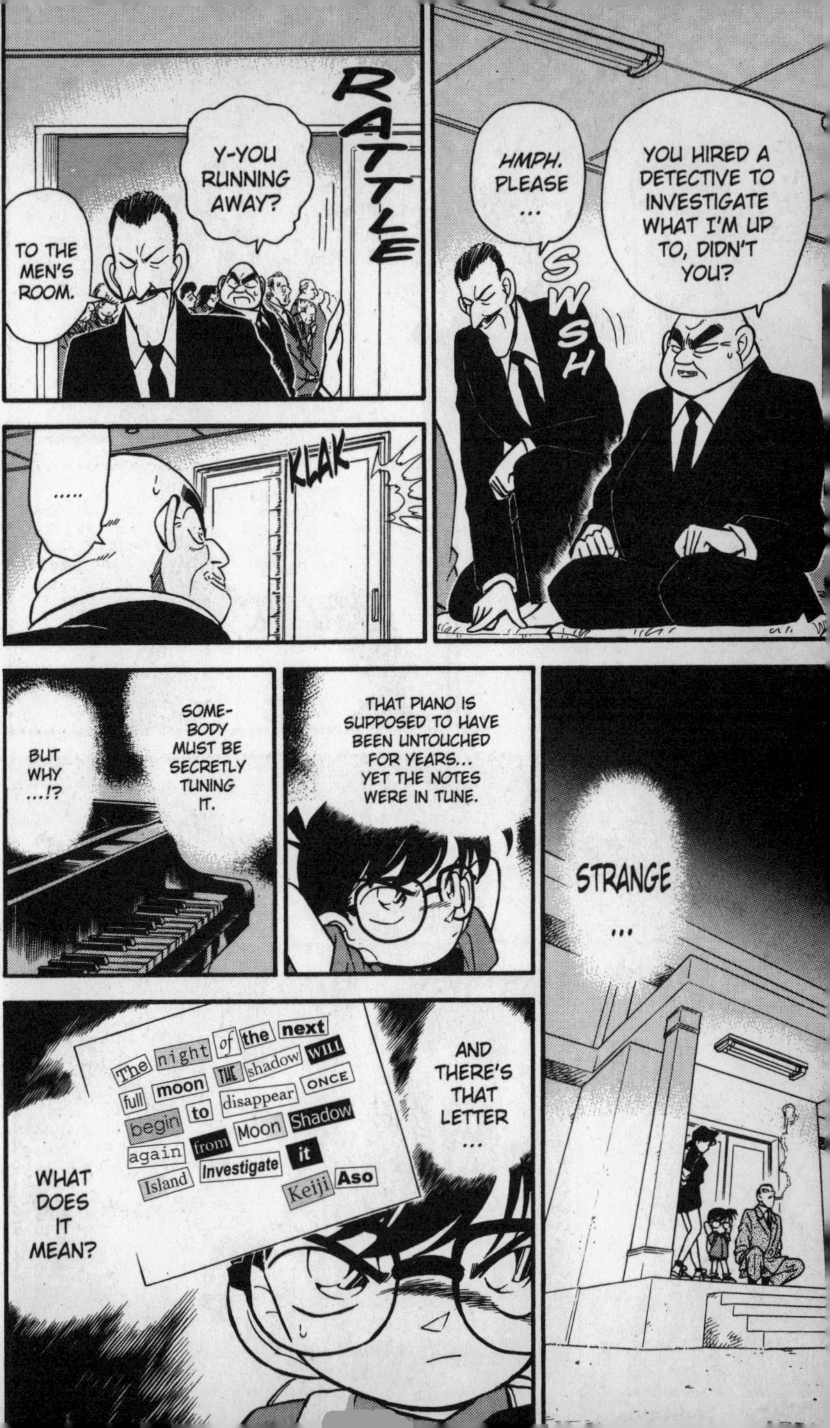
YOU HIRED A DETECTIVE TO INVESTIGATE WHAT I'M UP TO, DIDN'T YOU?
HMPH. PLEASE ...
SWSH
Y-YOU RUNNING AWAY?
TO THE MEN'S ROOM.
RATTLE
KLAK
.....
STRANGE ...
THAT PIANO IS SUPPOSED TO HAVE BEEN UNTOUCHED FOR YEARS... YET THE NOTES WERE IN TUNE.
SOME-BODY MUST BE SECRETLY TUNING IT.
BUT WHY ...!?
AND THERE'S THAT LETTER ...
The night of the next
full moon THE shadow WILL
begin to disappear ONCE
again from Moon Shadow
Island Investigate it
Keiji Aso
WHAT DOES IT MEAN?

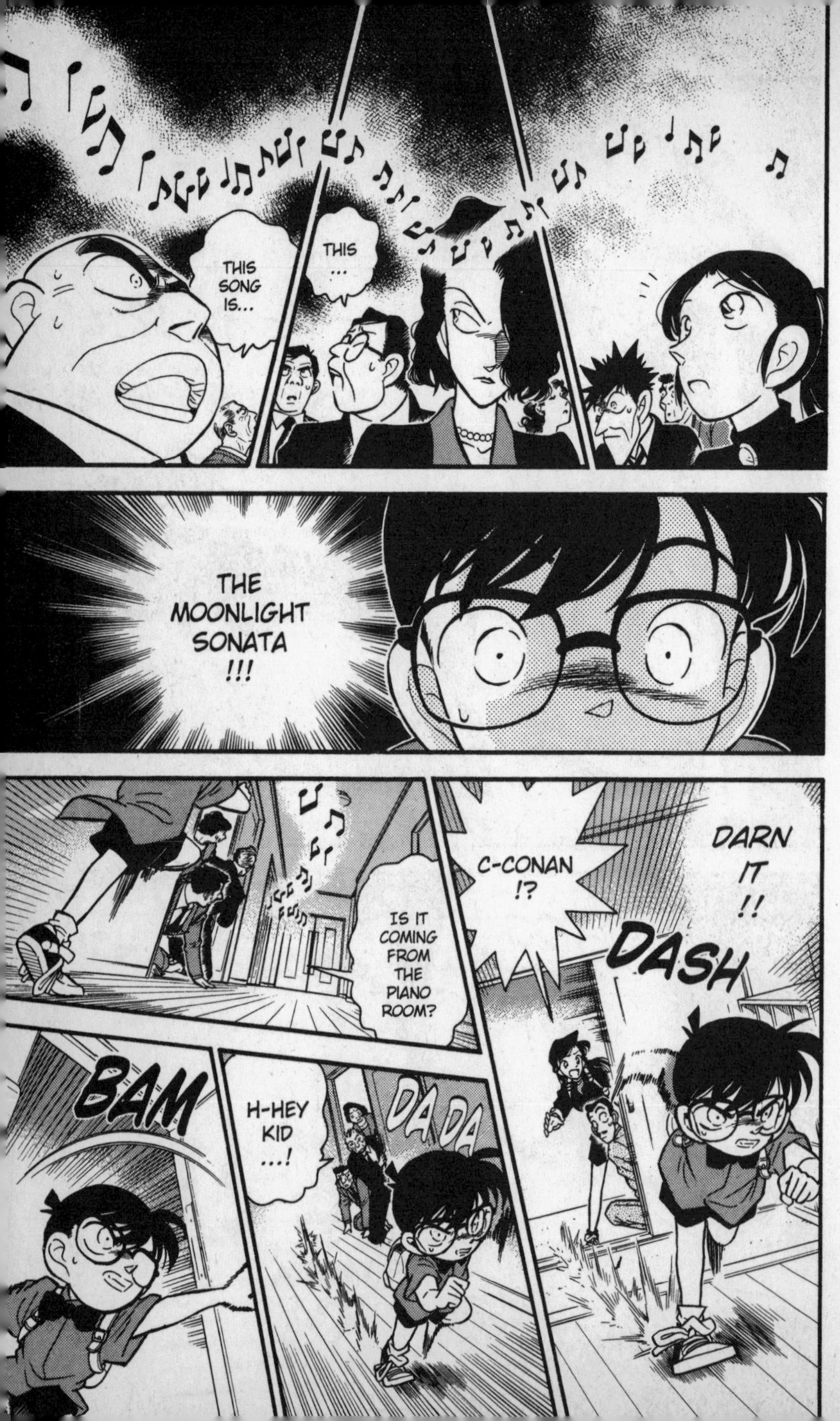
THIS ...
THIS SONG IS...
THE MOONLIGHT SONATA !!!
DARN IT !!
C-CONAN !?
DASH
IS IT COMING FROM THE PIANO ROOM?
DA DA
H-HEY KID ...!
BAM

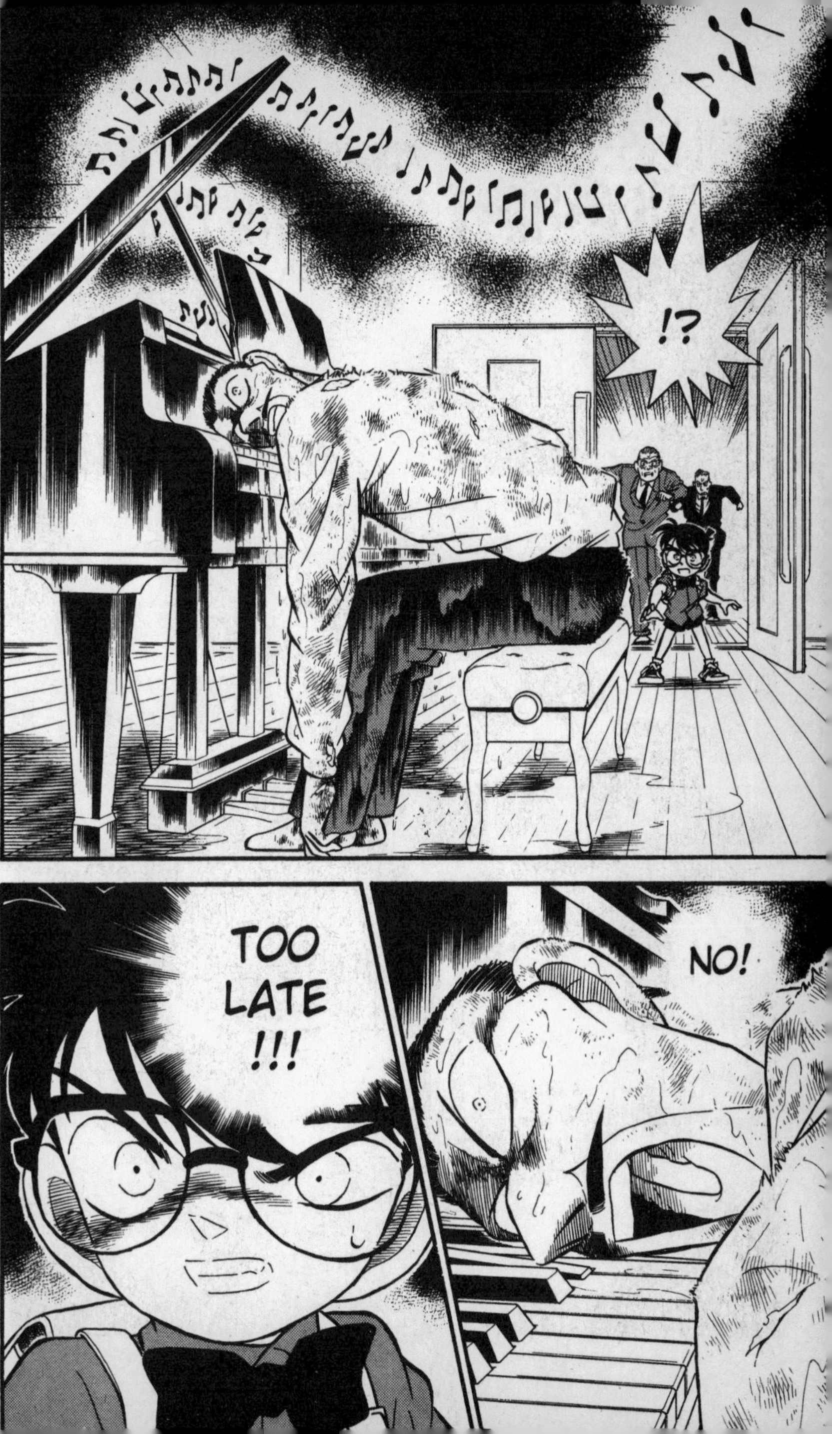
!?
NO!
TOO LATE !!!

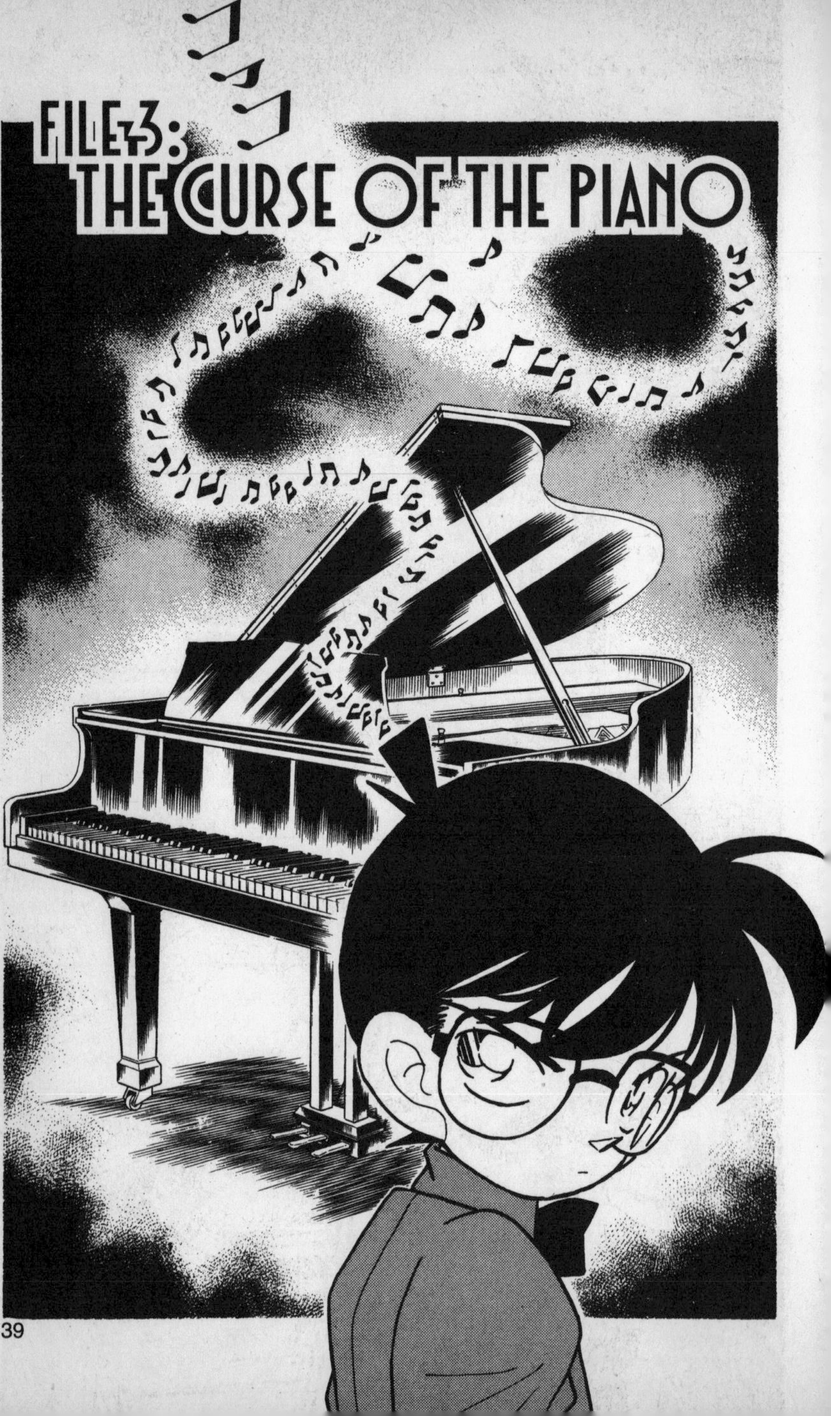
FILE 3:
THE CURSE OF THE PIANO

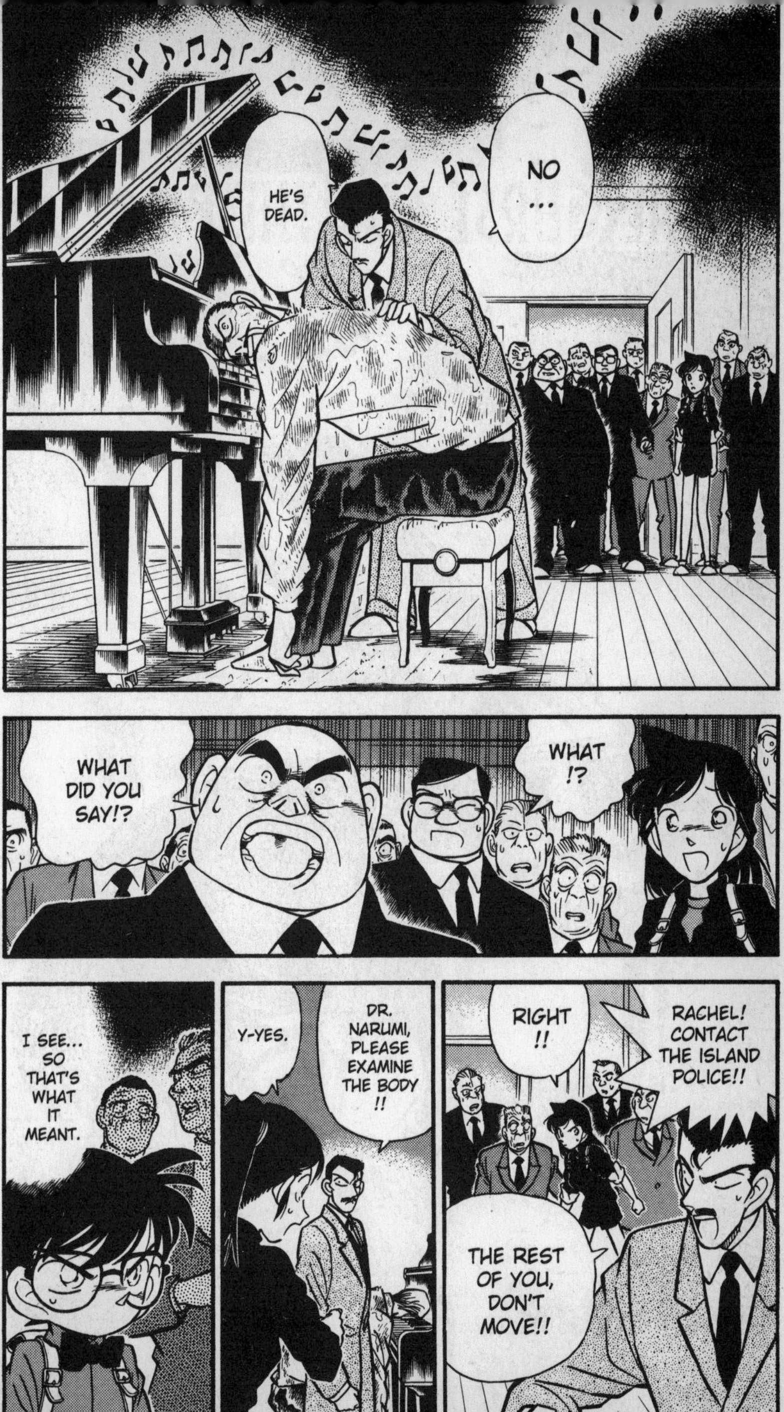
NO ...
HE'S DEAD.
WHAT !?
WHAT DID YOU SAY!?
RACHEL! CONTACT THE ISLAND POLICE!!
RIGHT !!
THE REST OF YOU, DON'T MOVE!!
DR. NARUMI, PLEASE EXAMINE THE BODY !!
Y-YES.
I SEE... SO THAT'S WHAT IT MEANT.

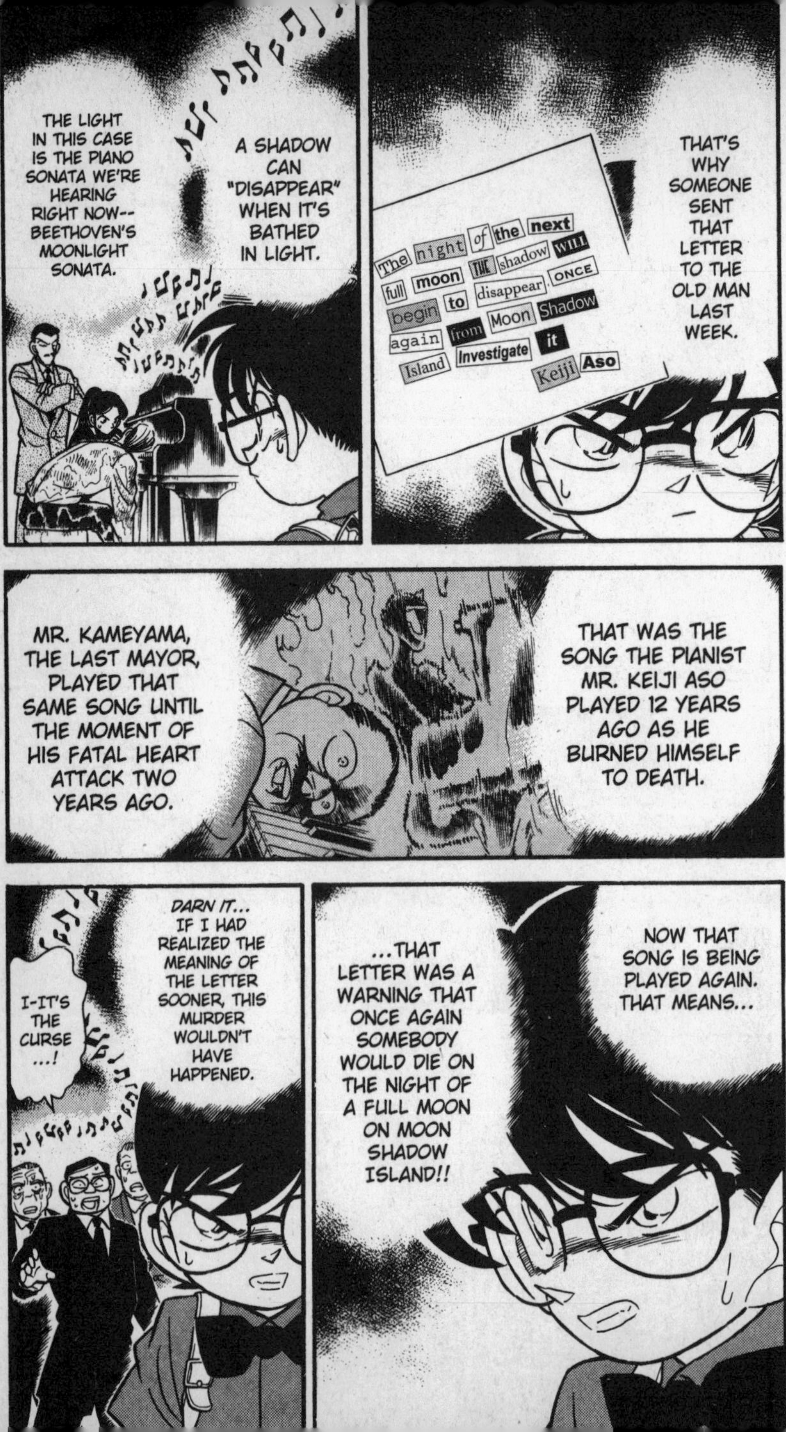

THAT'S WHY SOMEONE SENT THAT LETTER TO THE OLD MAN LAST WEEK.
The night of the next
full moon THE shadow WILL
begin to disappear ONCE
again from Moon Shadow
Island Investigate it
Keiji Aso
A SHADOW CAN "DISAPPEAR" WHEN IT'S BATHED IN LIGHT.
THE LIGHT IN THIS CASE IS THE PIANO SONATA WE'RE HEARING RIGHT NOW-- BEETHOVEN'S MOONLIGHT SONATA.
THAT WAS THE SONG THE PIANIST MR. KEIJI ASO PLAYED 12 YEARS AGO AS HE BURNED HIMSELF TO DEATH.
MR. KAMEYAMA, THE LAST MAYOR, PLAYED THAT SAME SONG UNTIL THE MOMENT OF HIS FATAL HEART ATTACK TWO YEARS AGO.
NOW THAT SONG IS BEING PLAYED AGAIN. THAT MEANS...
...THAT LETTER WAS A WARNING THAT ONCE AGAIN SOMEBODY WOULD DIE ON THE NIGHT OF A FULL MOON ON MOON SHADOW ISLAND!!
DARN IT... IF I HAD REALIZED THE MEANING OF THE LETTER SOONER, THIS MURDER WOULDN'T HAVE HAPPENED.
I-IT'S THE CURSE ...!

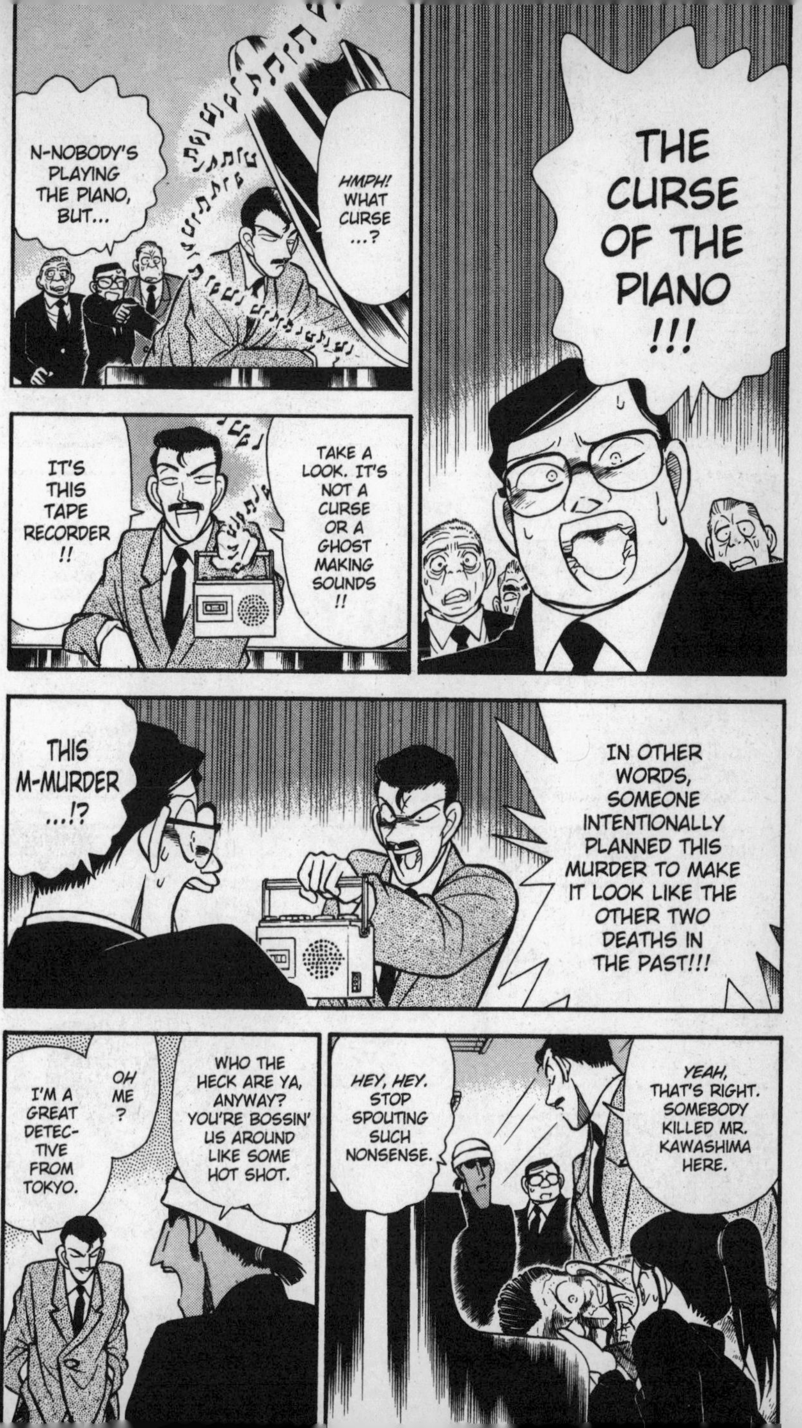
THE CURSE OF THE PIANO !!!
HMPH! WHAT CURSE ...?
N-NOBODY'S PLAYING THE PIANO, BUT...
TAKE A LOOK. IT'S NOT A CURSE OR A GHOST MAKING SOUNDS !!
IT'S THIS TAPE RECORDER !!
IN OTHER WORDS, SOMEONE INTENTIONALLY PLANNED THIS MURDER TO MAKE IT LOOK LIKE THE OTHER TWO DEATHS IN THE PAST!!!
THIS M-MURDER ...!?
YEAH, THAT'S RIGHT. SOMEBODY KILLED MR. KAWASHIMA HERE.
HEY, HEY. STOP SPOUTING SUCH NONSENSE.
WHO THE HECK ARE YA, ANYWAY? YOU'RE BOSSIN' US AROUND LIKE SOME HOT SHOT.
OH ME ?
I'M A GREAT DETEC-TIVE FROM TOKYO.

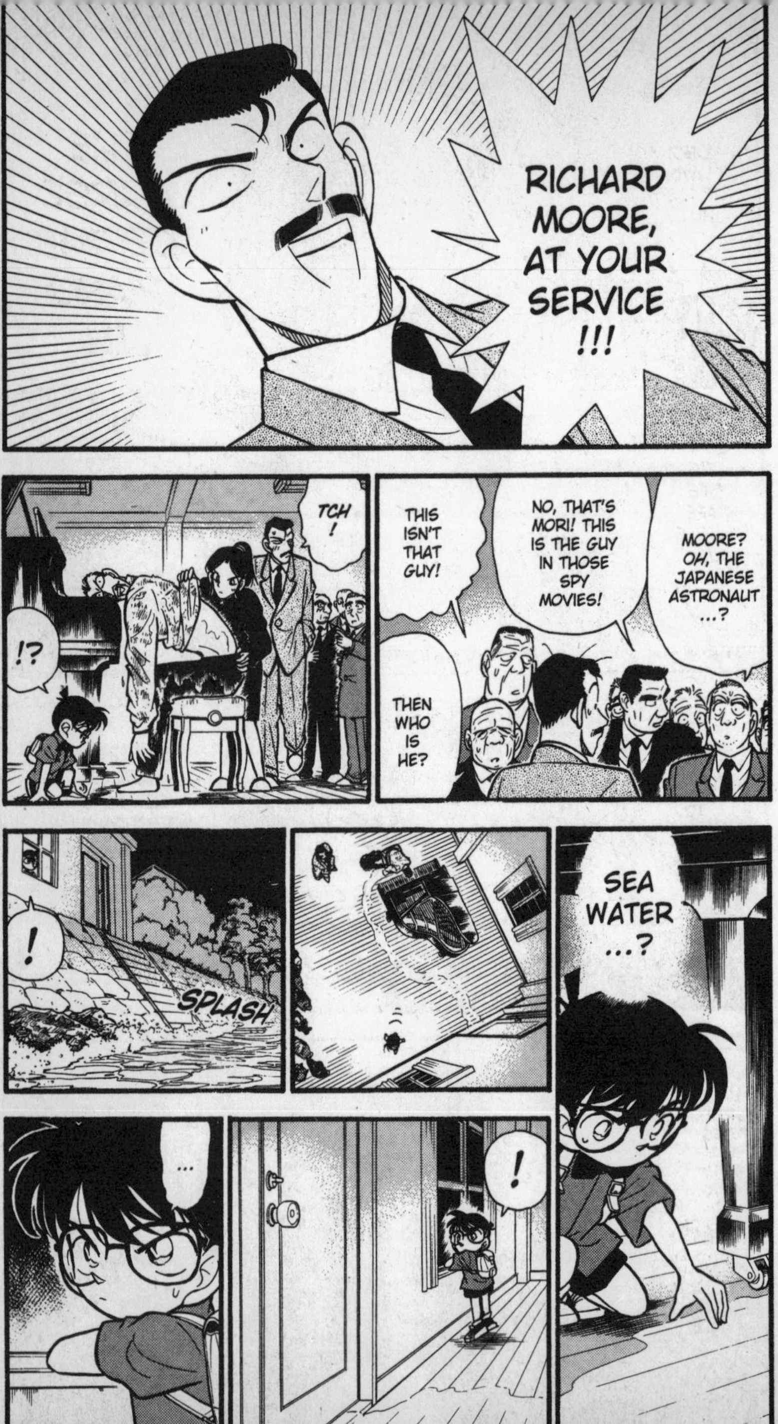
RICHARD MOORE, AT YOUR SERVICE !!!
MOORE? OH, THE JAPANESE ASTRONAUT ...?
NO, THAT'S MORI! THIS IS THE GUY IN THOSE SPY MOVIES!
THIS ISN'T THAT GUY!
THEN WHO IS HE?
TCH !
!?
SEA WATER ...?
!
SPLASH
!
...

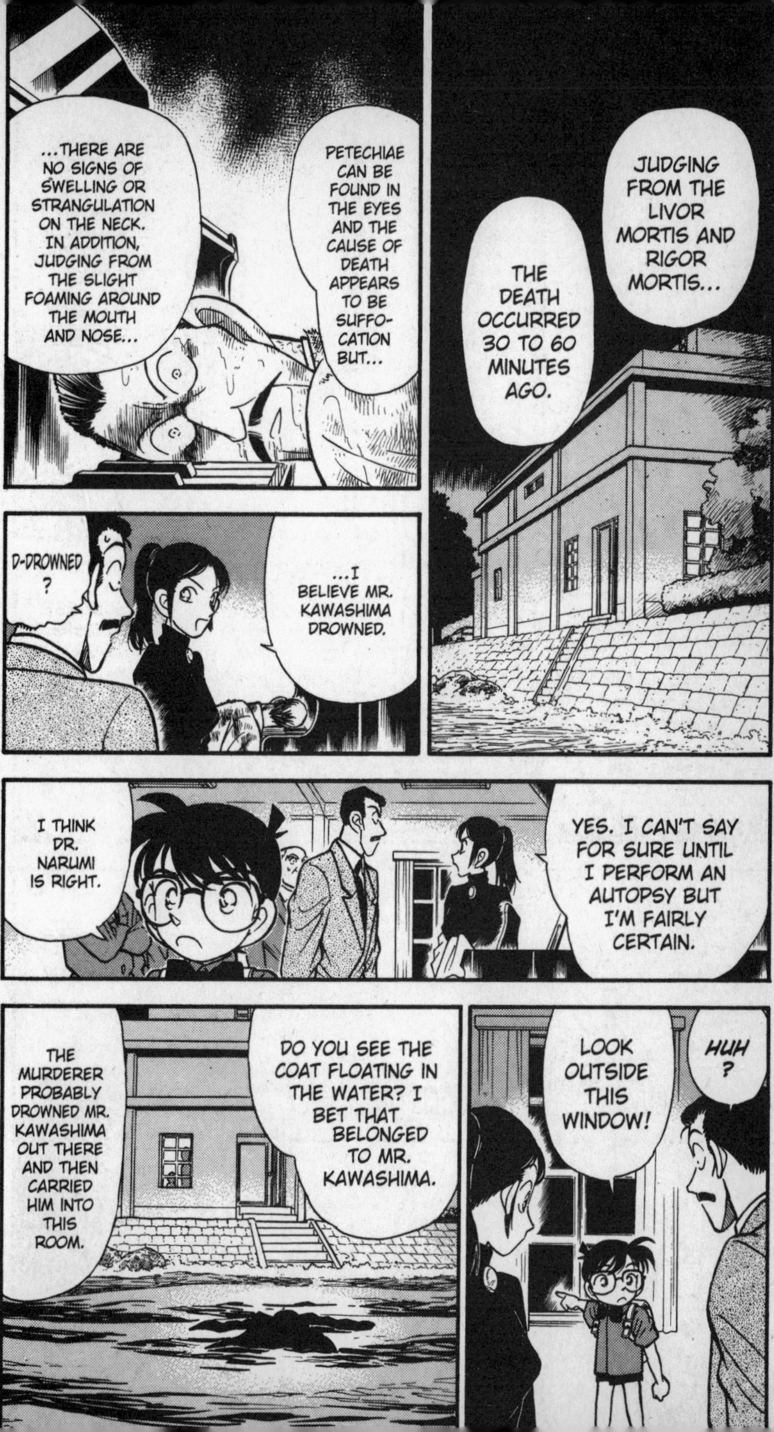
JUDGING FROM THE LIVOR MORTIS AND RIGOR MORTIS...
THE DEATH OCCURRED 30 TO 60 MINUTES AGO.
PETECHIAE CAN BE FOUND IN THE EYES AND THE CAUSE OF DEATH APPEARS TO BE SUFFOCATION BUT...
...THERE ARE NO SIGNS OF SWELLING OR STRANGULATION ON THE NECK. IN ADDITION, JUDGING FROM THE SLIGHT FOAMING AROUND THE MOUTH AND NOSE...
...I BELIEVE MR. KAWASHIMA DROWNED.
D-DROWNED?
YES. I CAN'T SAY FOR SURE UNTIL I PERFORM AN AUTOPSY BUT I'M FAIRLY CERTAIN.
I THINK DR. NARUMI IS RIGHT.
HUH?
LOOK OUTSIDE THIS WINDOW!
DO YOU SEE THE COAT FLOATING IN THE WATER? I BET THAT BELONGED TO MR. KAWASHIMA.
THE MURDERER PROBABLY DROWNED MR. KAWASHIMA OUT THERE AND THEN CARRIED HIM INTO THIS ROOM.

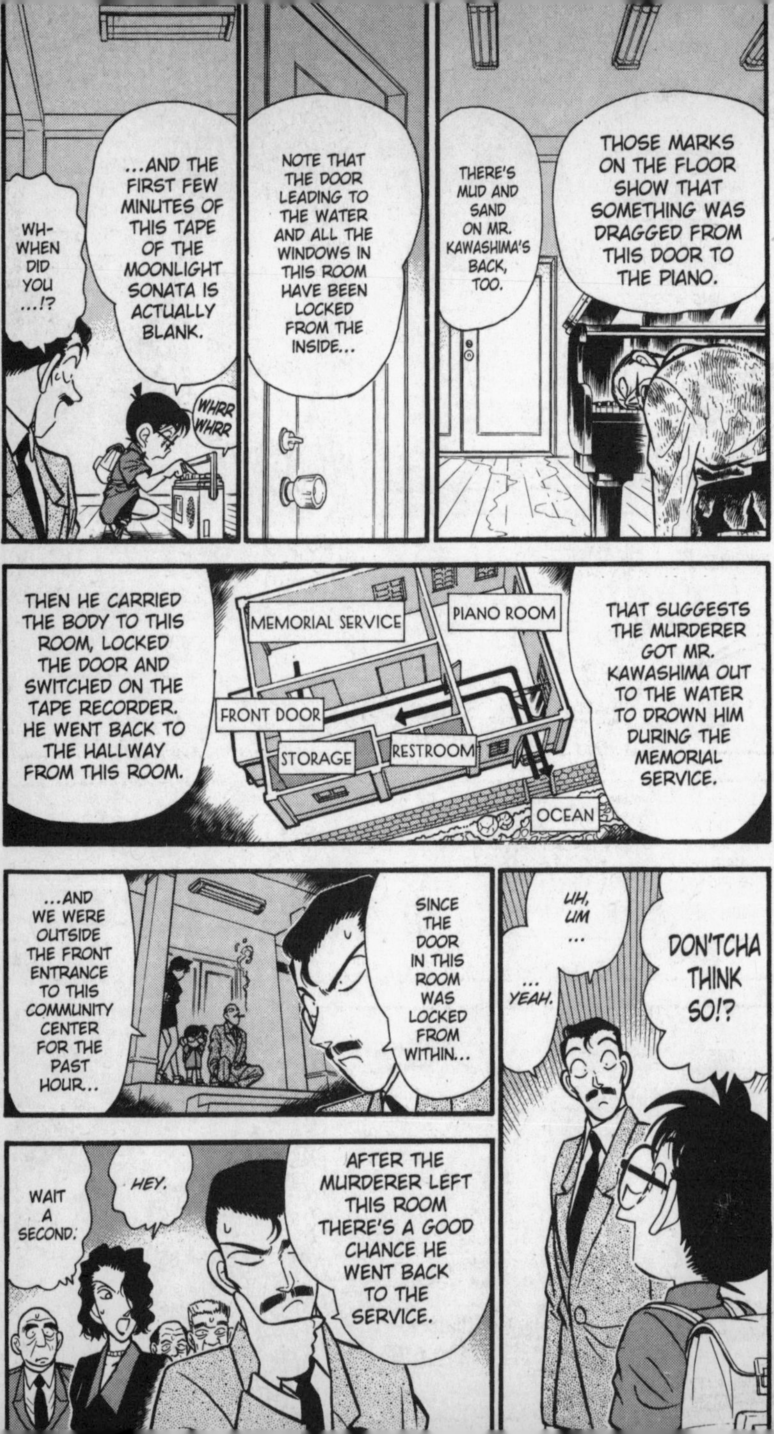
THOSE MARKS ON THE FLOOR SHOW THAT SOMETHING WAS DRAGGED FROM THIS DOOR TO THE PIANO.
THERE'S MUD AND SAND ON MR. KAWASHIMA'S BACK, TOO.
NOTE THAT THE DOOR LEADING TO THE WATER AND ALL THE WINDOWS IN THIS ROOM HAVE BEEN LOCKED FROM THE INSIDE...
...AND THE FIRST FEW MINUTES OF THIS TAPE OF THE MOONLIGHT SONATA IS ACTUALLY BLANK.
WHRR WHRR
WH-WHEN DID YOU ...!?
THAT SUGGESTS THE MURDERER GOT MR. KAWASHIMA OUT TO THE WATER TO DROWN HIM DURING THE MEMORIAL SERVICE.
PIANO ROOM
MEMORIAL SERVICE
FRONT DOOR
RESTROOM
STORAGE
OCEAN
THEN HE CARRIED THE BODY TO THIS ROOM, LOCKED THE DOOR AND SWITCHED ON THE TAPE RECORDER. HE WENT BACK TO THE HALLWAY FROM THIS ROOM.
DON'TCHA THINK SO!?
UH, UM ...
... YEAH.
SINCE THE DOOR IN THIS ROOM WAS LOCKED FROM WITHIN...
...AND WE WERE OUTSIDE THE FRONT ENTRANCE TO THIS COMMUNITY CENTER FOR THE PAST HOUR...
AFTER THE MURDERER LEFT THIS ROOM THERE'S A GOOD CHANCE HE WENT BACK TO THE SERVICE.
HEY.
WAIT A SECOND.

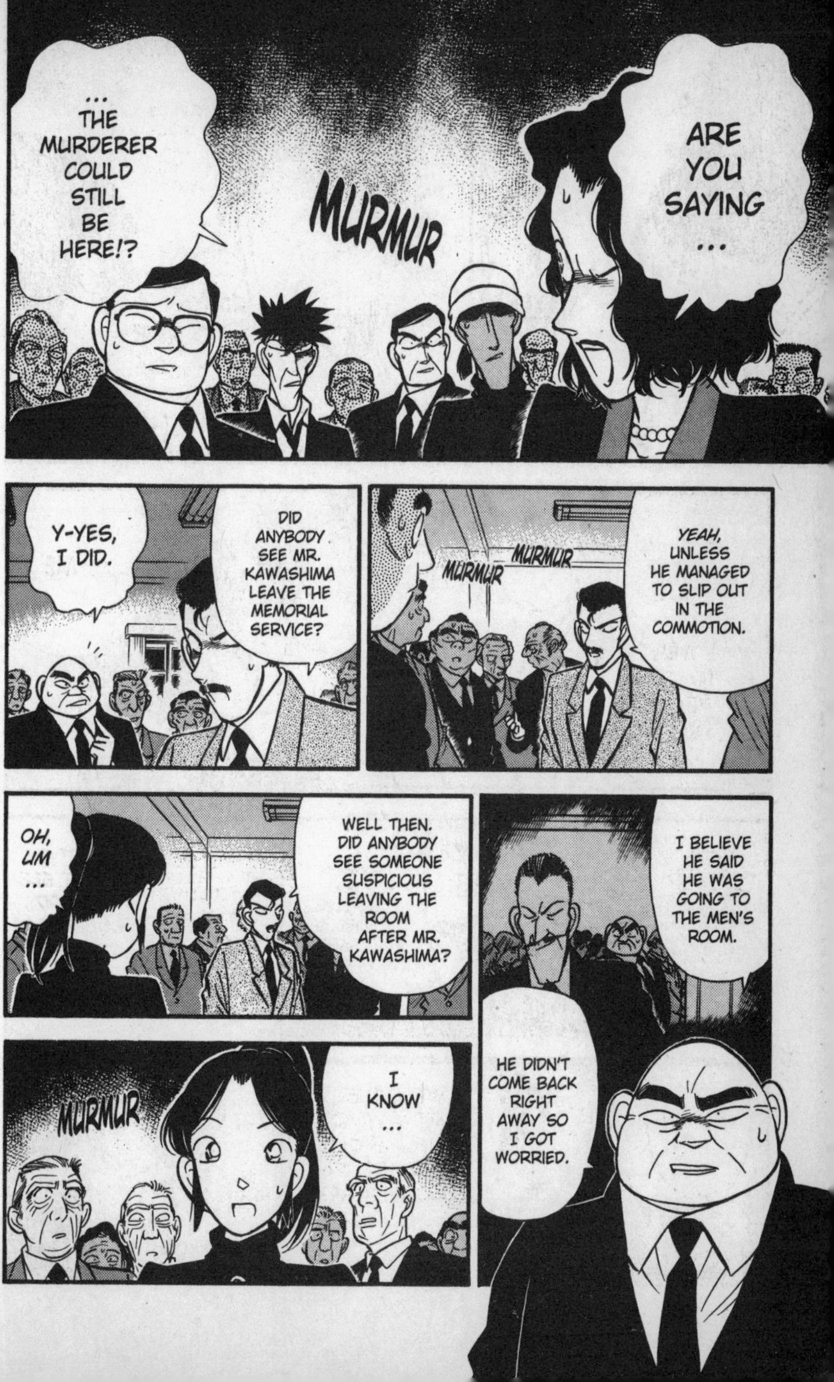
ARE YOU SAYING ...
MURMUR
... THE MURDERER COULD STILL BE HERE!?
MURMUR
MURMUR
YEAH, UNLESS HE MANAGED TO SLIP OUT IN THE COMMOTION.
DID ANYBODY SEE MR. KAWASHIMA LEAVE THE MEMORIAL SERVICE?
Y-YES, I DID.
I BELIEVE HE SAID HE WAS GOING TO THE MEN'S ROOM.
HE DIDN'T COME BACK RIGHT AWAY SO I GOT WORRIED.
WELL THEN. DID ANYBODY SEE SOMEONE SUSPICIOUS LEAVING THE ROOM AFTER MR. KAWASHIMA?
OH, UM ...
I KNOW ...
MURMUR

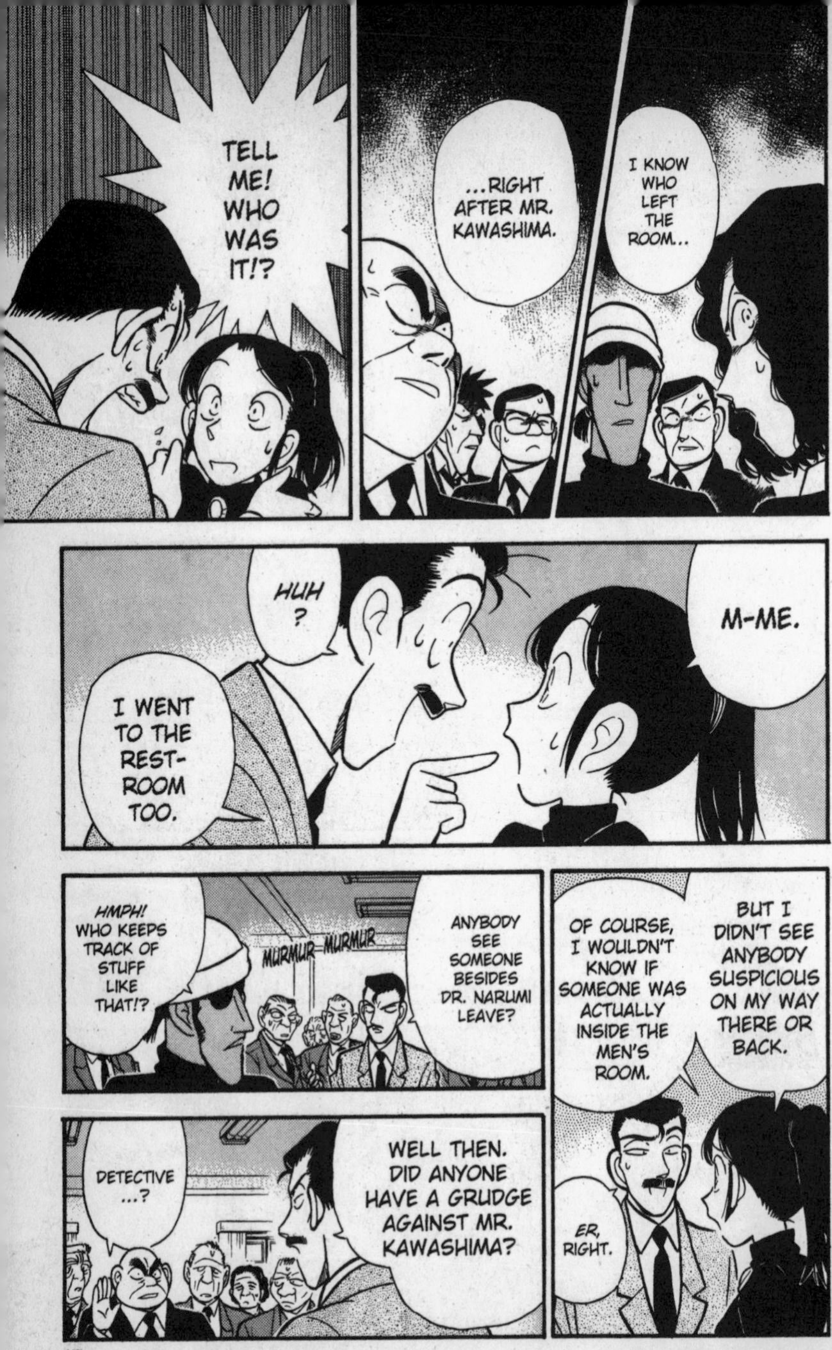
I KNOW WHO LEFT THE ROOM...
...RIGHT AFTER MR. KAWASHIMA.
TELL ME! WHO WAS IT!?
M-ME.
HUH?
I WENT TO THE REST-ROOM TOO.
BUT I DIDN'T SEE ANYBODY SUSPICIOUS ON MY WAY THERE OR BACK.
OF COURSE, I WOULDN'T KNOW IF SOMEONE WAS ACTUALLY INSIDE THE MEN'S ROOM.
ER, RIGHT.
ANYBODY SEE SOMEONE BESIDES DR. NARUMI LEAVE?
MURMUR MURMUR
HMPH! WHO KEEPS TRACK OF STUFF LIKE THAT!?
WELL THEN. DID ANYONE HAVE A GRUDGE AGAINST MR. KAWASHIMA?
DETECTIVE ...?

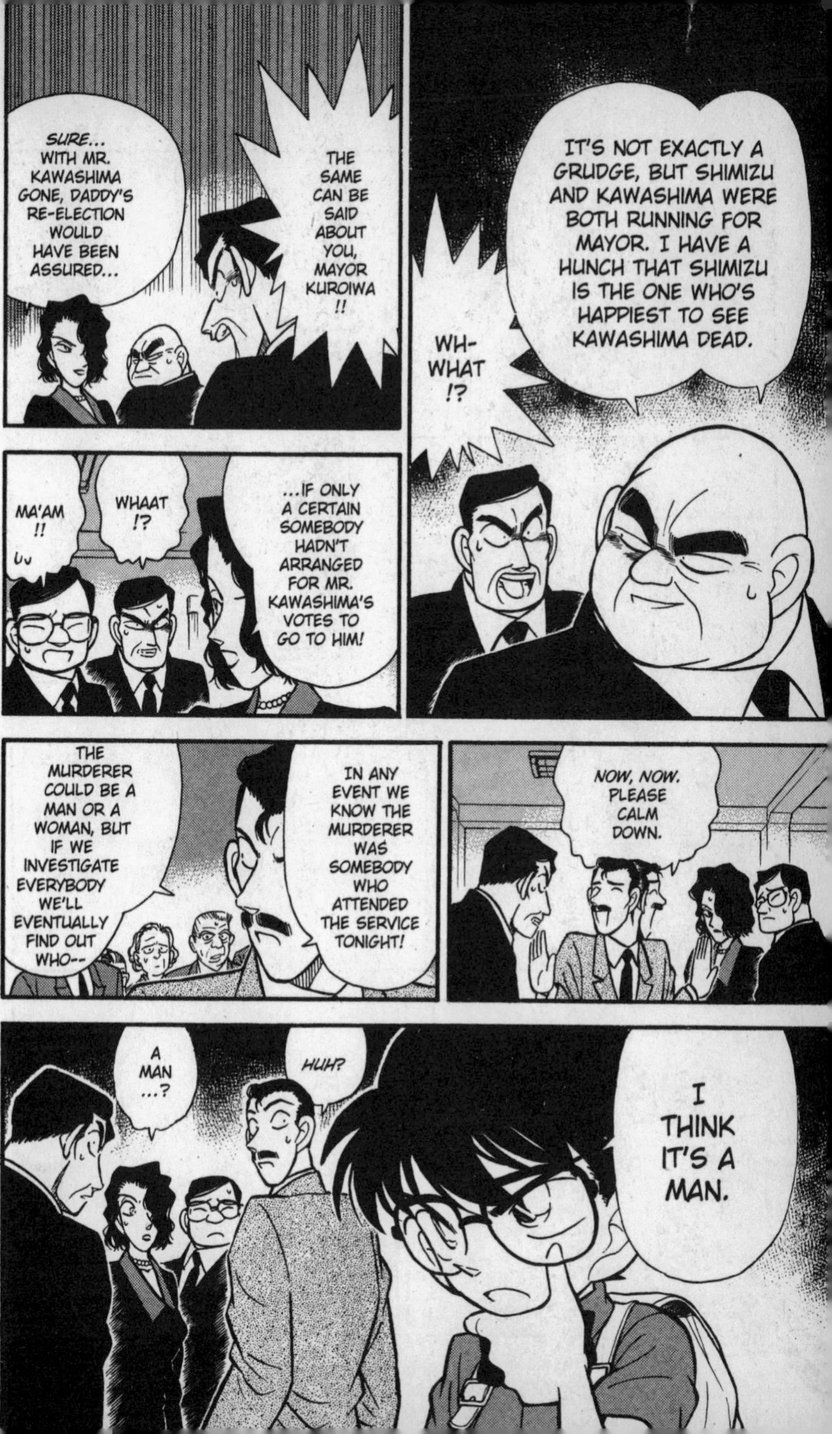
IT'S NOT EXACTLY A GRUDGE, BUT SHIMIZU AND KAWASHIMA WERE BOTH RUNNING FOR MAYOR. I HAVE A HUNCH THAT SHIMIZU IS THE ONE WHO'S HAPPIEST TO SEE KAWASHIMA DEAD.
WH- WHAT !?
THE SAME CAN BE SAID ABOUT YOU, MAYOR KUROIWA !!
SURE... WITH MR. KAWASHIMA GONE, DADDY'S RE-ELECTION WOULD HAVE BEEN ASSURED...
...IF ONLY A CERTAIN SOMEBODY HADN'T ARRANGED FOR MR. KAWASHIMA'S VOTES TO GO TO HIM!
WHAAT !?
MA'AM !!
NOW, NOW. PLEASE CALM DOWN.
IN ANY EVENT WE KNOW THE MURDERER WAS SOMEBODY WHO ATTENDED THE SERVICE TONIGHT!
THE MURDERER COULD BE A MAN OR A WOMAN, BUT IF WE INVESTIGATE EVERYBODY WE'LL EVENTUALLY FIND OUT WHO--
I THINK IT'S A MAN.
HUH?
A MAN ...?

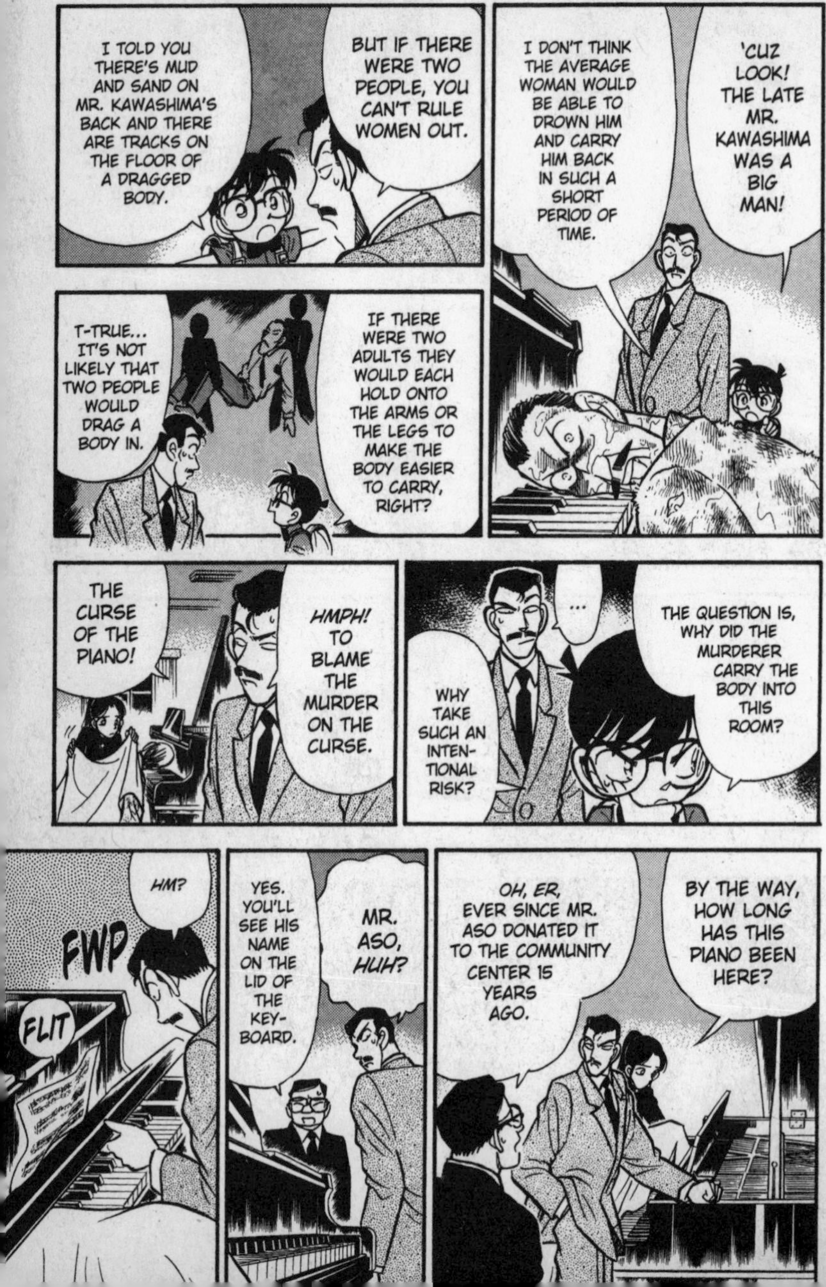
'CUZ LOOK! THE LATE MR. KAWASHIMA WAS A BIG MAN!
I DON'T THINK THE AVERAGE WOMAN WOULD BE ABLE TO DROWN HIM AND CARRY HIM BACK IN SUCH A SHORT PERIOD OF TIME.
BUT IF THERE WERE TWO PEOPLE, YOU CAN'T RULE WOMEN OUT.
I TOLD YOU THERE'S MUD AND SAND ON MR. KAWASHIMA'S BACK AND THERE ARE TRACKS ON THE FLOOR OF A DRAGGED BODY.
IF THERE WERE TWO ADULTS THEY WOULD EACH HOLD ONTO THE ARMS OR THE LEGS TO MAKE THE BODY EASIER TO CARRY, RIGHT?
T-TRUE... IT'S NOT LIKELY THAT TWO PEOPLE WOULD DRAG A BODY IN.
THE QUESTION IS, WHY DID THE MURDERER CARRY THE BODY INTO THIS ROOM?
...
WHY TAKE SUCH AN INTEN-TIONAL RISK?
HMPH! TO BLAME THE MURDER ON THE CURSE.
THE CURSE OF THE PIANO!
BY THE WAY, HOW LONG HAS THIS PIANO BEEN HERE?
OH, ER, EVER SINCE MR. ASO DONATED IT TO THE COMMUNITY CENTER 15 YEARS AGO.
MR. ASO, HUH?
YES. YOU'LL SEE HIS NAME ON THE LID OF THE KEY-BOARD.
HM?
FWP
FLIT

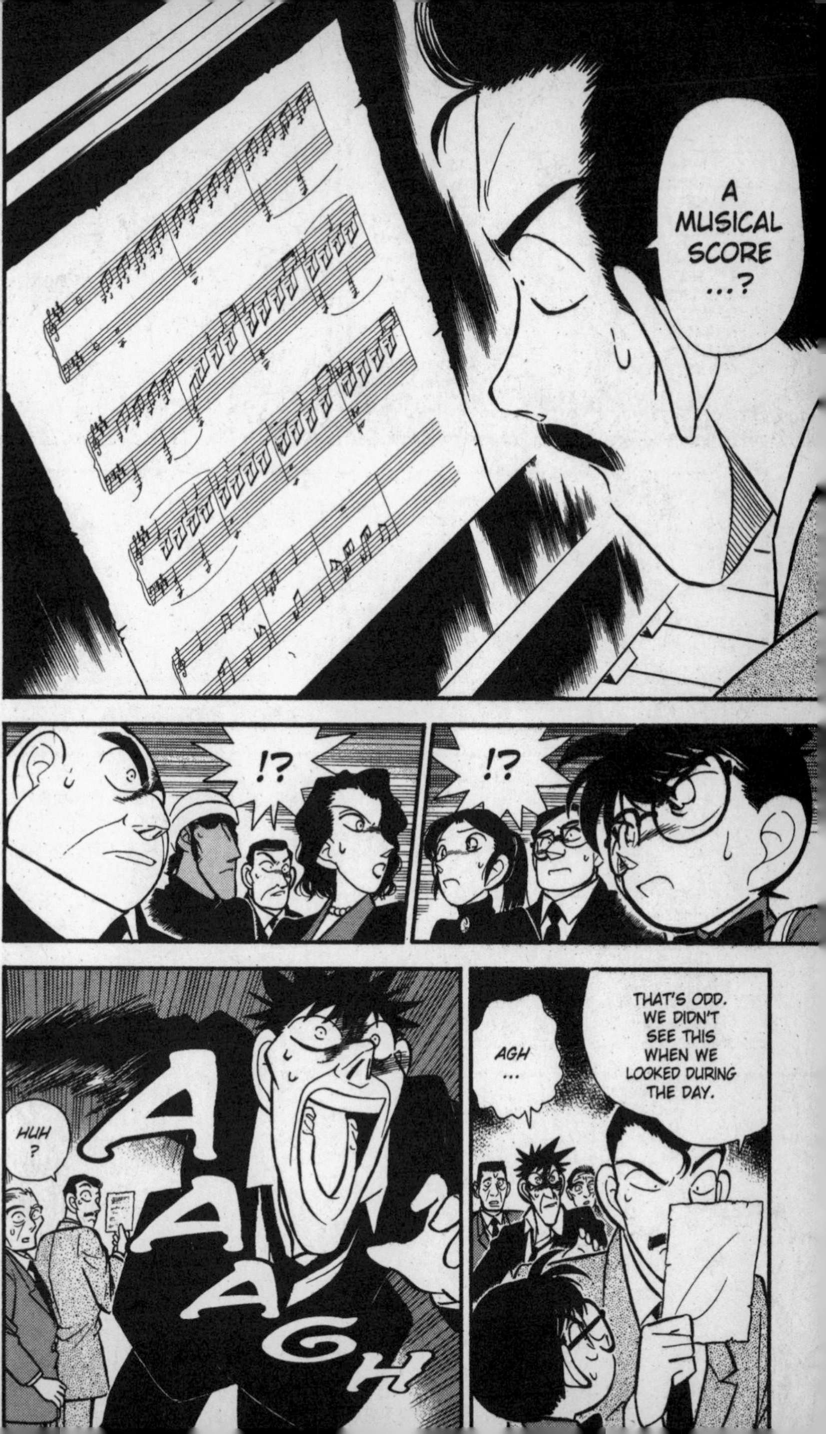
A MUSICAL SCORE ...?
!?
!?
THAT'S ODD. WE DIDN'T SEE THIS WHEN WE LOOKED DURING THE DAY.
AGH ...
AAAAGH
HUH ?

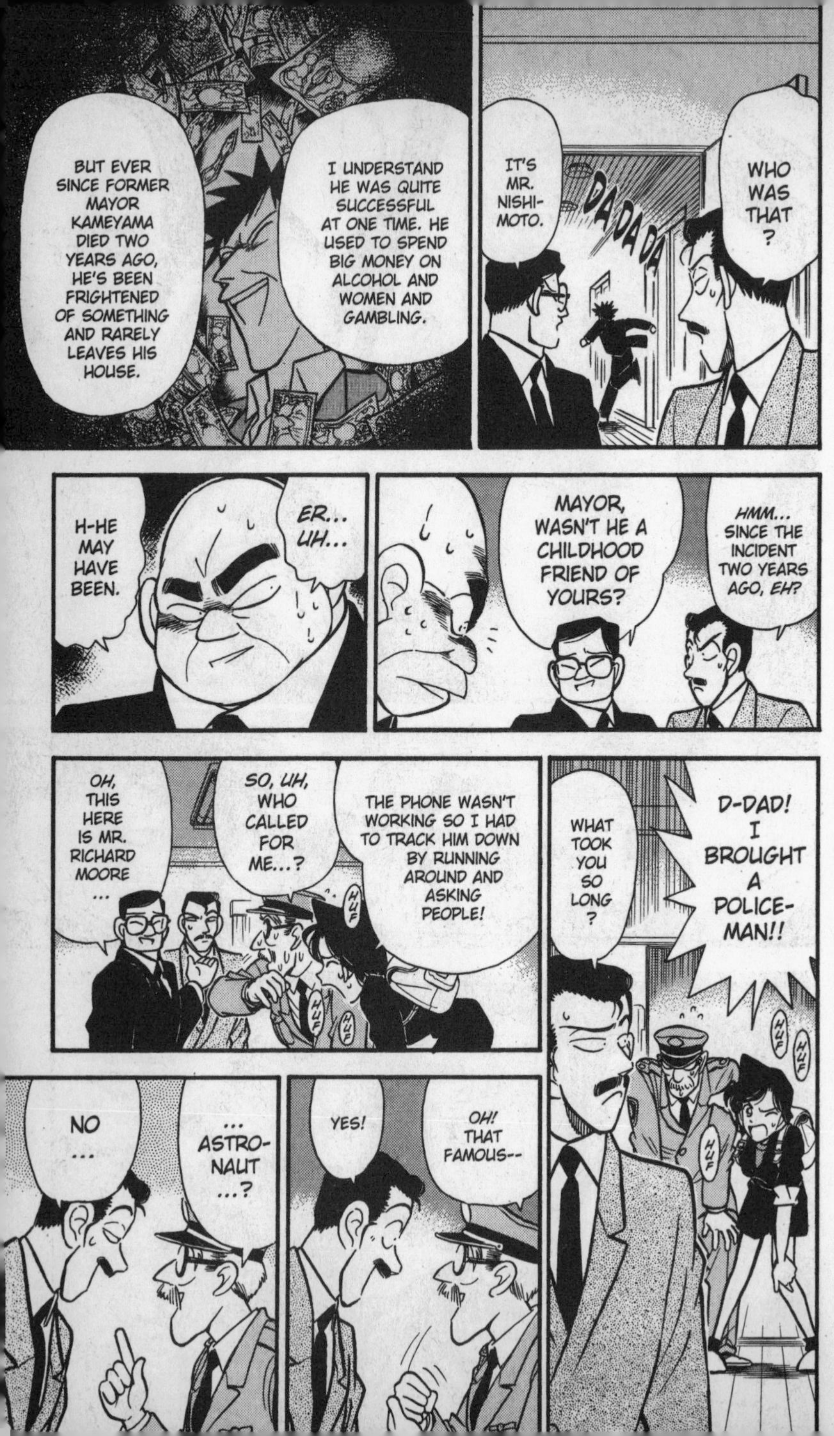
WHO WAS THAT?
IT'S MR. NISHIMOTO.
DA DA DA
I UNDERSTAND HE WAS QUITE SUCCESSFUL AT ONE TIME. HE USED TO SPEND BIG MONEY ON ALCOHOL AND WOMEN AND GAMBLING.
BUT EVER SINCE FORMER MAYOR KAMEYAMA DIED TWO YEARS AGO, HE'S BEEN FRIGHTENED OF SOMETHING AND RARELY LEAVES HIS HOUSE.
HMM... SINCE THE INCIDENT TWO YEARS AGO, EH?
MAYOR, WASN'T HE A CHILDHOOD FRIEND OF YOURS?
ER... UH...
H-HE MAY HAVE BEEN.
D-DAD! I BROUGHT A POLICE-MAN!!
HUF HUF
WHAT TOOK YOU SO LONG?
HUF
THE PHONE WASN'T WORKING SO I HAD TO TRACK HIM DOWN BY RUNNING AROUND AND ASKING PEOPLE!
HUF HUF
SO, UH, WHO CALLED FOR ME...?
HUF
OH, THIS HERE IS MR. RICHARD MOORE ...
OH! THAT FAMOUS--
YES!
... ASTRO-NAUT ...?
NO ...

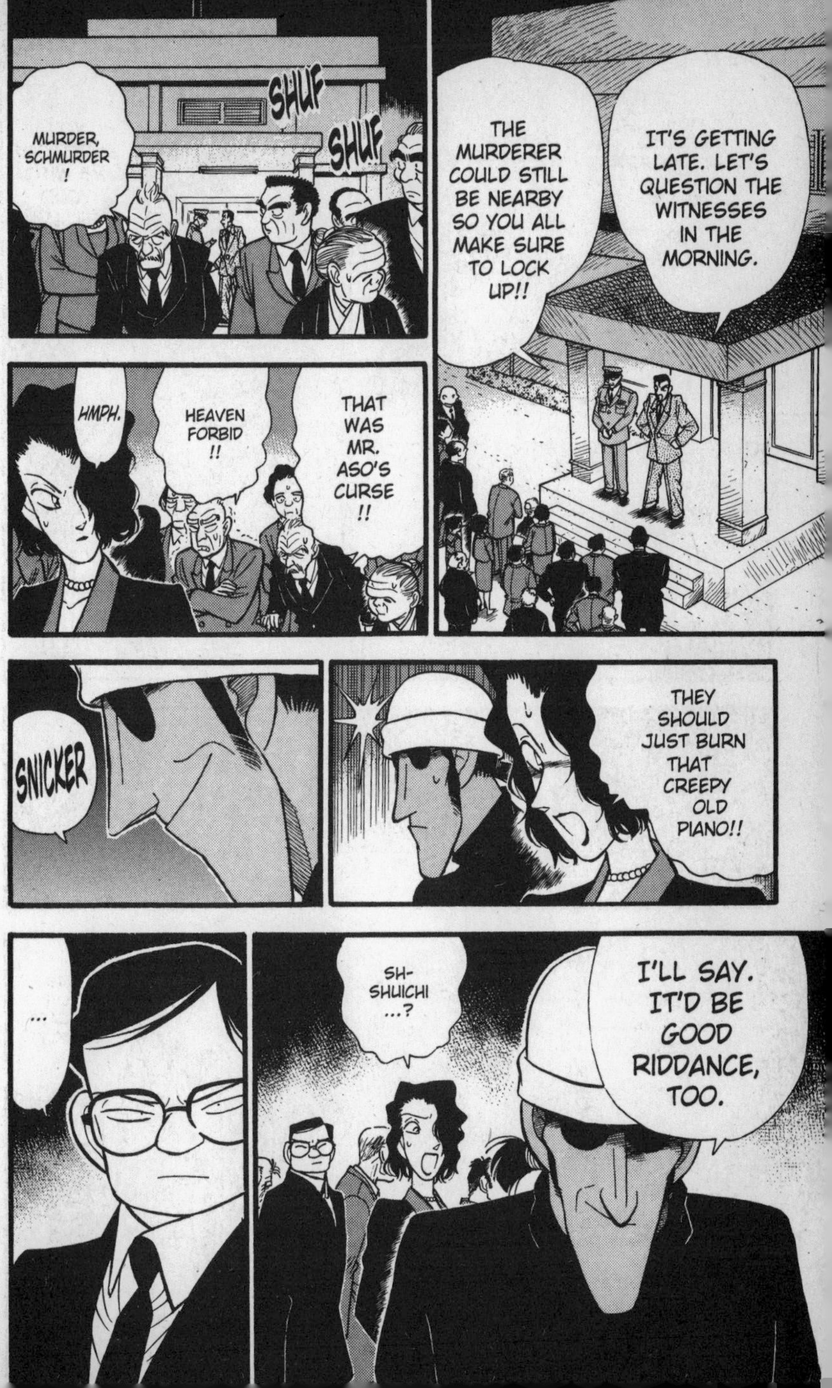
IT'S GETTING LATE. LET'S QUESTION THE WITNESSES IN THE MORNING.
THE MURDERER COULD STILL BE NEARBY SO YOU ALL MAKE SURE TO LOCK UP!!
SHUF
SHUF
MURDER, SCHMURDER!
THAT WAS MR. ASO'S CURSE!!
HEAVEN FORBID!!
HMPH.
THEY SHOULD JUST BURN THAT CREEPY OLD PIANO!!
SNICKER
I'LL SAY. IT'D BE GOOD RIDDANCE, TOO.
SH-SHUICHI...?
...

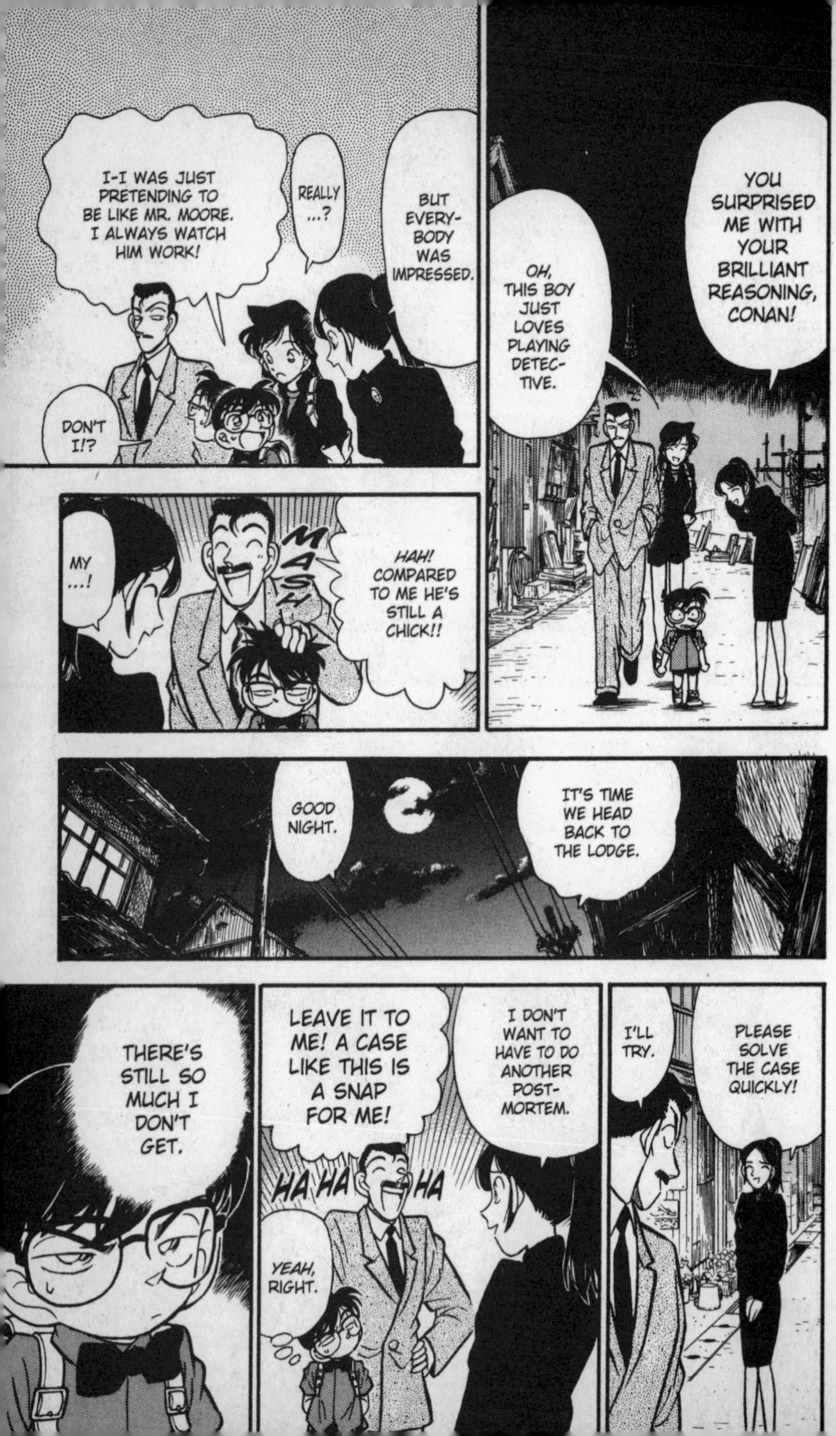
YOU SURPRISED ME WITH YOUR BRILLIANT REASONING, CONAN!
OH, THIS BOY JUST LOVES PLAYING DETEC-TIVE.
BUT EVERY-BODY WAS IMPRESSED.
REALLY ...?
I-I WAS JUST PRETENDING TO BE LIKE MR. MOORE. I ALWAYS WATCH HIM WORK!
DON'T I!?
HAH! COMPARED TO ME HE'S STILL A CHICK!!
MASH
MY ...!
IT'S TIME WE HEAD BACK TO THE LODGE.
GOOD NIGHT.
PLEASE SOLVE THE CASE QUICKLY!
I'LL TRY.
I DON'T WANT TO HAVE TO DO ANOTHER POST-MORTEM.
LEAVE IT TO ME! A CASE LIKE THIS IS A SNAP FOR ME!
HA HA HA
YEAH, RIGHT.
THERE'S STILL SO MUCH I DON'T GET.

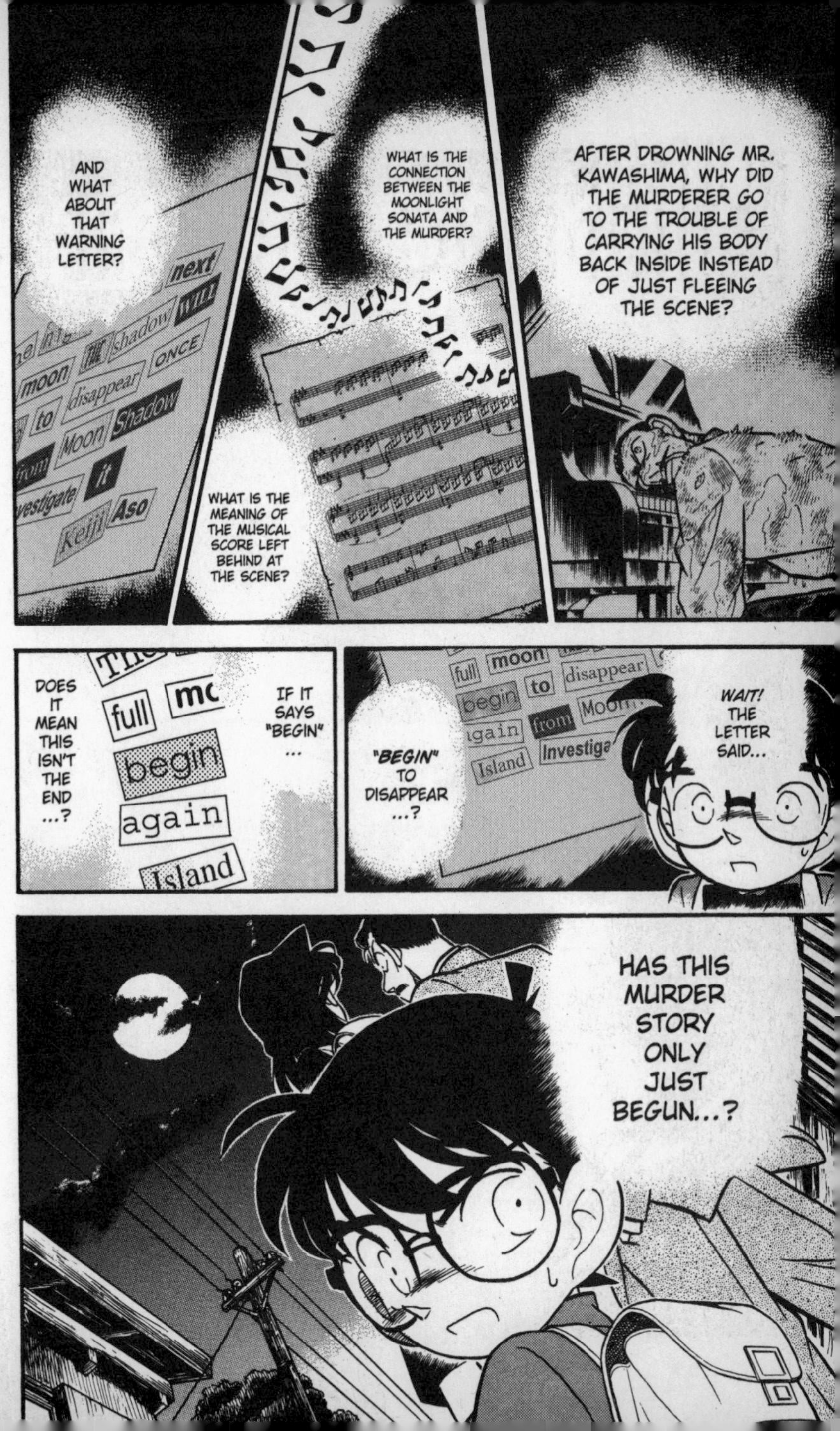
AFTER DROWNING MR. KAWASHIMA, WHY DID THE MURDERER GO TO THE TROUBLE OF CARRYING HIS BODY BACK INSIDE INSTEAD OF JUST FLEEING THE SCENE?
WHAT IS THE CONNECTION BETWEEN THE MOONLIGHT SONATA AND THE MURDER?
WHAT IS THE MEANING OF THE MUSICAL SCORE LEFT BEHIND AT THE SCENE?
AND WHAT ABOUT THAT WARNING LETTER?
WAIT! THE LETTER SAID...
"BEGIN" TO DISAPPEAR...?
IF IT SAYS "BEGIN"...
DOES IT MEAN THIS ISN'T THE END...?
HAS THIS MURDER STORY ONLY JUST BEGUN...?

FILE 4: THE MUSICAL SCORE

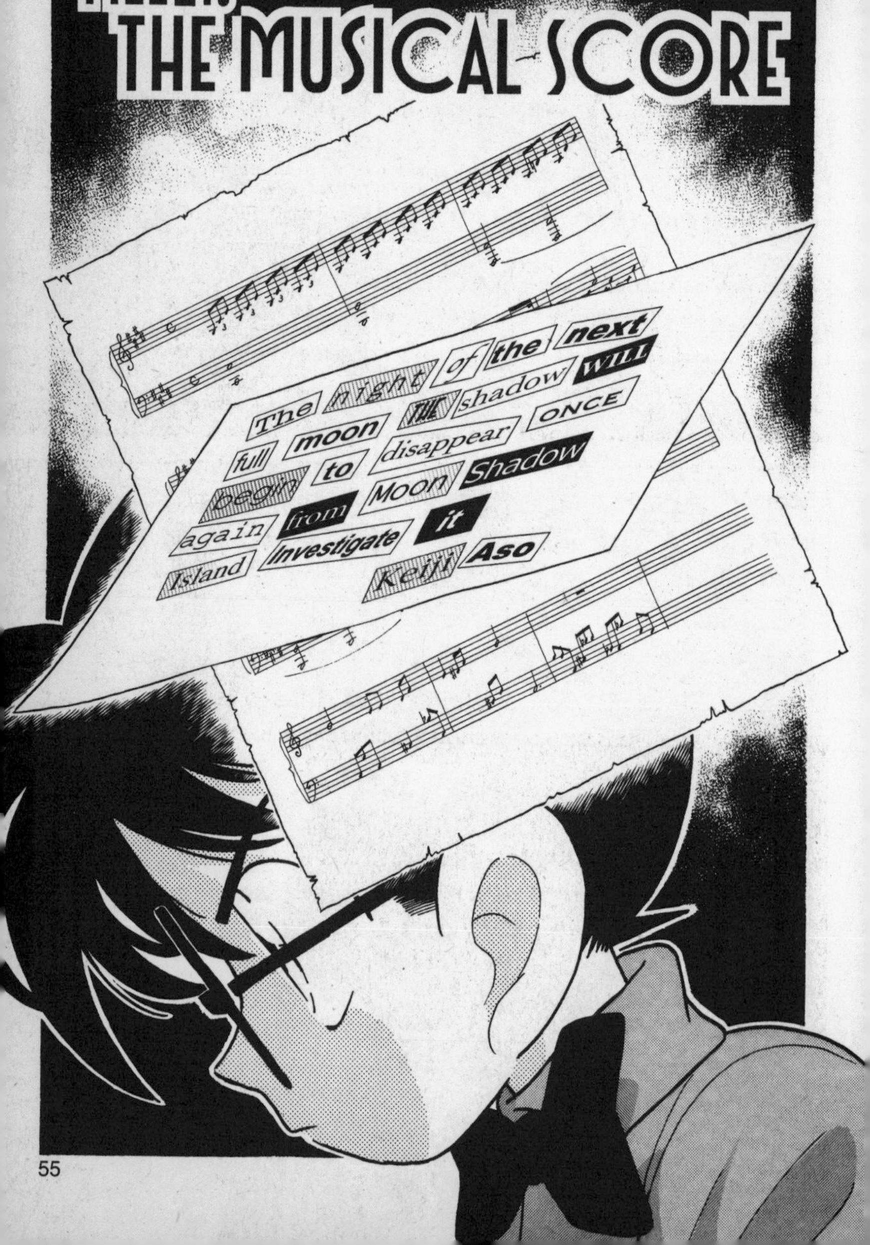
The night of the next
full moon THE shadow WILL
begin to disappear ONCE
again from Moon Shadow
Island Investigate it
Keiji Aso

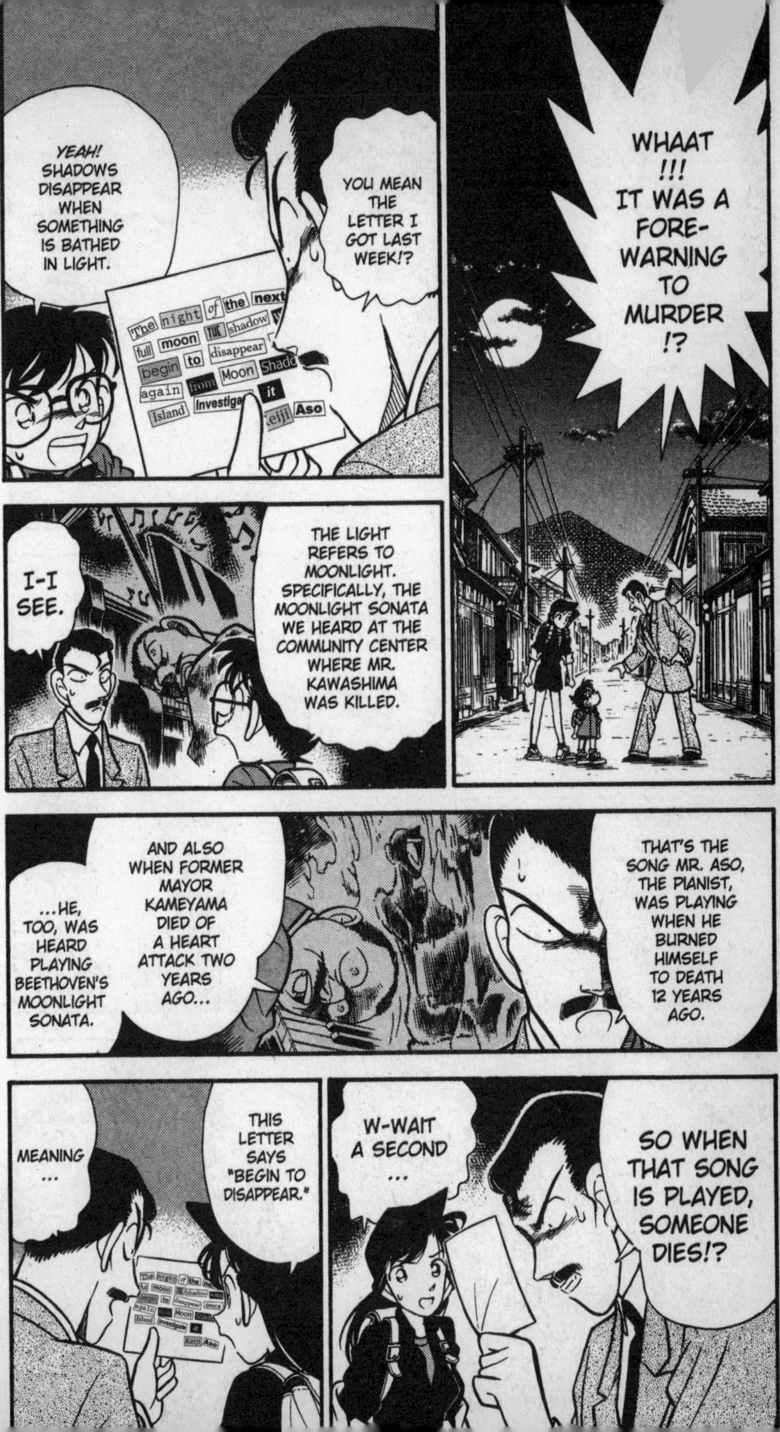
WHAAT !!! IT WAS A FORE-WARNING TO MURDER !?
YOU MEAN THE LETTER I GOT LAST WEEK!?
YEAH! SHADOWS DISAPPEAR WHEN SOMETHING IS BATHED IN LIGHT.
THE LIGHT REFERS TO MOONLIGHT. SPECIFICALLY, THE MOONLIGHT SONATA WE HEARD AT THE COMMUNITY CENTER WHERE MR. KAWASHIMA WAS KILLED.
I-I SEE.
THAT'S THE SONG MR. ASO, THE PIANIST, WAS PLAYING WHEN HE BURNED HIMSELF TO DEATH 12 YEARS AGO.
AND ALSO WHEN FORMER MAYOR KAMEYAMA DIED OF A HEART ATTACK TWO YEARS AGO...
...HE, TOO, WAS HEARD PLAYING BEETHOVEN'S MOONLIGHT SONATA.
SO WHEN THAT SONG IS PLAYED, SOMEONE DIES!?
W-WAIT A SECOND ...
THIS LETTER SAYS "BEGIN TO DISAPPEAR."
MEANING ...

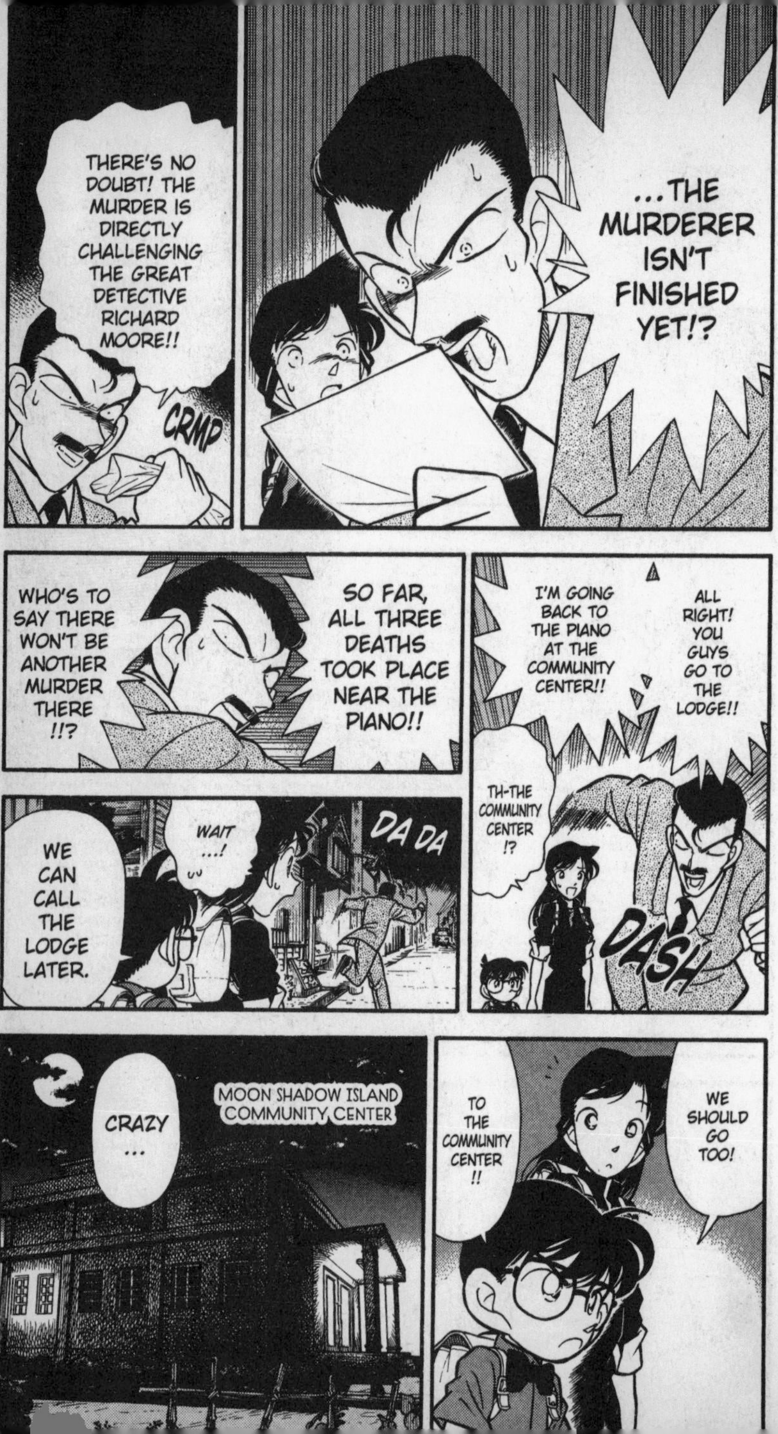
...THE MURDERER ISN'T FINISHED YET!?
THERE'S NO DOUBT! THE MURDER IS DIRECTLY CHALLENGING THE GREAT DETECTIVE RICHARD MOORE!!
CRMP
ALL RIGHT! YOU GUYS GO TO THE LODGE!!
I'M GOING BACK TO THE PIANO AT THE COMMUNITY CENTER!!
TH-THE COMMUNITY CENTER !?
DASH
SO FAR, ALL THREE DEATHS TOOK PLACE NEAR THE PIANO!!
WHO'S TO SAY THERE WON'T BE ANOTHER MURDER THERE !!?
DA DA
WAIT ...!
WE CAN CALL THE LODGE LATER.
WE SHOULD GO TOO!
TO THE COMMUNITY CENTER !!
MOON SHADOW ISLAND COMMUNITY CENTER
CRAZY ...

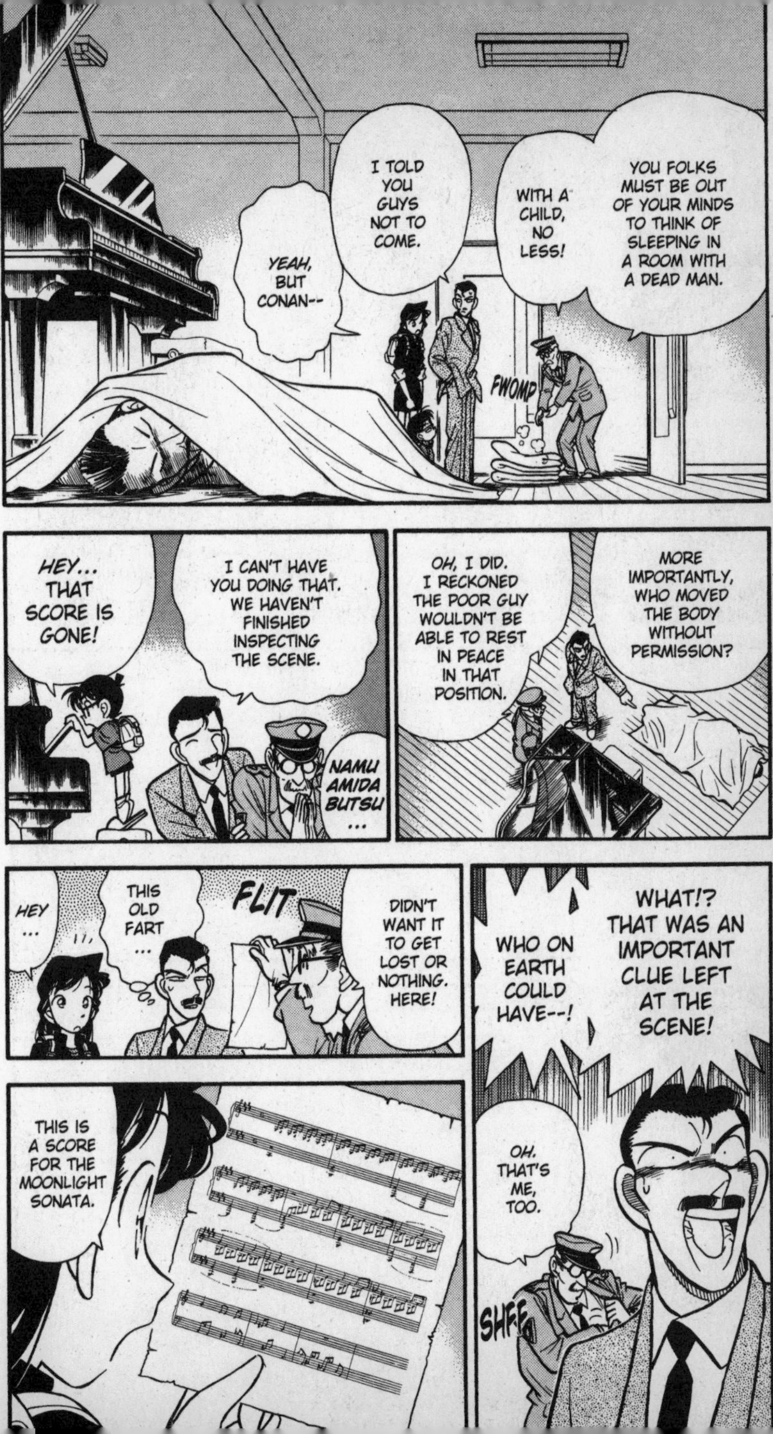
YOU FOLKS MUST BE OUT OF YOUR MINDS TO THINK OF SLEEPING IN A ROOM WITH A DEAD MAN.
WITH A CHILD, NO LESS!
I TOLD YOU GUYS NOT TO COME.
YEAH, BUT CONAN--
FWOMP
MORE IMPORTANTLY, WHO MOVED THE BODY WITHOUT PERMISSION?
OH, I DID. I RECKONED THE POOR GUY WOULDN'T BE ABLE TO REST IN PEACE IN THAT POSITION.
I CAN'T HAVE YOU DOING THAT. WE HAVEN'T FINISHED INSPECTING THE SCENE.
NAMU AMIDA BUTSU...
HEY... THAT SCORE IS GONE!
WHAT!? THAT WAS AN IMPORTANT CLUE LEFT AT THE SCENE!
WHO ON EARTH COULD HAVE--!
OH. THAT'S ME, TOO.
SHFF
DIDN'T WANT IT TO GET LOST OR NOTHING. HERE!
FLIT
THIS OLD FART...
HEY...
THIS IS A SCORE FOR THE MOONLIGHT SONATA.

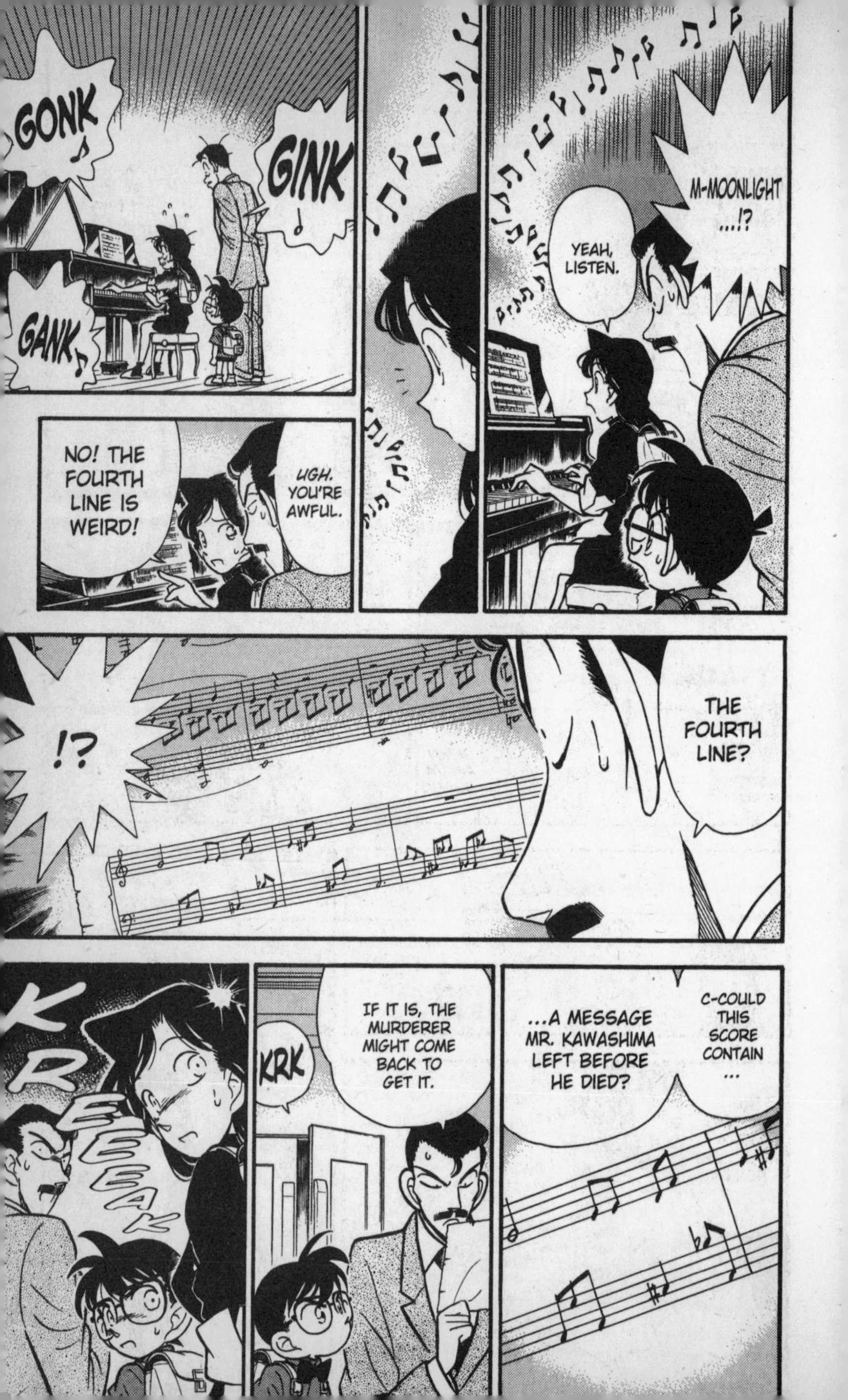
M-MOONLIGHT ...!?
YEAH, LISTEN.
GONK
GINK
GANK
UGH. YOU'RE AWFUL.
NO! THE FOURTH LINE IS WEIRD!
THE FOURTH LINE?
!?
C-COULD THIS SCORE CONTAIN ...
...A MESSAGE MR. KAWASHIMA LEFT BEFORE HE DIED?
IF IT IS, THE MURDERER MIGHT COME BACK TO GET IT.
KRK
KREEEEAK

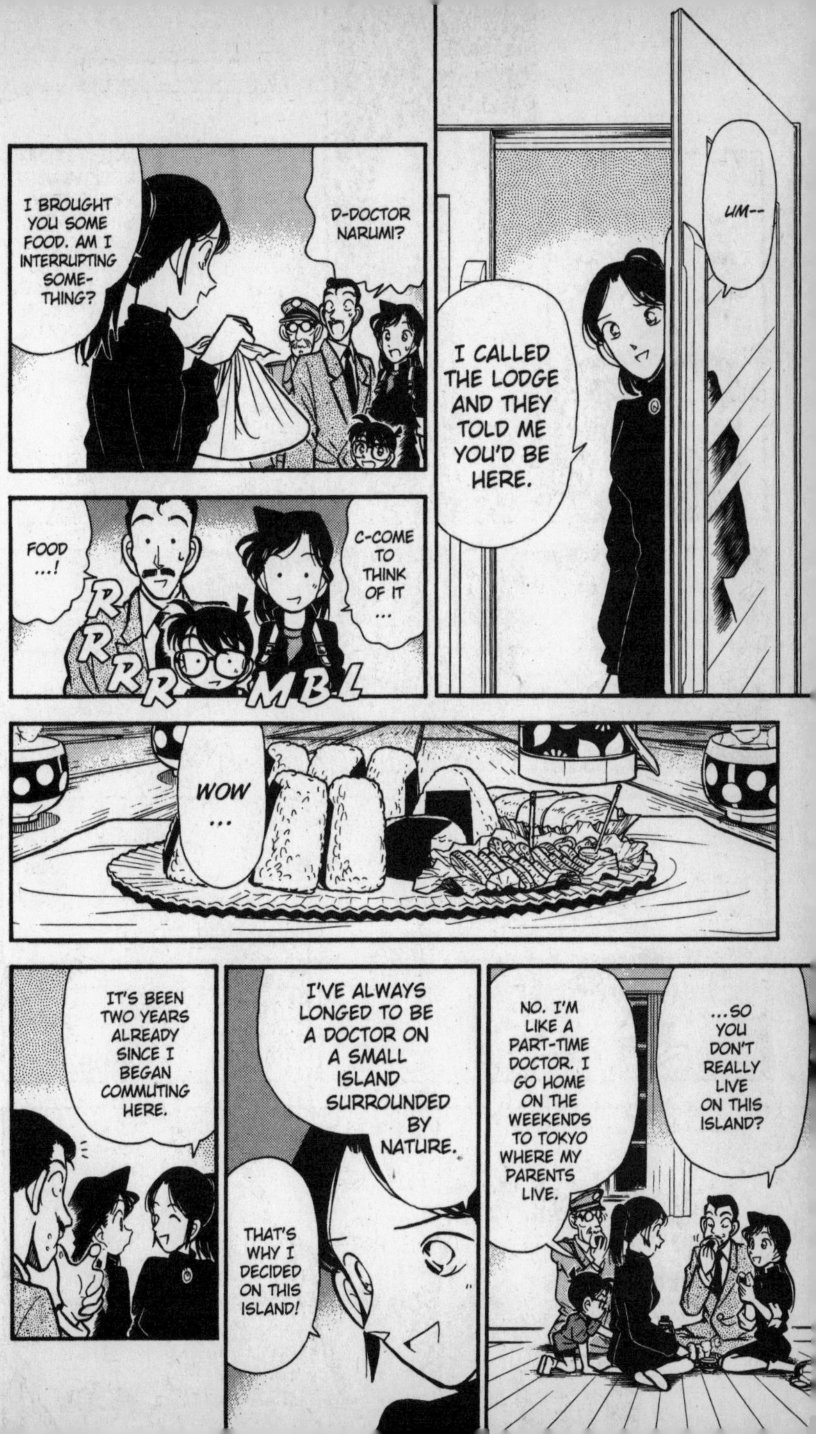
UM--
I CALLED THE LODGE AND THEY TOLD ME YOU'D BE HERE.
D-DOCTOR NARUMI?
I BROUGHT YOU SOME FOOD. AM I INTERRUPTING SOME-THING?
C-COME TO THINK OF IT...
FOOD...!
RRRRRMBL
WOW...
...SO YOU DON'T REALLY LIVE ON THIS ISLAND?
NO. I'M LIKE A PART-TIME DOCTOR. I GO HOME ON THE WEEKENDS TO TOKYO WHERE MY PARENTS LIVE.
I'VE ALWAYS LONGED TO BE A DOCTOR ON A SMALL ISLAND SURROUNDED BY NATURE.
THAT'S WHY I DECIDED ON THIS ISLAND!
IT'S BEEN TWO YEARS ALREADY SINCE I BEGAN COMMUTING HERE.

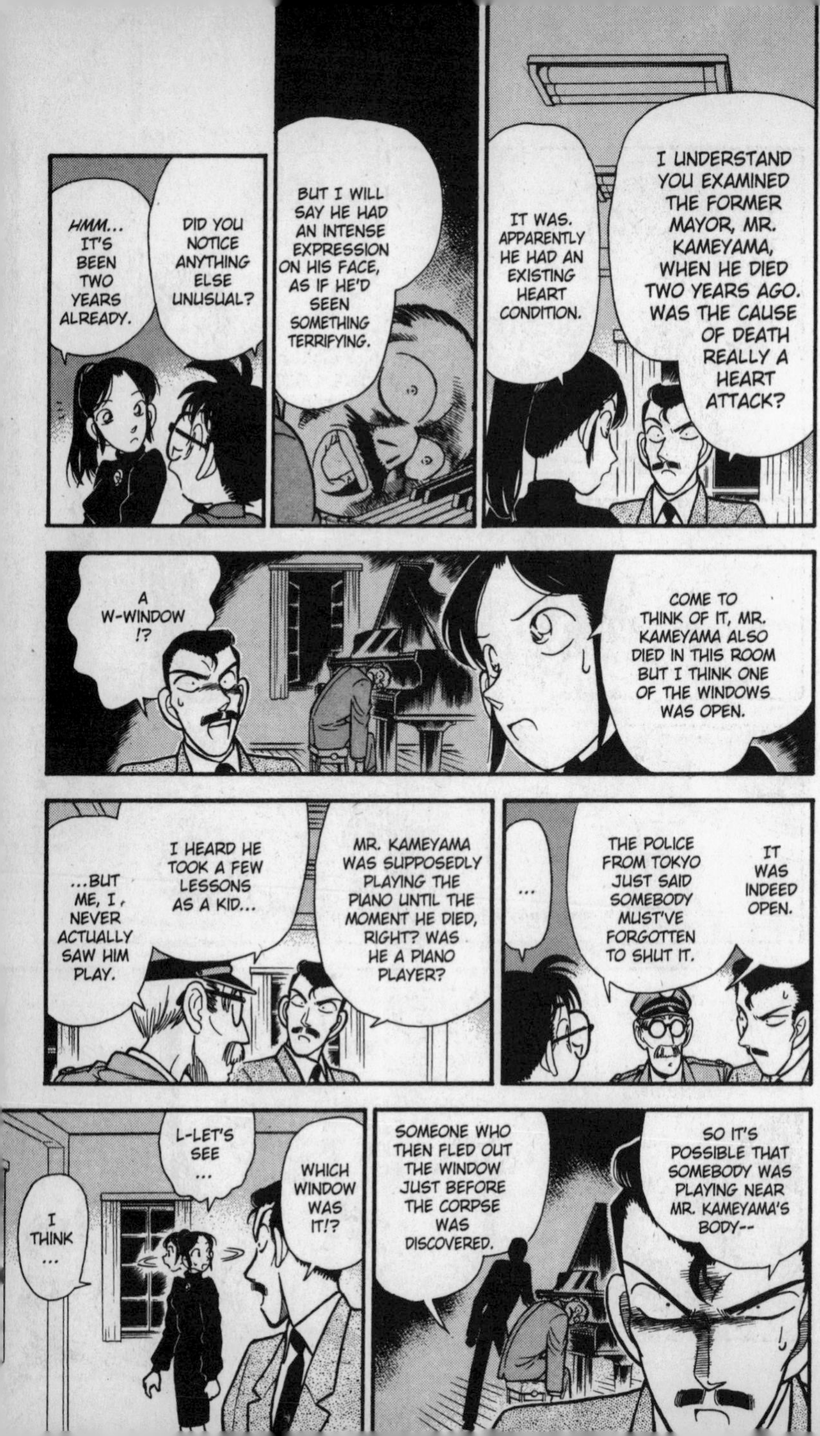
I UNDERSTAND YOU EXAMINED THE FORMER MAYOR, MR. KAMEYAMA, WHEN HE DIED TWO YEARS AGO. WAS THE CAUSE OF DEATH REALLY A HEART ATTACK?
IT WAS. APPARENTLY HE HAD AN EXISTING HEART CONDITION.
BUT I WILL SAY HE HAD AN INTENSE EXPRESSION ON HIS FACE, AS IF HE'D SEEN SOMETHING TERRIFYING.
DID YOU NOTICE ANYTHING ELSE UNUSUAL?
HMM... IT'S BEEN TWO YEARS ALREADY.
COME TO THINK OF IT, MR. KAMEYAMA ALSO DIED IN THIS ROOM BUT I THINK ONE OF THE WINDOWS WAS OPEN.
A W-WINDOW !?
IT WAS INDEED OPEN.
THE POLICE FROM TOKYO JUST SAID SOMEBODY MUST'VE FORGOTTEN TO SHUT IT.
...
MR. KAMEYAMA WAS SUPPOSEDLY PLAYING THE PIANO UNTIL THE MOMENT HE DIED, RIGHT? WAS HE A PIANO PLAYER?
I HEARD HE TOOK A FEW LESSONS AS A KID...
...BUT ME, I, NEVER ACTUALLY SAW HIM PLAY.
SO IT'S POSSIBLE THAT SOMEBODY WAS PLAYING NEAR MR. KAMEYAMA'S BODY--
SOMEONE WHO THEN FLED OUT THE WINDOW JUST BEFORE THE CORPSE WAS DISCOVERED.
WHICH WINDOW WAS IT!?
L-LET'S SEE ...
I THINK ...

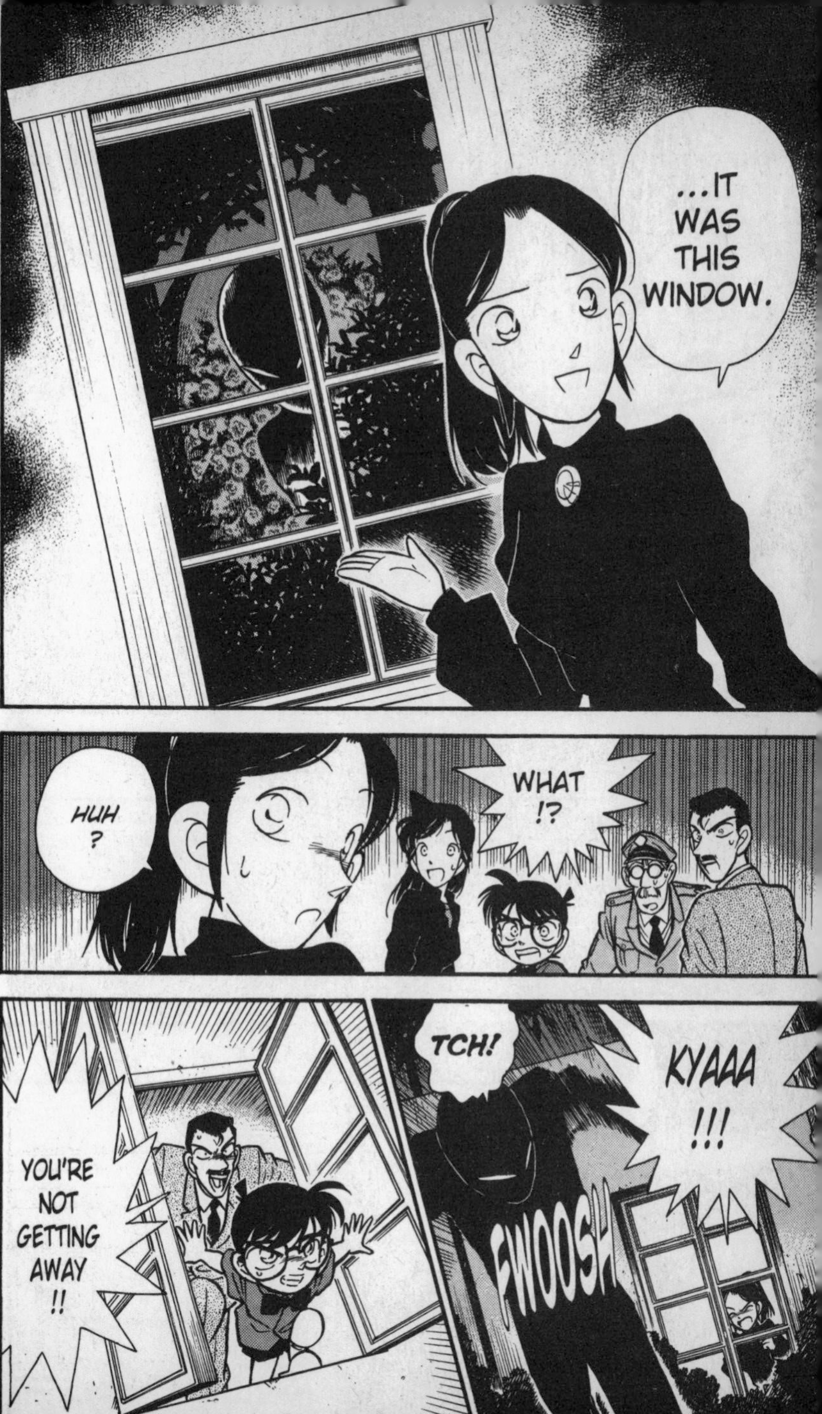
...IT WAS THIS WINDOW.
WHAT !?
HUH ?
KYAAA !!!
TCH!
SWOOSH
YOU'RE NOT GETTING AWAY !!

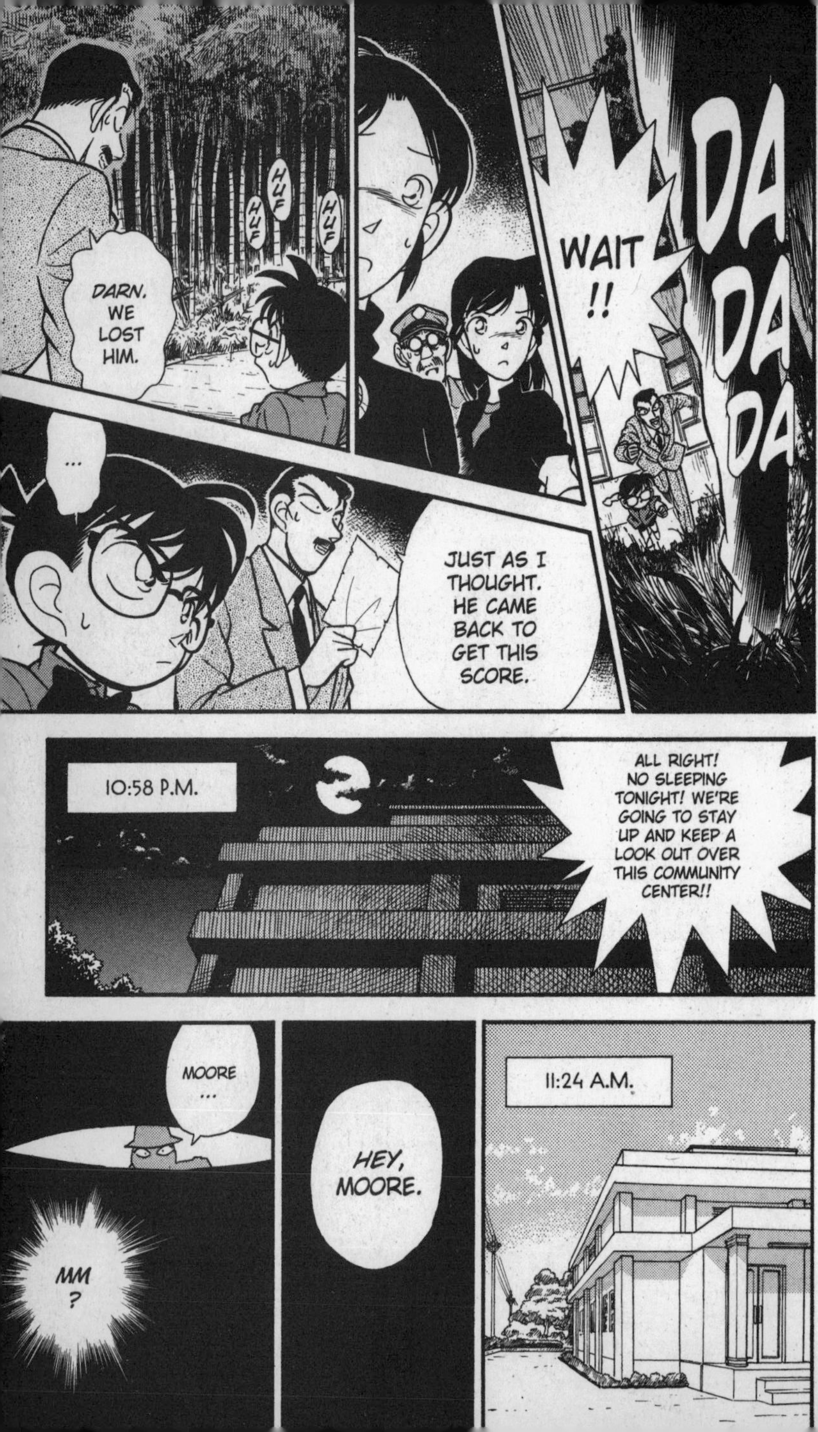
WAIT !!
DA DA DA
HUF HUF HUF
DARN. WE LOST HIM.
JUST AS I THOUGHT. HE CAME BACK TO GET THIS SCORE.
...
ALL RIGHT! NO SLEEPING TONIGHT! WE'RE GOING TO STAY UP AND KEEP A LOOK OUT OVER THIS COMMUNITY CENTER!!
10:58 P.M.
11:24 A.M.
HEY, MOORE.
MOORE ...
MM ?

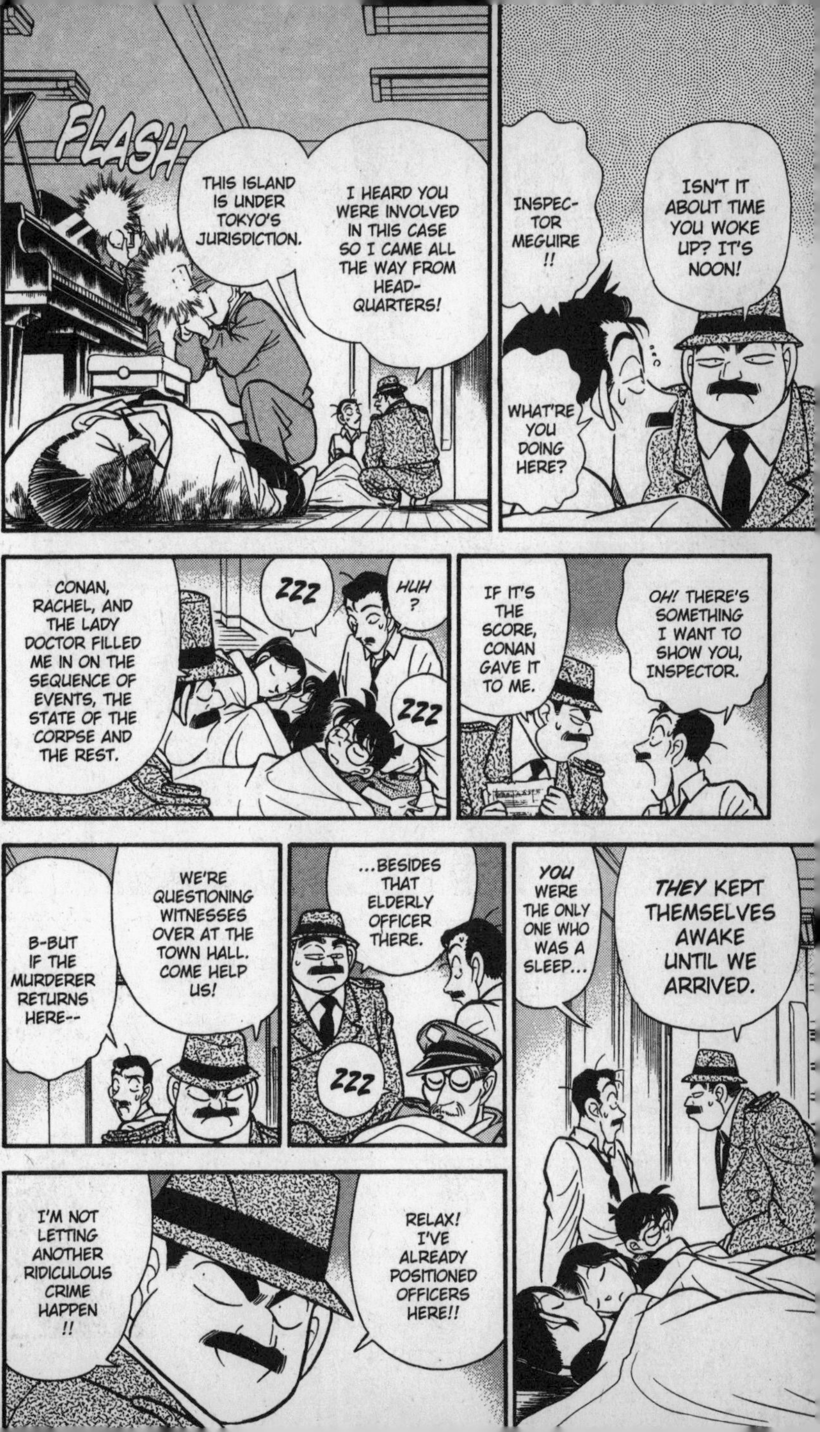
ISN'T IT ABOUT TIME YOU WOKE UP? IT'S NOON!
INSPECTOR MEGUIRE !!
WHAT'RE YOU DOING HERE?
I HEARD YOU WERE INVOLVED IN THIS CASE SO I CAME ALL THE WAY FROM HEADQUARTERS!
THIS ISLAND IS UNDER TOKYO'S JURISDICTION.
FLASH
OH! THERE'S SOMETHING I WANT TO SHOW YOU, INSPECTOR.
IF IT'S THE SCORE, CONAN GAVE IT TO ME.
HUH ?
ZZZ
ZZZ
CONAN, RACHEL, AND THE LADY DOCTOR FILLED ME IN ON THE SEQUENCE OF EVENTS, THE STATE OF THE CORPSE AND THE REST.
THEY KEPT THEMSELVES AWAKE UNTIL WE ARRIVED.
YOU WERE THE ONLY ONE WHO WAS A SLEEP...
...BESIDES THAT ELDERLY OFFICER THERE.
ZZZ
WE'RE QUESTIONING WITNESSES OVER AT THE TOWN HALL. COME HELP US!
B-BUT IF THE MURDERER RETURNS HERE--
RELAX! I'VE ALREADY POSITIONED OFFICERS HERE!!
I'M NOT LETTING ANOTHER RIDICULOUS CRIME HAPPEN !!

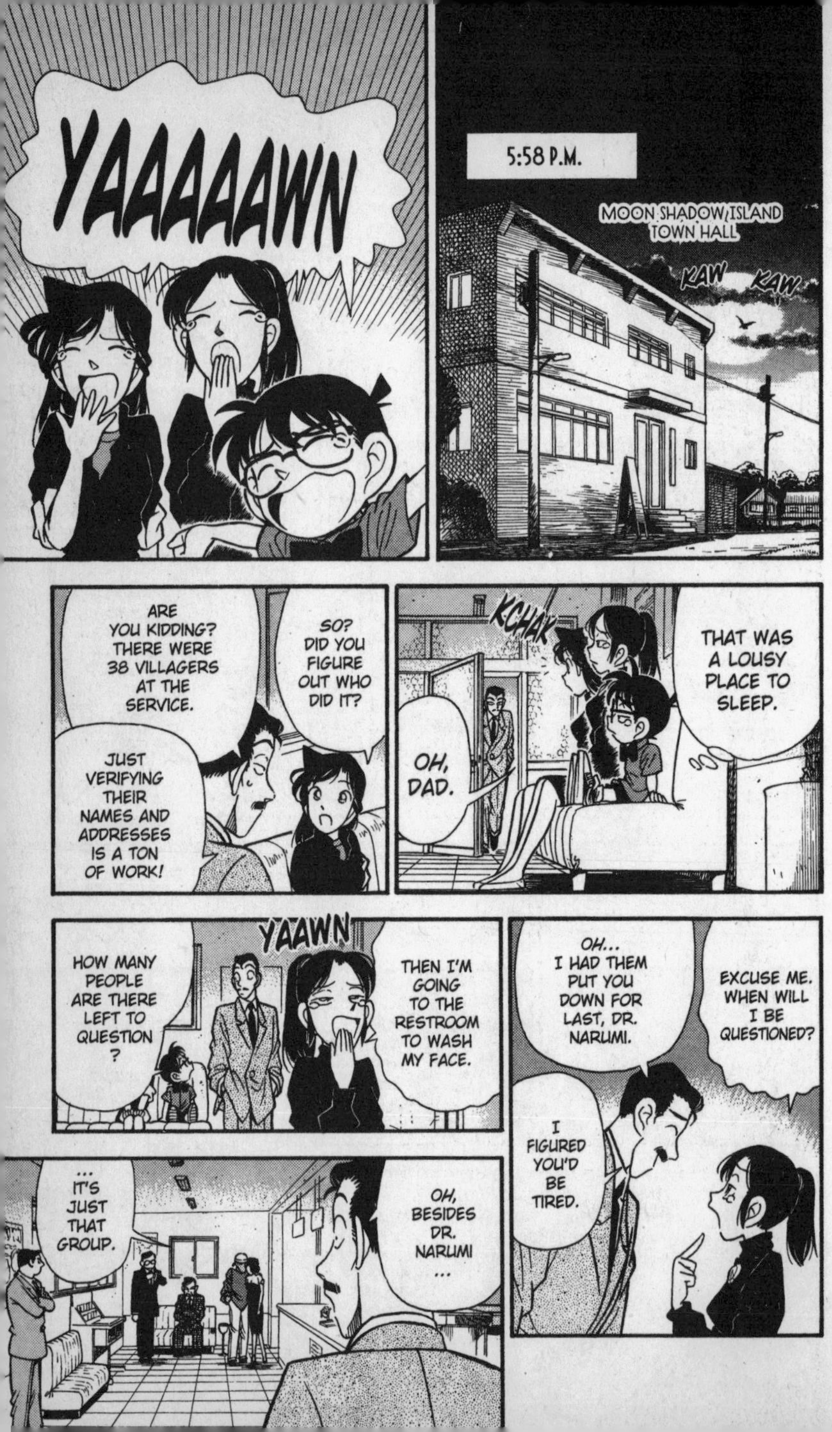
5:58 P.M.
MOON SHADOW ISLAND TOWN HALL
KAW
KAW
YAAAAAWN
KCHAK
THAT WAS A LOUSY PLACE TO SLEEP.
OH, DAD.
SO? DID YOU FIGURE OUT WHO DID IT?
ARE YOU KIDDING? THERE WERE 38 VILLAGERS AT THE SERVICE.
JUST VERIFYING THEIR NAMES AND ADDRESSES IS A TON OF WORK!
EXCUSE ME. WHEN WILL I BE QUESTIONED?
OH... I HAD THEM PUT YOU DOWN FOR LAST, DR. NARUMI.
I FIGURED YOU'D BE TIRED.
YAAWN
THEN I'M GOING TO THE RESTROOM TO WASH MY FACE.
HOW MANY PEOPLE ARE THERE LEFT TO QUESTION?
OH, BESIDES DR. NARUMI ...
... IT'S JUST THAT GROUP.

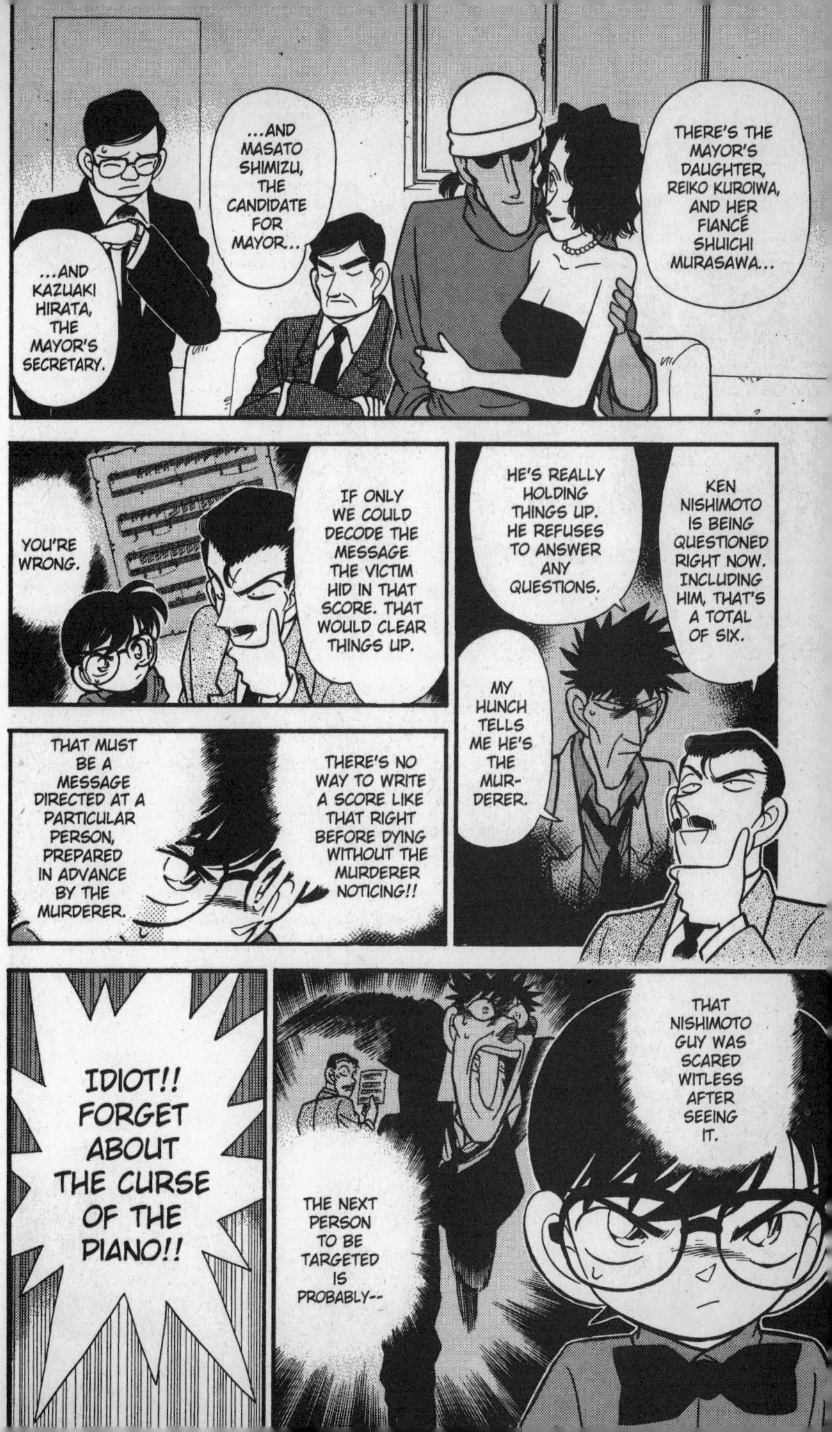
THERE'S THE MAYOR'S DAUGHTER, REIKO KUROIWA, AND HER FIANCÉ SHUICHI MURASAWA...
...AND MASATO SHIMIZU, THE CANDIDATE FOR MAYOR...
...AND KAZUAKI HIRATA, THE MAYOR'S SECRETARY.
KEN NISHIMOTO IS BEING QUESTIONED RIGHT NOW. INCLUDING HIM, THAT'S A TOTAL OF SIX.
HE'S REALLY HOLDING THINGS UP. HE REFUSES TO ANSWER ANY QUESTIONS.
MY HUNCH TELLS ME HE'S THE MUR-DERER.
IF ONLY WE COULD DECODE THE MESSAGE THE VICTIM HID IN THAT SCORE. THAT WOULD CLEAR THINGS UP.
YOU'RE WRONG.
THERE'S NO WAY TO WRITE A SCORE LIKE THAT RIGHT BEFORE DYING WITHOUT THE MURDERER NOTICING!!
THAT MUST BE A MESSAGE DIRECTED AT A PARTICULAR PERSON, PREPARED IN ADVANCE BY THE MURDERER.
THAT NISHIMOTO GUY WAS SCARED WITLESS AFTER SEEING IT.
THE NEXT PERSON TO BE TARGETED IS PROBABLY--
IDIOT!! FORGET ABOUT THE CURSE OF THE PIANO!!

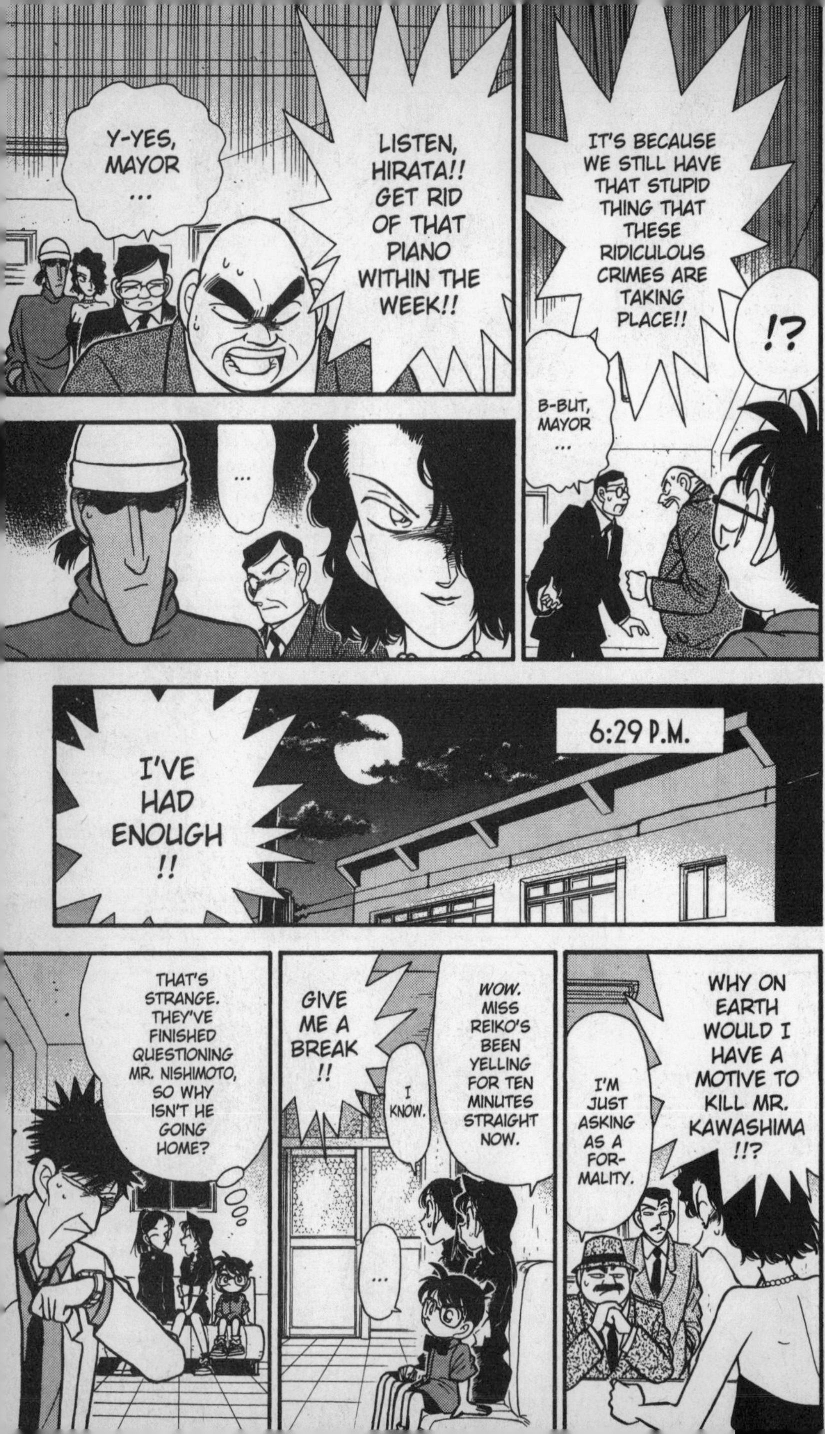
IT'S BECAUSE WE STILL HAVE THAT STUPID THING THAT THESE RIDICULOUS CRIMES ARE TAKING PLACE!!
!?
B-BUT, MAYOR ...
LISTEN, HIRATA!! GET RID OF THAT PIANO WITHIN THE WEEK!!
Y-YES, MAYOR ...
...
6:29 P.M.
I'VE HAD ENOUGH !!
WHY ON EARTH WOULD I HAVE A MOTIVE TO KILL MR. KAWASHIMA !!?
I'M JUST ASKING AS A FOR-MALITY.
WOW. MISS REIKO'S BEEN YELLING FOR TEN MINUTES STRAIGHT NOW.
I KNOW.
GIVE ME A BREAK !!
...
THAT'S STRANGE. THEY'VE FINISHED QUESTIONING MR. NISHIMOTO, SO WHY ISN'T HE GOING HOME?

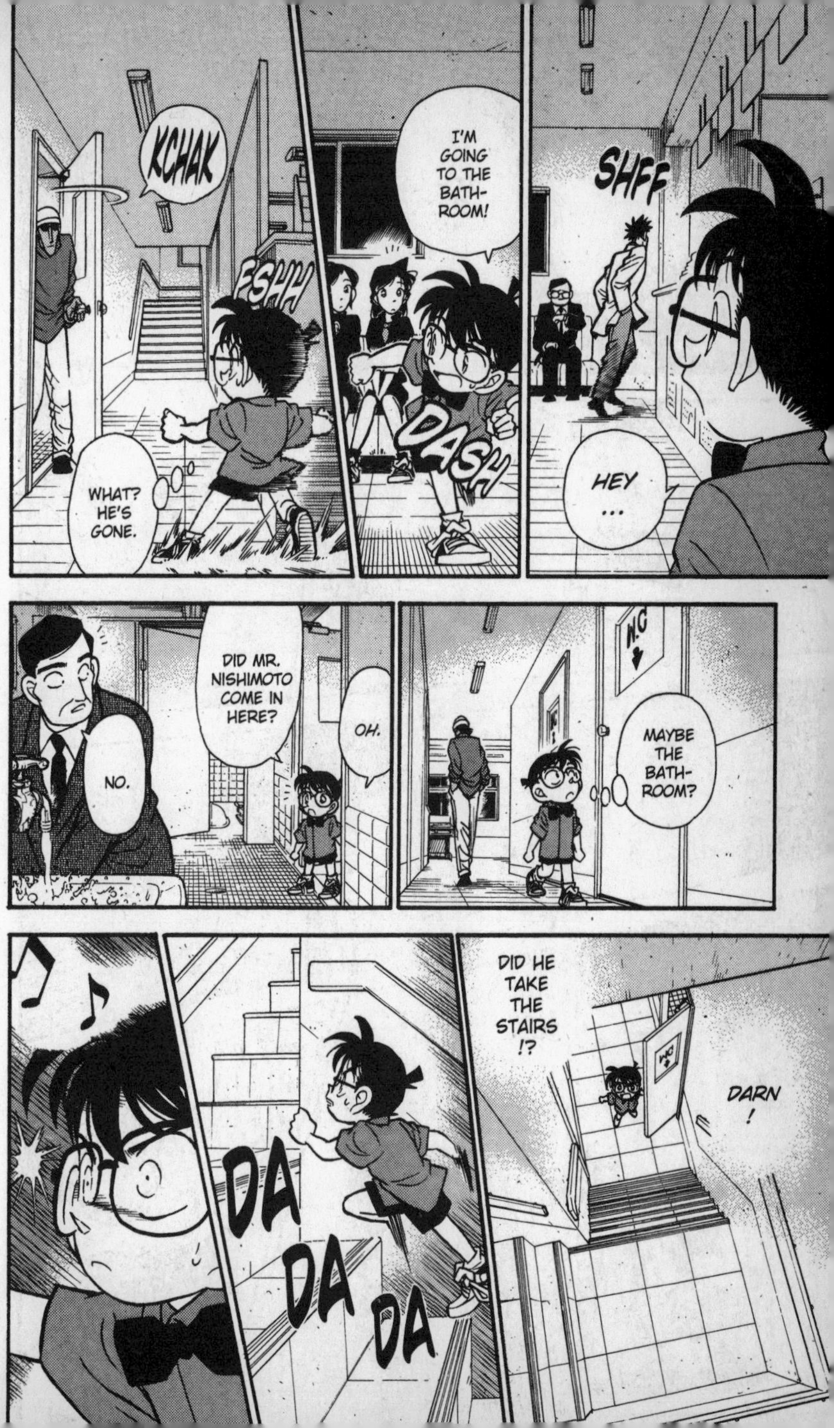
SHFF
HEY ...
I'M GOING TO THE BATH-ROOM!
DASH
KCHAK
FSHH
WHAT? HE'S GONE.
W.C
MAYBE THE BATH-ROOM?
DID MR. NISHIMOTO COME IN HERE?
OH.
NO.
DID HE TAKE THE STAIRS !?
DARN !
DA
DA
DA
DA

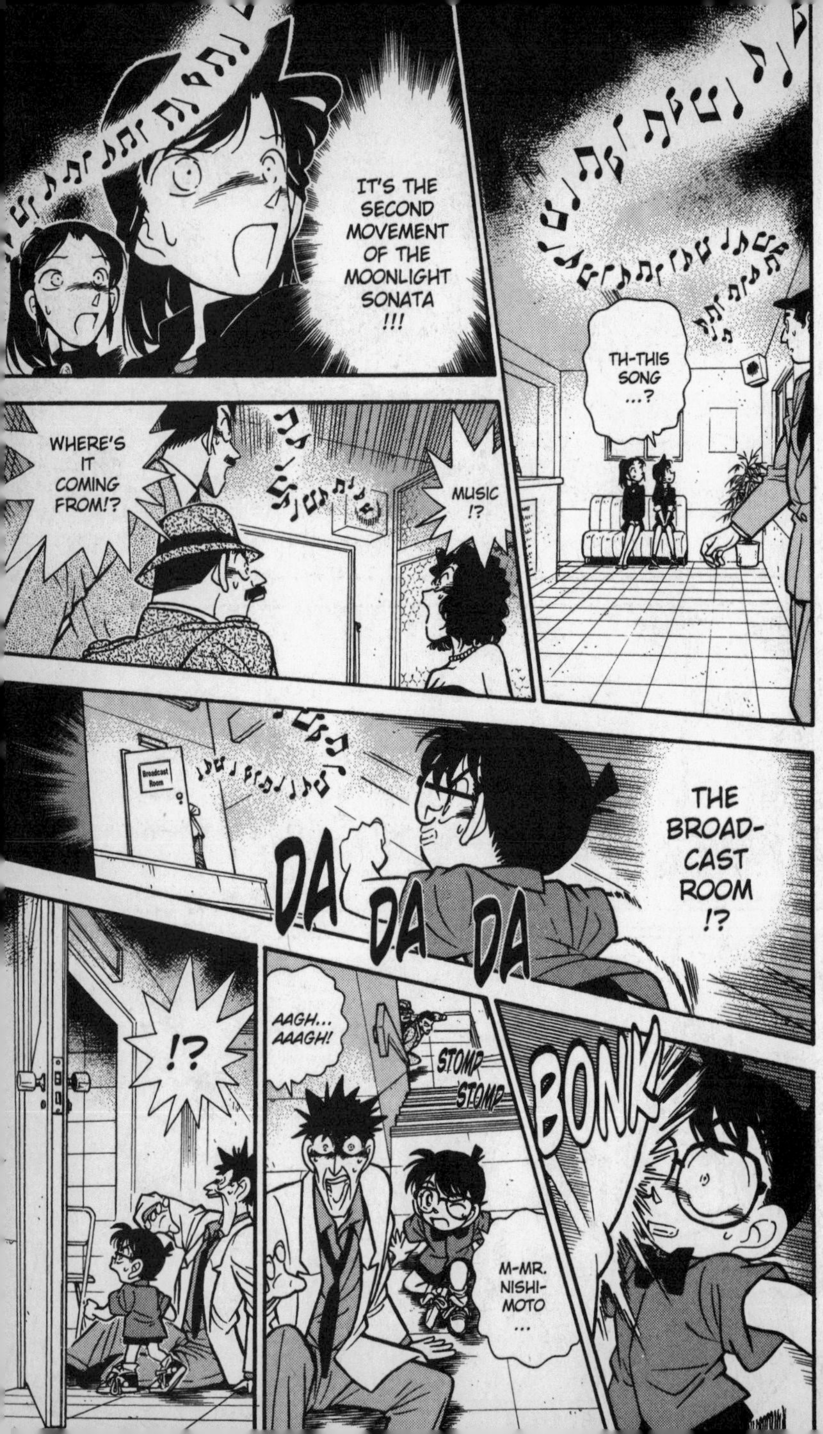
TH-THIS SONG ...?
IT'S THE SECOND MOVEMENT OF THE MOONLIGHT SONATA !!!
MUSIC !?
WHERE'S IT COMING FROM!?
THE BROAD-CAST ROOM !?
Broadcast Room
DA DA DA
BONK
AAGH... AAAGH!
STOMP STOMP
M-MR. NISHI-MOTO ...
!?

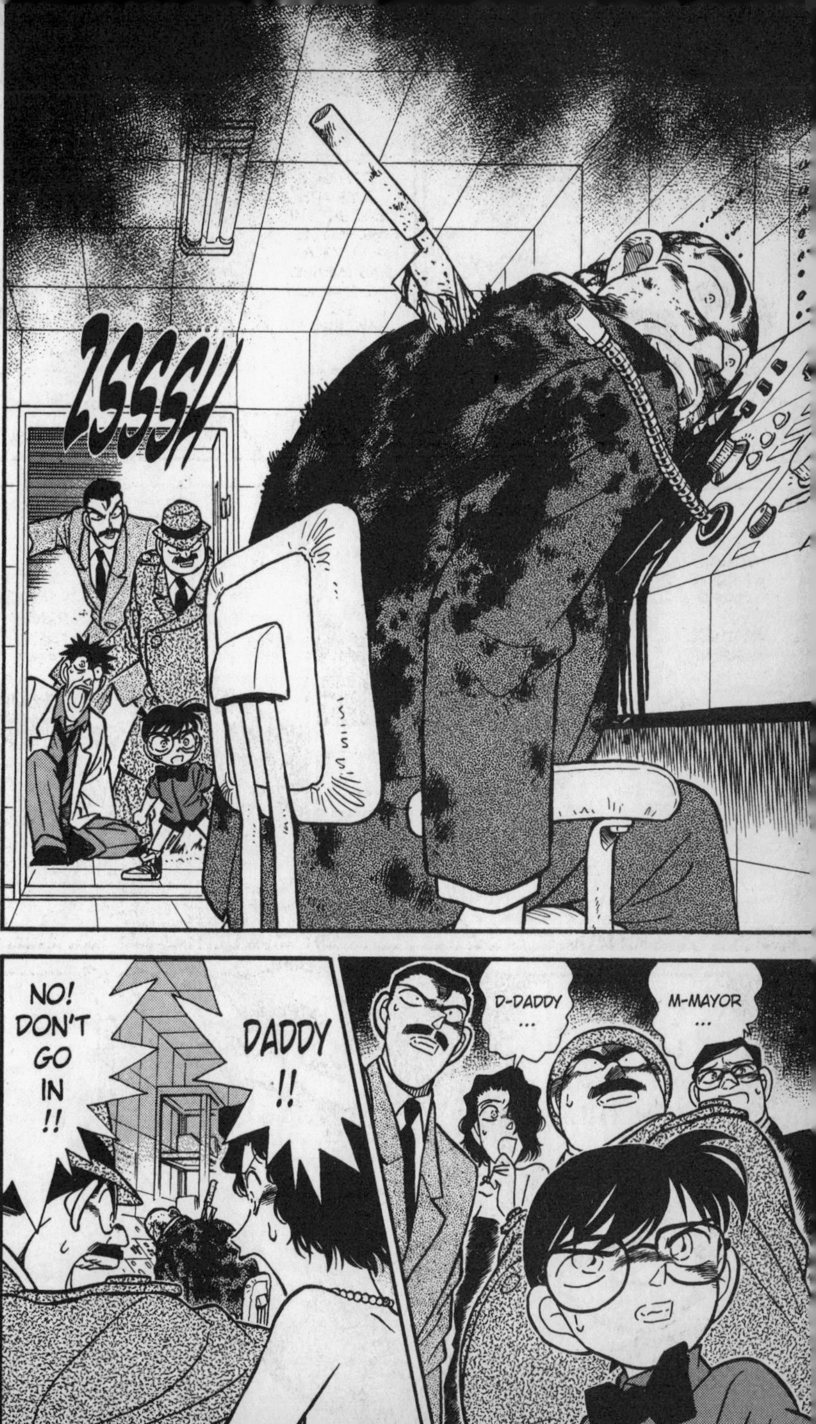
ZSSSH
M-MAYOR ...
D-DADDY ...
DADDY !!
NO! DON'T GO IN !!

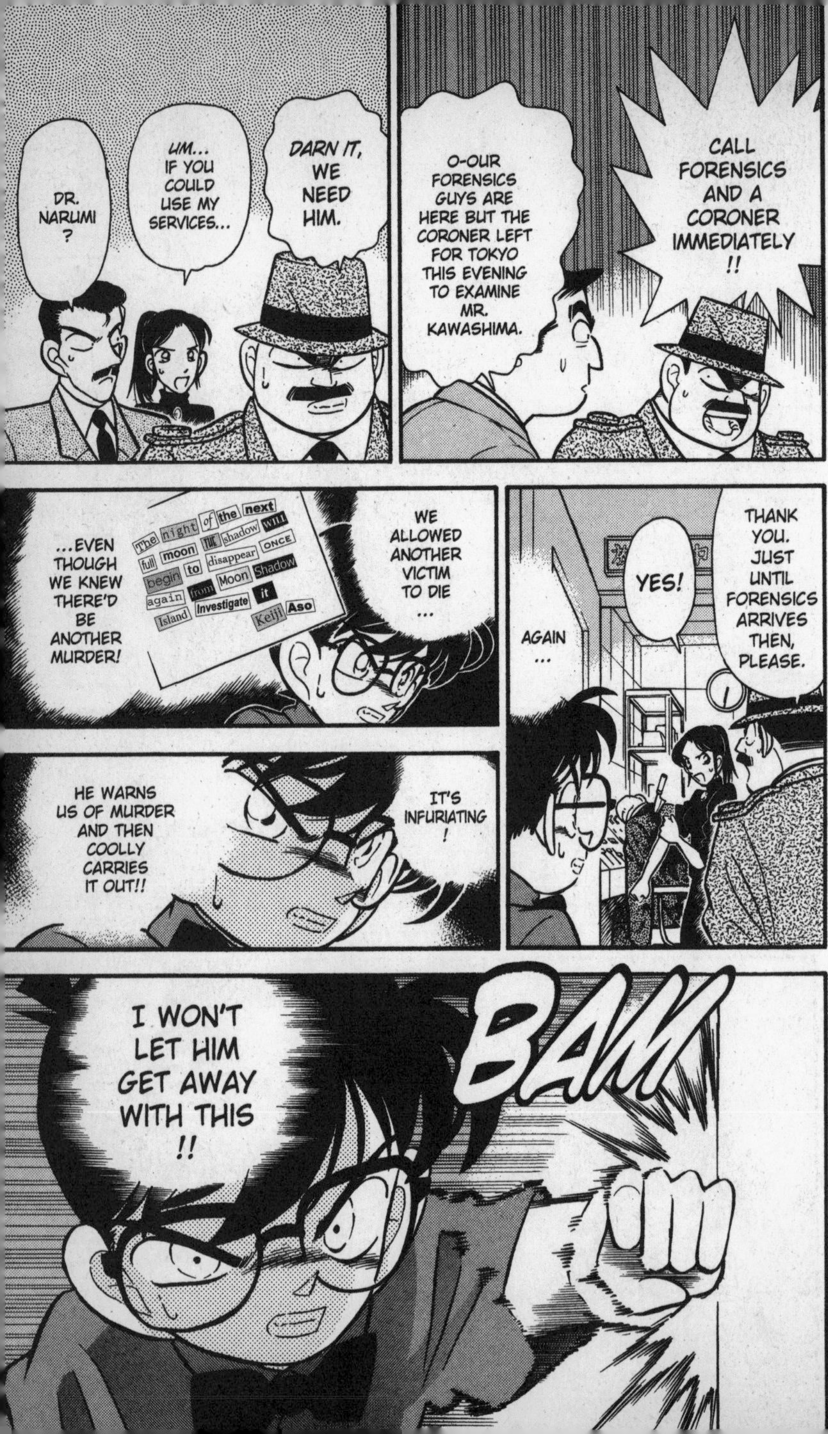
CALL FORENSICS AND A CORONER IMMEDIATELY !!
O-OUR FORENSICS GUYS ARE HERE BUT THE CORONER LEFT FOR TOKYO THIS EVENING TO EXAMINE MR. KAWASHIMA.
DARN IT, WE NEED HIM.
UM... IF YOU COULD USE MY SERVICES...
DR. NARUMI ?
THANK YOU. JUST UNTIL FORENSICS ARRIVES THEN, PLEASE.
YES!
AGAIN ...
WE ALLOWED ANOTHER VICTIM TO DIE ...
The night of the next WILL
full moon THE shadow ONCE
begin to disappear
again from Moon Shadow
Island Investigate it
Keiji Aso
...EVEN THOUGH WE KNEW THERE'D BE ANOTHER MURDER!
IT'S INFURIATING!
HE WARNS US OF MURDER AND THEN COOLLY CARRIES IT OUT!!
BAM
I WON'T LET HIM GET AWAY WITH THIS !!

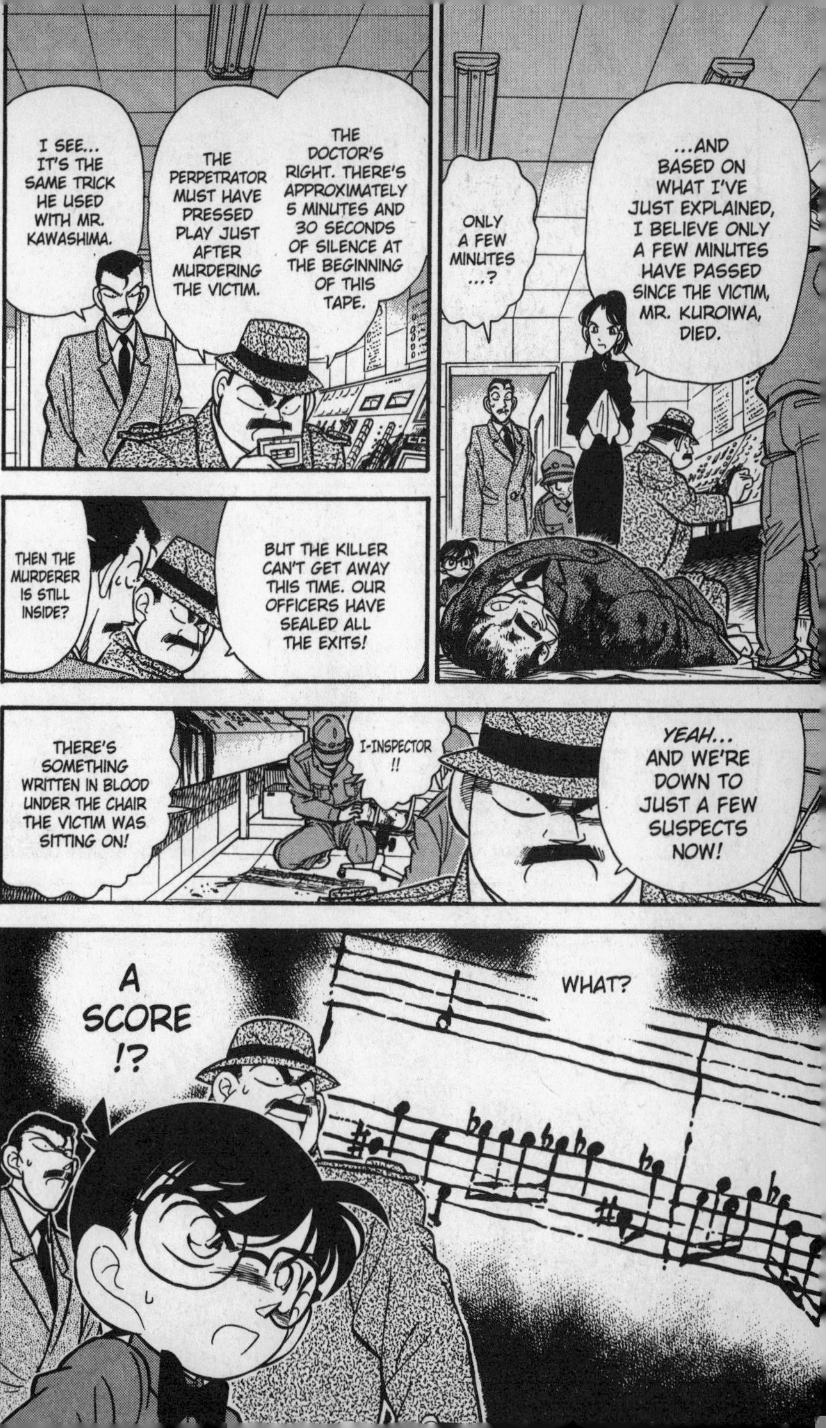
...AND BASED ON WHAT I'VE JUST EXPLAINED, I BELIEVE ONLY A FEW MINUTES HAVE PASSED SINCE THE VICTIM, MR. KUROIWA, DIED.
ONLY A FEW MINUTES ...?
THE DOCTOR'S RIGHT. THERE'S APPROXIMATELY 5 MINUTES AND 30 SECONDS OF SILENCE AT THE BEGINNING OF THIS TAPE.
THE PERPETRATOR MUST HAVE PRESSED PLAY JUST AFTER MURDERING THE VICTIM.
I SEE... IT'S THE SAME TRICK HE USED WITH MR. KAWASHIMA.
BUT THE KILLER CAN'T GET AWAY THIS TIME. OUR OFFICERS HAVE SEALED ALL THE EXITS!
THEN THE MURDERER IS STILL INSIDE?
YEAH... AND WE'RE DOWN TO JUST A FEW SUSPECTS NOW!
I-INSPECTOR !!
THERE'S SOMETHING WRITTEN IN BLOOD UNDER THE CHAIR THE VICTIM WAS SITTING ON!
WHAT?
A SCORE !?

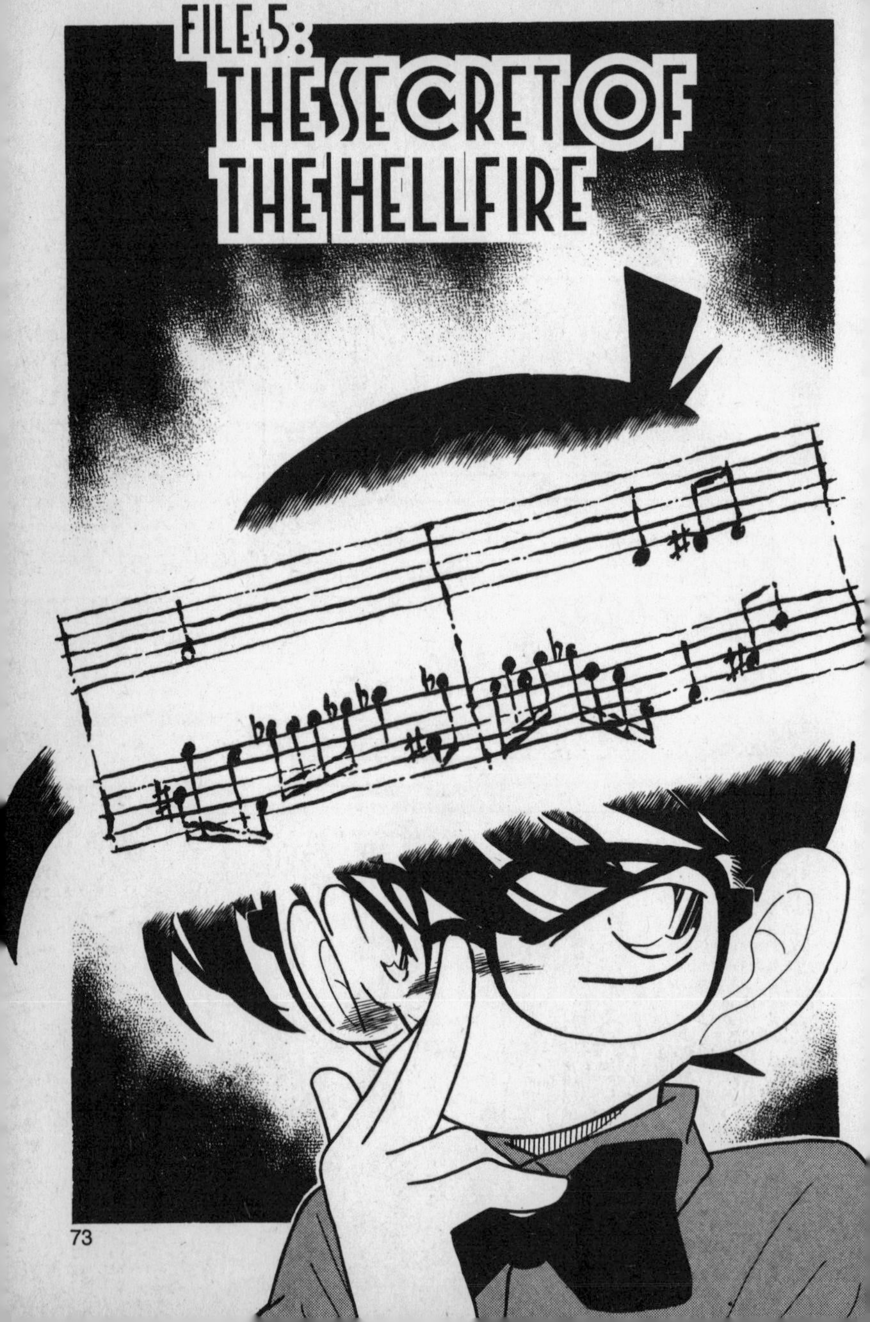
FILE 5:
THE SECRET OF
THE HELLFIRE

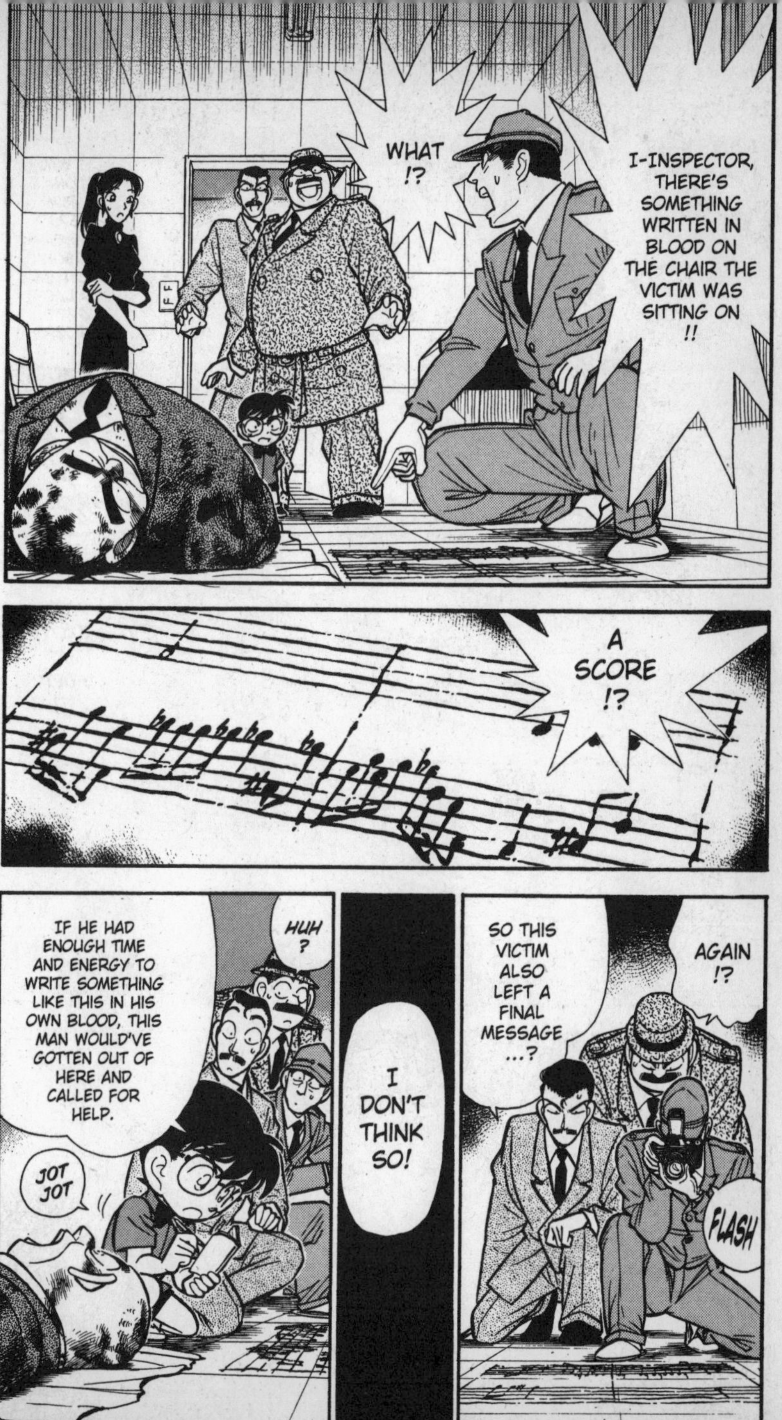
I-INSPECTOR, THERE'S SOMETHING WRITTEN IN BLOOD ON THE CHAIR THE VICTIM WAS SITTING ON !!
WHAT !?
A SCORE !?
AGAIN !?
SO THIS VICTIM ALSO LEFT A FINAL MESSAGE ...?
FLASH
I DON'T THINK SO!
HUH ?
IF HE HAD ENOUGH TIME AND ENERGY TO WRITE SOMETHING LIKE THIS IN HIS OWN BLOOD, THIS MAN WOULD'VE GOTTEN OUT OF HERE AND CALLED FOR HELP.
JOT JOT

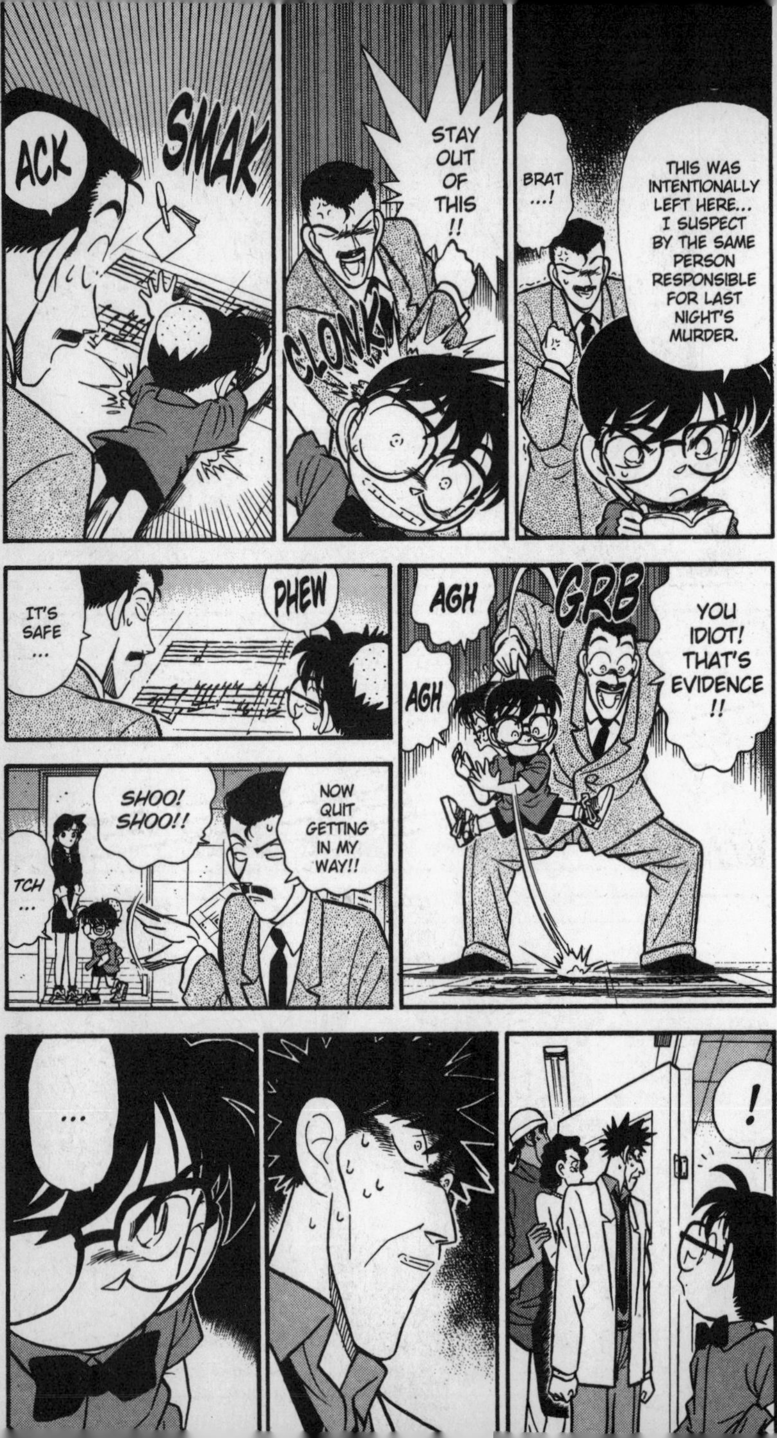
THIS WAS INTENTIONALLY LEFT HERE... I SUSPECT BY THE SAME PERSON RESPONSIBLE FOR LAST NIGHT'S MURDER.
BRAT ...!
STAY OUT OF THIS !!
CLONK
SMAK
ACK
YOU IDIOT! THAT'S EVIDENCE !!
GRB
AGH
AGH
PHEW
IT'S SAFE ...
NOW QUIT GETTING IN MY WAY!!
SHOO! SHOO!!
TCH ...
!
...

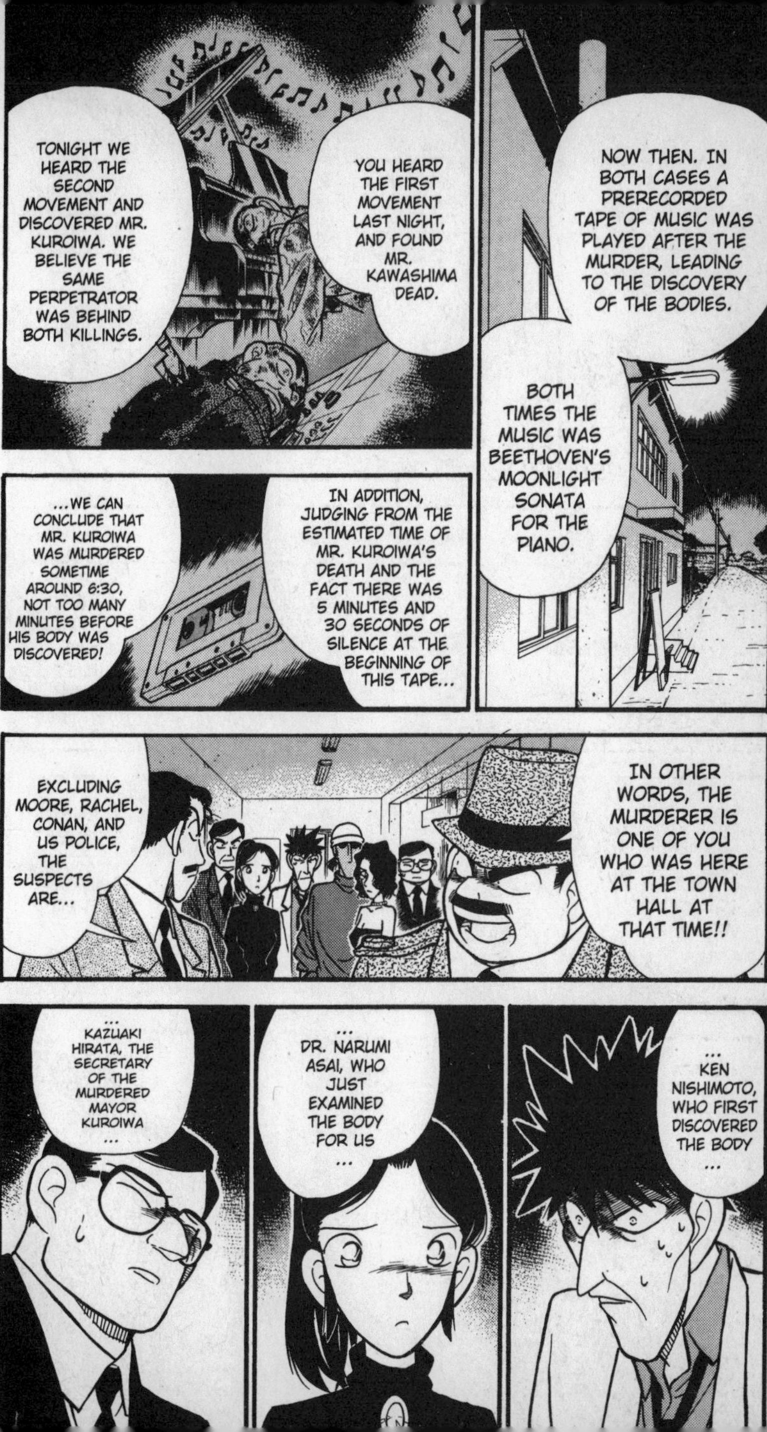
NOW THEN. IN BOTH CASES A PRERECORDED TAPE OF MUSIC WAS PLAYED AFTER THE MURDER, LEADING TO THE DISCOVERY OF THE BODIES.
BOTH TIMES THE MUSIC WAS BEETHOVEN'S MOONLIGHT SONATA FOR THE PIANO.
YOU HEARD THE FIRST MOVEMENT LAST NIGHT, AND FOUND MR. KAWASHIMA DEAD.
TONIGHT WE HEARD THE SECOND MOVEMENT AND DISCOVERED MR. KUROIWA. WE BELIEVE THE SAME PERPETRATOR WAS BEHIND BOTH KILLINGS.
IN ADDITION, JUDGING FROM THE ESTIMATED TIME OF MR. KUROIWA'S DEATH AND THE FACT THERE WAS 5 MINUTES AND 30 SECONDS OF SILENCE AT THE BEGINNING OF THIS TAPE...
...WE CAN CONCLUDE THAT MR. KUROIWA WAS MURDERED SOMETIME AROUND 6:30, NOT TOO MANY MINUTES BEFORE HIS BODY WAS DISCOVERED!
IN OTHER WORDS, THE MURDERER IS ONE OF YOU WHO WAS HERE AT THE TOWN HALL AT THAT TIME!!
EXCLUDING MOORE, RACHEL, CONAN, AND US POLICE, THE SUSPECTS ARE...
... KEN NISHIMOTO, WHO FIRST DISCOVERED THE BODY ...
... DR. NARUMI ASAI, WHO JUST EXAMINED THE BODY FOR US ...
... KAZUAKI HIRATA, THE SECRETARY OF THE MURDERED MAYOR KUROIWA ...

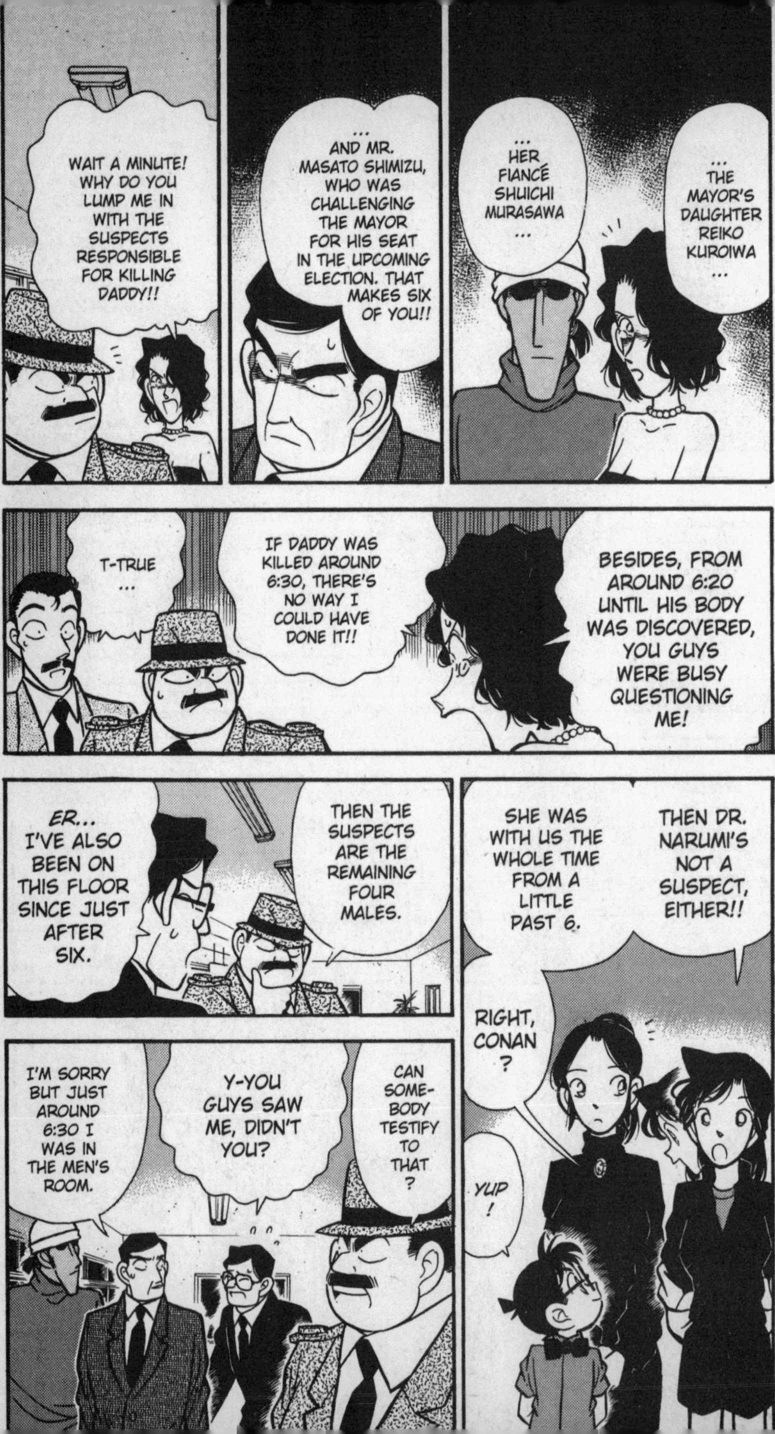

... THE MAYOR'S DAUGHTER REIKO KUROIWA ...
... HER FIANCÉ SHUICHI MURASAWA ...
... AND MR. MASATO SHIMIZU, WHO WAS CHALLENGING THE MAYOR FOR HIS SEAT IN THE UPCOMING ELECTION. THAT MAKES SIX OF YOU!!
WAIT A MINUTE! WHY DO YOU LUMP ME IN WITH THE SUSPECTS RESPONSIBLE FOR KILLING DADDY!!
BESIDES, FROM AROUND 6:20 UNTIL HIS BODY WAS DISCOVERED, YOU GUYS WERE BUSY QUESTIONING ME!
IF DADDY WAS KILLED AROUND 6:30, THERE'S NO WAY I COULD HAVE DONE IT!!
T-TRUE ...
THEN DR. NARUMI'S NOT A SUSPECT, EITHER!!
SHE WAS WITH US THE WHOLE TIME FROM A LITTLE PAST 6.
RIGHT, CONAN?
YUP!
THEN THE SUSPECTS ARE THE REMAINING FOUR MALES.
ER... I'VE ALSO BEEN ON THIS FLOOR SINCE JUST AFTER SIX.
CAN SOMEBODY TESTIFY TO THAT?
Y-YOU GUYS SAW ME, DIDN'T YOU?
I'M SORRY BUT JUST AROUND 6:30 I WAS IN THE MEN'S ROOM.

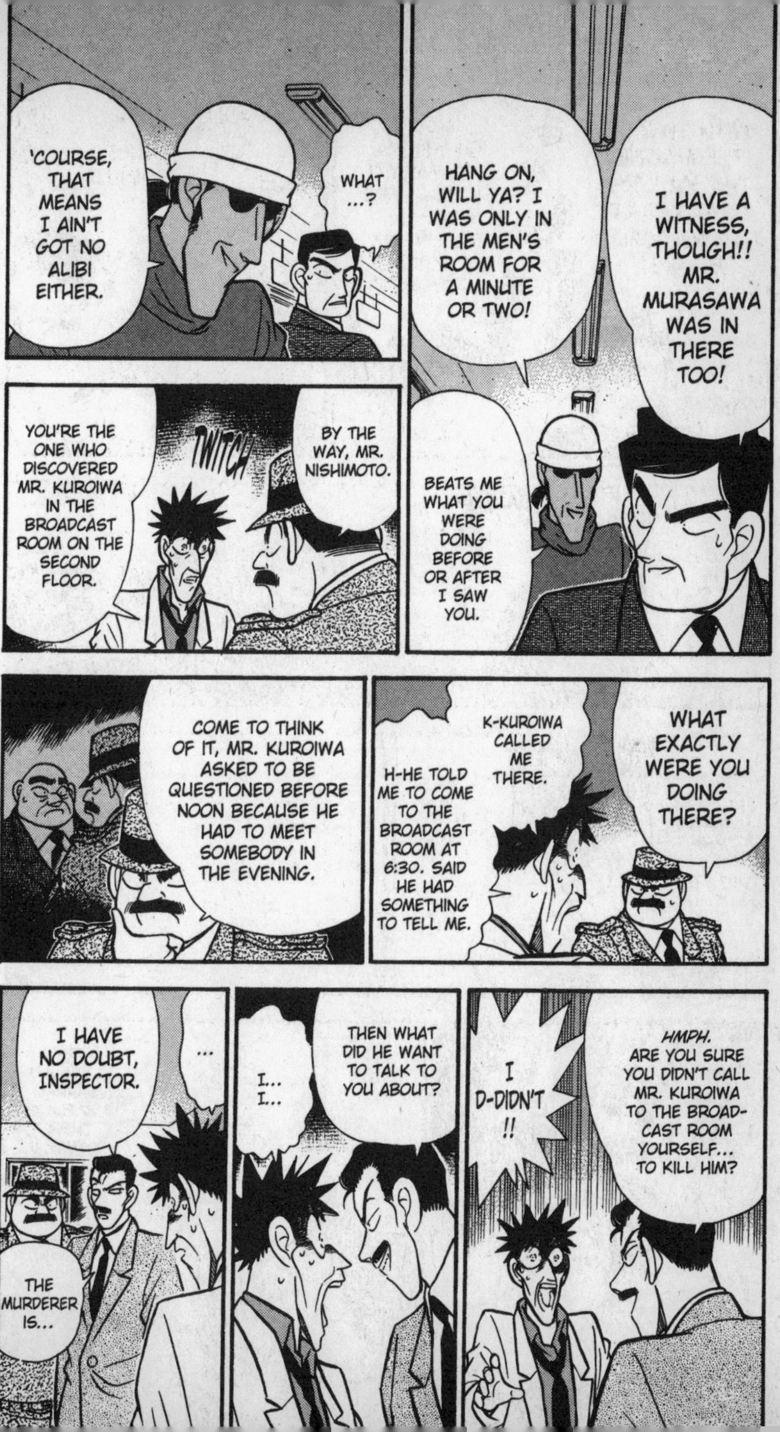
HANG ON, WILL YA? I WAS ONLY IN THE MEN'S ROOM FOR A MINUTE OR TWO!
I HAVE A WITNESS, THOUGH!! MR. MURASAWA WAS IN THERE TOO!
BEATS ME WHAT YOU WERE DOING BEFORE OR AFTER I SAW YOU.
WHAT ...?
'COURSE, THAT MEANS I AIN'T GOT NO ALIBI EITHER.
BY THE WAY, MR. NISHIMOTO.
TWITCH
YOU'RE THE ONE WHO DISCOVERED MR. KUROIWA IN THE BROADCAST ROOM ON THE SECOND FLOOR.
WHAT EXACTLY WERE YOU DOING THERE?
K-KUROIWA CALLED ME THERE.
H-HE TOLD ME TO COME TO THE BROADCAST ROOM AT 6:30. SAID HE HAD SOMETHING TO TELL ME.
COME TO THINK OF IT, MR. KUROIWA ASKED TO BE QUESTIONED BEFORE NOON BECAUSE HE HAD TO MEET SOMEBODY IN THE EVENING.
HMPH. ARE YOU SURE YOU DIDN'T CALL MR. KUROIWA TO THE BROAD-CAST ROOM YOURSELF... TO KILL HIM?
I D-DIDN'T !!
THEN WHAT DID HE WANT TO TALK TO YOU ABOUT?
I... I...
...
I HAVE NO DOUBT, INSPECTOR.
THE MURDERER IS...

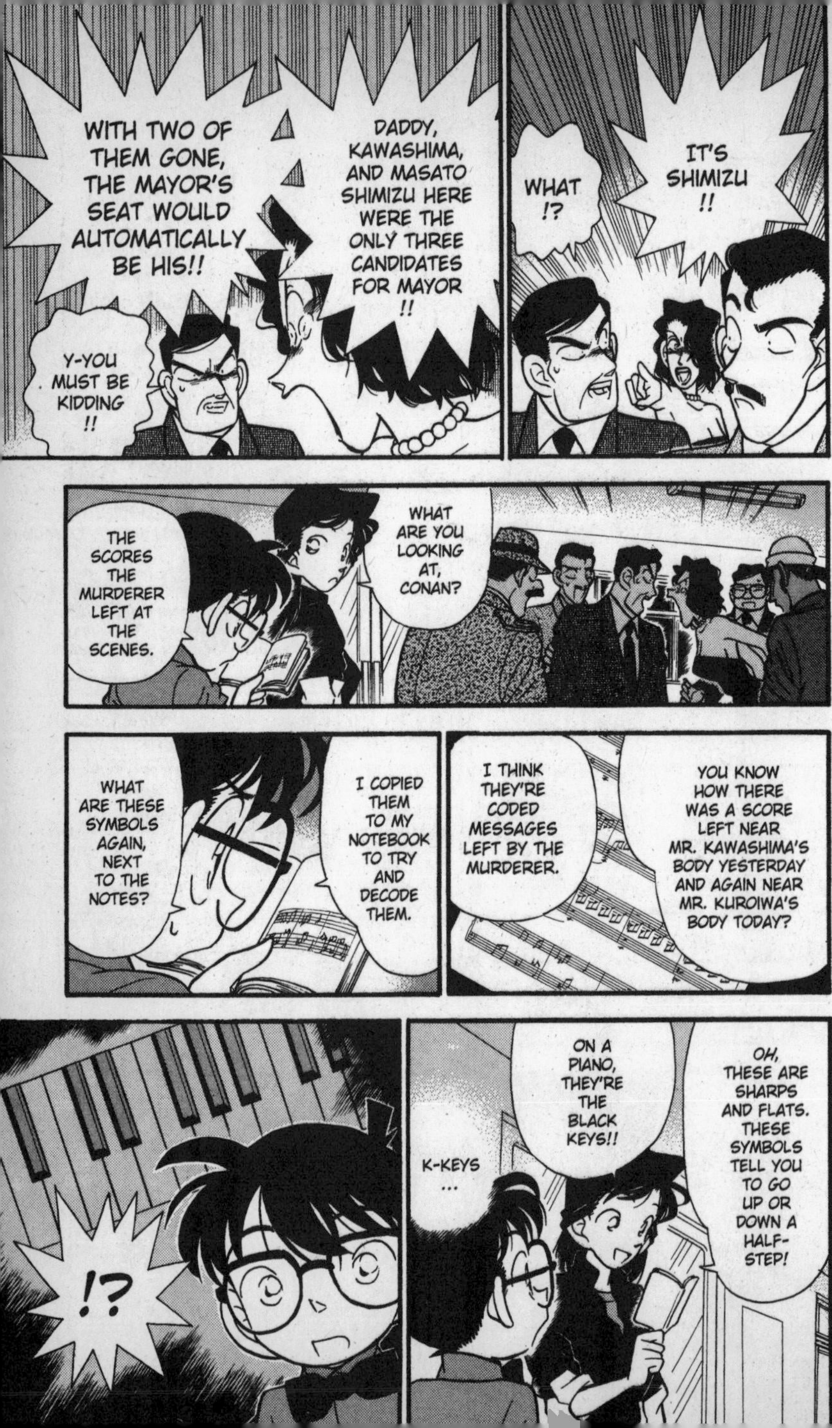
IT'S SHIMIZU !!
WHAT !?
DADDY, KAWASHIMA, AND MASATO SHIMIZU HERE WERE THE ONLY THREE CANDIDATES FOR MAYOR !!
WITH TWO OF THEM GONE, THE MAYOR'S SEAT WOULD AUTOMATICALLY BE HIS!!
Y-YOU MUST BE KIDDING !!
WHAT ARE YOU LOOKING AT, CONAN?
THE SCORES THE MURDERER LEFT AT THE SCENES.
YOU KNOW HOW THERE WAS A SCORE LEFT NEAR MR. KAWASHIMA'S BODY YESTERDAY AND AGAIN NEAR MR. KUROIWA'S BODY TODAY?
I THINK THEY'RE CODED MESSAGES LEFT BY THE MURDERER.
I COPIED THEM TO MY NOTEBOOK TO TRY AND DECODE THEM.
WHAT ARE THESE SYMBOLS AGAIN, NEXT TO THE NOTES?
OH, THESE ARE SHARPS AND FLATS. THESE SYMBOLS TELL YOU TO GO UP OR DOWN A HALF-STEP!
ON A PIANO, THEY'RE THE BLACK KEYS!!
K-KEYS ...
!?

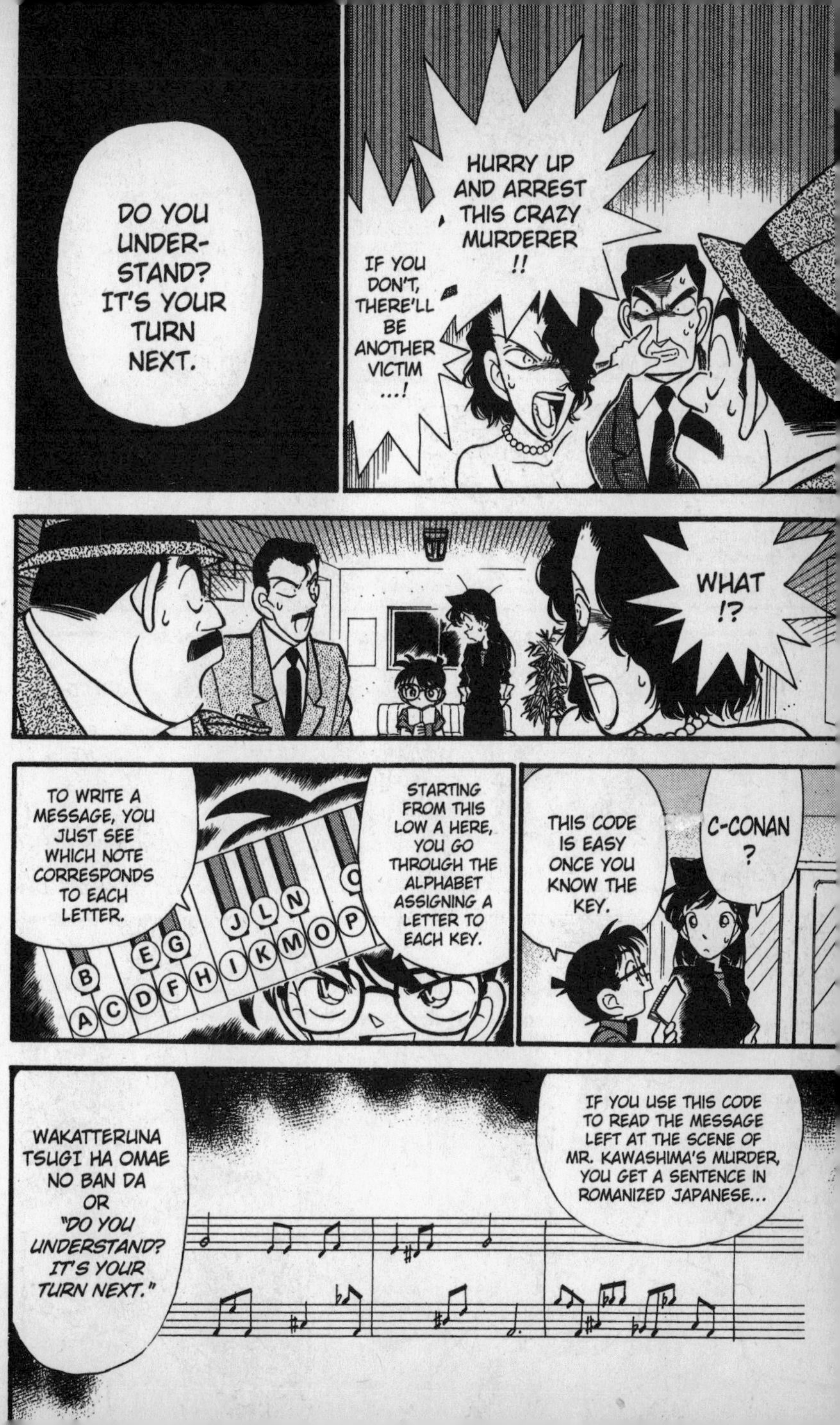
HURRY UP AND ARREST THIS CRAZY MURDERER !!
IF YOU DON'T, THERE'LL BE ANOTHER VICTIM ...!
DO YOU UNDER-STAND? IT'S YOUR TURN NEXT.
WHAT !?
C-CONAN ?
THIS CODE IS EASY ONCE YOU KNOW THE KEY.
STARTING FROM THIS LOW A HERE, YOU GO THROUGH THE ALPHABET ASSIGNING A LETTER TO EACH KEY.
TO WRITE A MESSAGE, YOU JUST SEE WHICH NOTE CORRESPONDS TO EACH LETTER.
B E G J L N O
A C D F H I K M O P
IF YOU USE THIS CODE TO READ THE MESSAGE LEFT AT THE SCENE OF MR. KAWASHIMA'S MURDER, YOU GET A SENTENCE IN ROMANIZED JAPANESE...
WAKATTERUNA TSUGI HA OMAE NO BAN DA OR "DO YOU UNDERSTAND? IT'S YOUR TURN NEXT."

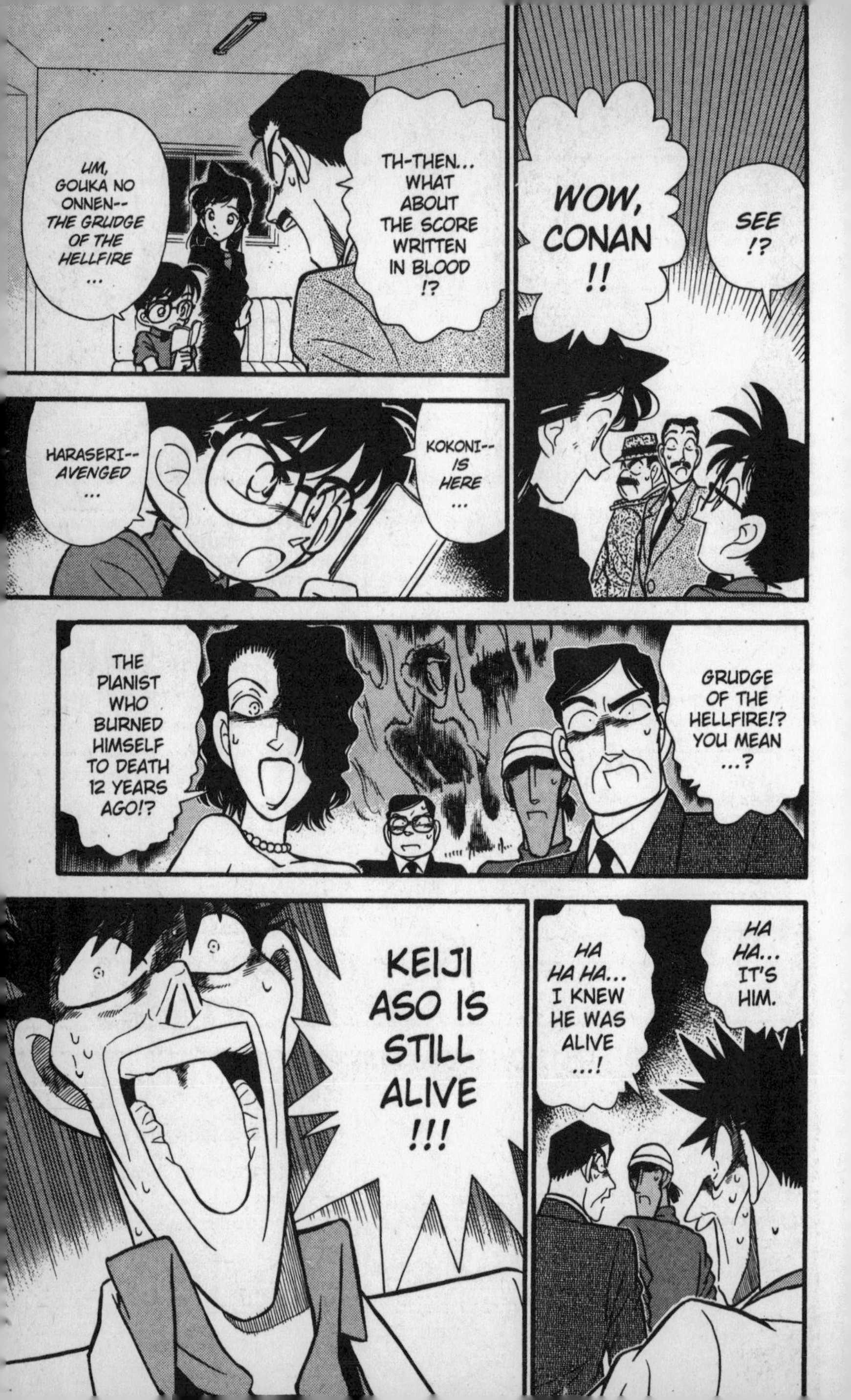
SEE !?
WOW, CONAN !!
TH-THEN... WHAT ABOUT THE SCORE WRITTEN IN BLOOD !?
UM, GOUKA NO ONNEN-- THE GRUDGE OF THE HELLFIRE ...
KOKONI-- IS HERE ...
HARASERI-- AVENGED ...
GRUDGE OF THE HELLFIRE!? YOU MEAN ...?
THE PIANIST WHO BURNED HIMSELF TO DEATH 12 YEARS AGO!?
HA HA... IT'S HIM.
HA HA HA... I KNEW HE WAS ALIVE ...!
KEIJI ASO IS STILL ALIVE !!!

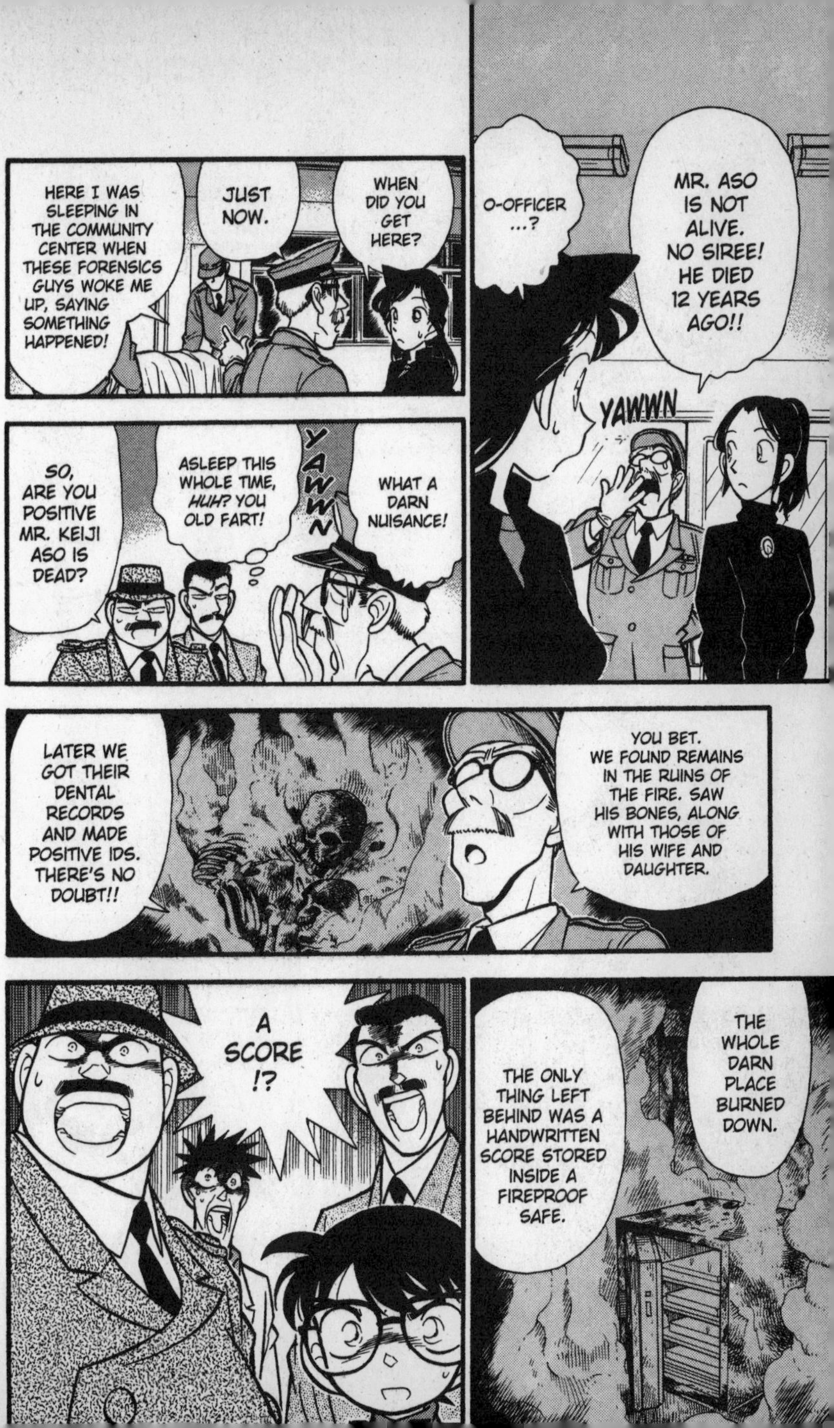
MR. ASO IS NOT ALIVE. NO SIREE! HE DIED 12 YEARS AGO!!
O-OFFICER ...?
YAWWN
WHEN DID YOU GET HERE?
JUST NOW.
HERE I WAS SLEEPING IN THE COMMUNITY CENTER WHEN THESE FORENSICS GUYS WOKE ME UP, SAYING SOMETHING HAPPENED!
WHAT A DARN NUISANCE!
YAWWN
ASLEEP THIS WHOLE TIME, *HUH*? YOU OLD FART!
SO, ARE YOU POSITIVE MR. KEIJI ASO IS DEAD?
YOU BET. WE FOUND REMAINS IN THE RUINS OF THE FIRE. SAW HIS BONES, ALONG WITH THOSE OF HIS WIFE AND DAUGHTER.
LATER WE GOT THEIR DENTAL RECORDS AND MADE POSITIVE IDS. THERE'S NO DOUBT!!
THE WHOLE DARN PLACE BURNED DOWN.
THE ONLY THING LEFT BEHIND WAS A HANDWRITTEN SCORE STORED INSIDE A FIREPROOF SAFE.
A SCORE !?

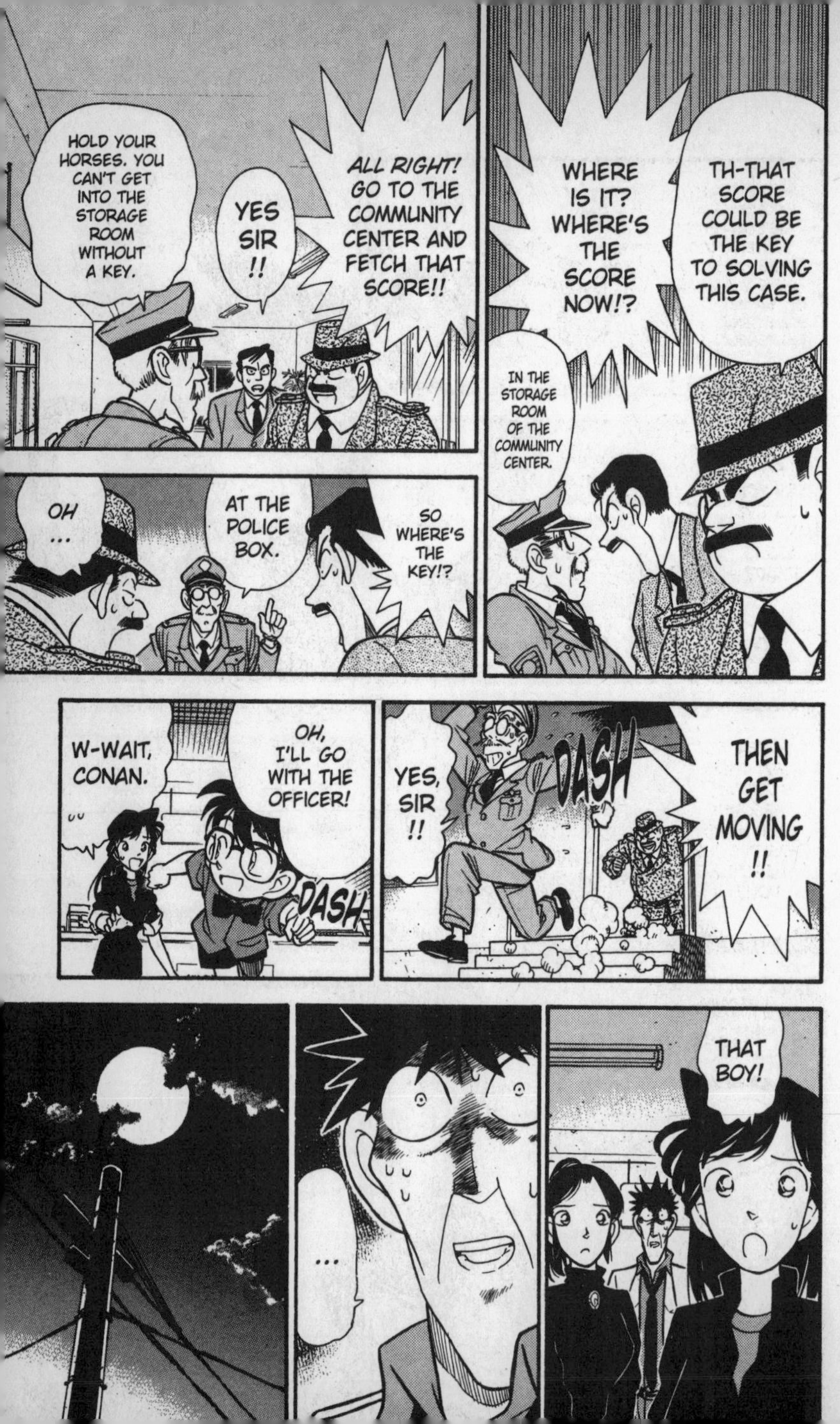
TH-THAT SCORE COULD BE THE KEY TO SOLVING THIS CASE.
WHERE IS IT? WHERE'S THE SCORE NOW!?
IN THE STORAGE ROOM OF THE COMMUNITY CENTER.
ALL RIGHT! GO TO THE COMMUNITY CENTER AND FETCH THAT SCORE!!
YES SIR !!
HOLD YOUR HORSES. YOU CAN'T GET INTO THE STORAGE ROOM WITHOUT A KEY.
SO WHERE'S THE KEY!?
AT THE POLICE BOX.
OH ...
THEN GET MOVING !!
DASH
YES, SIR !!
OH, I'LL GO WITH THE OFFICER!
DASH
W-WAIT, CONAN.
THAT BOY!
DASH
...

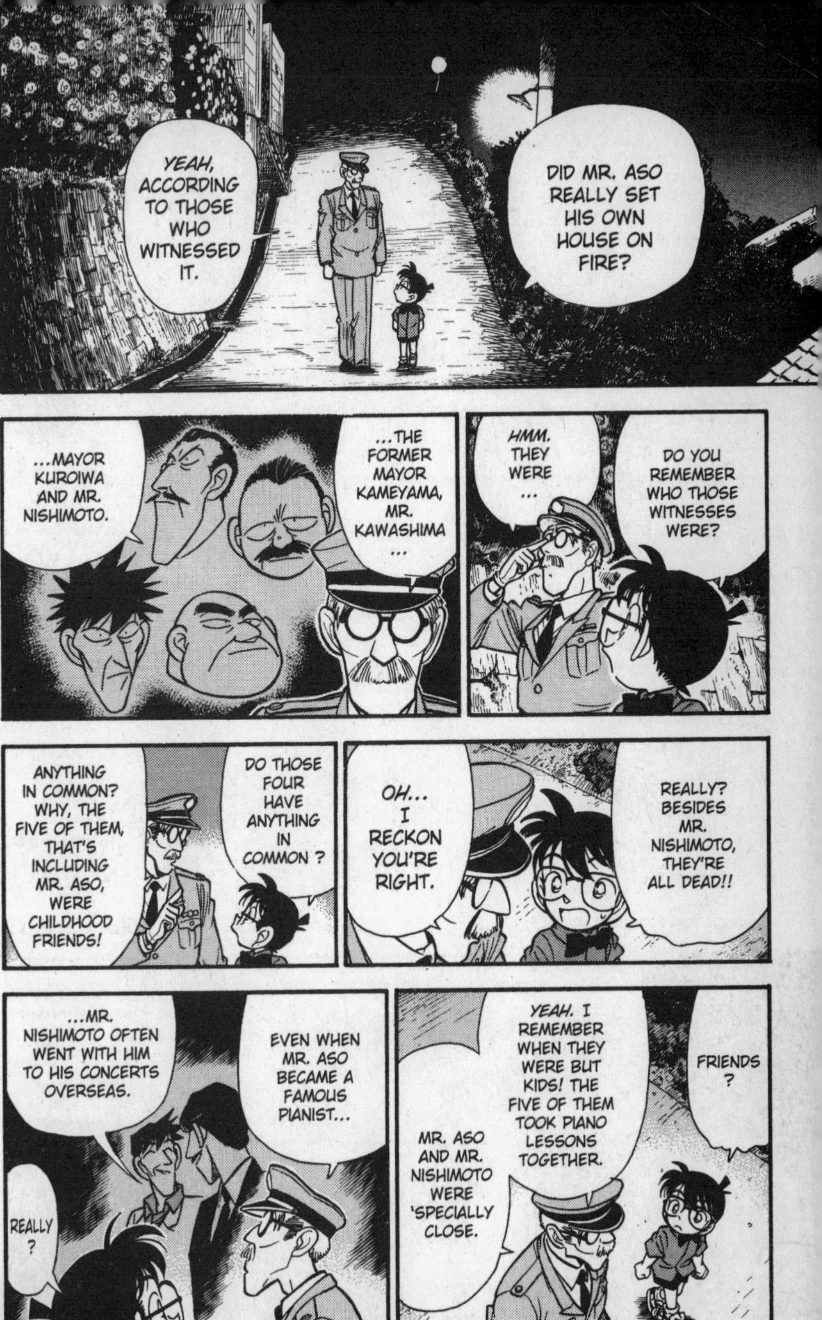
DID MR. ASO REALLY SET HIS OWN HOUSE ON FIRE?
YEAH, ACCORDING TO THOSE WHO WITNESSED IT.
DO YOU REMEMBER WHO THOSE WITNESSES WERE?
HMM. THEY WERE ...
...THE FORMER MAYOR KAMEYAMA, MR. KAWASHIMA ...
...MAYOR KUROIWA AND MR. NISHIMOTO.
REALLY? BESIDES MR. NISHIMOTO, THEY'RE ALL DEAD!!
OH... I RECKON YOU'RE RIGHT.
DO THOSE FOUR HAVE ANYTHING IN COMMON ?
ANYTHING IN COMMON? WHY, THE FIVE OF THEM, THAT'S INCLUDING MR. ASO, WERE CHILDHOOD FRIENDS!
FRIENDS ?
YEAH. I REMEMBER WHEN THEY WERE BUT KIDS! THE FIVE OF THEM TOOK PIANO LESSONS TOGETHER.
MR. ASO AND MR. NISHIMOTO WERE 'SPECIALLY CLOSE.
EVEN WHEN MR. ASO BECAME A FAMOUS PIANIST...
...MR. NISHIMOTO OFTEN WENT WITH HIM TO HIS CONCERTS OVERSEAS.
REALLY ?

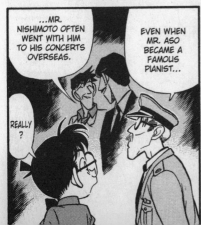

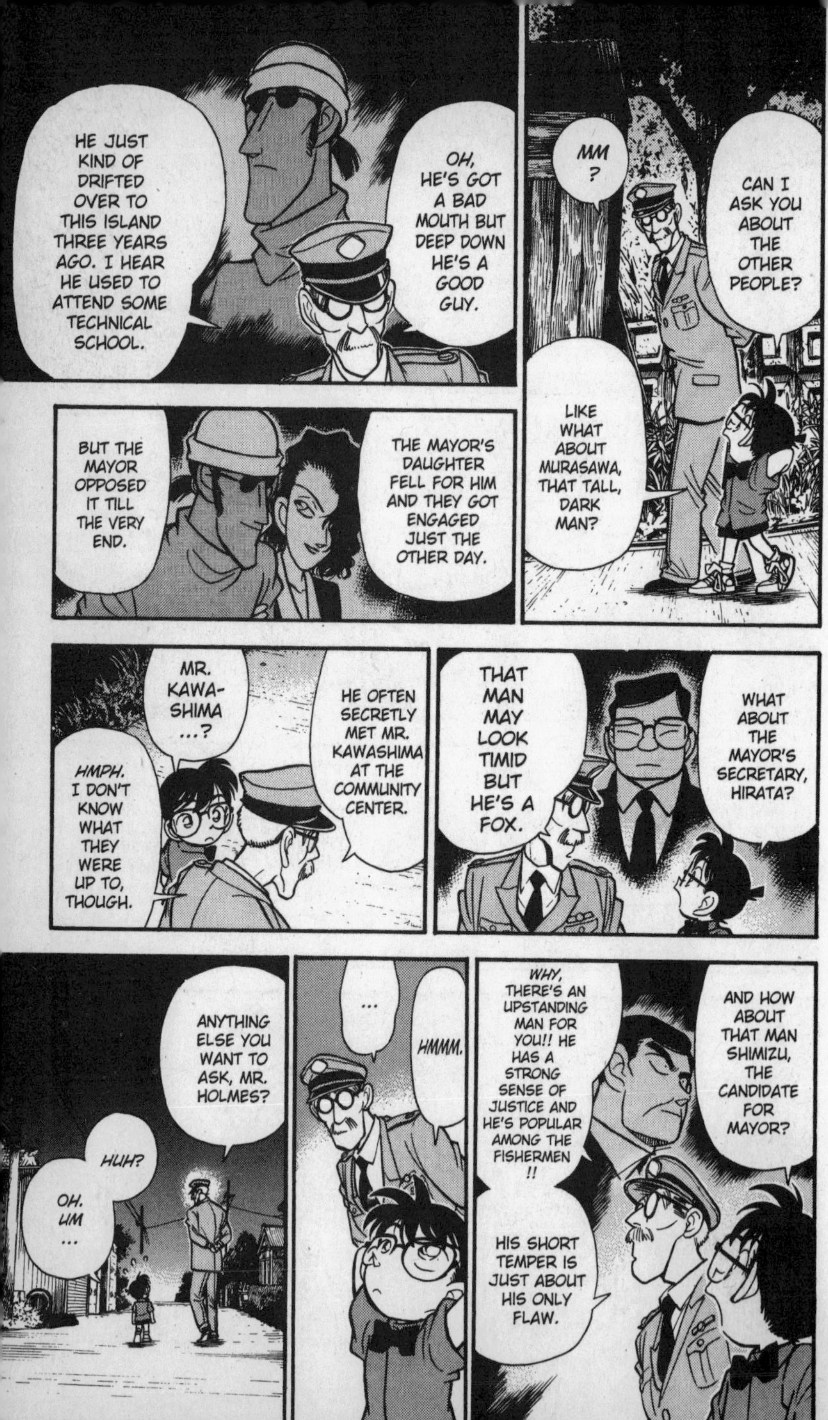
CAN I ASK YOU ABOUT THE OTHER PEOPLE?
MM ?
LIKE WHAT ABOUT MURASAWA, THAT TALL, DARK MAN?
OH, HE'S GOT A BAD MOUTH BUT DEEP DOWN HE'S A GOOD GUY.
HE JUST KIND OF DRIFTED OVER TO THIS ISLAND THREE YEARS AGO. I HEAR HE USED TO ATTEND SOME TECHNICAL SCHOOL.
THE MAYOR'S DAUGHTER FELL FOR HIM AND THEY GOT ENGAGED JUST THE OTHER DAY.
BUT THE MAYOR OPPOSED IT TILL THE VERY END.
WHAT ABOUT THE MAYOR'S SECRETARY, HIRATA?
THAT MAN MAY LOOK TIMID BUT HE'S A FOX.
HE OFTEN SECRETLY MET MR. KAWASHIMA AT THE COMMUNITY CENTER.
MR. KAWA-SHIMA ...?
HMPH. I DON'T KNOW WHAT THEY WERE UP TO, THOUGH.
AND HOW ABOUT THAT MAN SHIMIZU, THE CANDIDATE FOR MAYOR?
WHY, THERE'S AN UPSTANDING MAN FOR YOU!! HE HAS A STRONG SENSE OF JUSTICE AND HE'S POPULAR AMONG THE FISHERMEN !!
HIS SHORT TEMPER IS JUST ABOUT HIS ONLY FLAW.
HMMM.
...
ANYTHING ELSE YOU WANT TO ASK, MR. HOLMES?
HUH?
OH. UM ...

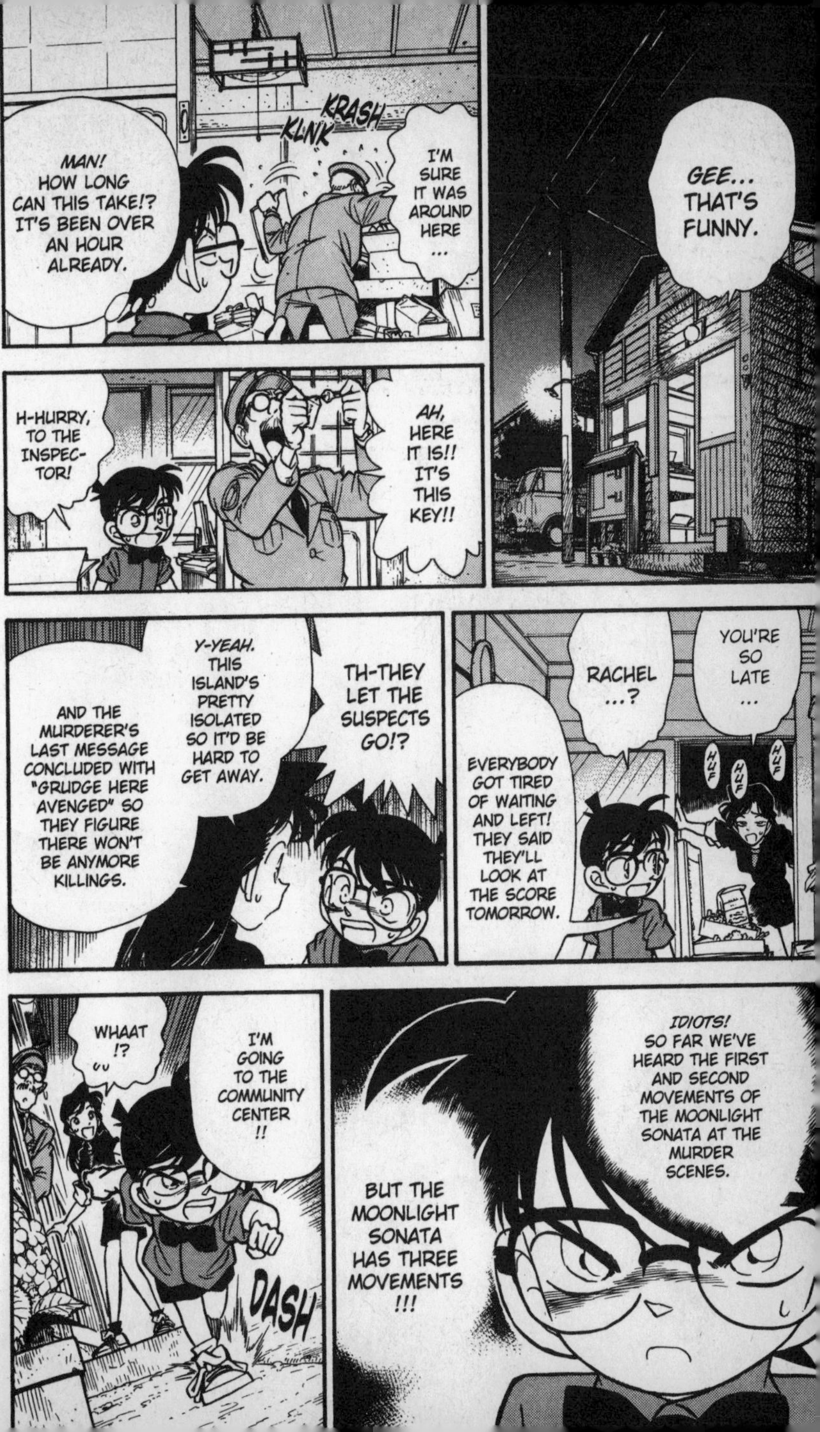
GEE... THAT'S FUNNY.
I'M SURE IT WAS AROUND HERE ...
KRASH
KLNK
MAN! HOW LONG CAN THIS TAKE!? IT'S BEEN OVER AN HOUR ALREADY.
AH, HERE IT IS!! IT'S THIS KEY!!
H-HURRY, TO THE INSPECTOR!
YOU'RE SO LATE ...
HUF
HUF
HUF
RACHEL ...?
EVERYBODY GOT TIRED OF WAITING AND LEFT! THEY SAID THEY'LL LOOK AT THE SCORE TOMORROW.
TH-THEY LET THE SUSPECTS GO!?
Y-YEAH. THIS ISLAND'S PRETTY ISOLATED SO IT'D BE HARD TO GET AWAY.
AND THE MURDERER'S LAST MESSAGE CONCLUDED WITH "GRUDGE HERE AVENGED" SO THEY FIGURE THERE WON'T BE ANYMORE KILLINGS.
IDIOTS! SO FAR WE'VE HEARD THE FIRST AND SECOND MOVEMENTS OF THE MOONLIGHT SONATA AT THE MURDER SCENES.
BUT THE MOONLIGHT SONATA HAS THREE MOVEMENTS !!!
I'M GOING TO THE COMMUNITY CENTER !!
WHAAT !?
DASH

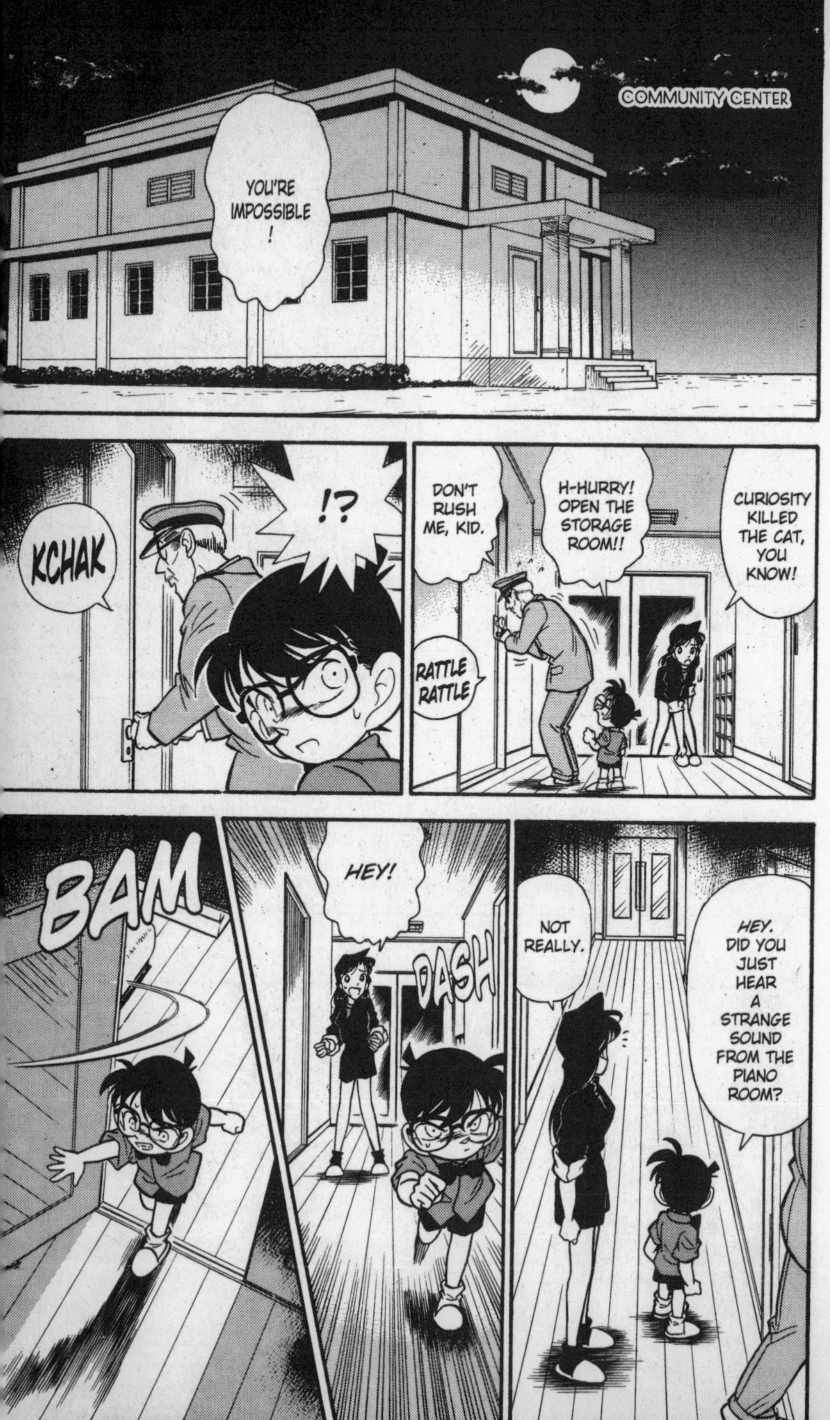
COMMUNITY CENTER
YOU'RE IMPOSSIBLE!
CURIOSITY KILLED THE CAT, YOU KNOW!
H-HURRY! OPEN THE STORAGE ROOM!!
DON'T RUSH ME, KID.
RATTLE RATTLE
!?
KCHAK
HEY. DID YOU JUST HEAR A STRANGE SOUND FROM THE PIANO ROOM?
NOT REALLY.
HEY!
DASH
BAM

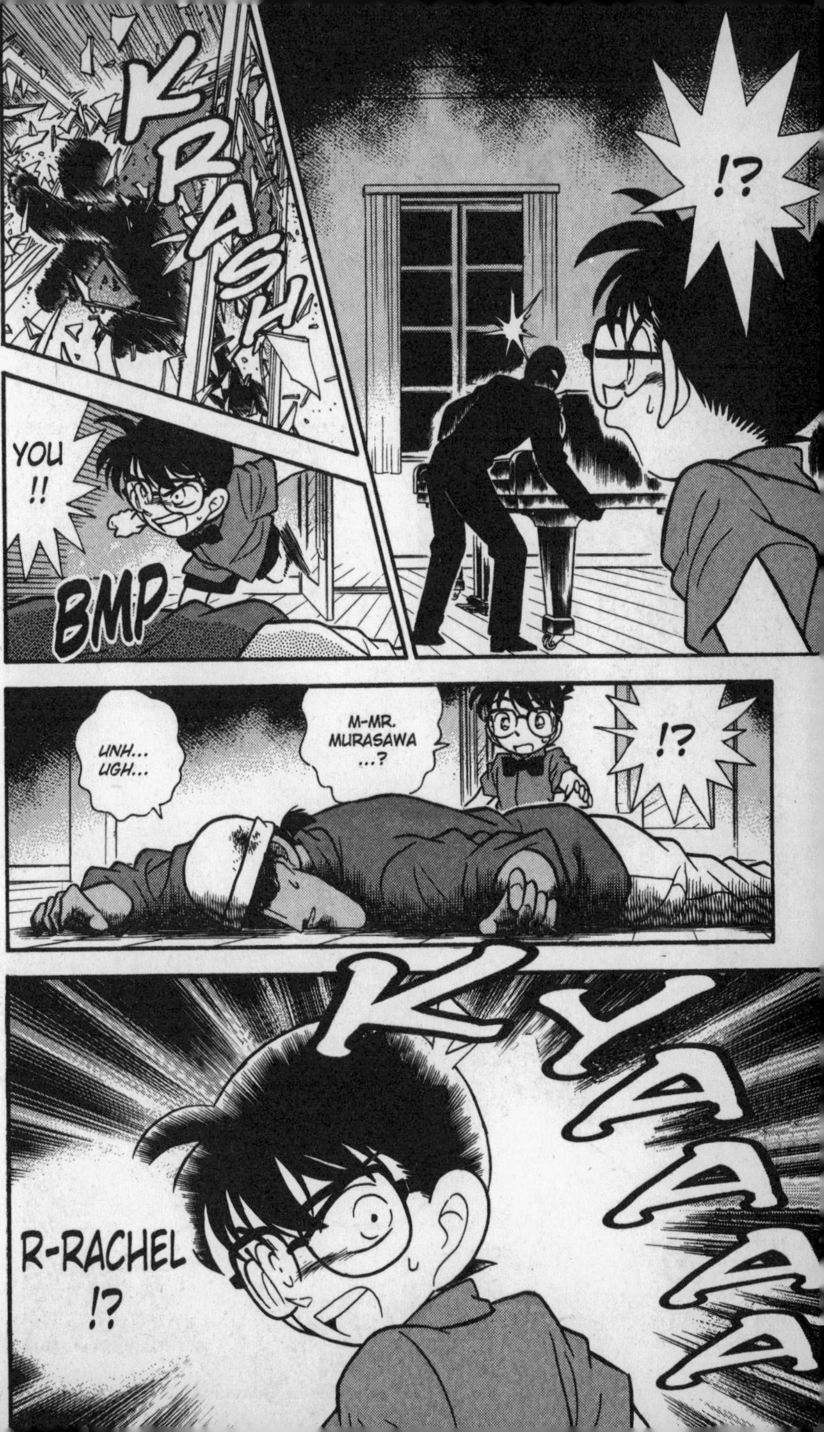
!?
KRASH
YOU !!
BMP
!?
M-MR. MURASAWA ...?
UNH... UGH...
KYAAAA
R-RACHEL !?

FILE 6: THE BLOOD-STAINED BUTTON

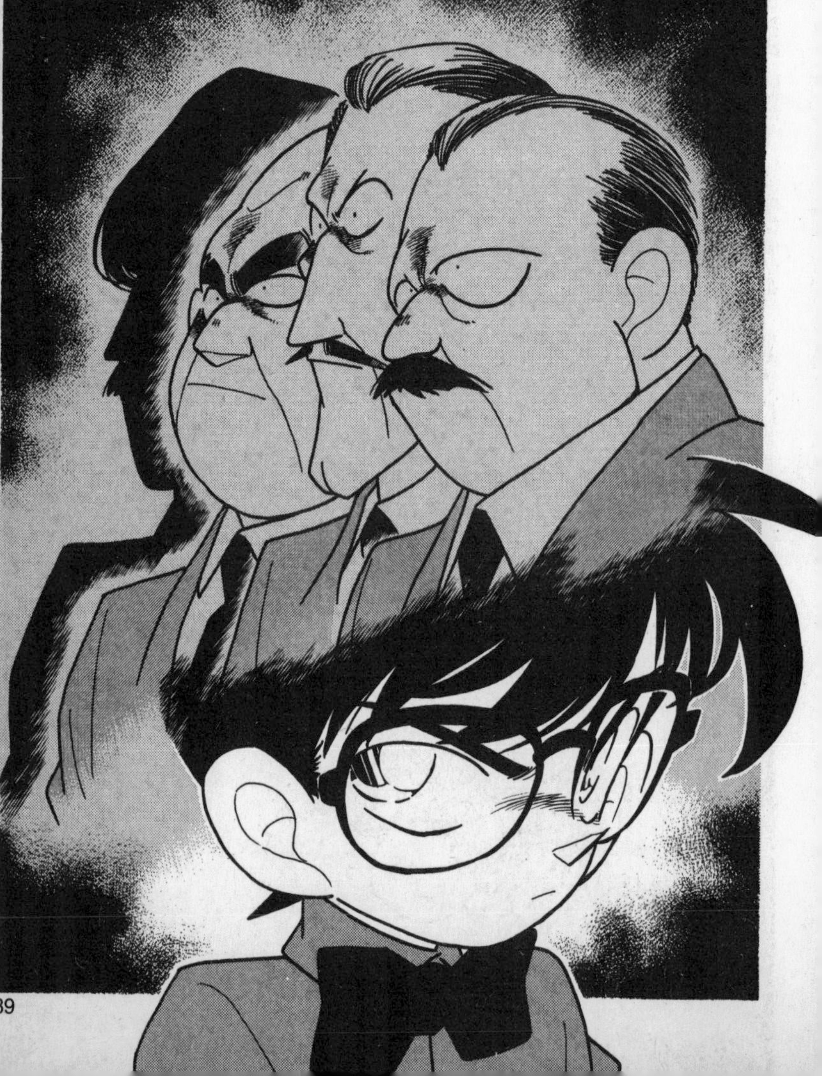

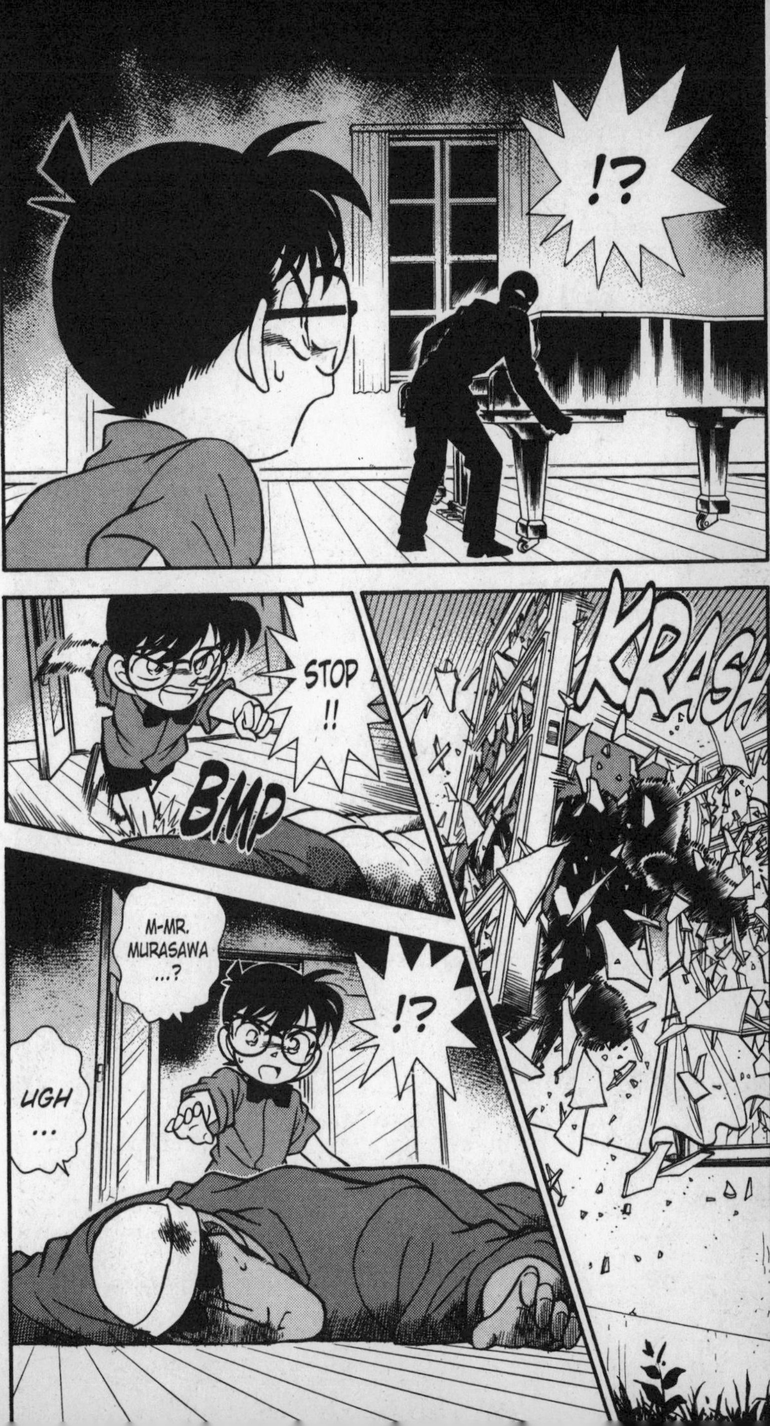
!?
KRASH
STOP !!
BMP
!?
M-MR. MURASAWA ...?
UGH ...

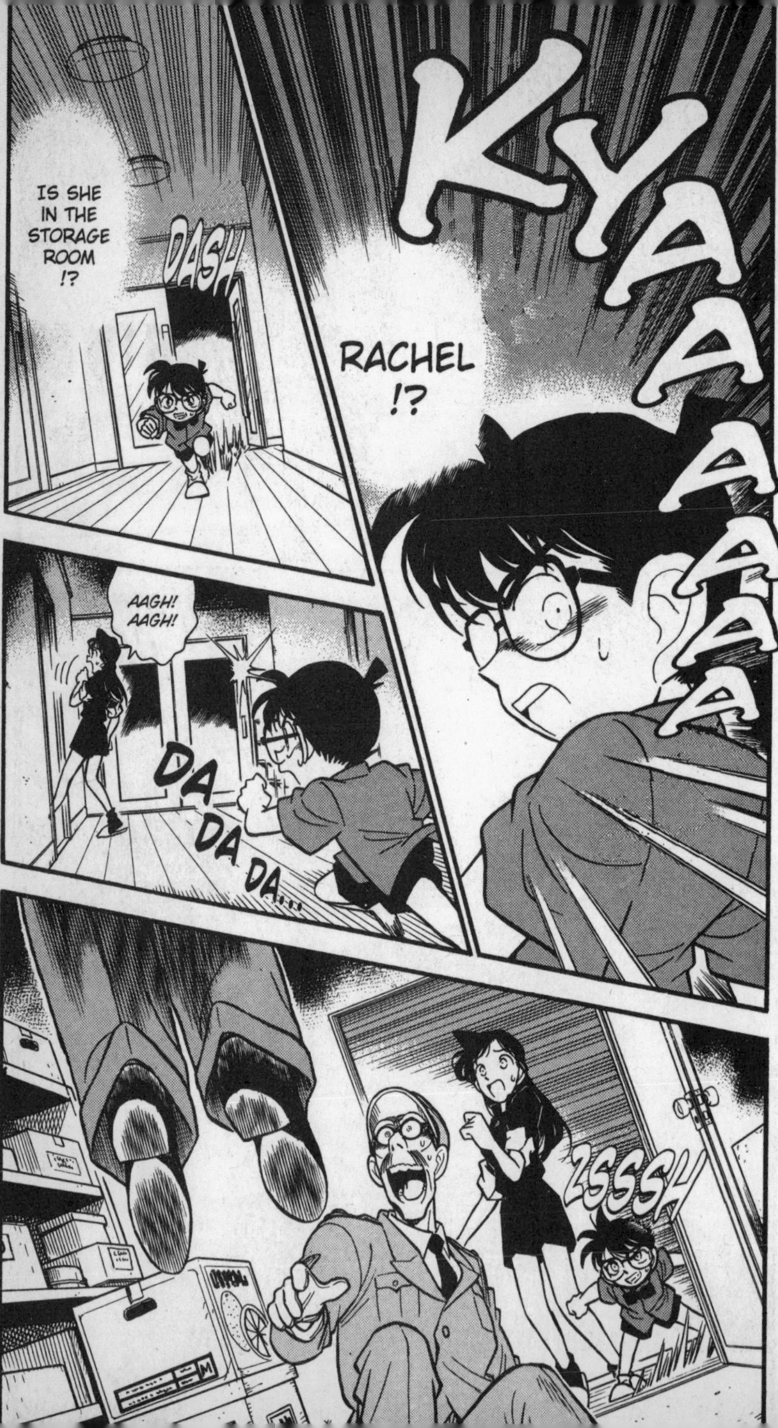
KYAAAAAAAA
RACHEL !?
IS SHE IN THE STORAGE ROOM !?
DASH
AAGH! AAGH!
DA DA DA...
ZSSSH

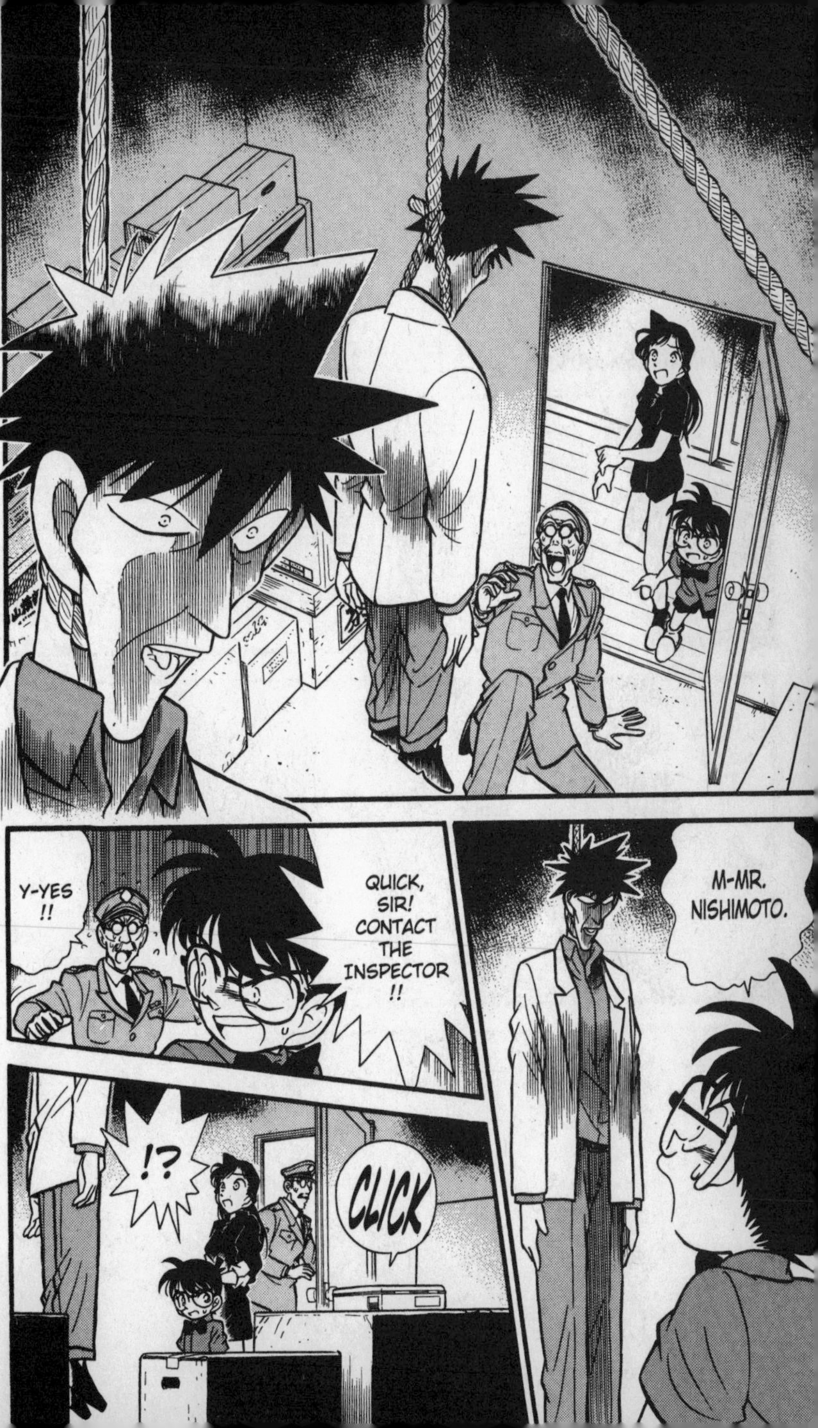
M-MR. NISHIMOTO.
QUICK, SIR! CONTACT THE INSPECTOR !!
Y-YES !!
CLICK
!?

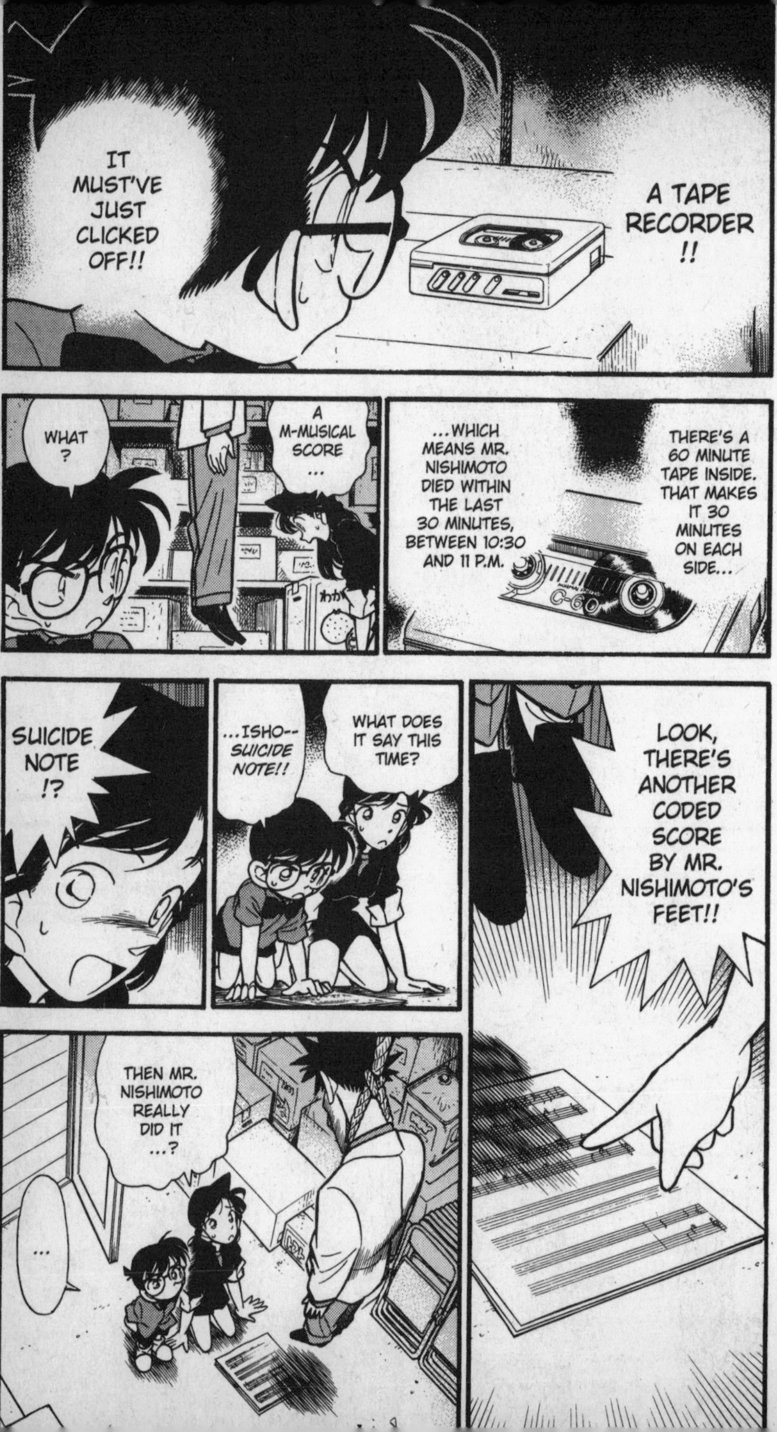
A TAPE RECORDER !!
IT MUST'VE JUST CLICKED OFF!!
THERE'S A 60 MINUTE TAPE INSIDE. THAT MAKES IT 30 MINUTES ON EACH SIDE...
...WHICH MEANS MR. NISHIMOTO DIED WITHIN THE LAST 30 MINUTES, BETWEEN 10:30 AND 11 P.M.
A M-MUSICAL SCORE ...
WHAT ?
LOOK, THERE'S ANOTHER CODED SCORE BY MR. NISHIMOTO'S FEET!!
WHAT DOES IT SAY THIS TIME?
...ISHO-- SUICIDE NOTE!!
SUICIDE NOTE !?
THEN MR. NISHIMOTO REALLY DID IT ...?
...

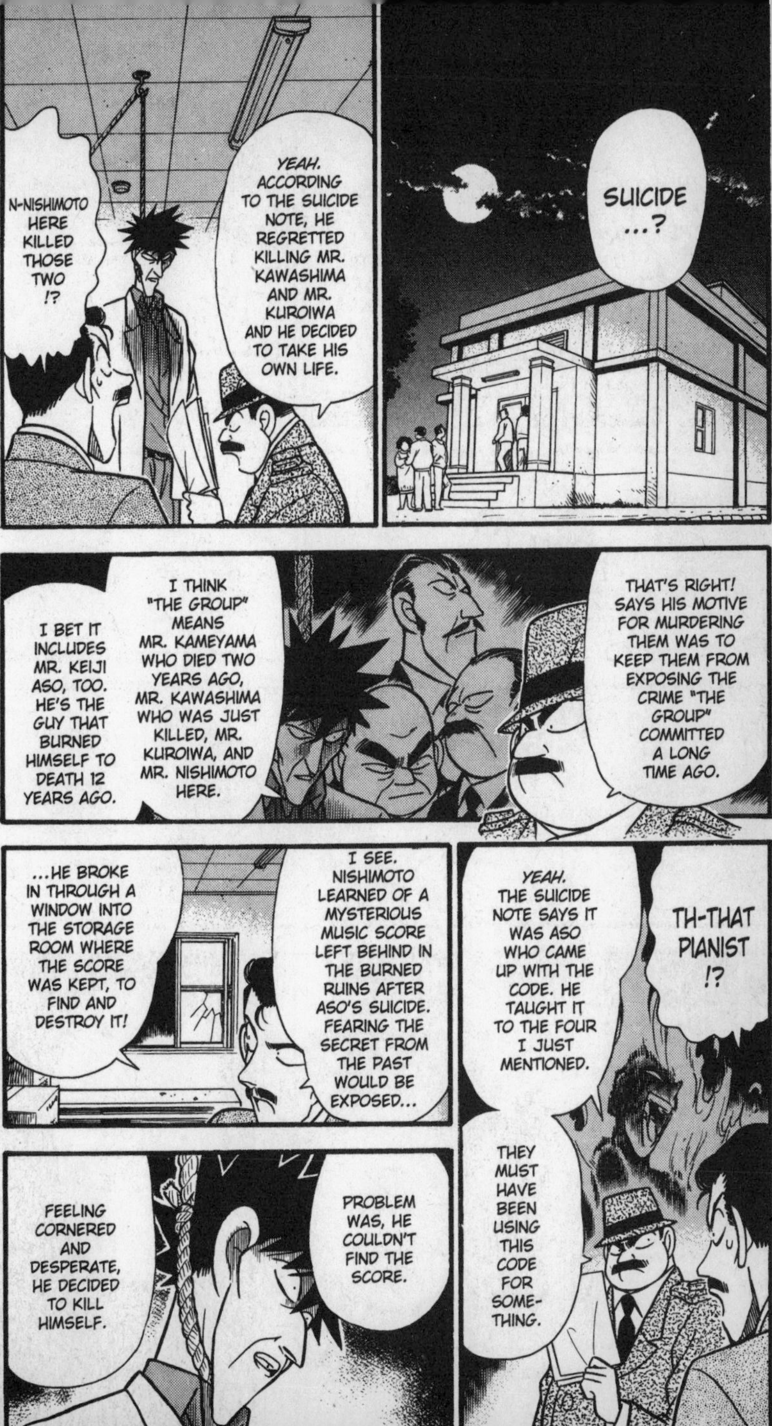
SUICIDE ...?
N-NISHIMOTO HERE KILLED THOSE TWO !?
YEAH. ACCORDING TO THE SUICIDE NOTE, HE REGRETTED KILLING MR. KAWASHIMA AND MR. KUROIWA AND HE DECIDED TO TAKE HIS OWN LIFE.
THAT'S RIGHT! SAYS HIS MOTIVE FOR MURDERING THEM WAS TO KEEP THEM FROM EXPOSING THE CRIME "THE GROUP" COMMITTED A LONG TIME AGO.
I THINK "THE GROUP" MEANS MR. KAMEYAMA WHO DIED TWO YEARS AGO, MR. KAWASHIMA WHO WAS JUST KILLED, MR. KUROIWA, AND MR. NISHIMOTO HERE.
I BET IT INCLUDES MR. KEIJI ASO, TOO. HE'S THE GUY THAT BURNED HIMSELF TO DEATH 12 YEARS AGO.
TH-THAT PIANIST !?
YEAH. THE SUICIDE NOTE SAYS IT WAS ASO WHO CAME UP WITH THE CODE. HE TAUGHT IT TO THE FOUR I JUST MENTIONED.
THEY MUST HAVE BEEN USING THIS CODE FOR SOME-THING.
I SEE. NISHIMOTO LEARNED OF A MYSTERIOUS MUSIC SCORE LEFT BEHIND IN THE BURNED RUINS AFTER ASO'S SUICIDE. FEARING THE SECRET FROM THE PAST WOULD BE EXPOSED...
...HE BROKE IN THROUGH A WINDOW INTO THE STORAGE ROOM WHERE THE SCORE WAS KEPT, TO FIND AND DESTROY IT!
PROBLEM WAS, HE COULDN'T FIND THE SCORE.
FEELING CORNERED AND DESPERATE, HE DECIDED TO KILL HIMSELF.

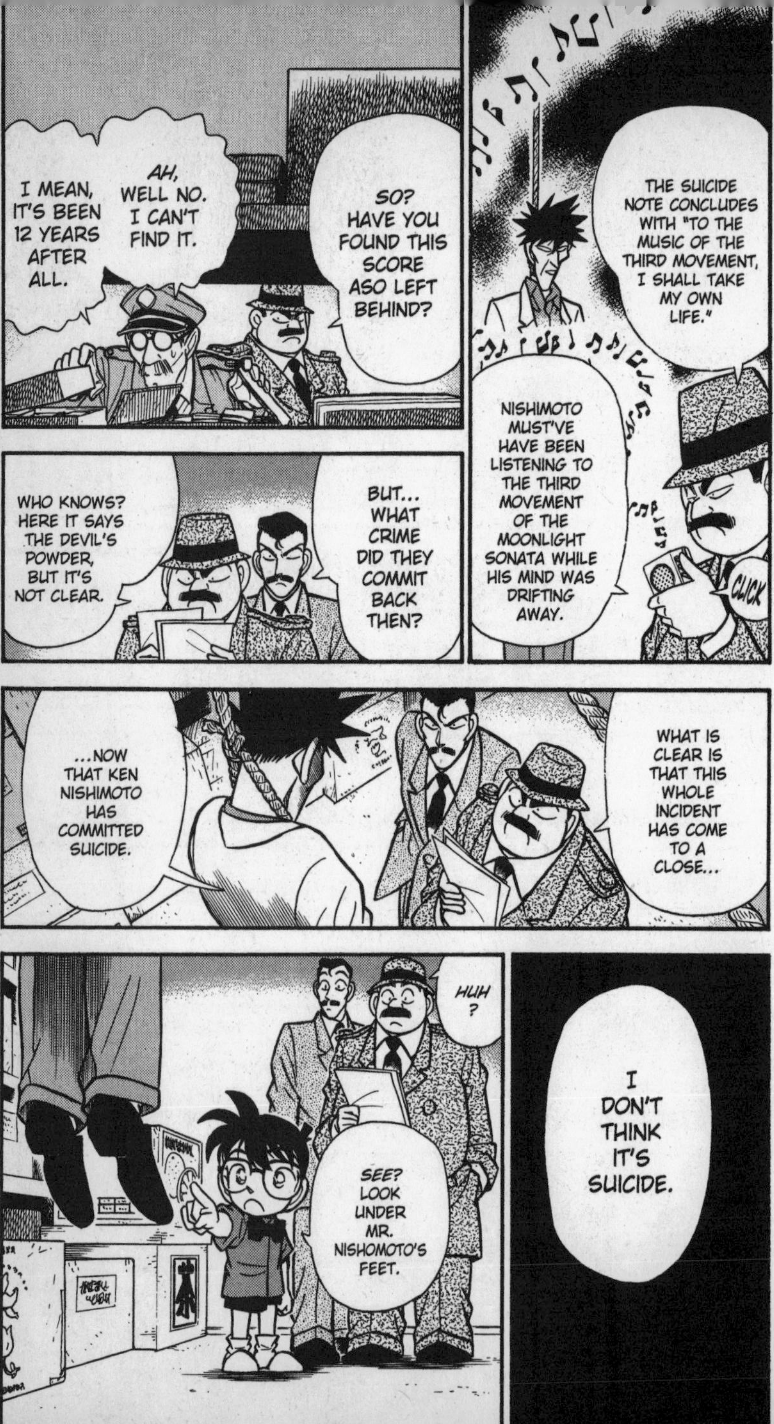
THE SUICIDE NOTE CONCLUDES WITH "TO THE MUSIC OF THE THIRD MOVEMENT, I SHALL TAKE MY OWN LIFE."
NISHIMOTO MUST'VE HAVE BEEN LISTENING TO THE THIRD MOVEMENT OF THE MOONLIGHT SONATA WHILE HIS MIND WAS DRIFTING AWAY.
CLICK
SO? HAVE YOU FOUND THIS SCORE ASO LEFT BEHIND?
AH, WELL NO. I CAN'T FIND IT.
I MEAN, IT'S BEEN 12 YEARS AFTER ALL.
BUT... WHAT CRIME DID THEY COMMIT BACK THEN?
WHO KNOWS? HERE IT SAYS THE DEVIL'S POWDER, BUT IT'S NOT CLEAR.
WHAT IS CLEAR IS THAT THIS WHOLE INCIDENT HAS COME TO A CLOSE...
...NOW THAT KEN NISHIMOTO HAS COMMITTED SUICIDE.
I DON'T THINK IT'S SUICIDE.
HUH?
SEE? LOOK UNDER MR. NISHOMOTO'S FEET.

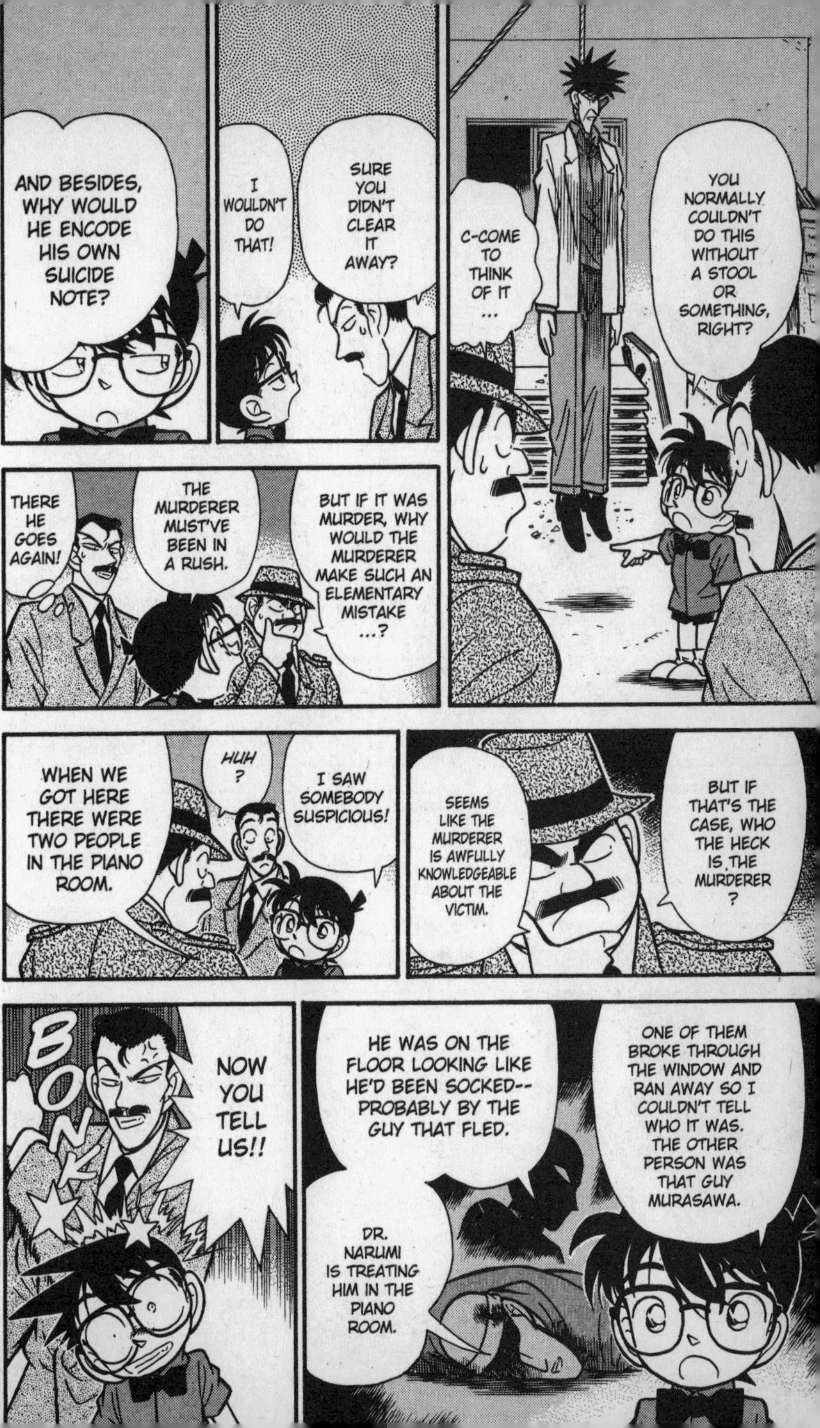
YOU NORMALLY COULDN'T DO THIS WITHOUT A STOOL OR SOMETHING, RIGHT?
C-COME TO THINK OF IT ...
SURE YOU DIDN'T CLEAR IT AWAY?
I WOULDN'T DO THAT!
AND BESIDES, WHY WOULD HE ENCODE HIS OWN SUICIDE NOTE?
BUT IF IT WAS MURDER, WHY WOULD THE MURDERER MAKE SUCH AN ELEMENTARY MISTAKE ...?
THE MURDERER MUST'VE BEEN IN A RUSH.
THERE HE GOES AGAIN!
BUT IF THAT'S THE CASE, WHO THE HECK IS THE MURDERER?
SEEMS LIKE THE MURDERER IS AWFULLY KNOWLEDGEABLE ABOUT THE VICTIM.
I SAW SOMEBODY SUSPICIOUS!
HUH?
WHEN WE GOT HERE THERE WERE TWO PEOPLE IN THE PIANO ROOM.
ONE OF THEM BROKE THROUGH THE WINDOW AND RAN AWAY SO I COULDN'T TELL WHO IT WAS. THE OTHER PERSON WAS THAT GUY MURASAWA.
HE WAS ON THE FLOOR LOOKING LIKE HE'D BEEN SOCKED--PROBABLY BY THE GUY THAT FLED.
DR. NARUMI IS TREATING HIM IN THE PIANO ROOM.
NOW YOU TELL US!!
BONK

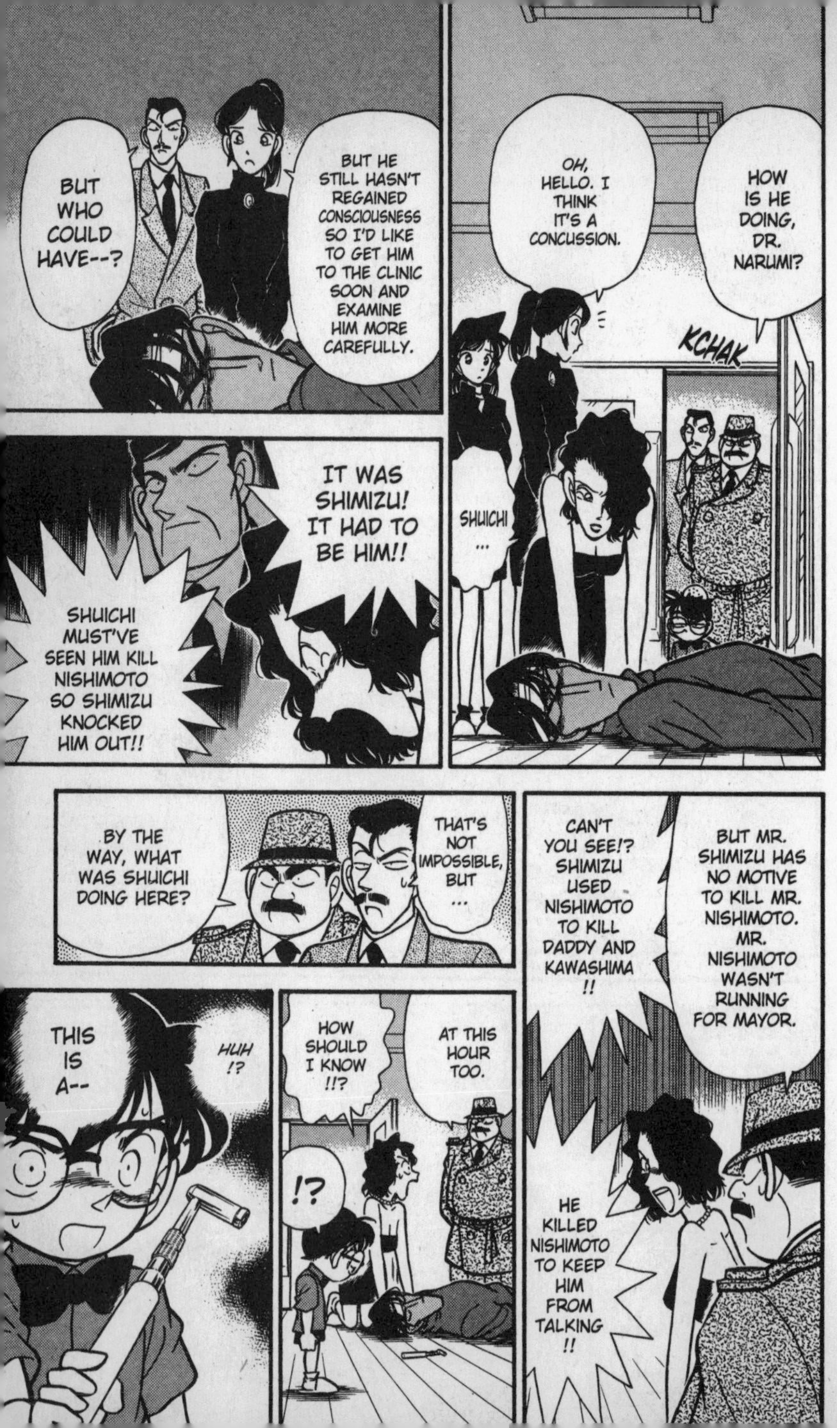
HOW IS HE DOING, DR. NARUMI?
KCHAK
OH, HELLO. I THINK IT'S A CONCUSSION.
SHUICHI ...
BUT HE STILL HASN'T REGAINED CONSCIOUSNESS SO I'D LIKE TO GET HIM TO THE CLINIC SOON AND EXAMINE HIM MORE CAREFULLY.
BUT WHO COULD HAVE--?
IT WAS SHIMIZU! IT HAD TO BE HIM!!
SHUICHI MUST'VE SEEN HIM KILL NISHIMOTO SO SHIMIZU KNOCKED HIM OUT!!
BUT MR. SHIMIZU HAS NO MOTIVE TO KILL MR. NISHIMOTO. MR. NISHIMOTO WASN'T RUNNING FOR MAYOR.
CAN'T YOU SEE!? SHIMIZU USED NISHIMOTO TO KILL DADDY AND KAWASHIMA !!
HE KILLED NISHIMOTO TO KEEP HIM FROM TALKING !!
THAT'S NOT IMPOSSIBLE, BUT ...
BY THE WAY, WHAT WAS SHUICHI DOING HERE?
AT THIS HOUR TOO.
HOW SHOULD I KNOW !!?
!?
HUH !?
THIS IS A--

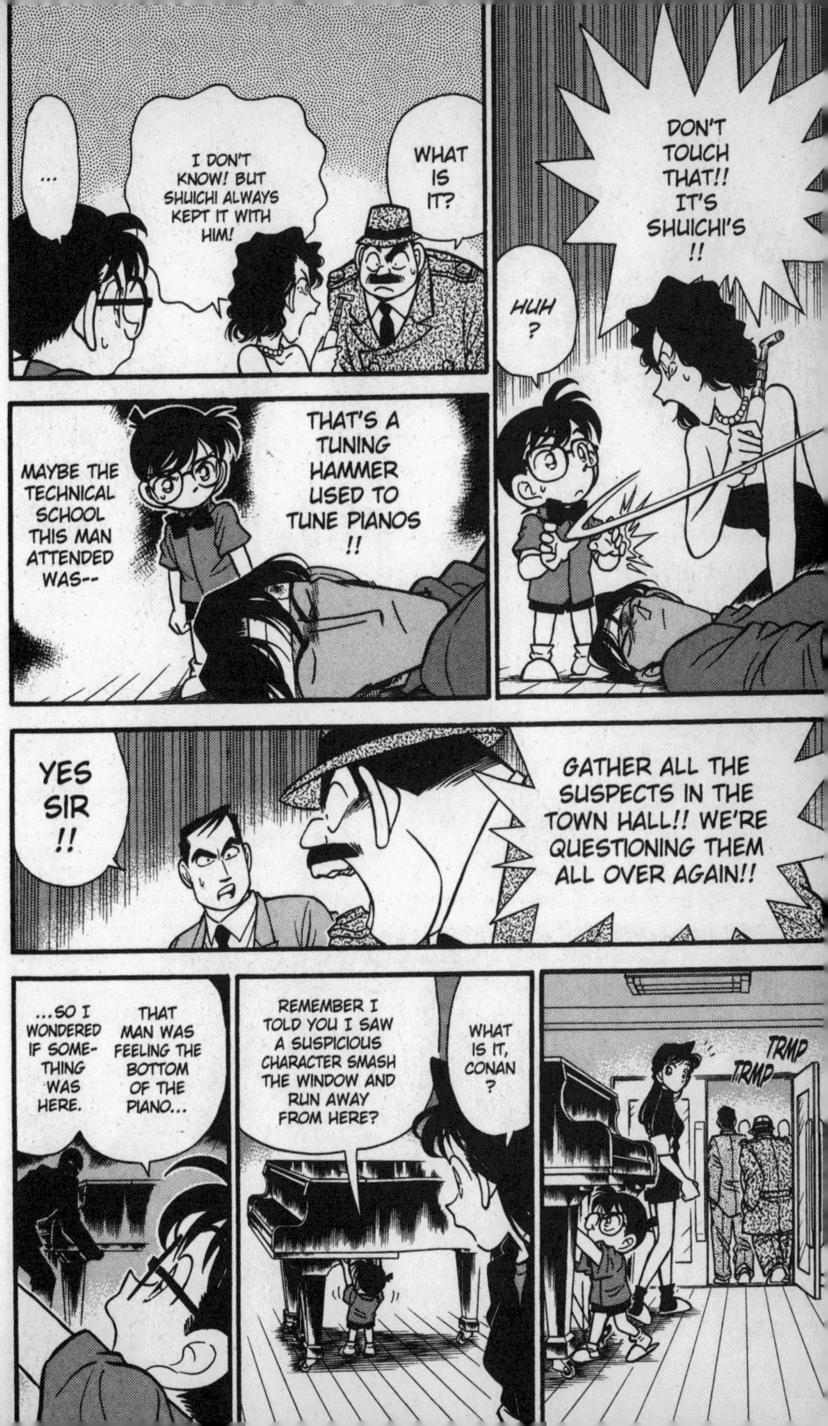
DON'T TOUCH THAT!! IT'S SHUICHI'S !!
HUH ?
WHAT IS IT?
I DON'T KNOW! BUT SHUICHI ALWAYS KEPT IT WITH HIM!
...
THAT'S A TUNING HAMMER USED TO TUNE PIANOS !!
MAYBE THE TECHNICAL SCHOOL THIS MAN ATTENDED WAS--
GATHER ALL THE SUSPECTS IN THE TOWN HALL!! WE'RE QUESTIONING THEM ALL OVER AGAIN!!
YES SIR !!
TRMP TRMP
WHAT IS IT, CONAN ?
REMEMBER I TOLD YOU I SAW A SUSPICIOUS CHARACTER SMASH THE WINDOW AND RUN AWAY FROM HERE?
THAT MAN WAS FEELING THE BOTTOM OF THE PIANO...
...SO I WONDERED IF SOME-THING WAS HERE.

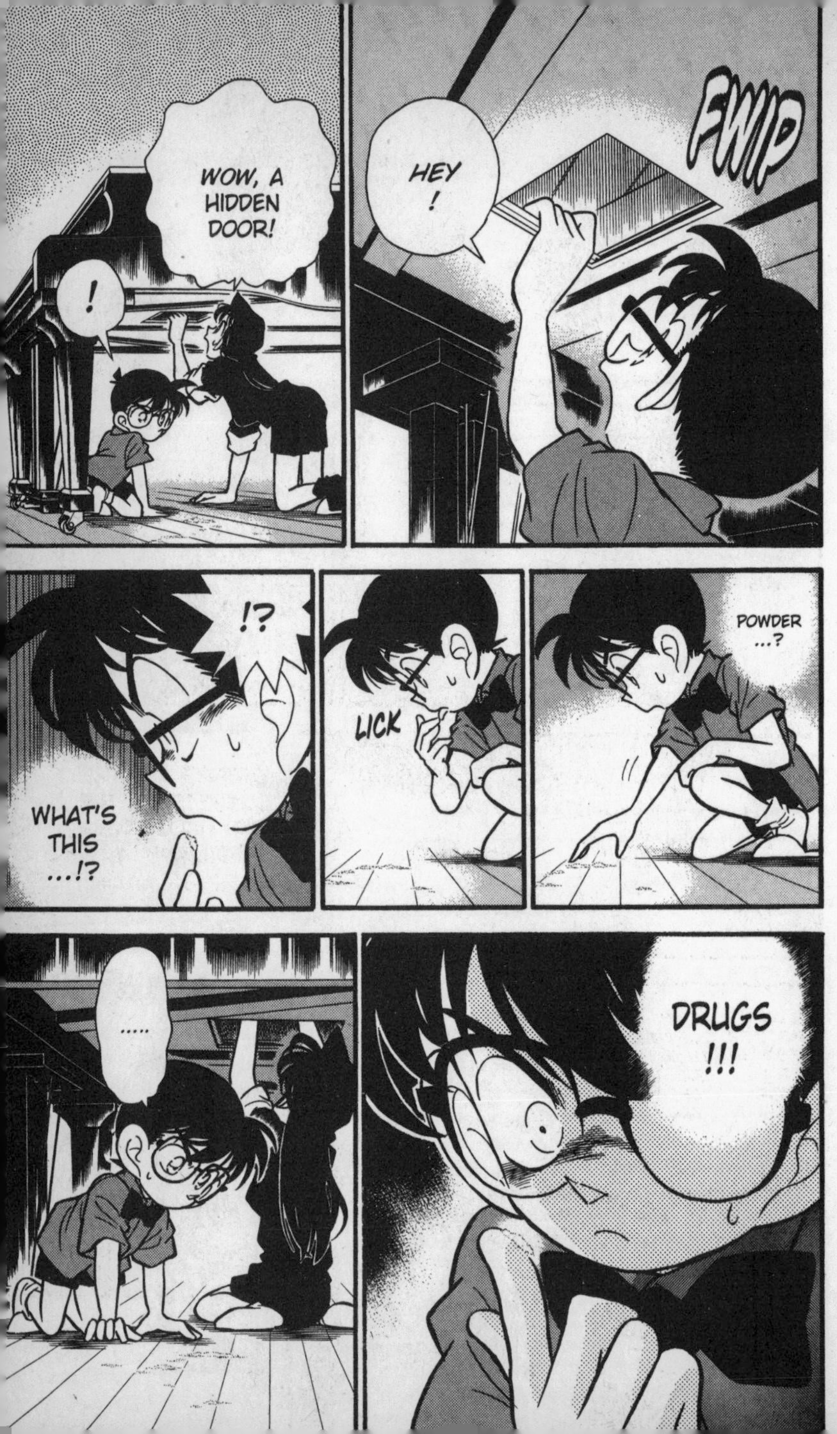
FWIP
HEY !
WOW, A HIDDEN DOOR!
!
POWDER ...?
LICK
!?
WHAT'S THIS ...!?
DRUGS !!!
.....

MOON SHADOW ISLAND TOWN HALL
THREE CRIMES WERE COMMITTED ON THIS ISLAND!
IN EACH CASE, THE PERPETRATOR PLAYED THAT SONG AT THE SCENE OF THE CRIME AND LEFT BEHIND A CODED MESSAGE! AND ALL THREE MURDERS REQUIRED PHYSICAL STRENGTH!
IN THE FIRST INCIDENT SOMEONE DROWNED MR. KAWASHIMA IN THE OCEAN AND THEN CARRIED HIM TO THE PIANO ROOM IN THE COMMUNITY CENTER.
IN THE SECOND INCIDENT SOMEONE STABBED MR. KUROIWA IN THE BROADCAST ROOM HERE IN THE TOWN HALL.
AND IN THE THIRD, SOMEONE HANGED MR. NISHIMOTO IN THE STORAGE ROOM OF THE COMMUNITY CENTER TO MAKE IT LOOK LIKE A SUICIDE.
THERE'S NO DOUBT THAT THE SAME PERSON WAS RESPONSIBLE FOR ALL THREE!! AND IT'S SOMEONE STRONG ENOUGH TO DO ALL THAT!!
DR. NARUMI, WHAT IS THE ESTIMATED TIME OF DEATH FOR MR. NISHIMOTO?
I BELIEVE IT WAS BETWEEN 10 AND 11 P.M.
WE LET YOU LEAVE THIS TOWN HALL AROUND TEN LAST NIGHT.
THAT MEANS THAT THE THIRD MURDER IS LIKE THE FIRST ONE IN THAT WE CANNOT IDENTIFY THE SUSPECT!
BUT WITH THE SECOND MURDER, THE ESTIMATED TIME OF DEATH AND THE LENGTH OF SILENCE AT THE BEGINNING OF THAT TAPE ...
... ESTABLISH ALIBIS FOR REIKO KUROIWA AND DOCTOR NARUMI ASAI.
THAT MEANS THE SUSPECT IS AMONG THOSE WHO WERE HERE IN THE TOWN HALL DURING THAT TIME BUT DON'T HAVE AN ALIBI.

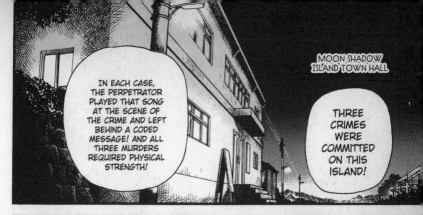

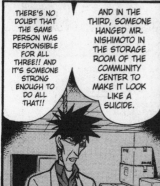

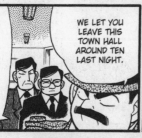

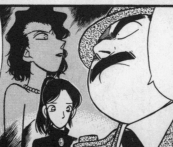

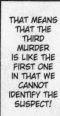

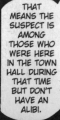

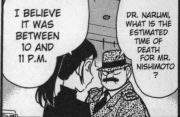

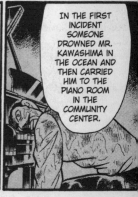

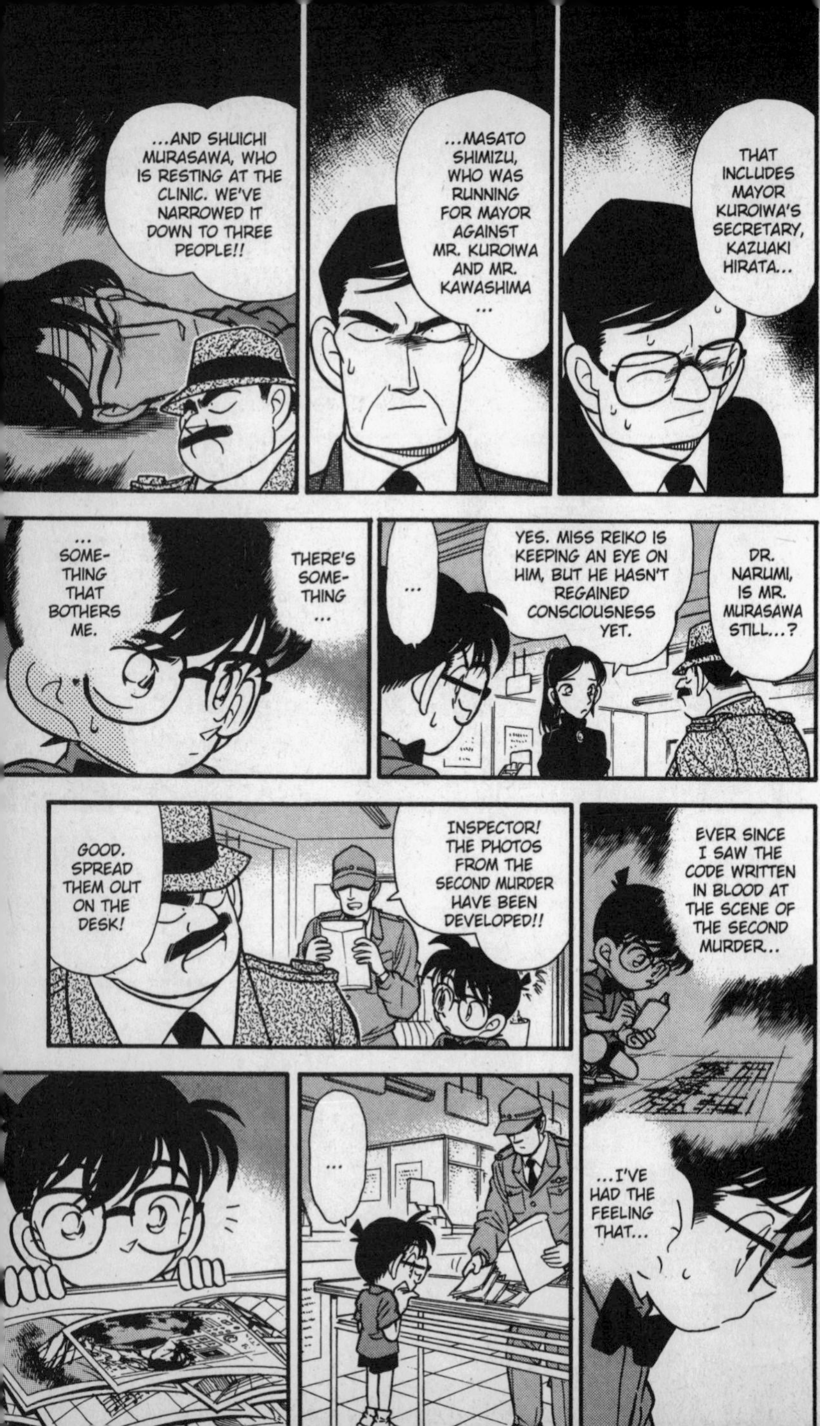
THAT INCLUDES MAYOR KUROIWA'S SECRETARY, KAZUAKI HIRATA...
...MASATO SHIMIZU, WHO WAS RUNNING FOR MAYOR AGAINST MR. KUROIWA AND MR. KAWASHIMA ...
...AND SHUICHI MURASAWA, WHO IS RESTING AT THE CLINIC. WE'VE NARROWED IT DOWN TO THREE PEOPLE!!
DR. NARUMI, IS MR. MURASAWA STILL...?
YES. MISS REIKO IS KEEPING AN EYE ON HIM, BUT HE HASN'T REGAINED CONSCIOUSNESS YET.
...
THERE'S SOME-THING ...
... SOME-THING THAT BOTHERS ME.
EVER SINCE I SAW THE CODE WRITTEN IN BLOOD AT THE SCENE OF THE SECOND MURDER...
...I'VE HAD THE FEELING THAT...
INSPECTOR! THE PHOTOS FROM THE SECOND MURDER HAVE BEEN DEVELOPED!!
GOOD. SPREAD THEM OUT ON THE DESK!
...

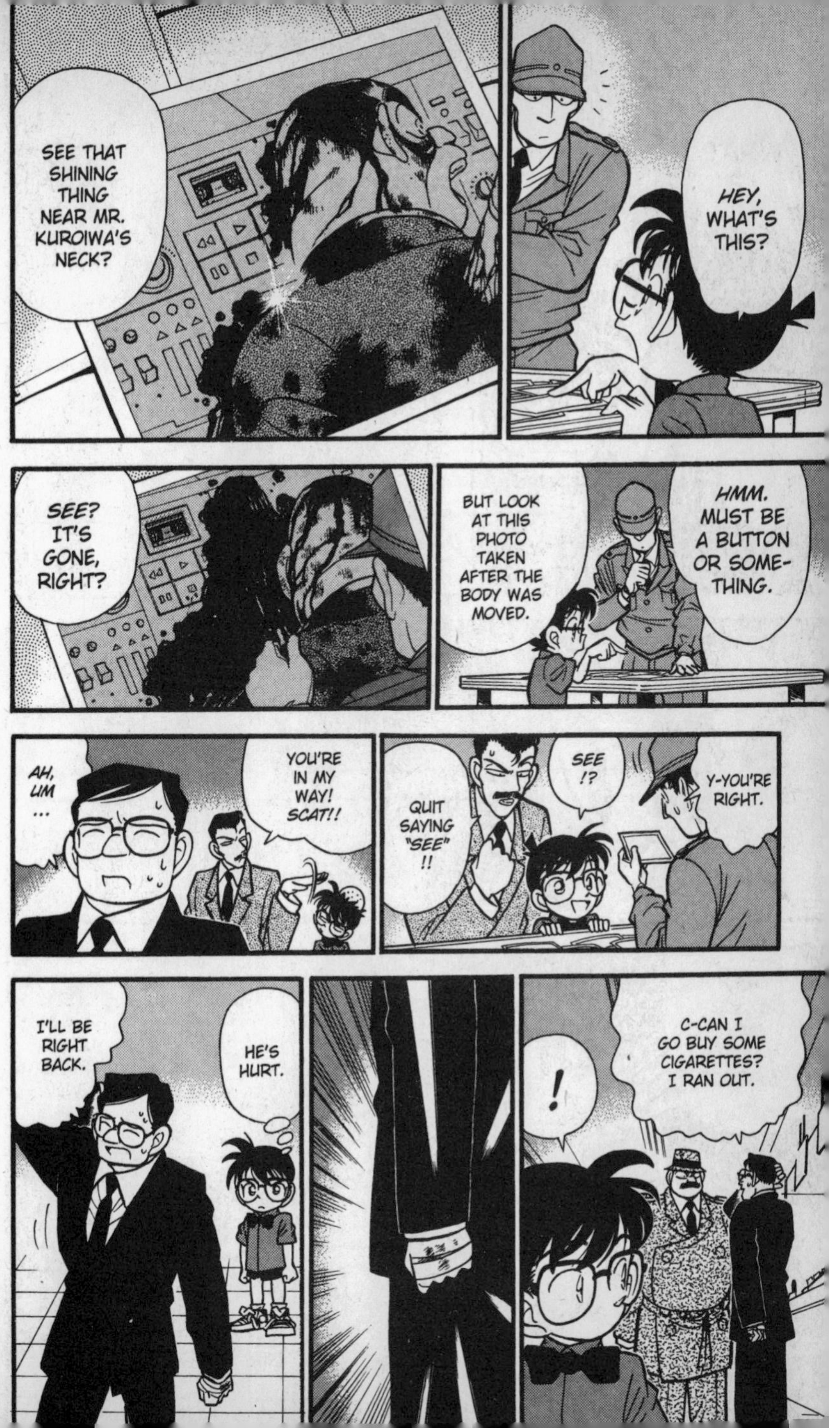
HEY, WHAT'S THIS?
SEE THAT SHINING THING NEAR MR. KUROIWA'S NECK?
HMM. MUST BE A BUTTON OR SOME-THING.
BUT LOOK AT THIS PHOTO TAKEN AFTER THE BODY WAS MOVED.
SEE? IT'S GONE, RIGHT?
Y-YOU'RE RIGHT.
SEE !?
QUIT SAYING "SEE" !!
YOU'RE IN MY WAY! SCAT!!
AH, UM ...
C-CAN I GO BUY SOME CIGARETTES? I RAN OUT.
!
HE'S HURT.
I'LL BE RIGHT BACK.

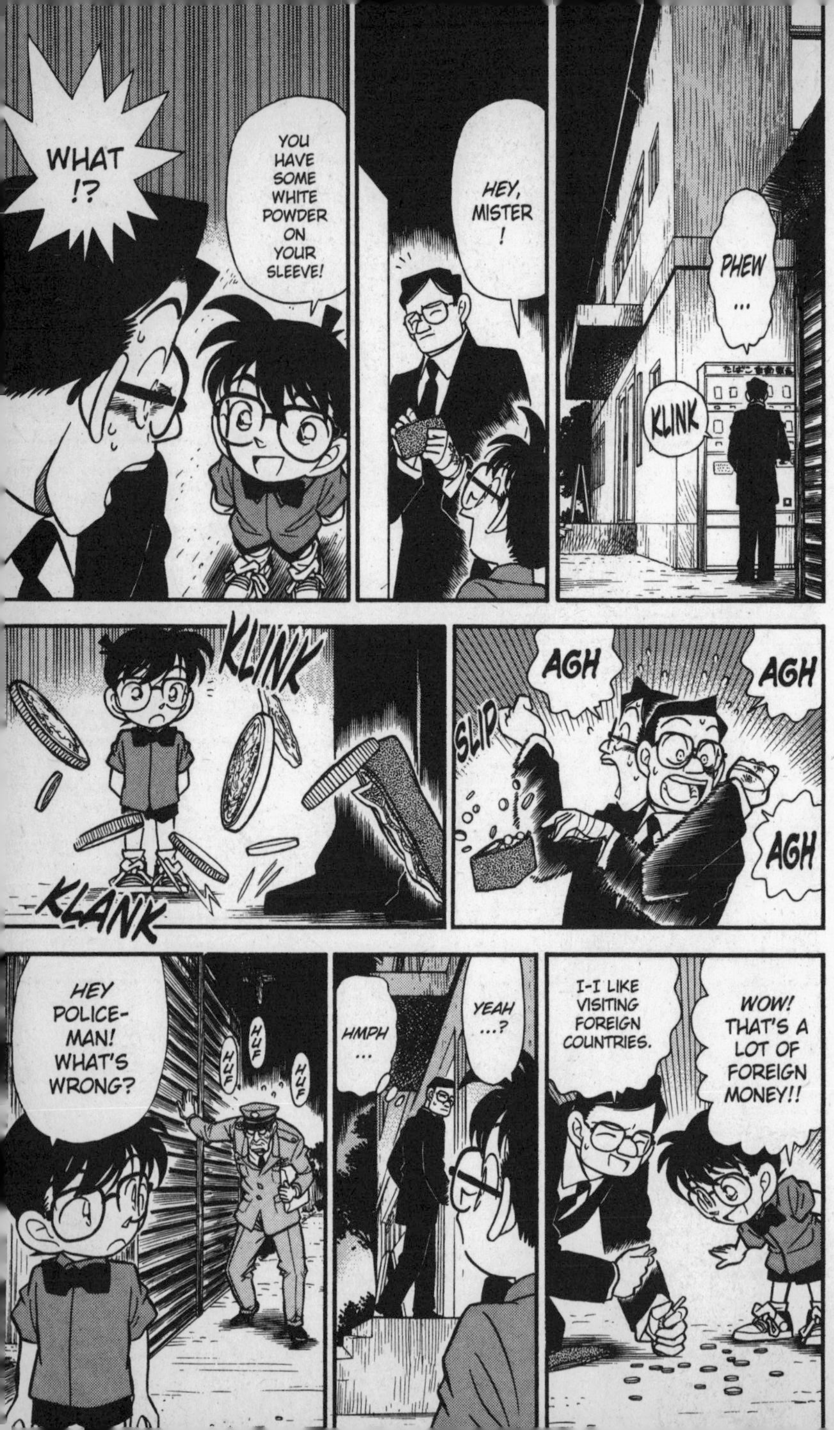
PHEW ...
KLINK
HEY, MISTER !
YOU HAVE SOME WHITE POWDER ON YOUR SLEEVE!
WHAT !?
AGH
AGH
SLIP
AGH
KLINK
KLANK
WOW! THAT'S A LOT OF FOREIGN MONEY!!
I-I LIKE VISITING FOREIGN COUNTRIES.
YEAH ...?
HMPH ...
HUF
HUF
HUF
HEY POLICE-MAN! WHAT'S WRONG?

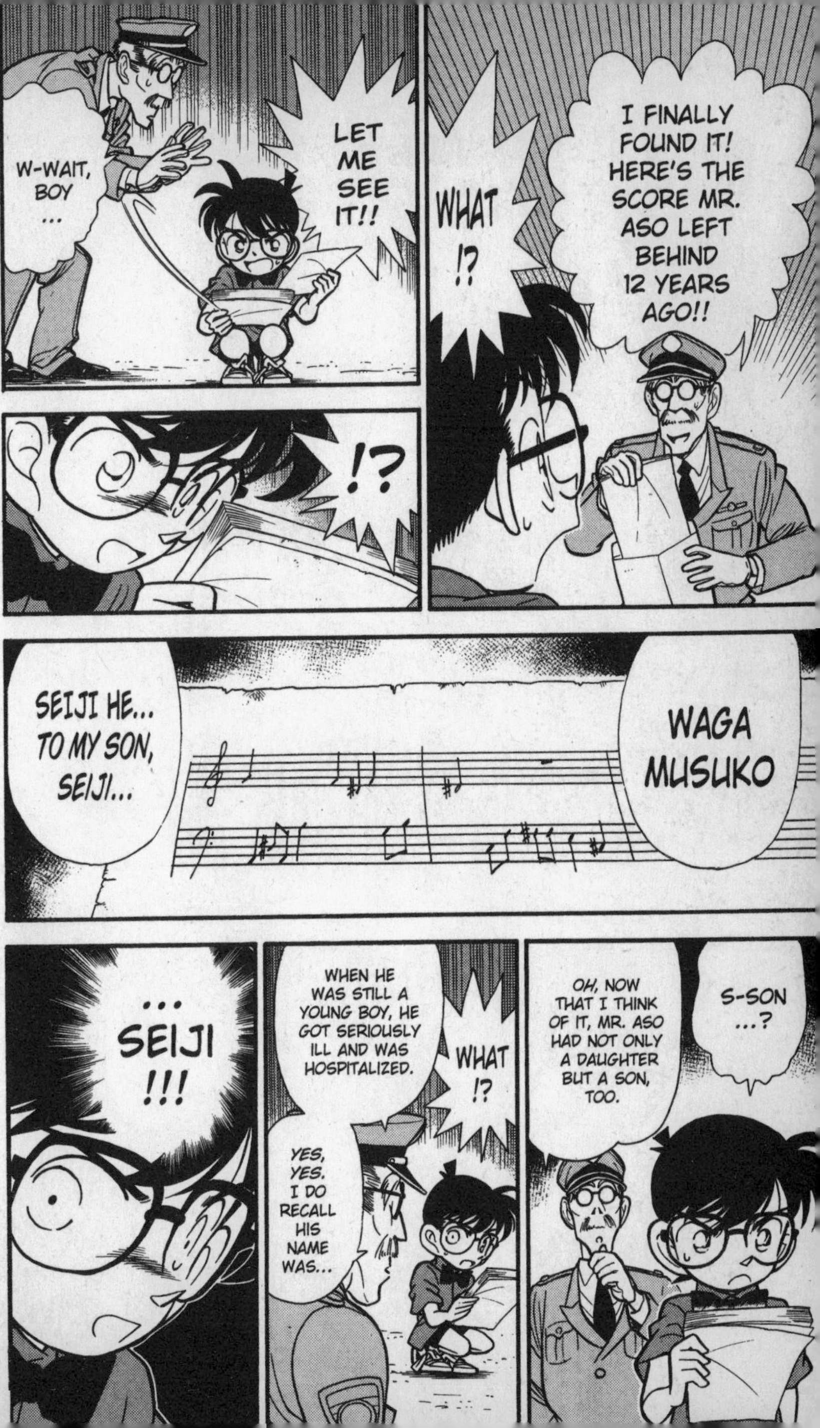
I FINALLY FOUND IT! HERE'S THE SCORE MR. ASO LEFT BEHIND 12 YEARS AGO!!
WHAT !?
LET ME SEE IT!!
W-WAIT, BOY ...
!?
WAGA MUSUKO
SEIJI HE... TO MY SON, SEIJI...
S-SON ...?
OH, NOW THAT I THINK OF IT, MR. ASO HAD NOT ONLY A DAUGHTER BUT A SON, TOO.
WHAT !?
WHEN HE WAS STILL A YOUNG BOY, HE GOT SERIOUSLY ILL AND WAS HOSPITALIZED.
YES, YES. I DO RECALL HIS NAME WAS...
... SEIJI !!!

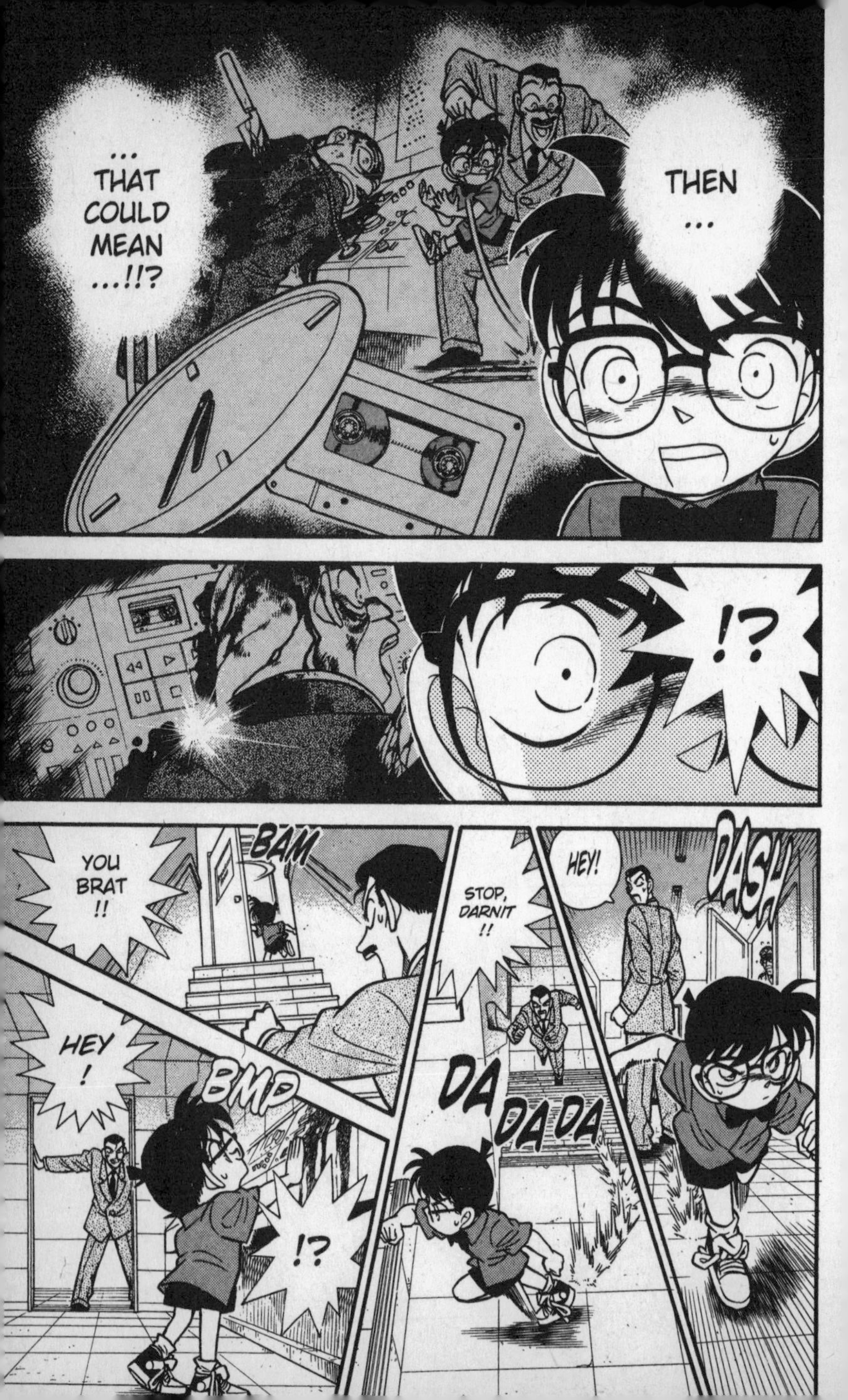
THEN ...
... THAT COULD MEAN ...!!?
!?
DASH
HEY!
STOP, DARNIT !!
DA DA DA
BAM
YOU BRAT !!
HEY !
BMP
!?

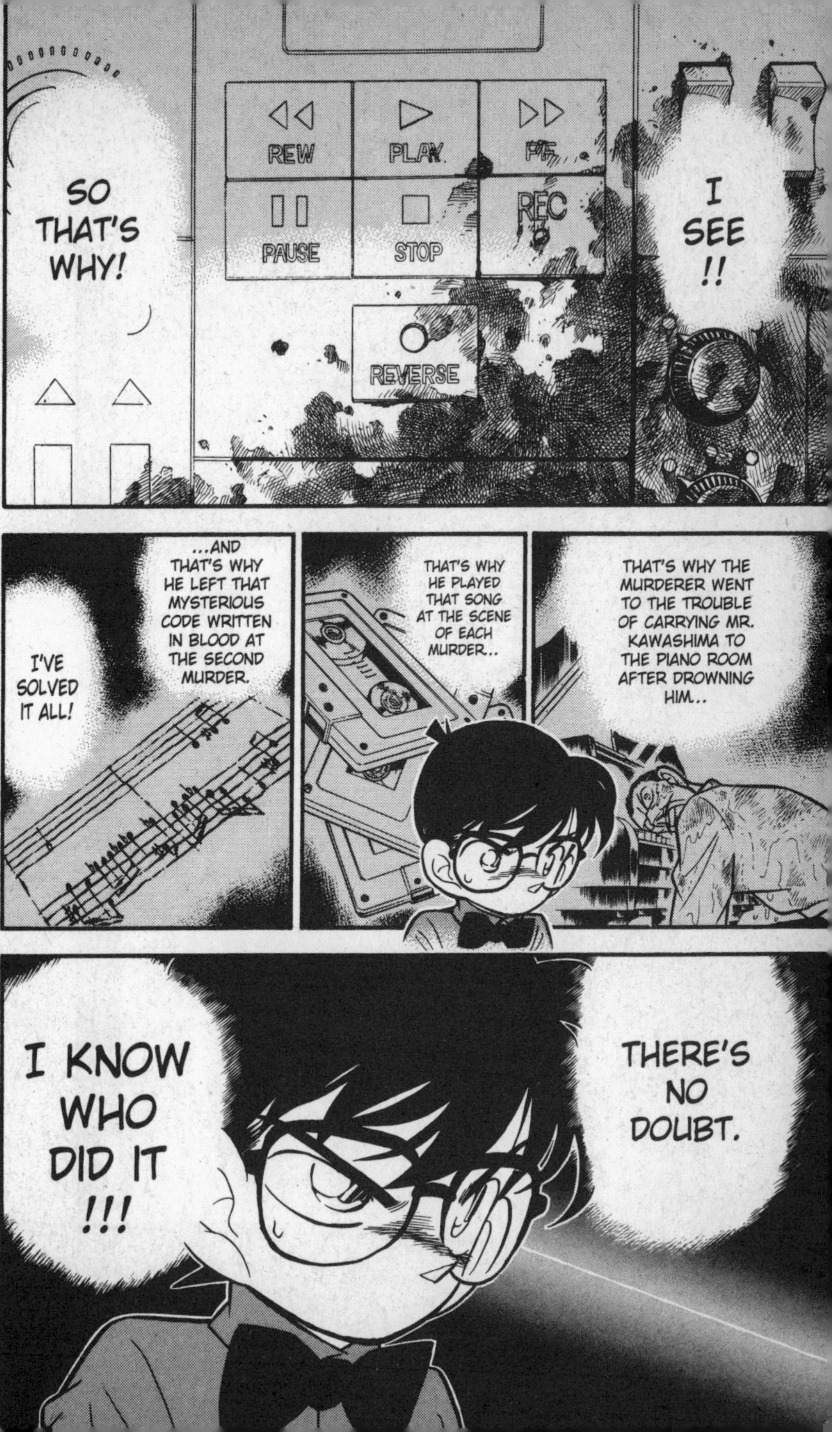
I SEE!!
REW
PLAY
REC
PAUSE
STOP
REVERSE
SO THAT'S WHY!
THAT'S WHY THE MURDERER WENT TO THE TROUBLE OF CARRYING MR. KAWASHIMA TO THE PIANO ROOM AFTER DROWNING HIM...
THAT'S WHY HE PLAYED THAT SONG AT THE SCENE OF EACH MURDER...
...AND THAT'S WHY HE LEFT THAT MYSTERIOUS CODE WRITTEN IN BLOOD AT THE SECOND MURDER.
I'VE SOLVED IT ALL!
THERE'S NO DOUBT.
I KNOW WHO DID IT!!!

FILE 7:

THE SECRET
BEHIND A NAME!!

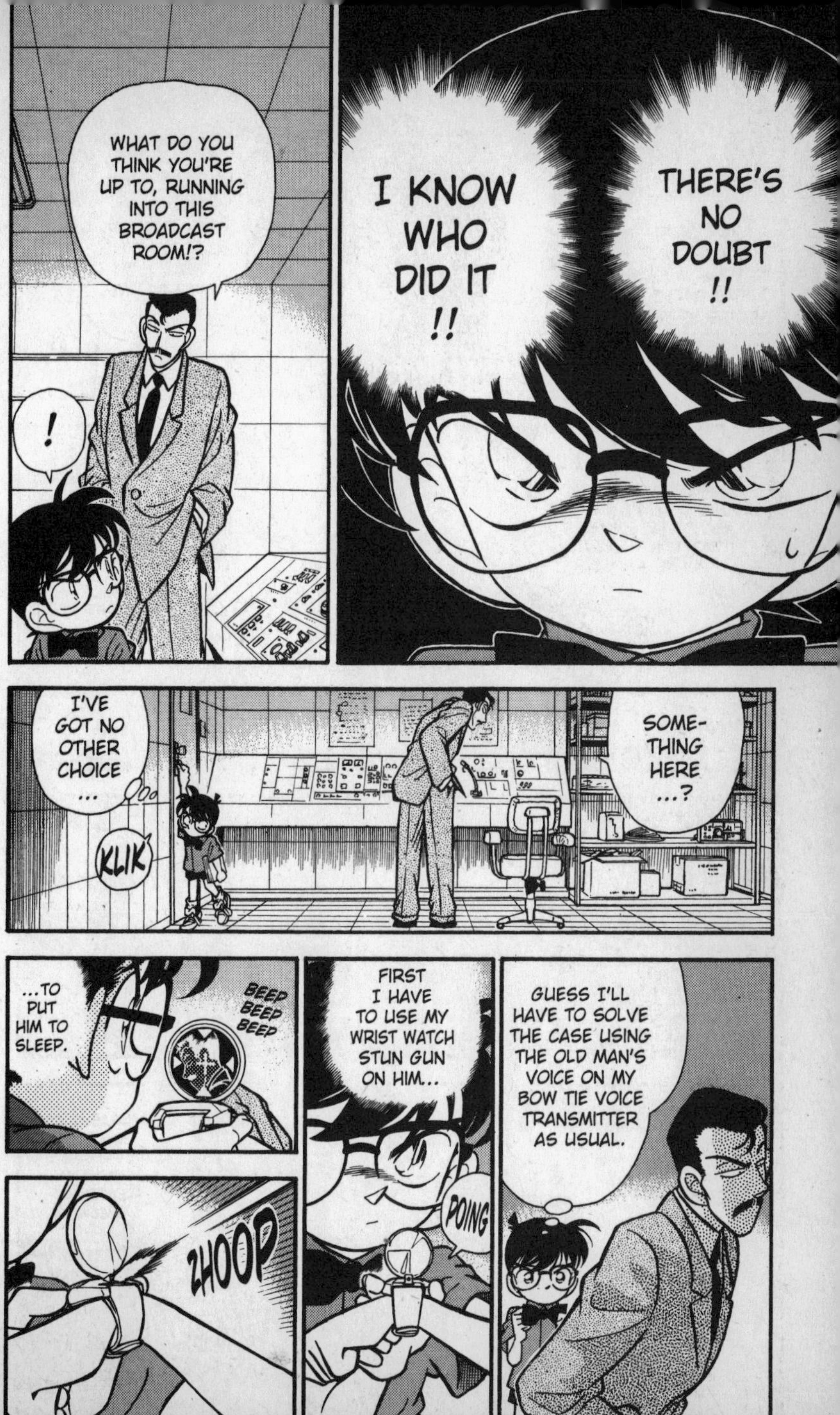
THERE'S NO DOUBT !!
I KNOW WHO DID IT !!
WHAT DO YOU THINK YOU'RE UP TO, RUNNING INTO THIS BROADCAST ROOM!?
!
SOME-THING HERE ...?
I'VE GOT NO OTHER CHOICE ...
KLIK
GUESS I'LL HAVE TO SOLVE THE CASE USING THE OLD MAN'S VOICE ON MY BOW TIE VOICE TRANSMITTER AS USUAL.
FIRST I HAVE TO USE MY WRIST WATCH STUN GUN ON HIM...
POING
...TO PUT HIM TO SLEEP.
BEEP BEEP BEEP
ZHOOP

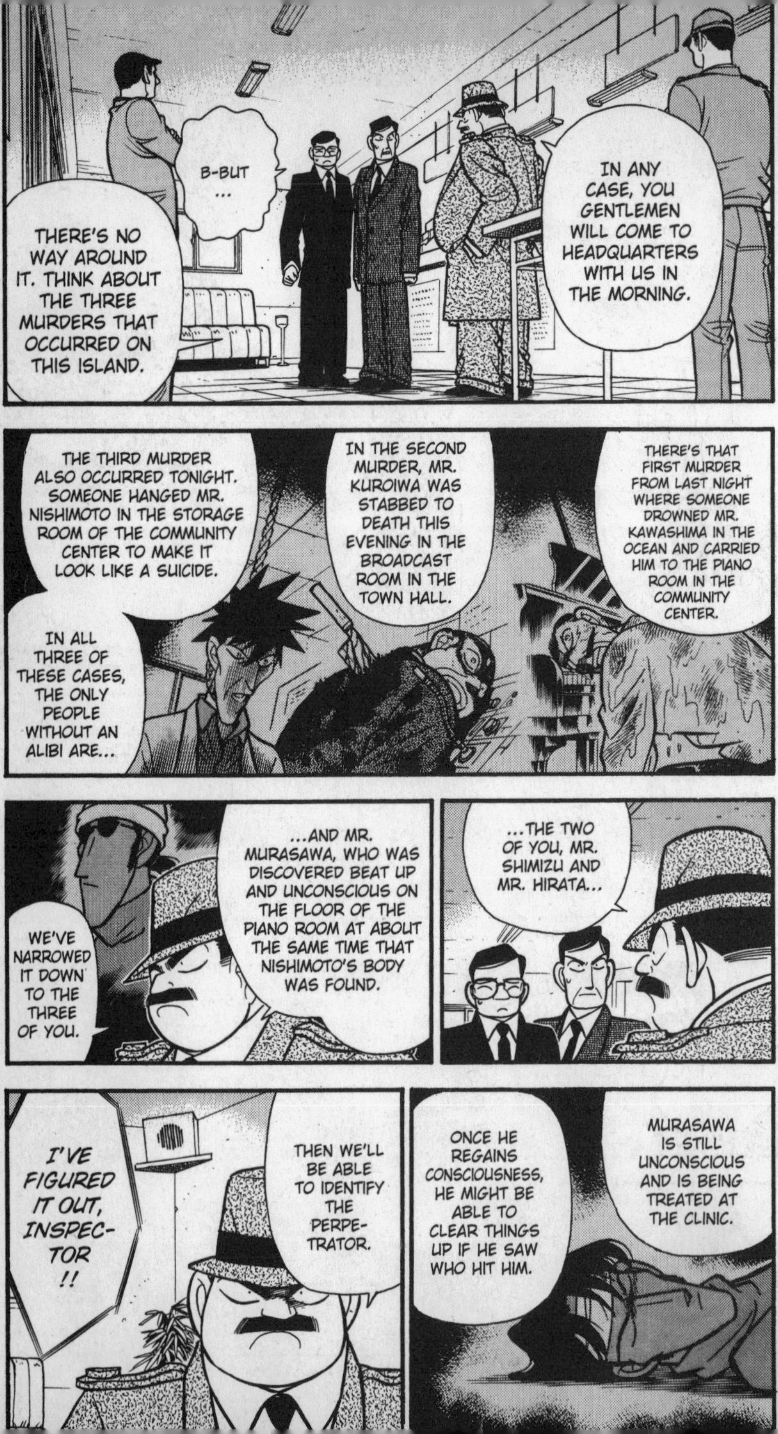
IN ANY CASE, YOU GENTLEMEN WILL COME TO HEADQUARTERS WITH US IN THE MORNING.
B-BUT ...
THERE'S NO WAY AROUND IT. THINK ABOUT THE THREE MURDERS THAT OCCURRED ON THIS ISLAND.
THERE'S THAT FIRST MURDER FROM LAST NIGHT WHERE SOMEONE DROWNED MR. KAWASHIMA IN THE OCEAN AND CARRIED HIM TO THE PIANO ROOM IN THE COMMUNITY CENTER.
IN THE SECOND MURDER, MR. KUROIWA WAS STABBED TO DEATH THIS EVENING IN THE BROADCAST ROOM IN THE TOWN HALL.
THE THIRD MURDER ALSO OCCURRED TONIGHT. SOMEONE HANGED MR. NISHIMOTO IN THE STORAGE ROOM OF THE COMMUNITY CENTER TO MAKE IT LOOK LIKE A SUICIDE.
IN ALL THREE OF THESE CASES, THE ONLY PEOPLE WITHOUT AN ALIBI ARE...
...THE TWO OF YOU, MR. SHIMIZU AND MR. HIRATA...
...AND MR. MURASAWA, WHO WAS DISCOVERED BEAT UP AND UNCONSCIOUS ON THE FLOOR OF THE PIANO ROOM AT ABOUT THE SAME TIME THAT NISHIMOTO'S BODY WAS FOUND.
WE'VE NARROWED IT DOWN TO THE THREE OF YOU.
MURASAWA IS STILL UNCONSCIOUS AND IS BEING TREATED AT THE CLINIC.
ONCE HE REGAINS CONSCIOUSNESS, HE MIGHT BE ABLE TO CLEAR THINGS UP IF HE SAW WHO HIT HIM.
THEN WE'LL BE ABLE TO IDENTIFY THE PERPETRATOR.
I'VE FIGURED IT OUT, INSPECTOR !!

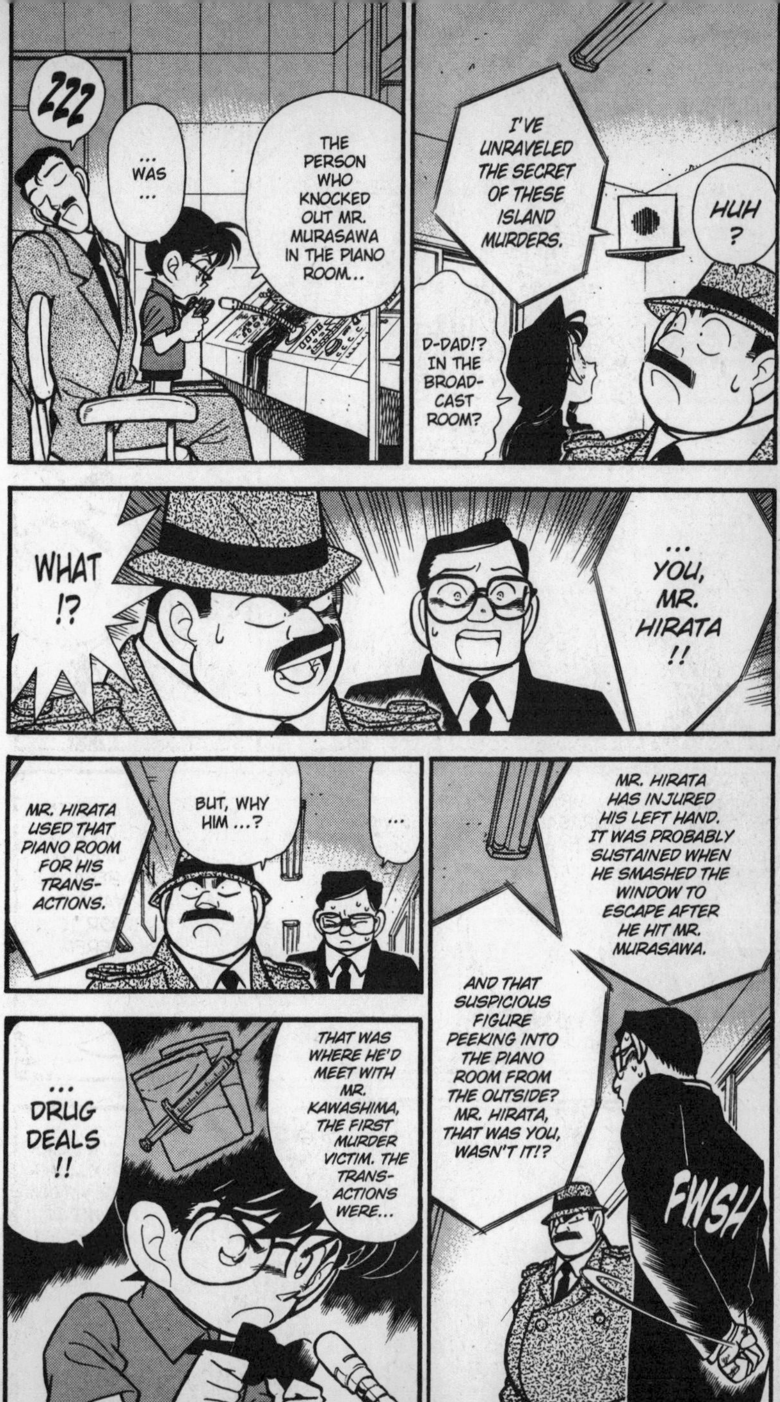

I'VE UNRAVELED THE SECRET OF THESE ISLAND MURDERS.
HUH ?
D-DAD!? IN THE BROAD-CAST ROOM?
THE PERSON WHO KNOCKED OUT MR. MURASAWA IN THE PIANO ROOM...
... WAS ...
ZZZ
... YOU, MR. HIRATA !!
WHAT !?
MR. HIRATA HAS INJURED HIS LEFT HAND. IT WAS PROBABLY SUSTAINED WHEN HE SMASHED THE WINDOW TO ESCAPE AFTER HE HIT MR. MURASAWA.
AND THAT SUSPICIOUS FIGURE PEEKING INTO THE PIANO ROOM FROM THE OUTSIDE? MR. HIRATA, THAT WAS YOU, WASN'T IT!?
FWSH
...
BUT, WHY HIM ...?
MR. HIRATA USED THAT PIANO ROOM FOR HIS TRANS-ACTIONS.
THAT WAS WHERE HE'D MEET WITH MR. KAWASHIMA, THE FIRST MURDER VICTIM. THE TRANS-ACTIONS WERE...
... DRUG DEALS !!

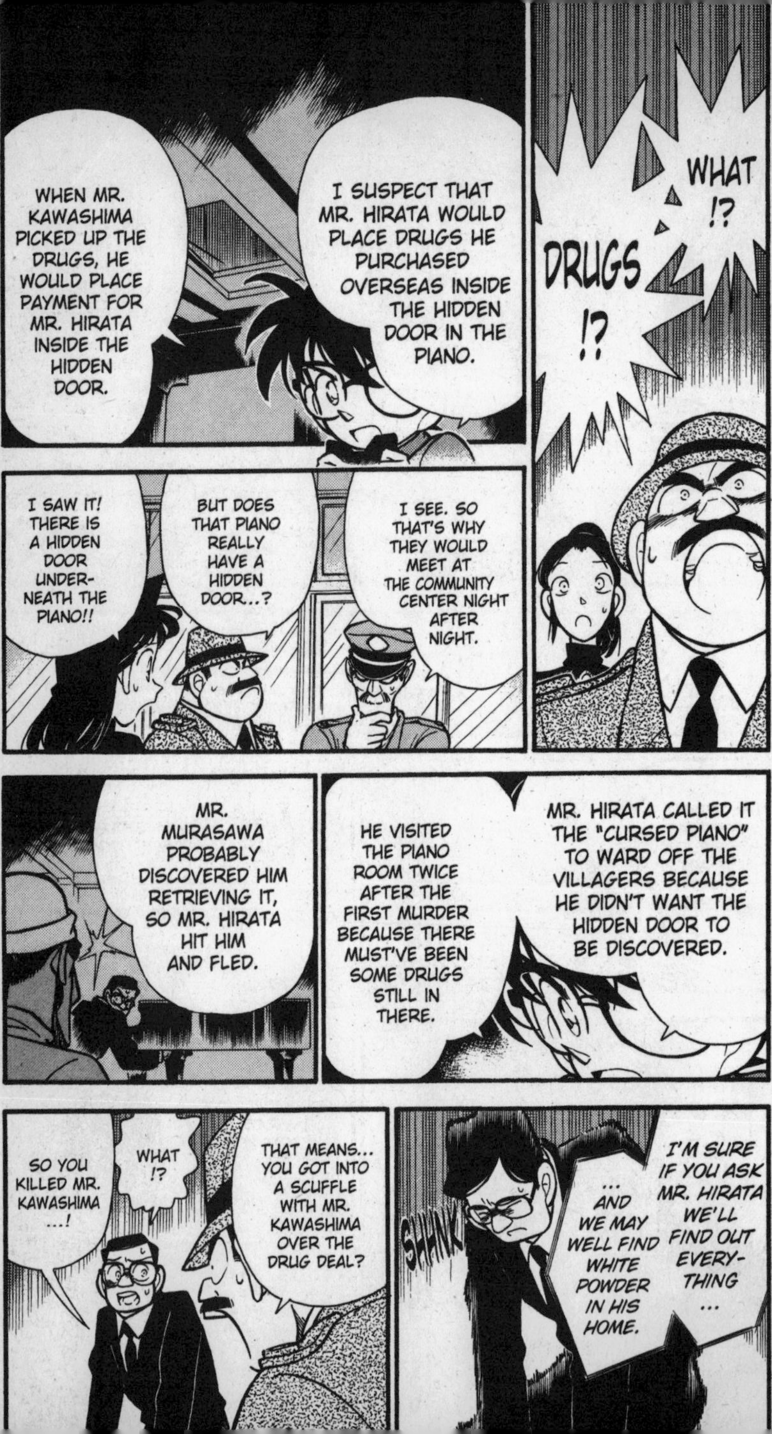
WHAT !?
DRUGS !?
I SUSPECT THAT MR. HIRATA WOULD PLACE DRUGS HE PURCHASED OVERSEAS INSIDE THE HIDDEN DOOR IN THE PIANO.
WHEN MR. KAWASHIMA PICKED UP THE DRUGS, HE WOULD PLACE PAYMENT FOR MR. HIRATA INSIDE THE HIDDEN DOOR.
I SEE. SO THAT'S WHY THEY WOULD MEET AT THE COMMUNITY CENTER NIGHT AFTER NIGHT.
BUT DOES THAT PIANO REALLY HAVE A HIDDEN DOOR...?
I SAW IT! THERE IS A HIDDEN DOOR UNDER-NEATH THE PIANO!!
MR. HIRATA CALLED IT THE "CURSED PIANO" TO WARD OFF THE VILLAGERS BECAUSE HE DIDN'T WANT THE HIDDEN DOOR TO BE DISCOVERED.
HE VISITED THE PIANO ROOM TWICE AFTER THE FIRST MURDER BECAUSE THERE MUST'VE BEEN SOME DRUGS STILL IN THERE.
MR. MURASAWA PROBABLY DISCOVERED HIM RETRIEVING IT, SO MR. HIRATA HIT HIM AND FLED.
I'M SURE IF YOU ASK MR. HIRATA WE'LL FIND OUT EVERY-THING...
...AND WE MAY WELL FIND WHITE POWDER IN HIS HOME.
THAT MEANS... YOU GOT INTO A SCUFFLE WITH MR. KAWASHIMA OVER THE DRUG DEAL?
WHAT !?
SO YOU KILLED MR. KAWASHIMA ...!

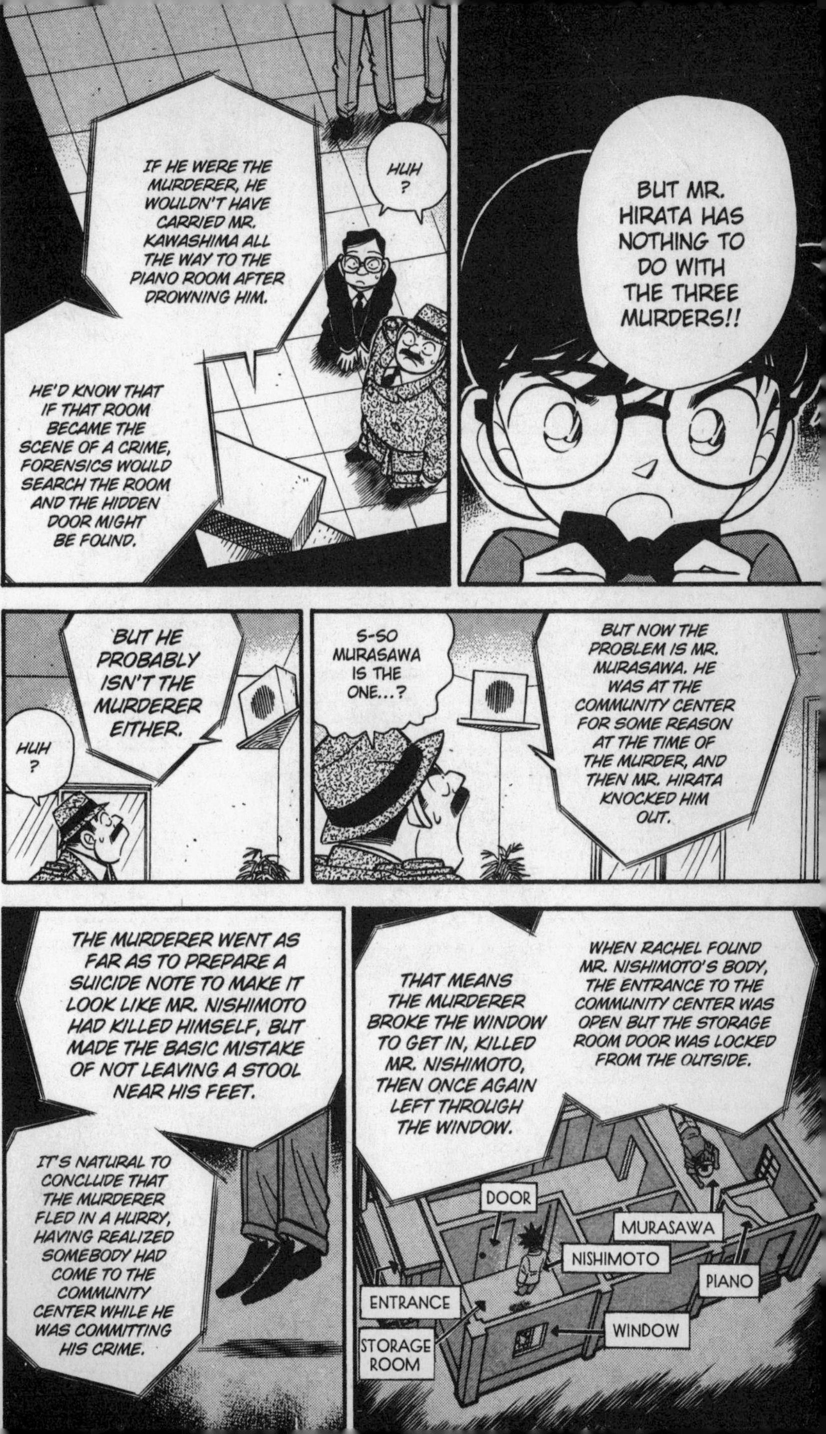
BUT MR. HIRATA HAS NOTHING TO DO WITH THE THREE MURDERS!!
HUH ?
IF HE WERE THE MURDERER, HE WOULDN'T HAVE CARRIED MR. KAWASHIMA ALL THE WAY TO THE PIANO ROOM AFTER DROWNING HIM.
HE'D KNOW THAT IF THAT ROOM BECAME THE SCENE OF A CRIME, FORENSICS WOULD SEARCH THE ROOM AND THE HIDDEN DOOR MIGHT BE FOUND.
BUT NOW THE PROBLEM IS MR. MURASAWA. HE WAS AT THE COMMUNITY CENTER FOR SOME REASON AT THE TIME OF THE MURDER, AND THEN MR. HIRATA KNOCKED HIM OUT.
S-SO MURASAWA IS THE ONE...?
BUT HE PROBABLY ISN'T THE MURDERER EITHER.
HUH ?
WHEN RACHEL FOUND MR. NISHIMOTO'S BODY, THE ENTRANCE TO THE COMMUNITY CENTER WAS OPEN BUT THE STORAGE ROOM DOOR WAS LOCKED FROM THE OUTSIDE.
THAT MEANS THE MURDERER BROKE THE WINDOW TO GET IN, KILLED MR. NISHIMOTO, THEN ONCE AGAIN LEFT THROUGH THE WINDOW.
DOOR
MURASAWA
NISHIMOTO
PIANO
ENTRANCE
WINDOW
STORAGE ROOM
THE MURDERER WENT AS FAR AS TO PREPARE A SUICIDE NOTE TO MAKE IT LOOK LIKE MR. NISHIMOTO HAD KILLED HIMSELF, BUT MADE THE BASIC MISTAKE OF NOT LEAVING A STOOL NEAR HIS FEET.
IT'S NATURAL TO CONCLUDE THAT THE MURDERER FLED IN A HURRY, HAVING REALIZED SOMEBODY HAD COME TO THE COMMUNITY CENTER WHILE HE WAS COMMITTING HIS CRIME.

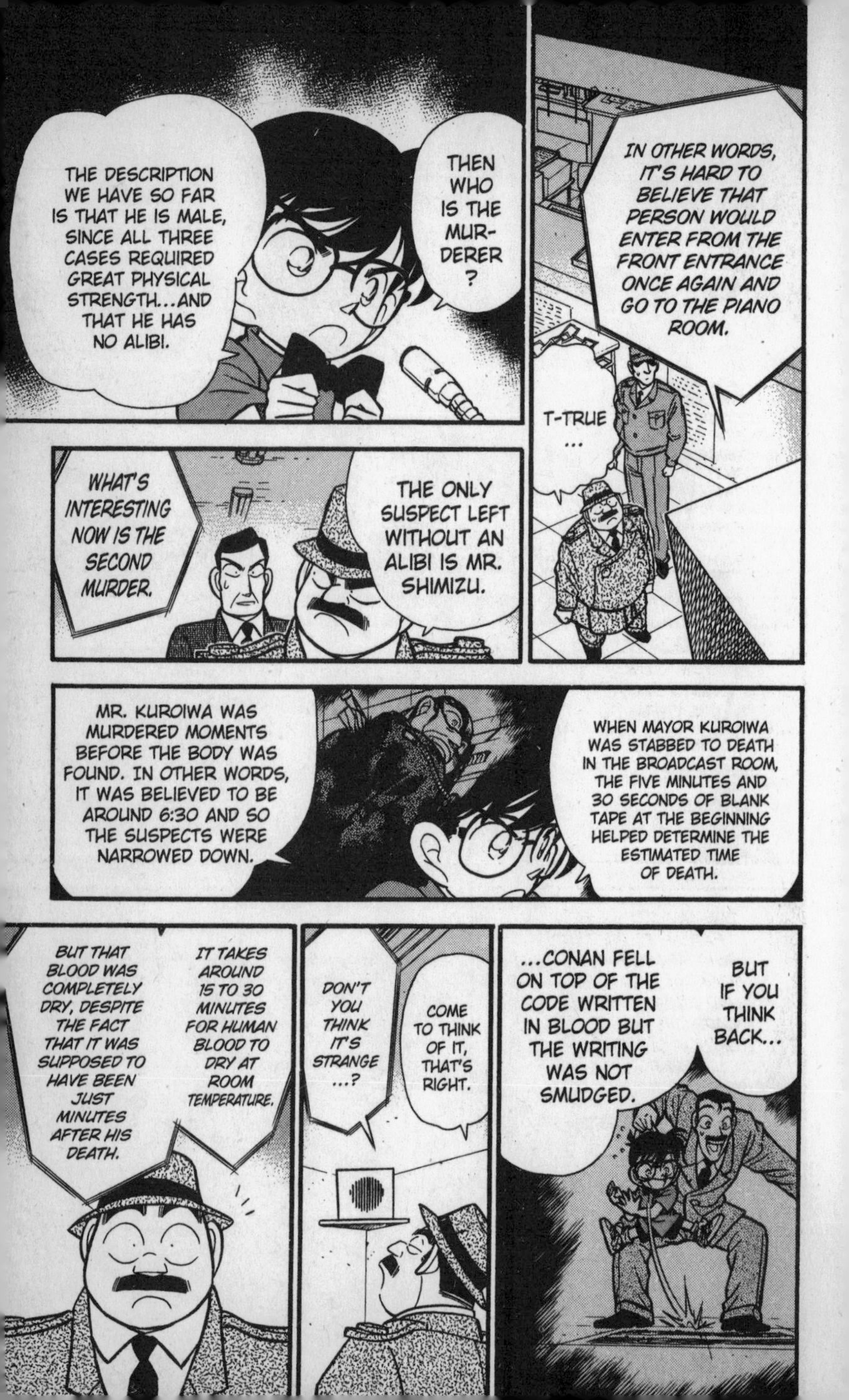
IN OTHER WORDS, IT'S HARD TO BELIEVE THAT PERSON WOULD ENTER FROM THE FRONT ENTRANCE ONCE AGAIN AND GO TO THE PIANO ROOM.
T-TRUE ...
THEN WHO IS THE MUR-DERER ?
THE DESCRIPTION WE HAVE SO FAR IS THAT HE IS MALE, SINCE ALL THREE CASES REQUIRED GREAT PHYSICAL STRENGTH...AND THAT HE HAS NO ALIBI.
THE ONLY SUSPECT LEFT WITHOUT AN ALIBI IS MR. SHIMIZU.
WHAT'S INTERESTING NOW IS THE SECOND MURDER.
WHEN MAYOR KUROIWA WAS STABBED TO DEATH IN THE BROADCAST ROOM, THE FIVE MINUTES AND 30 SECONDS OF BLANK TAPE AT THE BEGINNING HELPED DETERMINE THE ESTIMATED TIME OF DEATH.
MR. KUROIWA WAS MURDERED MOMENTS BEFORE THE BODY WAS FOUND. IN OTHER WORDS, IT WAS BELIEVED TO BE AROUND 6:30 AND SO THE SUSPECTS WERE NARROWED DOWN.
BUT IF YOU THINK BACK...
...CONAN FELL ON TOP OF THE CODE WRITTEN IN BLOOD BUT THE WRITING WAS NOT SMUDGED.
COME TO THINK OF IT, THAT'S RIGHT.
DON'T YOU THINK IT'S STRANGE ...?
IT TAKES AROUND 15 TO 30 MINUTES FOR HUMAN BLOOD TO DRY AT ROOM TEMPERATURE.
BUT THAT BLOOD WAS COMPLETELY DRY, DESPITE THE FACT THAT IT WAS SUPPOSED TO HAVE BEEN JUST MINUTES AFTER HIS DEATH.

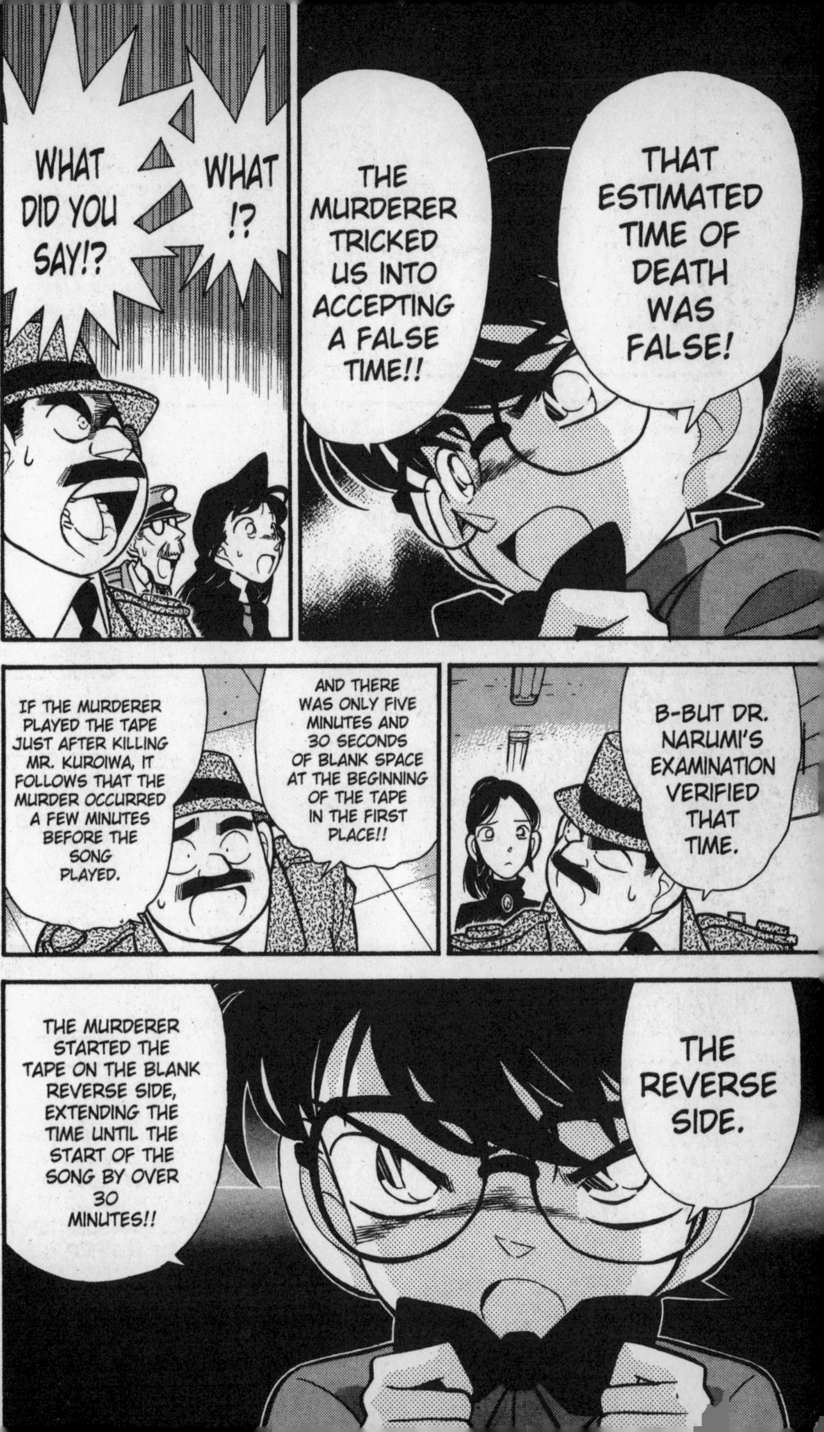
THAT ESTIMATED TIME OF DEATH WAS FALSE!
THE MURDERER TRICKED US INTO ACCEPTING A FALSE TIME!!
WHAT !?
WHAT DID YOU SAY!?
B-BUT DR. NARUMI'S EXAMINATION VERIFIED THAT TIME.
AND THERE WAS ONLY FIVE MINUTES AND 30 SECONDS OF BLANK SPACE AT THE BEGINNING OF THE TAPE IN THE FIRST PLACE!!
IF THE MURDERER PLAYED THE TAPE JUST AFTER KILLING MR. KUROIWA, IT FOLLOWS THAT THE MURDER OCCURRED A FEW MINUTES BEFORE THE SONG PLAYED.
THE REVERSE SIDE.
THE MURDERER STARTED THE TAPE ON THE BLANK REVERSE SIDE, EXTENDING THE TIME UNTIL THE START OF THE SONG BY OVER 30 MINUTES!!

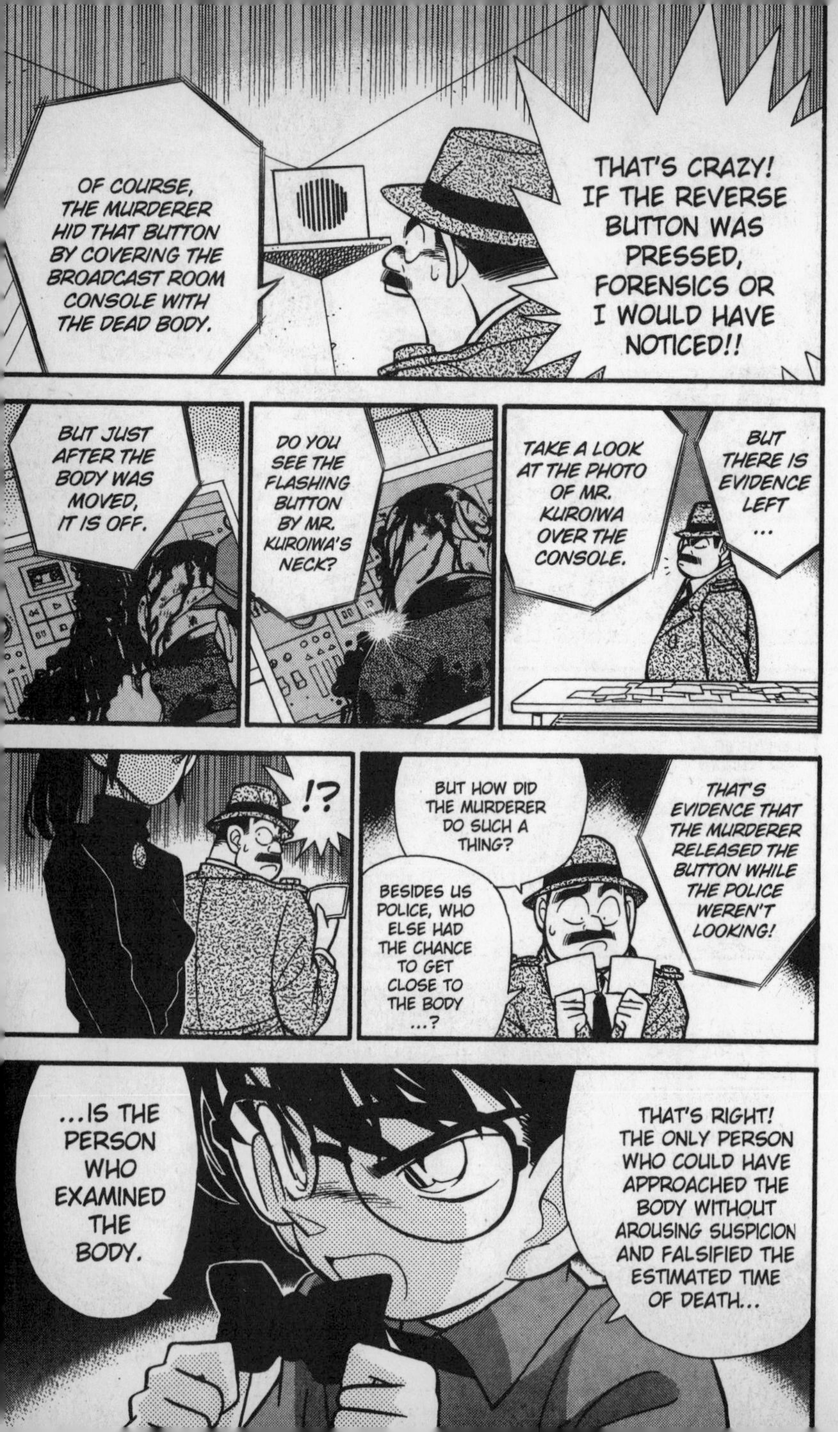
THAT'S CRAZY! IF THE REVERSE BUTTON WAS PRESSED, FORENSICS OR I WOULD HAVE NOTICED!!
OF COURSE, THE MURDERER HID THAT BUTTON BY COVERING THE BROADCAST ROOM CONSOLE WITH THE DEAD BODY.
BUT THERE IS EVIDENCE LEFT...
TAKE A LOOK AT THE PHOTO OF MR. KUROIWA OVER THE CONSOLE.
DO YOU SEE THE FLASHING BUTTON BY MR. KUROIWA'S NECK?
BUT JUST AFTER THE BODY WAS MOVED, IT IS OFF.
THAT'S EVIDENCE THAT THE MURDERER RELEASED THE BUTTON WHILE THE POLICE WEREN'T LOOKING!
BUT HOW DID THE MURDERER DO SUCH A THING?
BESIDES US POLICE, WHO ELSE HAD THE CHANCE TO GET CLOSE TO THE BODY...?
!?
THAT'S RIGHT! THE ONLY PERSON WHO COULD HAVE APPROACHED THE BODY WITHOUT AROUSING SUSPICION AND FALSIFIED THE ESTIMATED TIME OF DEATH...
...IS THE PERSON WHO EXAMINED THE BODY.

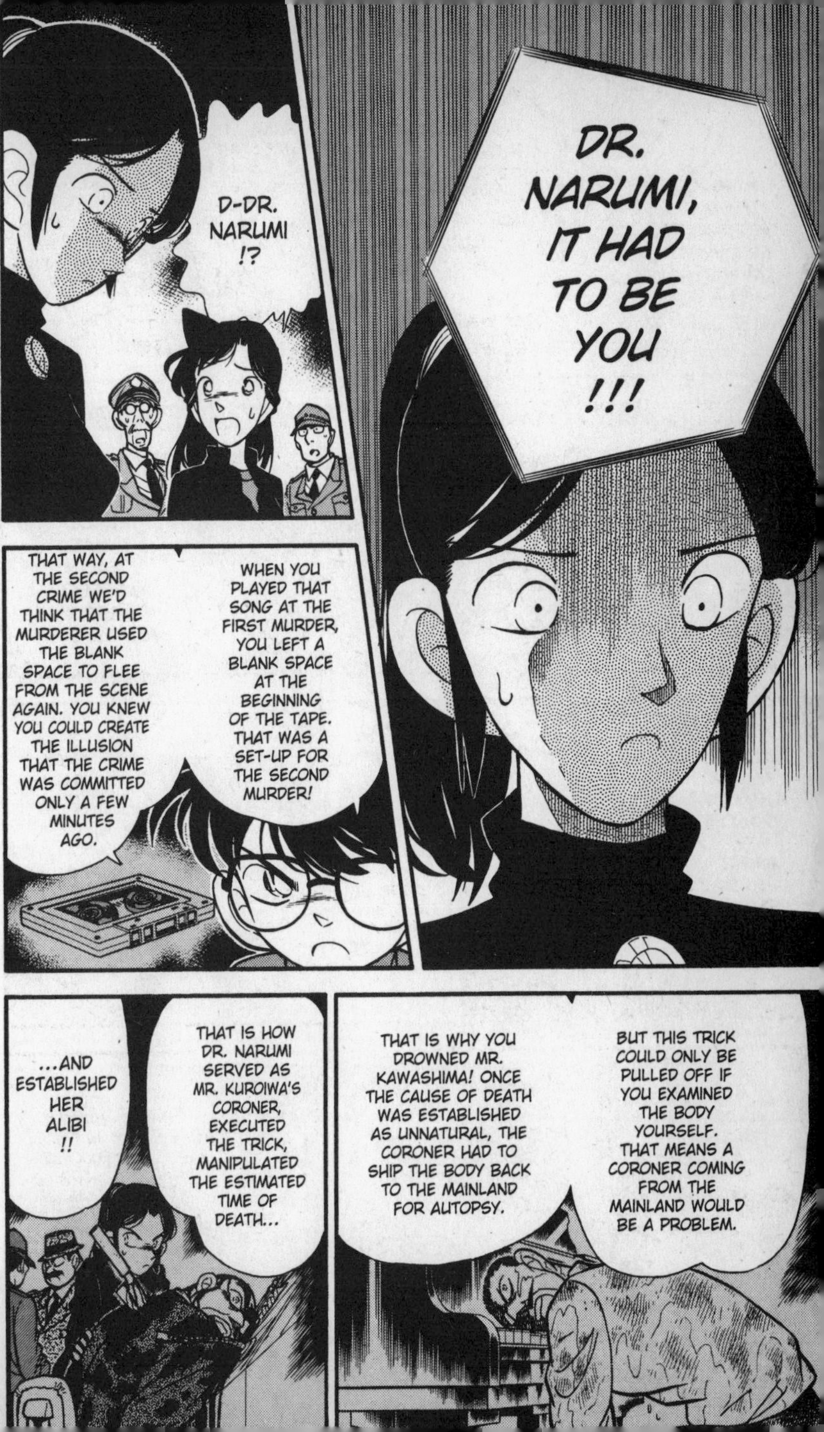
DR. NARUMI, IT HAD TO BE YOU !!!
D-DR. NARUMI !?
WHEN YOU PLAYED THAT SONG AT THE FIRST MURDER, YOU LEFT A BLANK SPACE AT THE BEGINNING OF THE TAPE. THAT WAS A SET-UP FOR THE SECOND MURDER!
THAT WAY, AT THE SECOND CRIME WE'D THINK THAT THE MURDERER USED THE BLANK SPACE TO FLEE FROM THE SCENE AGAIN. YOU KNEW YOU COULD CREATE THE ILLUSION THAT THE CRIME WAS COMMITTED ONLY A FEW MINUTES AGO.
BUT THIS TRICK COULD ONLY BE PULLED OFF IF YOU EXAMINED THE BODY YOURSELF. THAT MEANS A CORONER COMING FROM THE MAINLAND WOULD BE A PROBLEM.
THAT IS WHY YOU DROWNED MR. KAWASHIMA! ONCE THE CAUSE OF DEATH WAS ESTABLISHED AS UNNATURAL, THE CORONER HAD TO SHIP THE BODY BACK TO THE MAINLAND FOR AUTOPSY.
THAT IS HOW DR. NARUMI SERVED AS MR. KUROIWA'S CORONER, EXECUTED THE TRICK, MANIPULATED THE ESTIMATED TIME OF DEATH...
...AND ESTABLISHED HER ALIBI !!

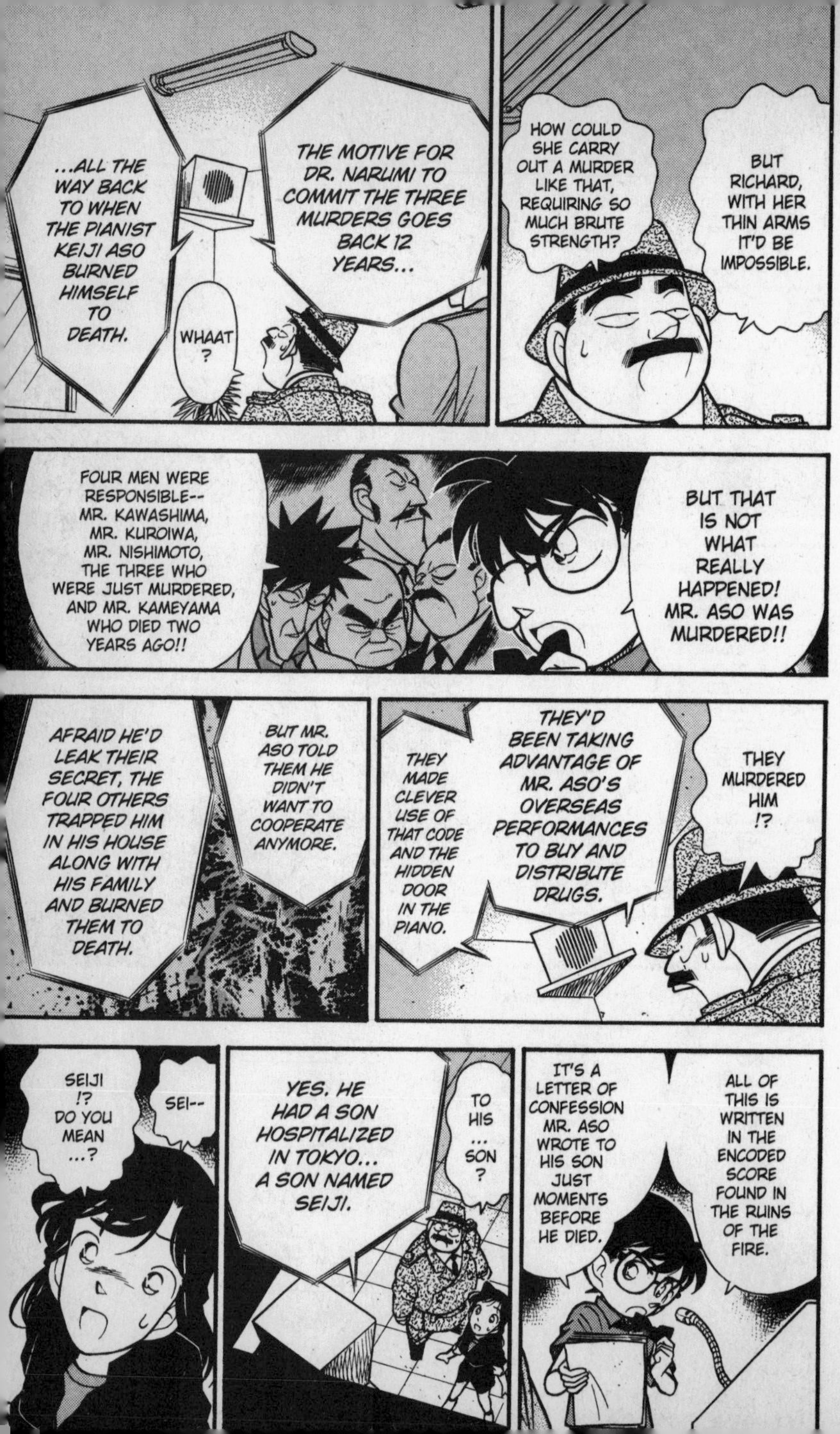
BUT RICHARD, WITH HER THIN ARMS IT'D BE IMPOSSIBLE.
HOW COULD SHE CARRY OUT A MURDER LIKE THAT, REQUIRING SO MUCH BRUTE STRENGTH?
THE MOTIVE FOR DR. NARUMI TO COMMIT THE THREE MURDERS GOES BACK 12 YEARS...
...ALL THE WAY BACK TO WHEN THE PIANIST KEIJI ASO BURNED HIMSELF TO DEATH.
WHAAT?
BUT THAT IS NOT WHAT REALLY HAPPENED! MR. ASO WAS MURDERED!!
FOUR MEN WERE RESPONSIBLE-- MR. KAWASHIMA, MR. KUROIWA, MR. NISHIMOTO, THE THREE WHO WERE JUST MURDERED, AND MR. KAMEYAMA WHO DIED TWO YEARS AGO!!
THEY MURDERED HIM !?
THEY'D BEEN TAKING ADVANTAGE OF MR. ASO'S OVERSEAS PERFORMANCES TO BUY AND DISTRIBUTE DRUGS.
THEY MADE CLEVER USE OF THAT CODE AND THE HIDDEN DOOR IN THE PIANO.
BUT MR. ASO TOLD THEM HE DIDN'T WANT TO COOPERATE ANYMORE.
AFRAID HE'D LEAK THEIR SECRET, THE FOUR OTHERS TRAPPED HIM IN HIS HOUSE ALONG WITH HIS FAMILY AND BURNED THEM TO DEATH.
ALL OF THIS IS WRITTEN IN THE ENCODED SCORE FOUND IN THE RUINS OF THE FIRE.
IT'S A LETTER OF CONFESSION MR. ASO WROTE TO HIS SON JUST MOMENTS BEFORE HE DIED.
TO HIS ... SON?
YES. HE HAD A SON HOSPITALIZED IN TOKYO... A SON NAMED SEIJI.
SEI--
SEIJI !? DO YOU MEAN ...?

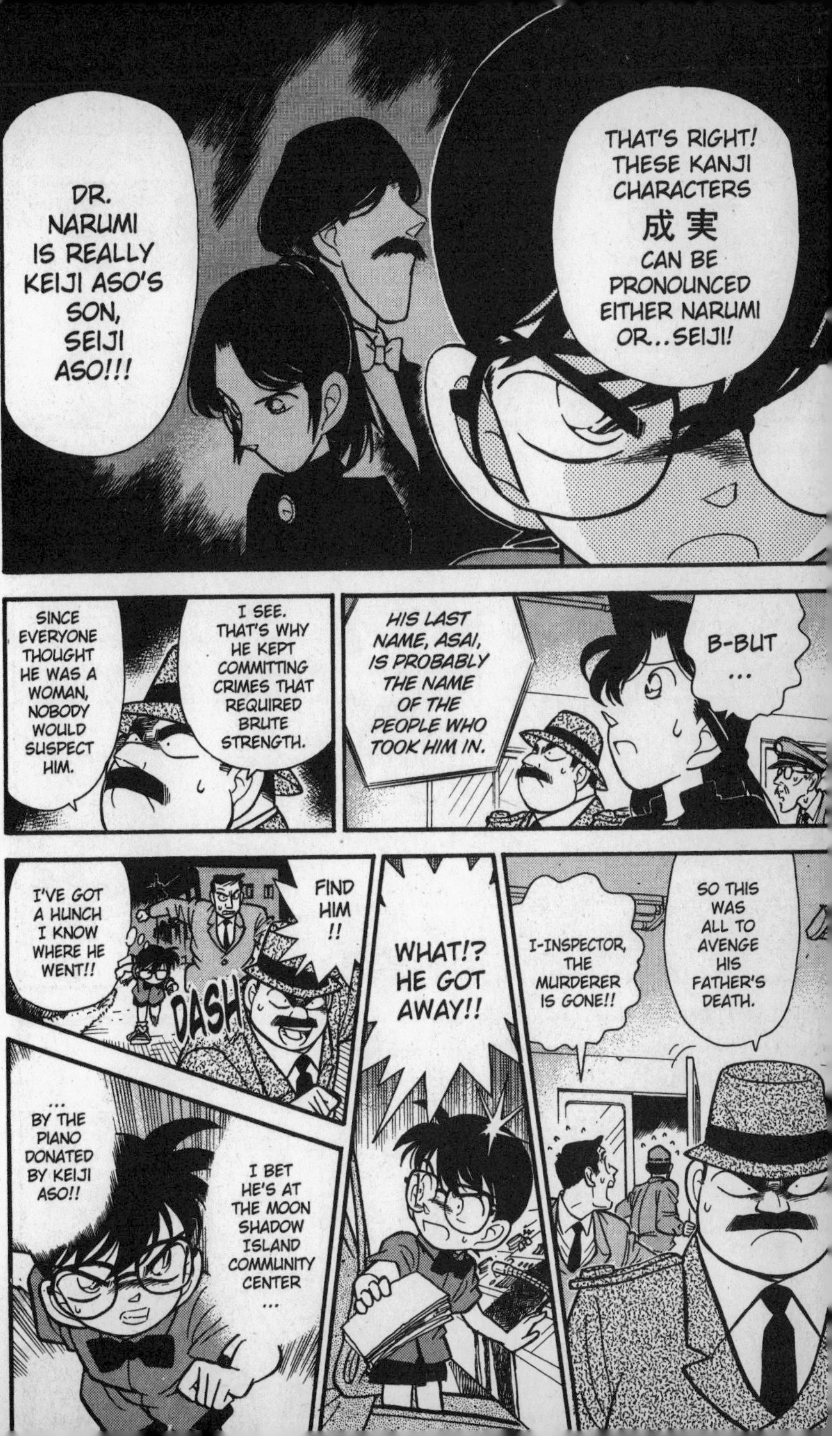
THAT'S RIGHT! THESE KANJI CHARACTERS 成実 CAN BE PRONOUNCED EITHER NARUMI OR...SEIJI!
DR. NARUMI IS REALLY KEIJI ASO'S SON, SEIJI ASO!!!
B-BUT ...
HIS LAST NAME, ASAI, IS PROBABLY THE NAME OF THE PEOPLE WHO TOOK HIM IN.
I SEE. THAT'S WHY HE KEPT COMMITTING CRIMES THAT REQUIRED BRUTE STRENGTH.
SINCE EVERYONE THOUGHT HE WAS A WOMAN, NOBODY WOULD SUSPECT HIM.
SO THIS WAS ALL TO AVENGE HIS FATHER'S DEATH.
I-INSPECTOR, THE MURDERER IS GONE!!
WHAT!? HE GOT AWAY!!
FIND HIM !!
I'VE GOT A HUNCH I KNOW WHERE HE WENT!!
DASH
I BET HE'S AT THE MOON SHADOW ISLAND COMMUNITY CENTER ...
... BY THE PIANO DONATED BY KEIJI ASO!!

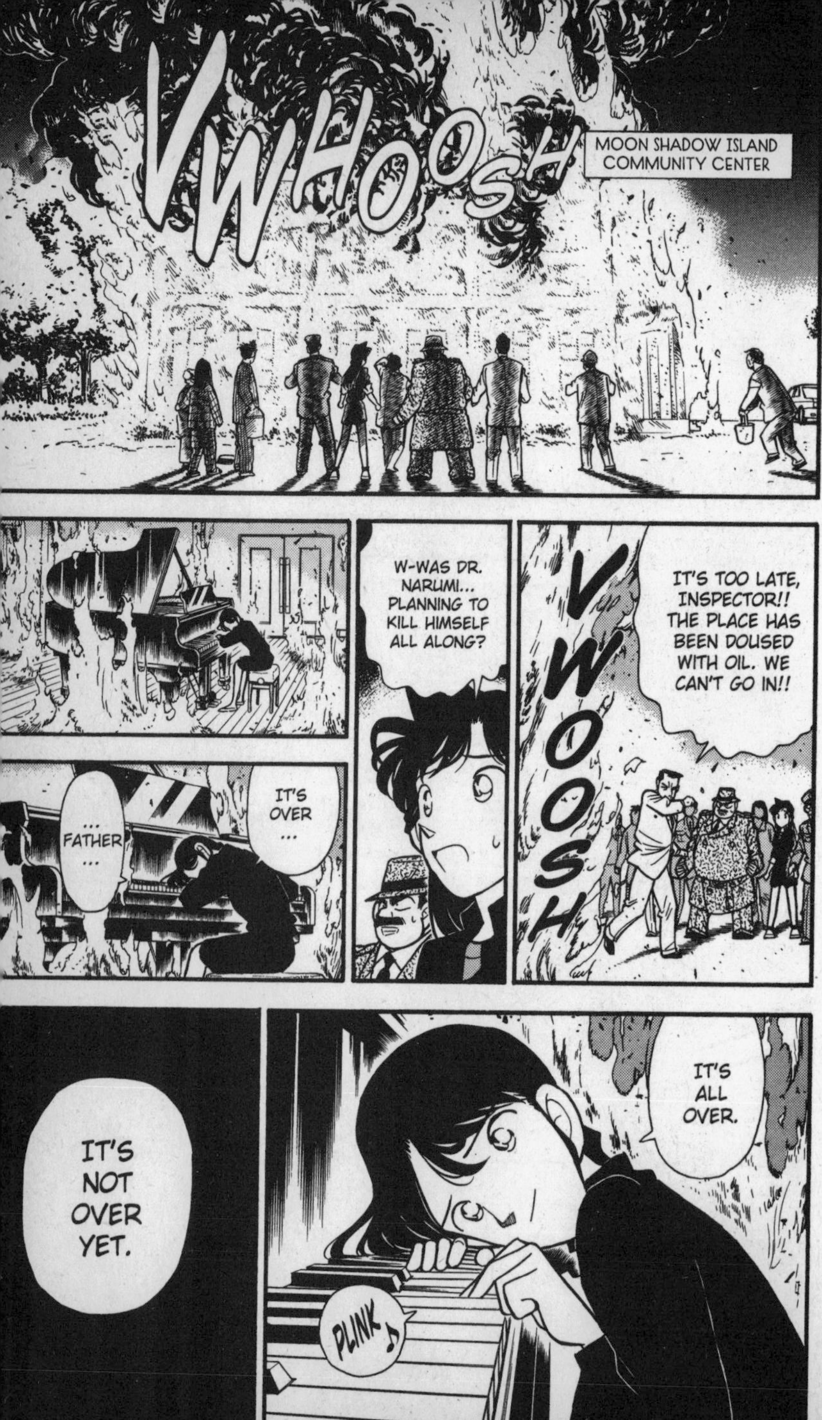
MOON SHADOW ISLAND COMMUNITY CENTER
VWHOOSH
IT'S TOO LATE, INSPECTOR!! THE PLACE HAS BEEN DOUSED WITH OIL. WE CAN'T GO IN!!
VWHOOSH
W-WAS DR. NARUMI... PLANNING TO KILL HIMSELF ALL ALONG?
IT'S OVER ...
... FATHER ...
IT'S ALL OVER.
PLINK
IT'S NOT OVER YET.

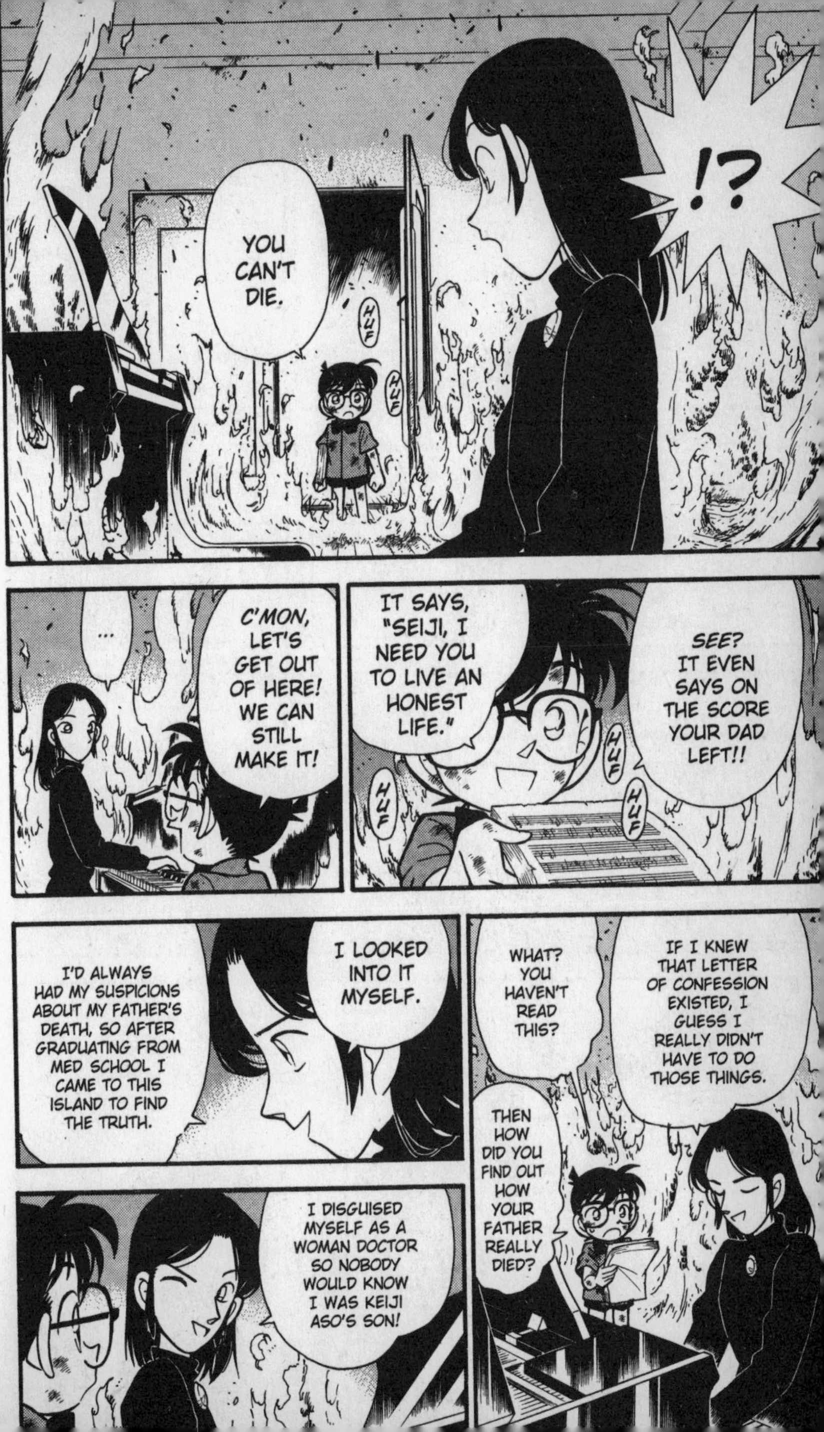
!?
YOU CAN'T DIE.
HUF
HUF
SEE? IT EVEN SAYS ON THE SCORE YOUR DAD LEFT!!
HUF
HUF
IT SAYS, "SEIJI, I NEED YOU TO LIVE AN HONEST LIFE."
HUF
C'MON, LET'S GET OUT OF HERE! WE CAN STILL MAKE IT!
...
IF I KNEW THAT LETTER OF CONFESSION EXISTED, I GUESS I REALLY DIDN'T HAVE TO DO THOSE THINGS.
WHAT? YOU HAVEN'T READ THIS?
THEN HOW DID YOU FIND OUT HOW YOUR FATHER REALLY DIED?
I LOOKED INTO IT MYSELF.
I'D ALWAYS HAD MY SUSPICIONS ABOUT MY FATHER'S DEATH, SO AFTER GRADUATING FROM MED SCHOOL I CAME TO THIS ISLAND TO FIND THE TRUTH.
I DISGUISED MYSELF AS A WOMAN DOCTOR SO NOBODY WOULD KNOW I WAS KEIJI ASO'S SON!

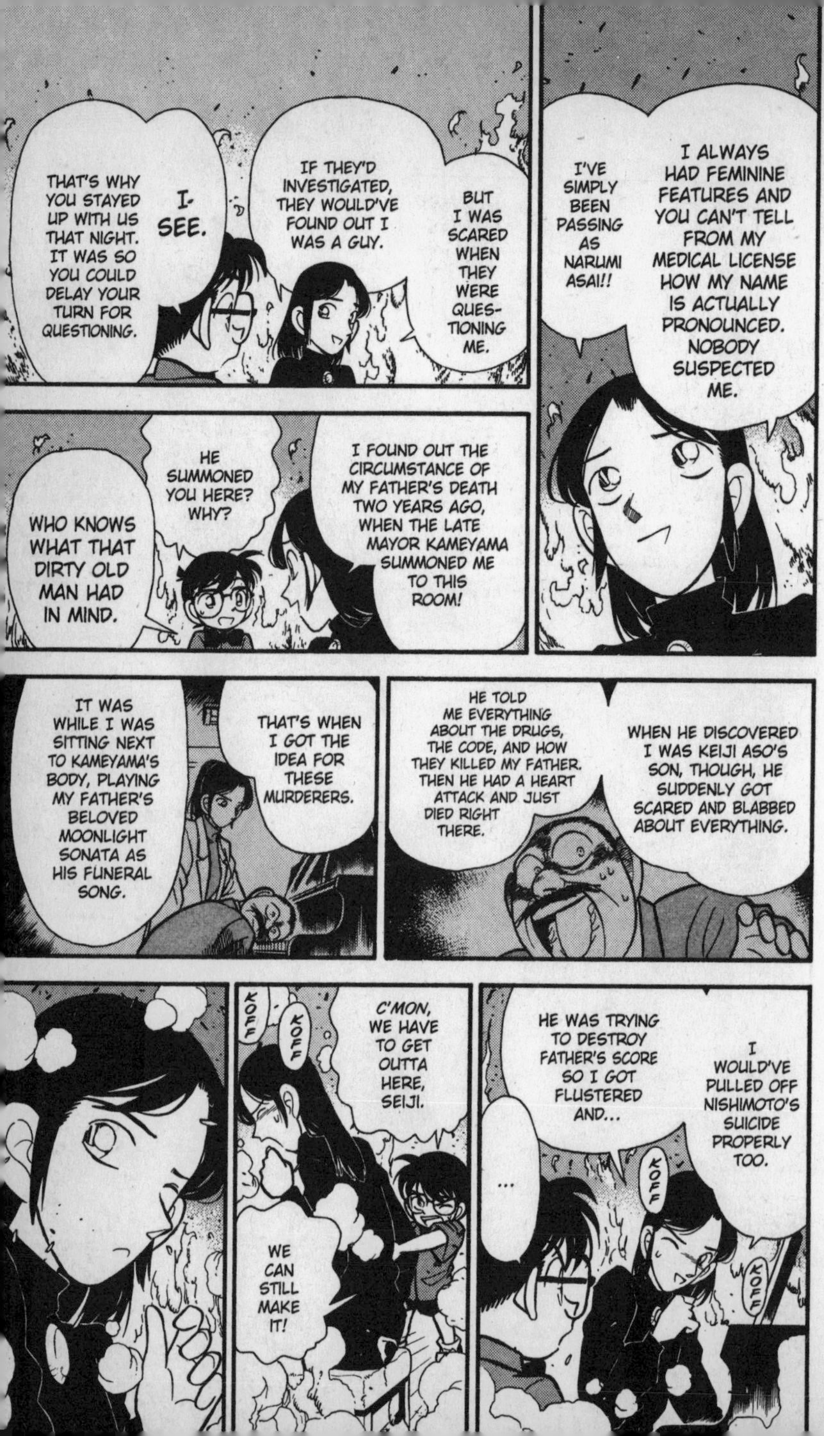
I ALWAYS HAD FEMININE FEATURES AND YOU CAN'T TELL FROM MY MEDICAL LICENSE HOW MY NAME IS ACTUALLY PRONOUNCED. NOBODY SUSPECTED ME.
I'VE SIMPLY BEEN PASSING AS NARUMI ASAI!!
BUT I WAS SCARED WHEN THEY WERE QUESTIONING ME.
IF THEY'D INVESTIGATED, THEY WOULD'VE FOUND OUT I WAS A GUY.
I- SEE.
THAT'S WHY YOU STAYED UP WITH US THAT NIGHT. IT WAS SO YOU COULD DELAY YOUR TURN FOR QUESTIONING.
I FOUND OUT THE CIRCUMSTANCE OF MY FATHER'S DEATH TWO YEARS AGO, WHEN THE LATE MAYOR KAMEYAMA SUMMONED ME TO THIS ROOM!
HE SUMMONED YOU HERE? WHY?
WHO KNOWS WHAT THAT DIRTY OLD MAN HAD IN MIND.
WHEN HE DISCOVERED I WAS KEIJI ASO'S SON, THOUGH, HE SUDDENLY GOT SCARED AND BLABBED ABOUT EVERYTHING.
HE TOLD ME EVERYTHING ABOUT THE DRUGS, THE CODE, AND HOW THEY KILLED MY FATHER. THEN HE HAD A HEART ATTACK AND JUST DIED RIGHT THERE.
THAT'S WHEN I GOT THE IDEA FOR THESE MURDERERS.
IT WAS WHILE I WAS SITTING NEXT TO KAMEYAMA'S BODY, PLAYING MY FATHER'S BELOVED MOONLIGHT SONATA AS HIS FUNERAL SONG.
I WOULD'VE PULLED OFF NISHIMOTO'S SUICIDE PROPERLY TOO.
HE WAS TRYING TO DESTROY FATHER'S SCORE SO I GOT FLUSTERED AND...
KOFF
KOFF
...
KOFF
KOFF
C'MON, WE HAVE TO GET OUTTA HERE, SEIJI.
WE CAN STILL MAKE IT!

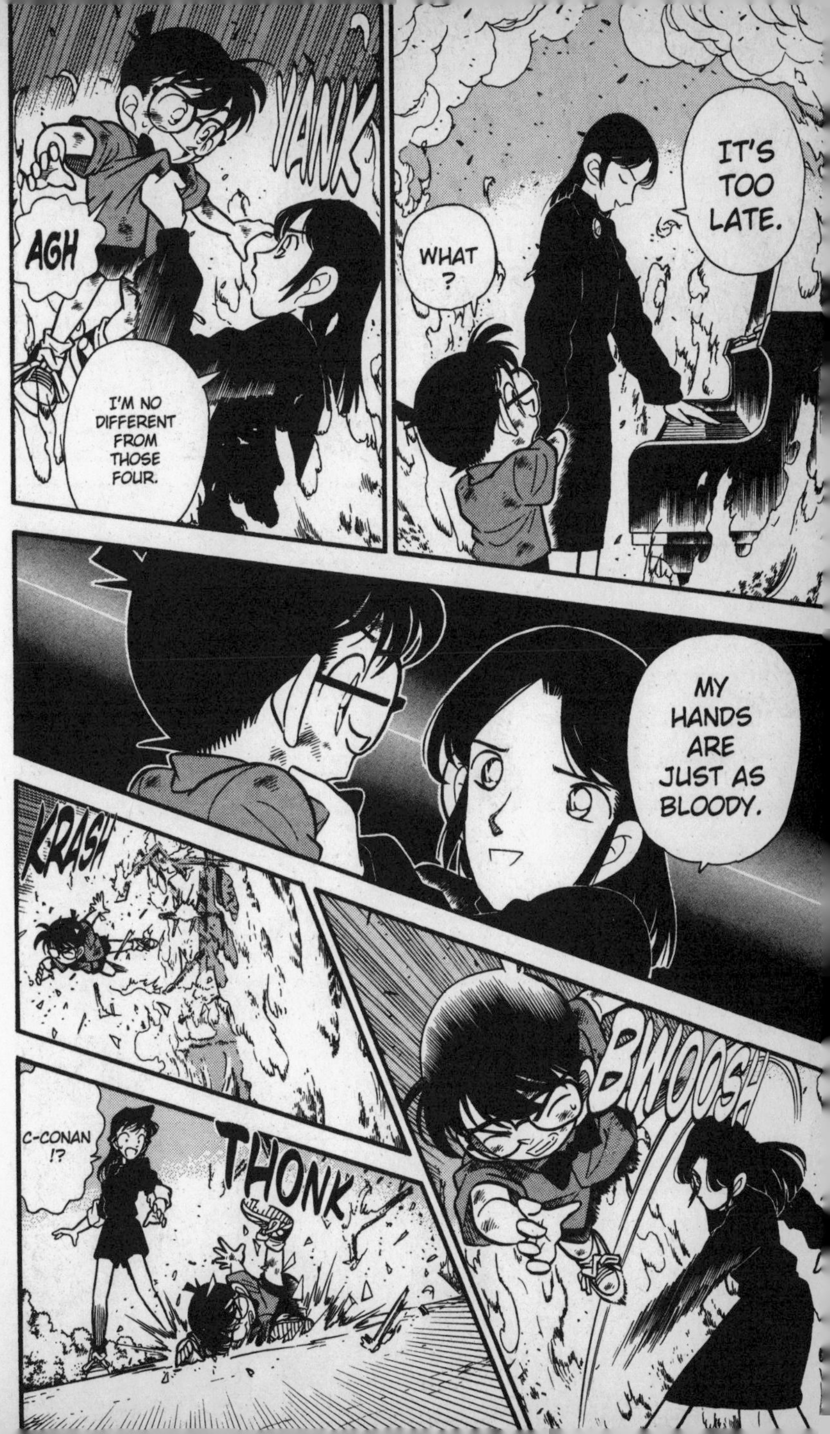
IT'S TOO LATE.
WHAT ?
YANK
AGH
I'M NO DIFFERENT FROM THOSE FOUR.
MY HANDS ARE JUST AS BLOODY.
BWOOSH
KRASH
THONK
C-CONAN !?

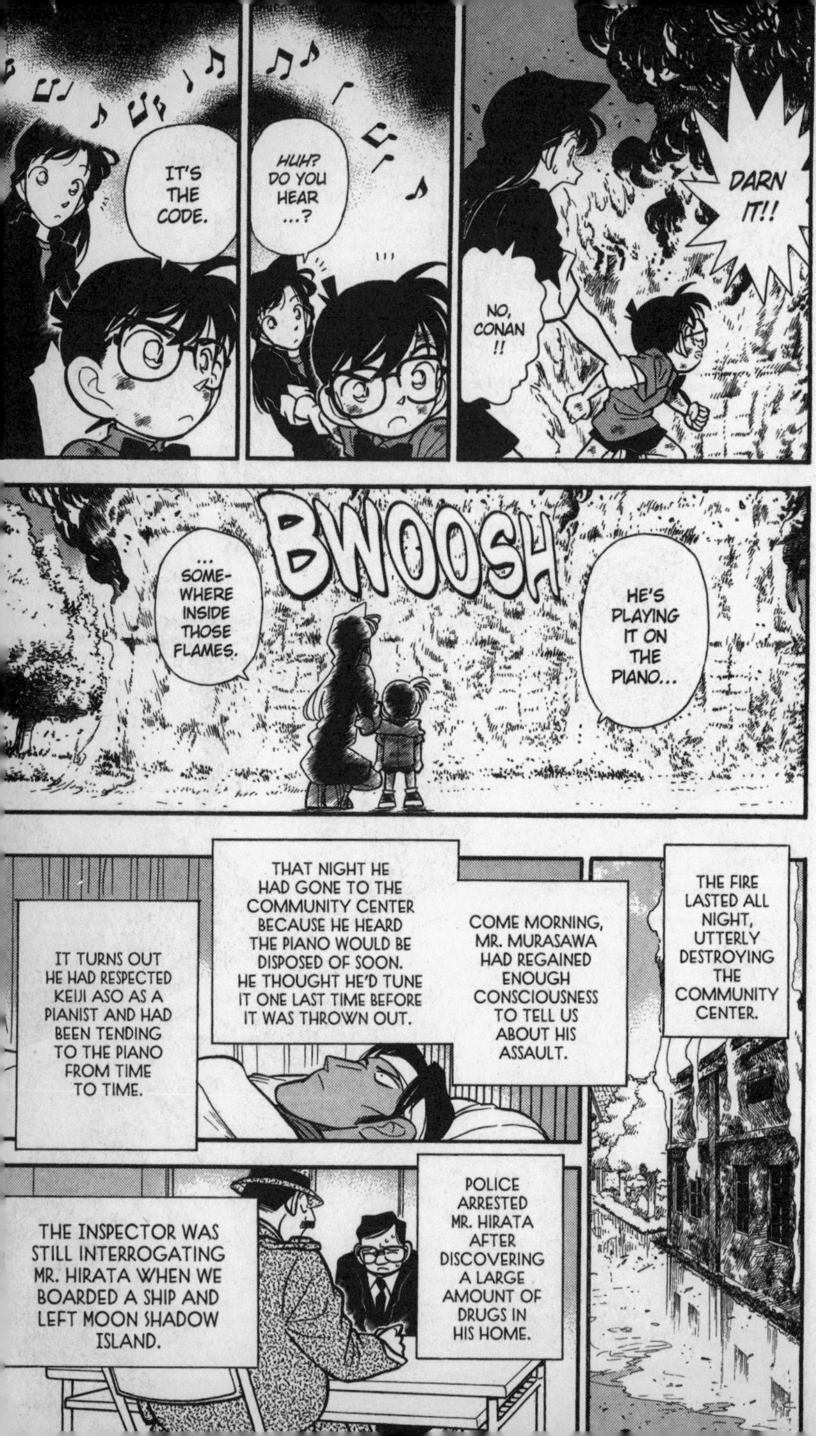
DARN IT!!
NO, CONAN !!
HUH? DO YOU HEAR ...?
IT'S THE CODE.
BWOOSH
HE'S PLAYING IT ON THE PIANO...
... SOME-WHERE INSIDE THOSE FLAMES.
THE FIRE LASTED ALL NIGHT, UTTERLY DESTROYING THE COMMUNITY CENTER.
COME MORNING, MR. MURASAWA HAD REGAINED ENOUGH CONSCIOUSNESS TO TELL US ABOUT HIS ASSAULT.
THAT NIGHT HE HAD GONE TO THE COMMUNITY CENTER BECAUSE HE HEARD THE PIANO WOULD BE DISPOSED OF SOON. HE THOUGHT HE'D TUNE IT ONE LAST TIME BEFORE IT WAS THROWN OUT.
IT TURNS OUT HE HAD RESPECTED KEIJI ASO AS A PIANIST AND HAD BEEN TENDING TO THE PIANO FROM TIME TO TIME.
POLICE ARRESTED MR. HIRATA AFTER DISCOVERING A LARGE AMOUNT OF DRUGS IN HIS HOME.
THE INSPECTOR WAS STILL INTERROGATING MR. HIRATA WHEN WE BOARDED A SHIP AND LEFT MOON SHADOW ISLAND.

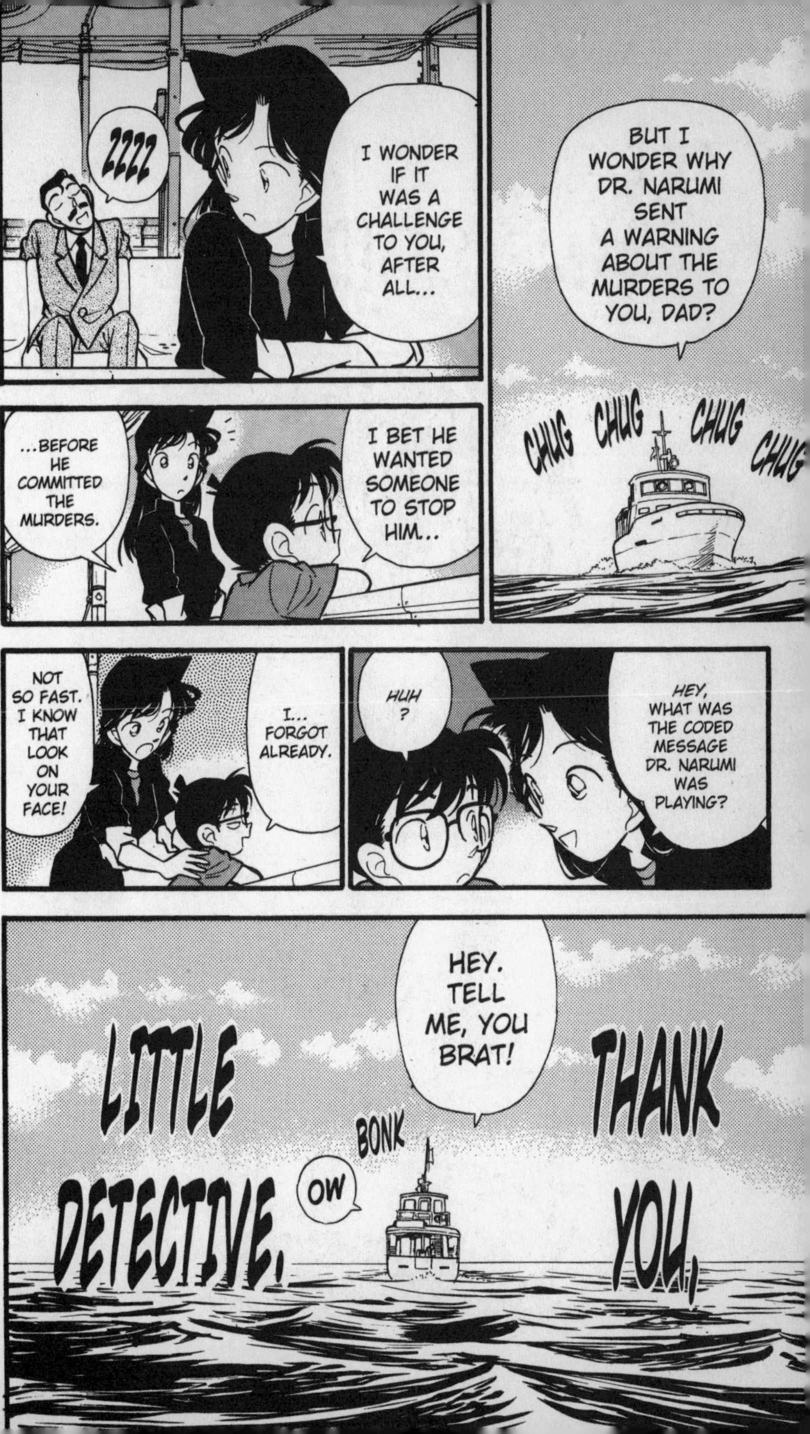
BUT I WONDER WHY DR. NARUMI SENT A WARNING ABOUT THE MURDERS TO YOU, DAD?
CHUG CHUG CHUG CHUG
I WONDER IF IT WAS A CHALLENGE TO YOU, AFTER ALL...
ZZZZ
I BET HE WANTED SOMEONE TO STOP HIM...
...BEFORE HE COMMITTED THE MURDERS.
HEY, WHAT WAS THE CODED MESSAGE DR. NARUMI WAS PLAYING?
HUH?
I... FORGOT ALREADY.
NOT SO FAST. I KNOW THAT LOOK ON YOUR FACE!
THANK YOU,
HEY. TELL ME, YOU BRAT!
BONK
OW
LITTLE DETECTIVE.

FILE 8: JIMMY'S GIRLFRIEND!!

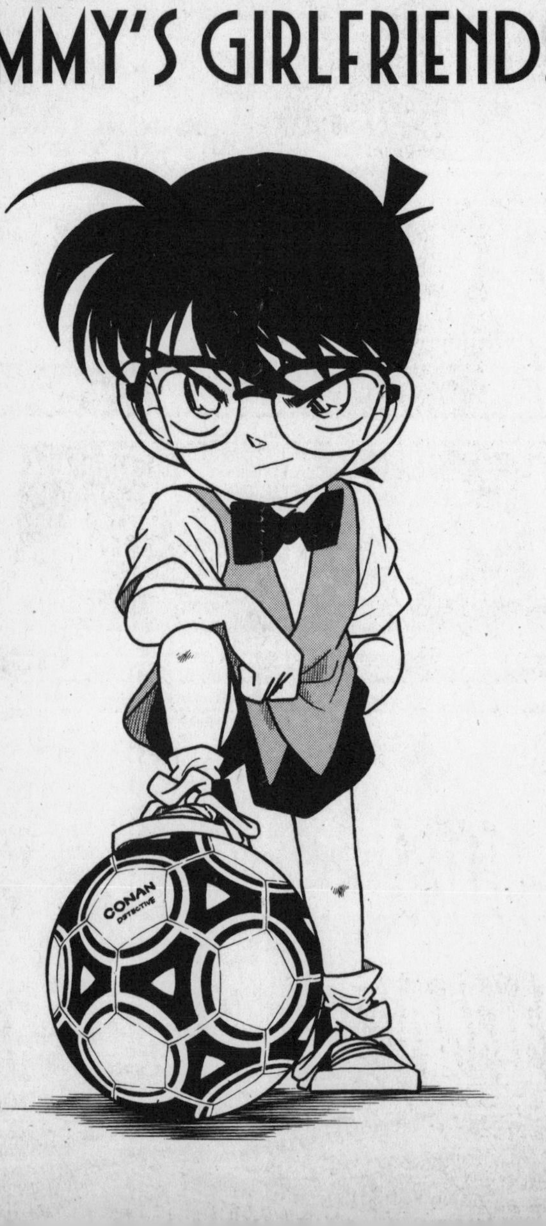
CONAN
DETECTIVE

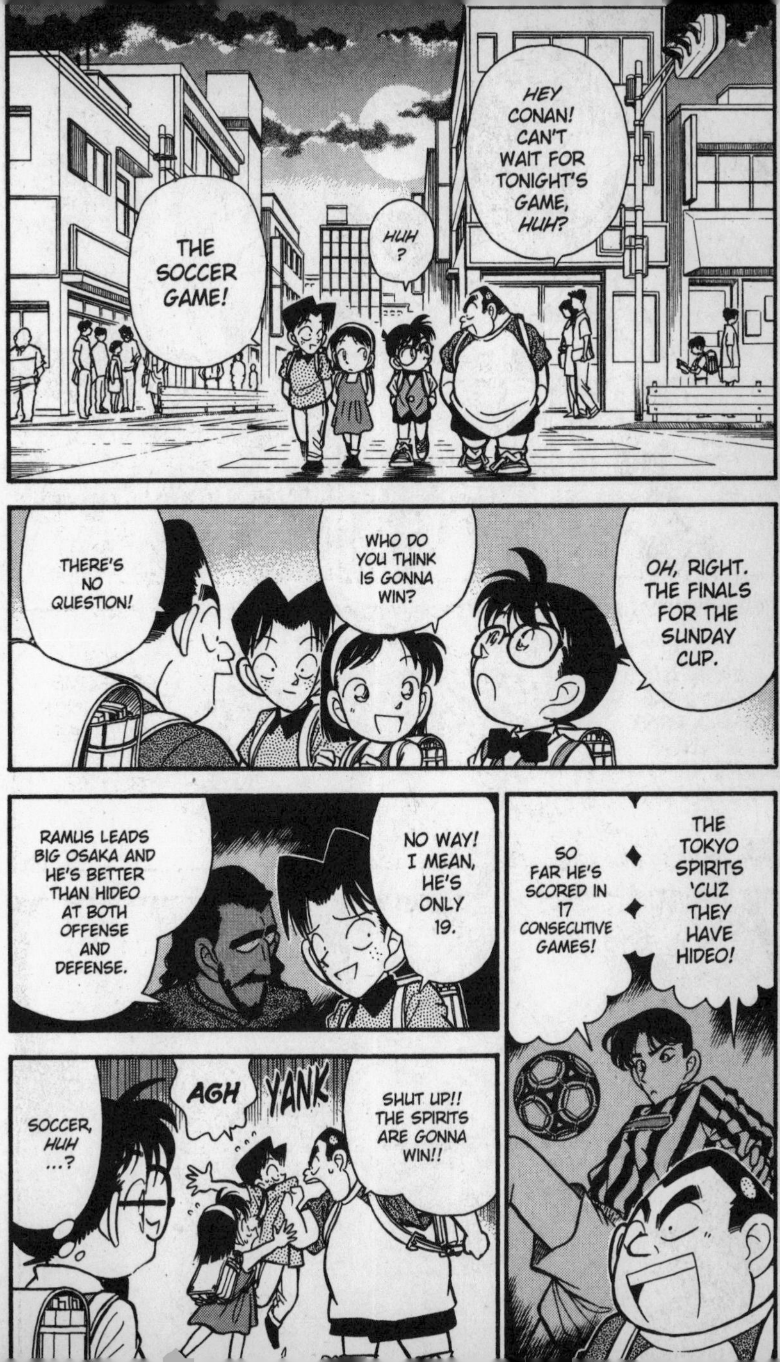
HEY CONAN! CAN'T WAIT FOR TONIGHT'S GAME, HUH?
HUH ?
THE SOCCER GAME!
OH, RIGHT. THE FINALS FOR THE SUNDAY CUP.
WHO DO YOU THINK IS GONNA WIN?
THERE'S NO QUESTION!
THE TOKYO SPIRITS 'CUZ THEY HAVE HIDEO!
SO FAR HE'S SCORED IN 17 CONSECUTIVE GAMES!
NO WAY! I MEAN, HE'S ONLY 19.
RAMUS LEADS BIG OSAKA AND HE'S BETTER THAN HIDEO AT BOTH OFFENSE AND DEFENSE.
SHUT UP!! THE SPIRITS ARE GONNA WIN!!
YANK
AGH
SOCCER, HUH ...?

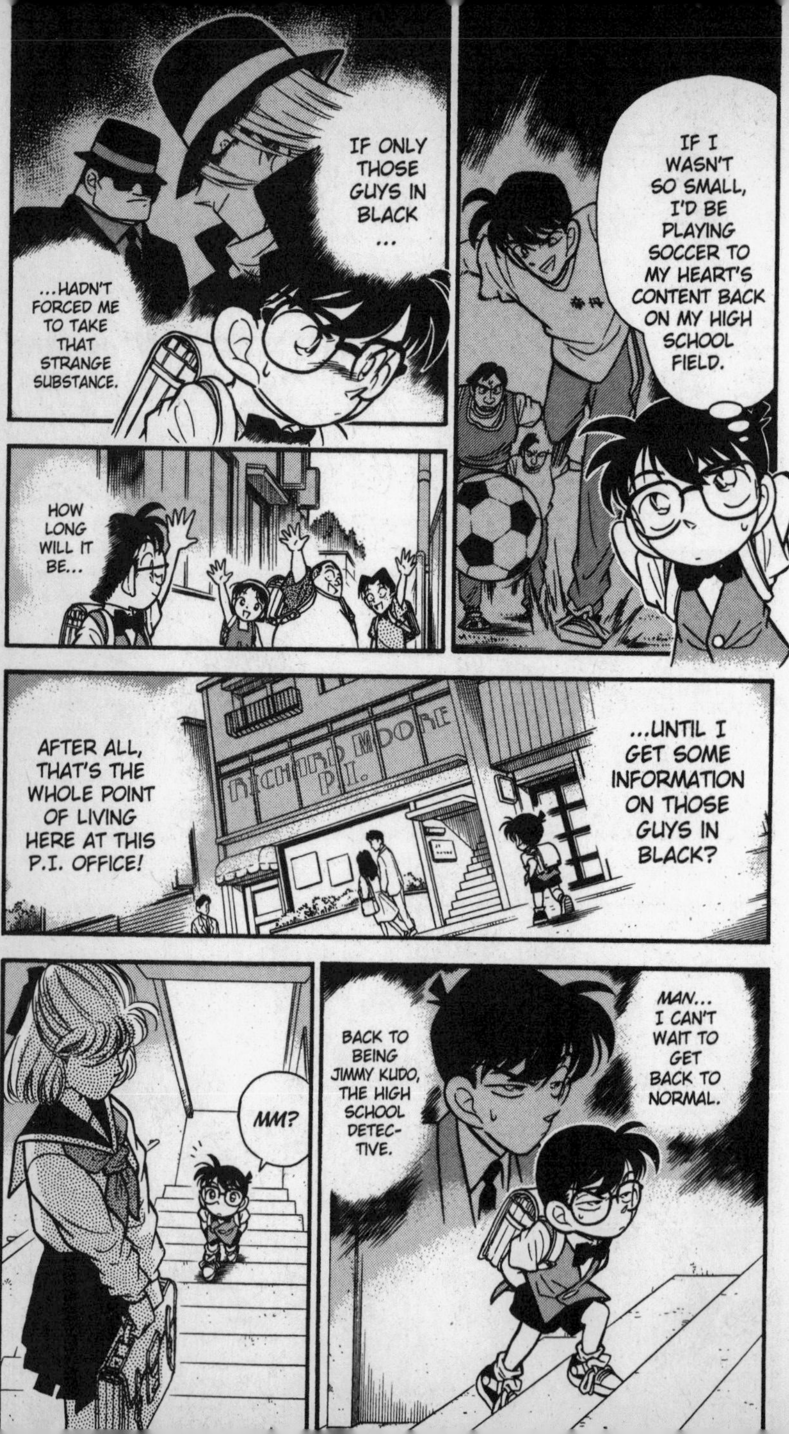

IF I WASN'T SO SMALL, I'D BE PLAYING SOCCER TO MY HEART'S CONTENT BACK ON MY HIGH SCHOOL FIELD.
IF ONLY THOSE GUYS IN BLACK ...
...HADN'T FORCED ME TO TAKE THAT STRANGE SUBSTANCE.
HOW LONG WILL IT BE...
...UNTIL I GET SOME INFORMATION ON THOSE GUYS IN BLACK?
RICHARD MOORE P.I.
AFTER ALL, THAT'S THE WHOLE POINT OF LIVING HERE AT THIS P.I. OFFICE!
MAN... I CAN'T WAIT TO GET BACK TO NORMAL.
BACK TO BEING JIMMY KUDO, THE HIGH SCHOOL DETECTIVE.
MM?

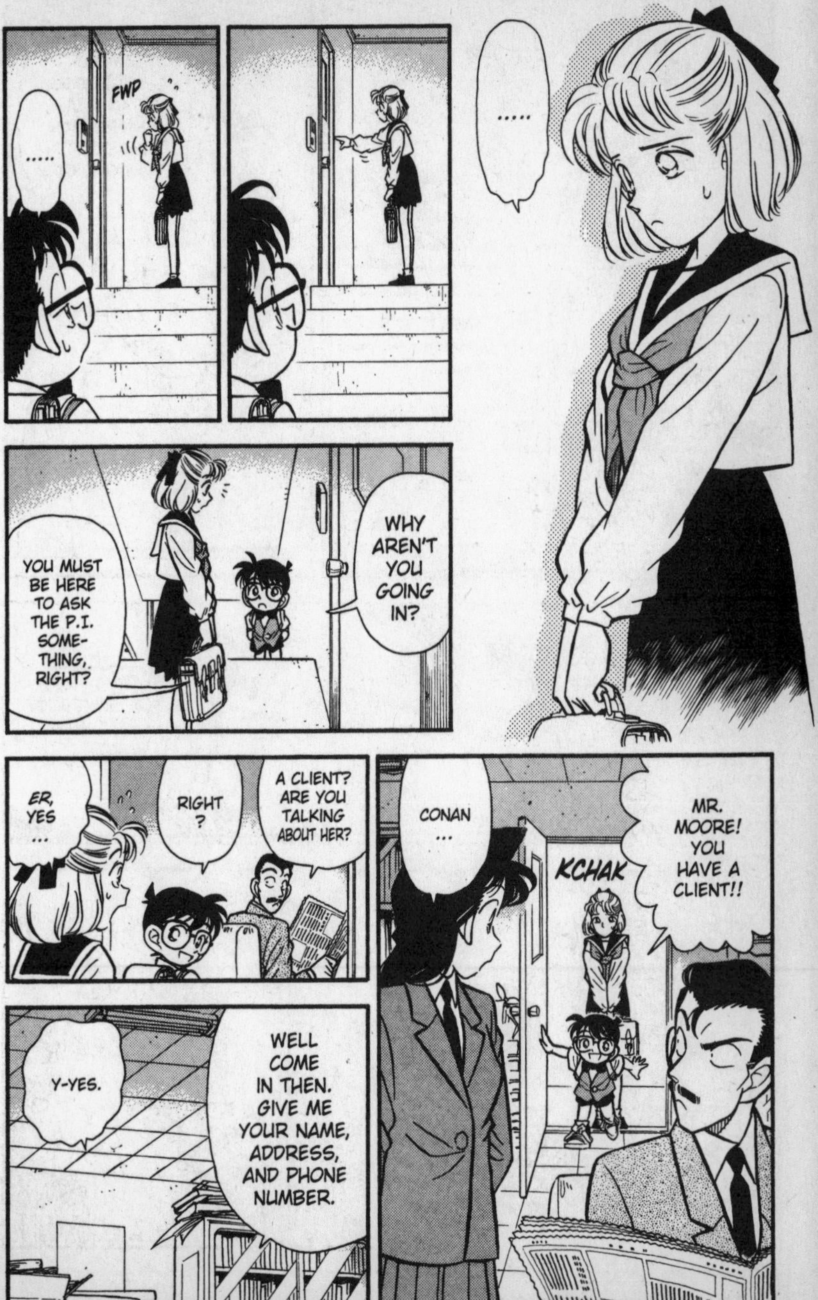
......
FWP
......
WHY AREN'T YOU GOING IN?
YOU MUST BE HERE TO ASK THE P.I. SOMETHING, RIGHT?
MR. MOORE! YOU HAVE A CLIENT!!
KCHAK
CONAN ...
A CLIENT? ARE YOU TALKING ABOUT HER?
RIGHT ?
ER, YES ...
WELL COME IN THEN. GIVE ME YOUR NAME, ADDRESS, AND PHONE NUMBER.
Y-YES.

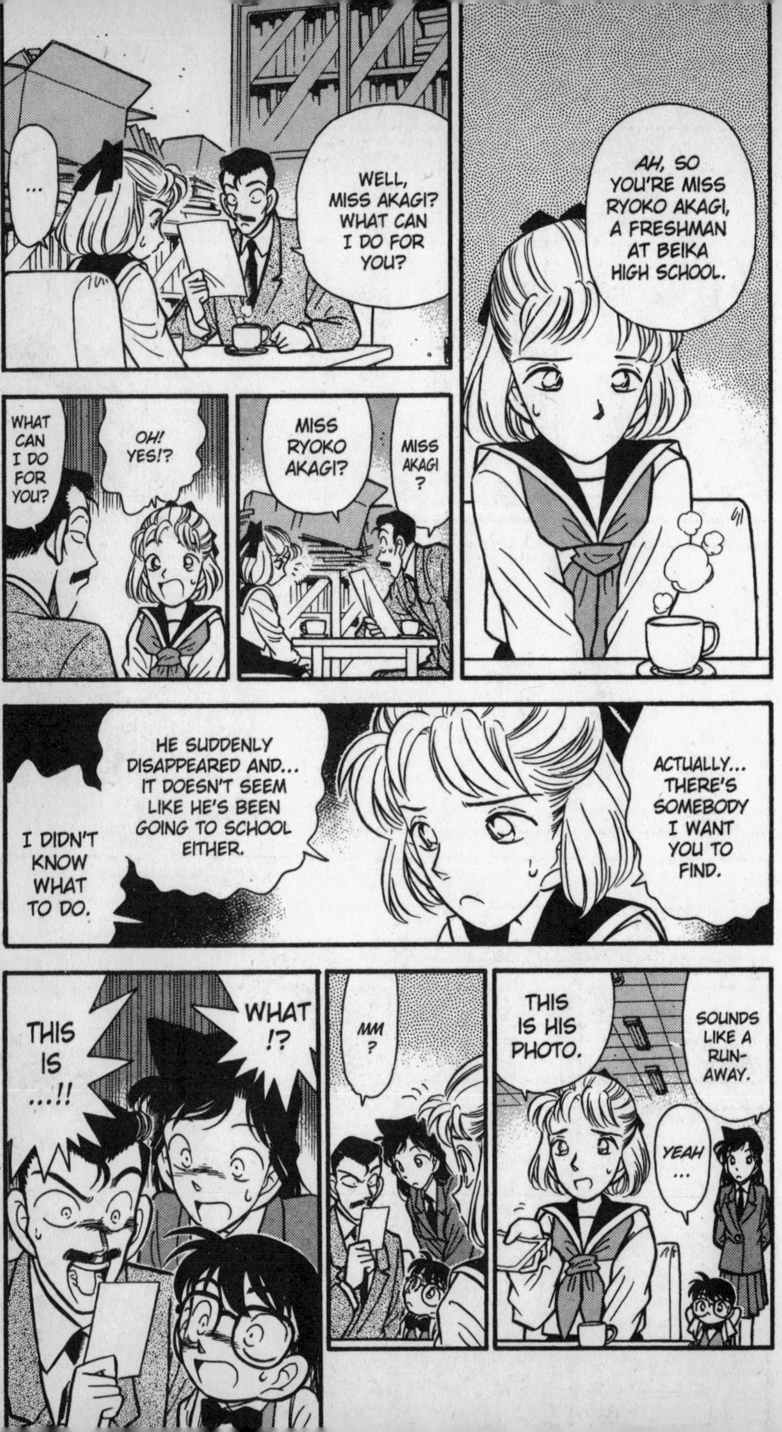
AH, SO YOU'RE MISS RYOKO AKAGI, A FRESHMAN AT BEIKA HIGH SCHOOL.
WELL, MISS AKAGI? WHAT CAN I DO FOR YOU?
...
MISS AKAGI ?
MISS RYOKO AKAGI?
OH! YES!?
WHAT CAN I DO FOR YOU?
ACTUALLY... THERE'S SOMEBODY I WANT YOU TO FIND.
HE SUDDENLY DISAPPEARED AND... IT DOESN'T SEEM LIKE HE'S BEEN GOING TO SCHOOL EITHER.
I DIDN'T KNOW WHAT TO DO.
SOUNDS LIKE A RUN-AWAY.
THIS IS HIS PHOTO.
YEAH ...
MM ?
WHAT !?
THIS IS ...!!

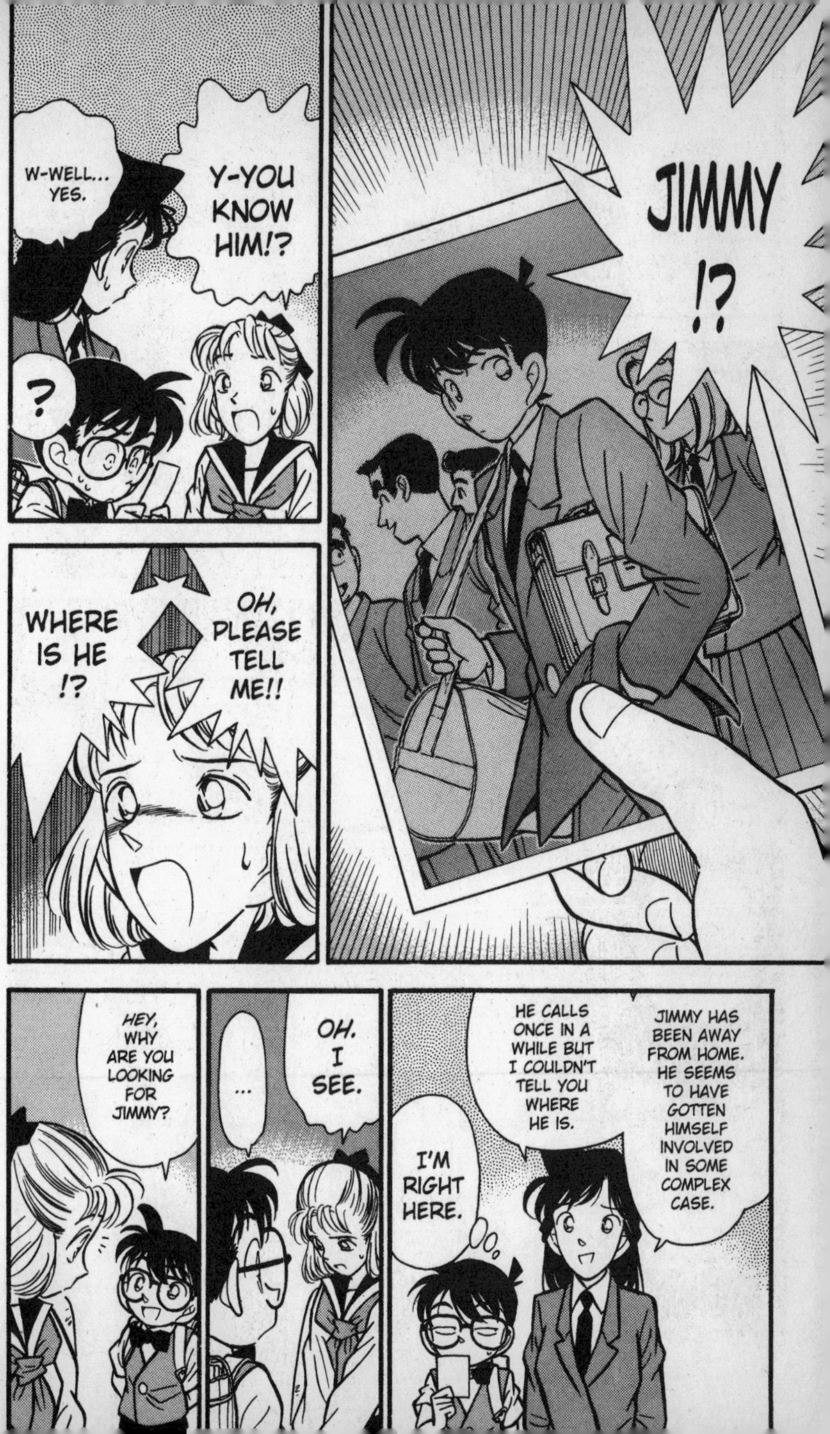
JIMMY !?
Y-YOU KNOW HIM!?
W-WELL... YES.
?
OH, PLEASE TELL ME!!
WHERE IS HE !?
JIMMY HAS BEEN AWAY FROM HOME. HE SEEMS TO HAVE GOTTEN HIMSELF INVOLVED IN SOME COMPLEX CASE.
HE CALLS ONCE IN A WHILE BUT I COULDN'T TELL YOU WHERE HE IS.
I'M RIGHT HERE.
OH. I SEE.
...
HEY, WHY ARE YOU LOOKING FOR JIMMY?

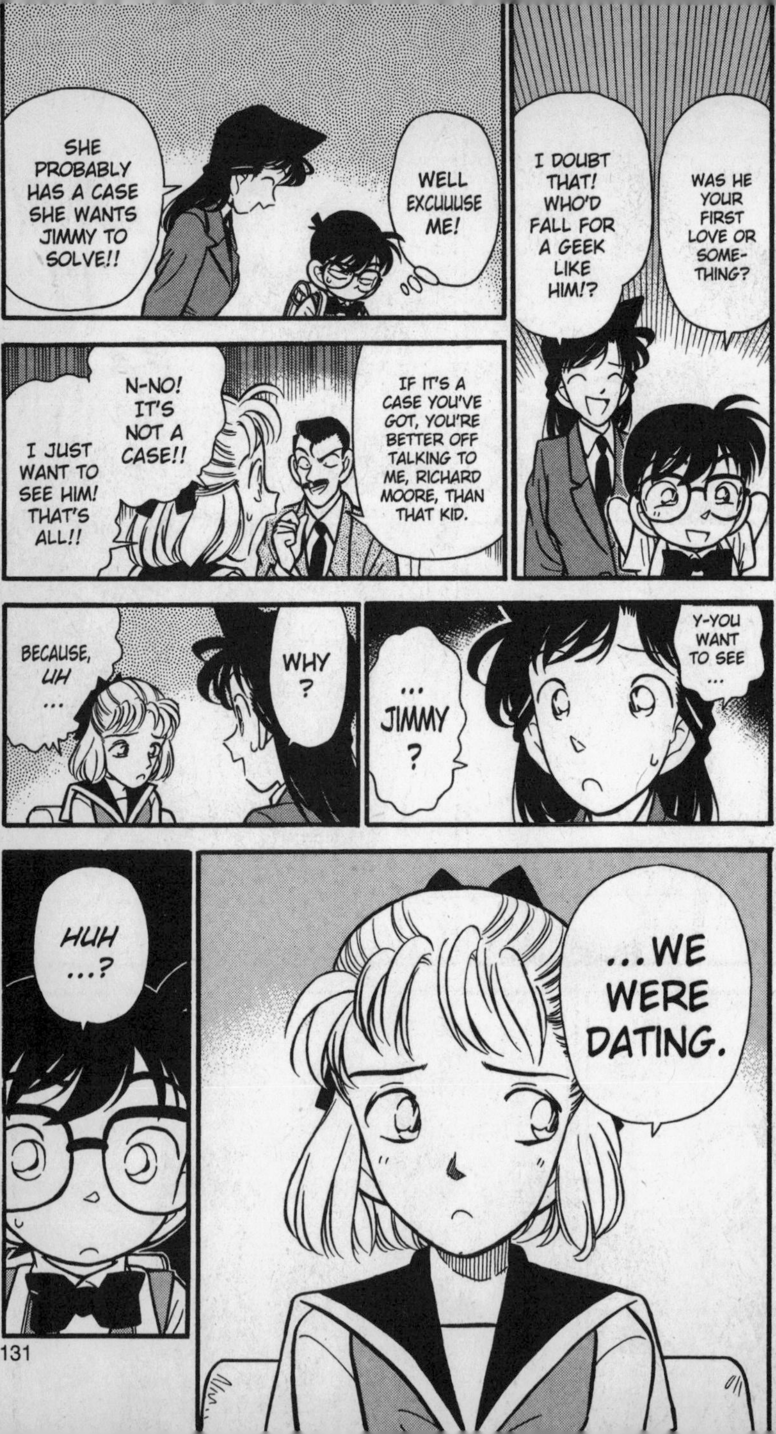
WAS HE YOUR FIRST LOVE OR SOME-THING?
I DOUBT THAT! WHO'D FALL FOR A GEEK LIKE HIM!?
WELL EXCUUUSE ME!
SHE PROBABLY HAS A CASE SHE WANTS JIMMY TO SOLVE!!
IF IT'S A CASE YOU'VE GOT, YOU'RE BETTER OFF TALKING TO ME, RICHARD MOORE, THAN THAT KID.
N-NO! IT'S NOT A CASE!!
I JUST WANT TO SEE HIM! THAT'S ALL!!
Y-YOU WANT TO SEE ...
... JIMMY ?
WHY ?
BECAUSE, *UH* ...
...WE WERE DATING.
HUH ...?

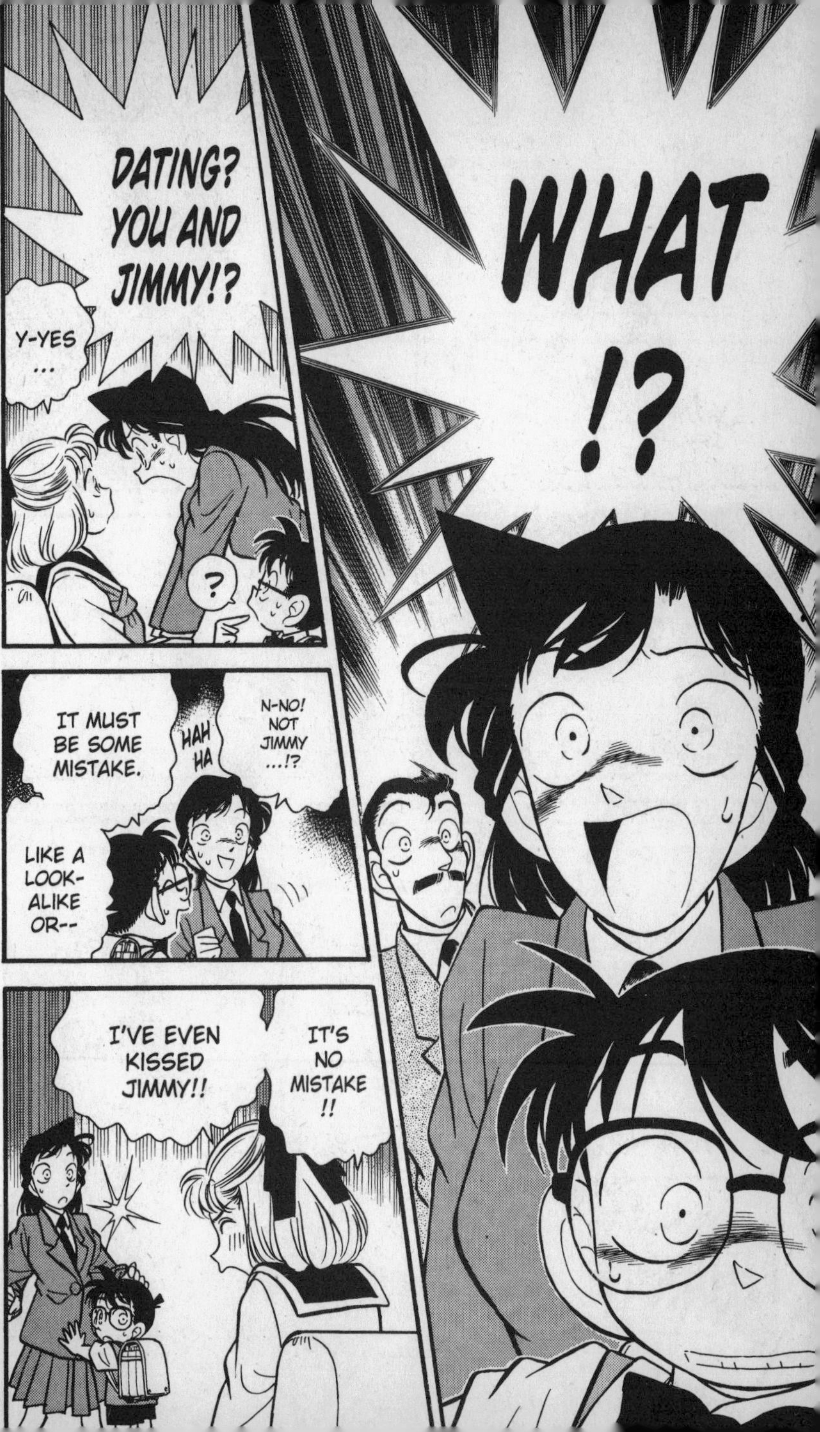
WHAT !?
DATING? YOU AND JIMMY!?
Y-YES ...
?
N-NO! NOT JIMMY ...!?
HAH HA
IT MUST BE SOME MISTAKE.
LIKE A LOOK-ALIKE OR--
IT'S NO MISTAKE !!
I'VE EVEN KISSED JIMMY!!

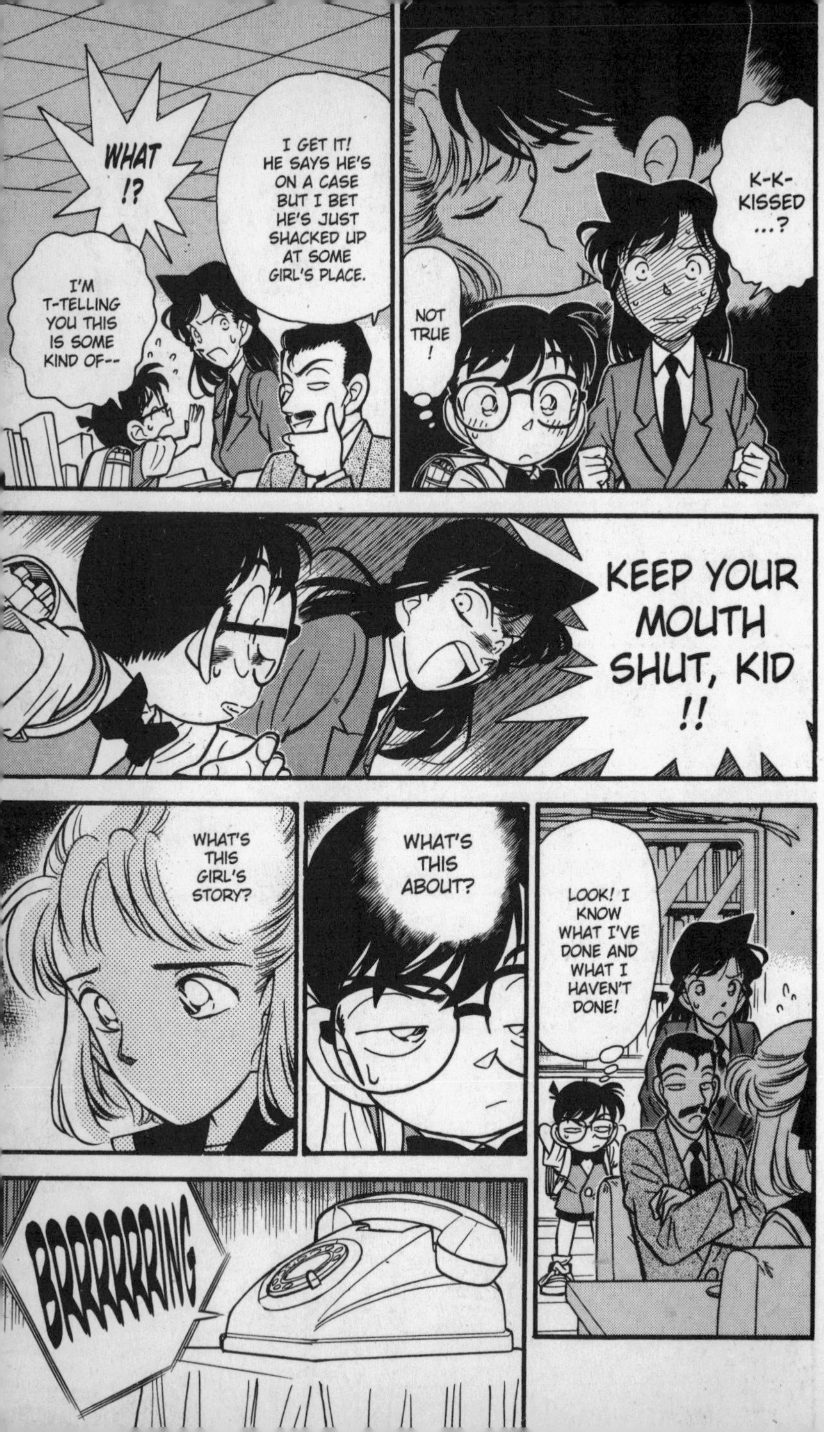
K-K-KISSED ...?
NOT TRUE !
I GET IT! HE SAYS HE'S ON A CASE BUT I BET HE'S JUST SHACKED UP AT SOME GIRL'S PLACE.
WHAT !?
I'M T-TELLING YOU THIS IS SOME KIND OF--
KEEP YOUR MOUTH SHUT, KID !!
LOOK! I KNOW WHAT I'VE DONE AND WHAT I HAVEN'T DONE!
WHAT'S THIS ABOUT?
WHAT'S THIS GIRL'S STORY?
BRRRRRING

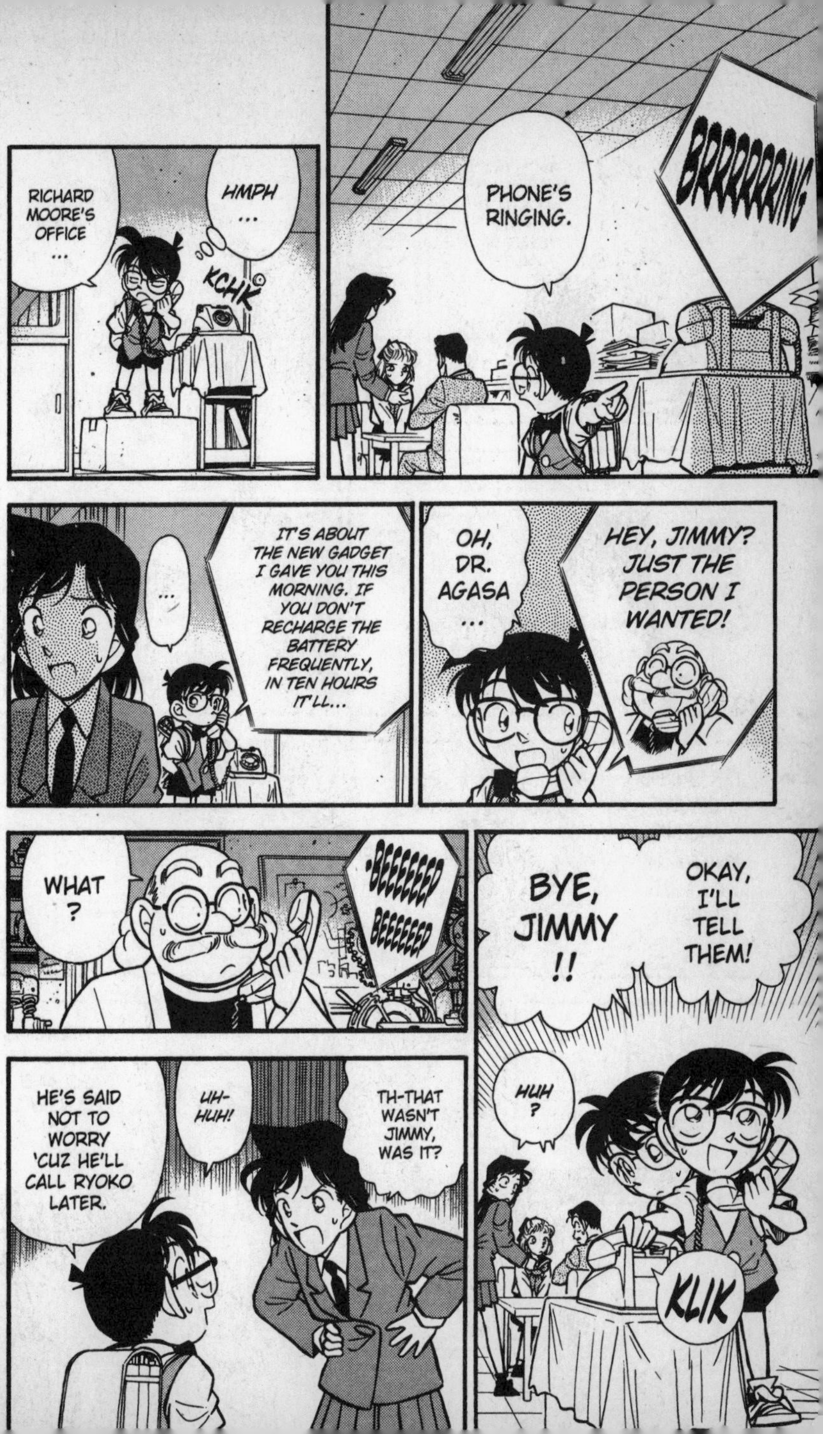
BRRRRRING
PHONE'S RINGING.
HMPH ...
RICHARD MOORE'S OFFICE ...
KCHK
HEY, JIMMY? JUST THE PERSON I WANTED!
OH, DR. AGASA ...
IT'S ABOUT THE NEW GADGET I GAVE YOU THIS MORNING. IF YOU DON'T RECHARGE THE BATTERY FREQUENTLY, IN TEN HOURS IT'LL...
...
OKAY, I'LL TELL THEM!
BYE, JIMMY !!
HUH ?
KLIK
BEEEEEEP BEEEEEEP
WHAT ?
TH-THAT WASN'T JIMMY, WAS IT?
UH-HUH!
HE'S SAID NOT TO WORRY 'CUZ HE'LL CALL RYOKO LATER.

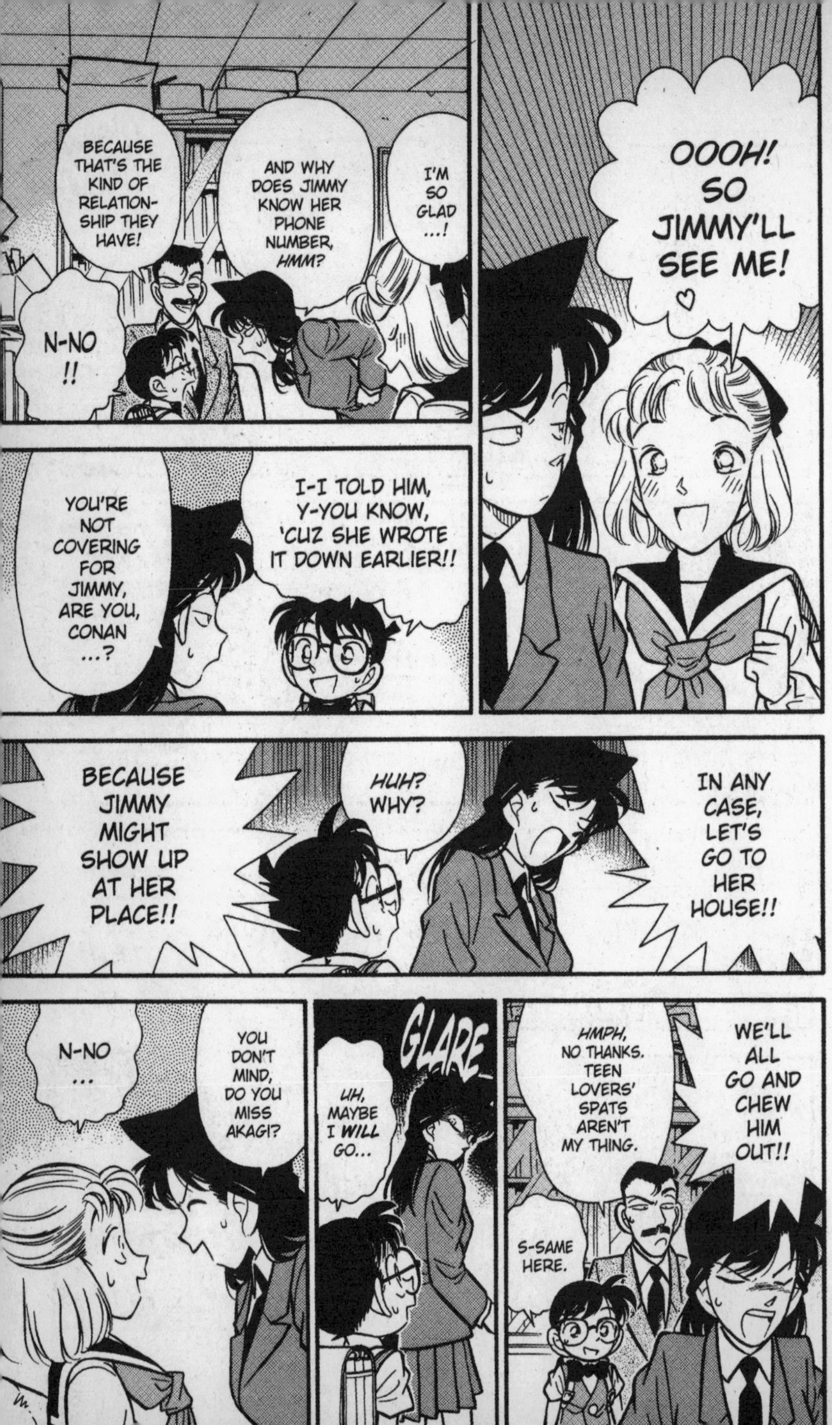
OOOH! SO JIMMY'LL SEE ME!
I'M SO GLAD ...!
AND WHY DOES JIMMY KNOW HER PHONE NUMBER, *HMM?*
BECAUSE THAT'S THE KIND OF RELATION-SHIP THEY HAVE!
N-NO !!
I-I TOLD HIM, Y-YOU KNOW, 'CUZ SHE WROTE IT DOWN EARLIER!!
YOU'RE NOT COVERING FOR JIMMY, ARE YOU, CONAN ...?
IN ANY CASE, LET'S GO TO HER HOUSE!!
HUH? WHY?
BECAUSE JIMMY MIGHT SHOW UP AT HER PLACE!!
WE'LL ALL GO AND CHEW HIM OUT!!
HMPH, NO THANKS. TEEN LOVERS' SPATS AREN'T MY THING.
S-SAME HERE.
GLARE
UH, MAYBE I *WILL* GO...
YOU DON'T MIND, DO YOU MISS AKAGI?
N-NO ...

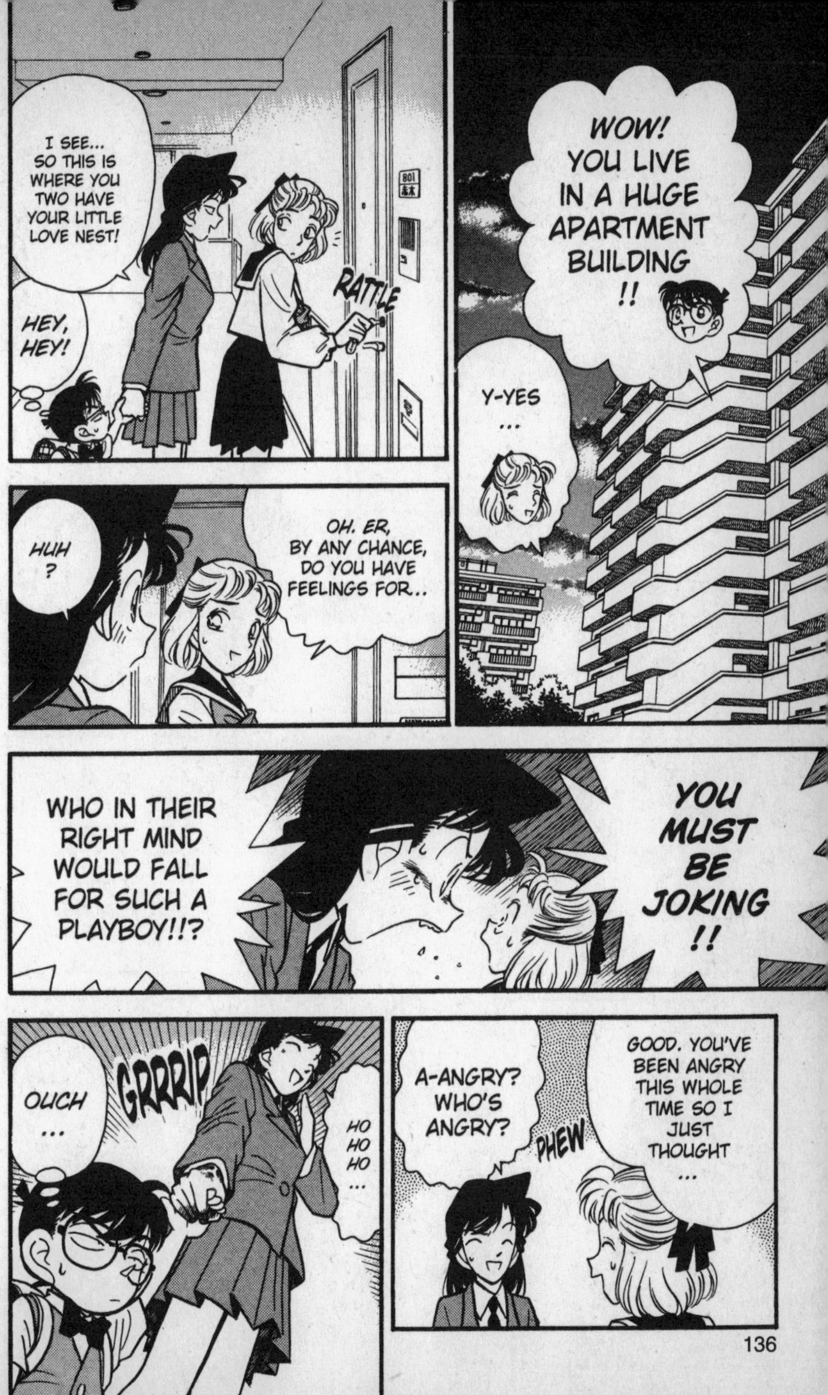
WOW! YOU LIVE IN A HUGE APARTMENT BUILDING !!
Y-YES ...
I SEE... SO THIS IS WHERE YOU TWO HAVE YOUR LITTLE LOVE NEST!
RATTLE
HEY, HEY!
OH. ER, BY ANY CHANCE, DO YOU HAVE FEELINGS FOR..
HUH ?
YOU MUST BE JOKING !!
WHO IN THEIR RIGHT MIND WOULD FALL FOR SUCH A PLAYBOY!!?
GOOD. YOU'VE BEEN ANGRY THIS WHOLE TIME SO I JUST THOUGHT ...
A-ANGRY? WHO'S ANGRY?
PHEW
HO HO HO ...
GRRRIP
OUCH ...

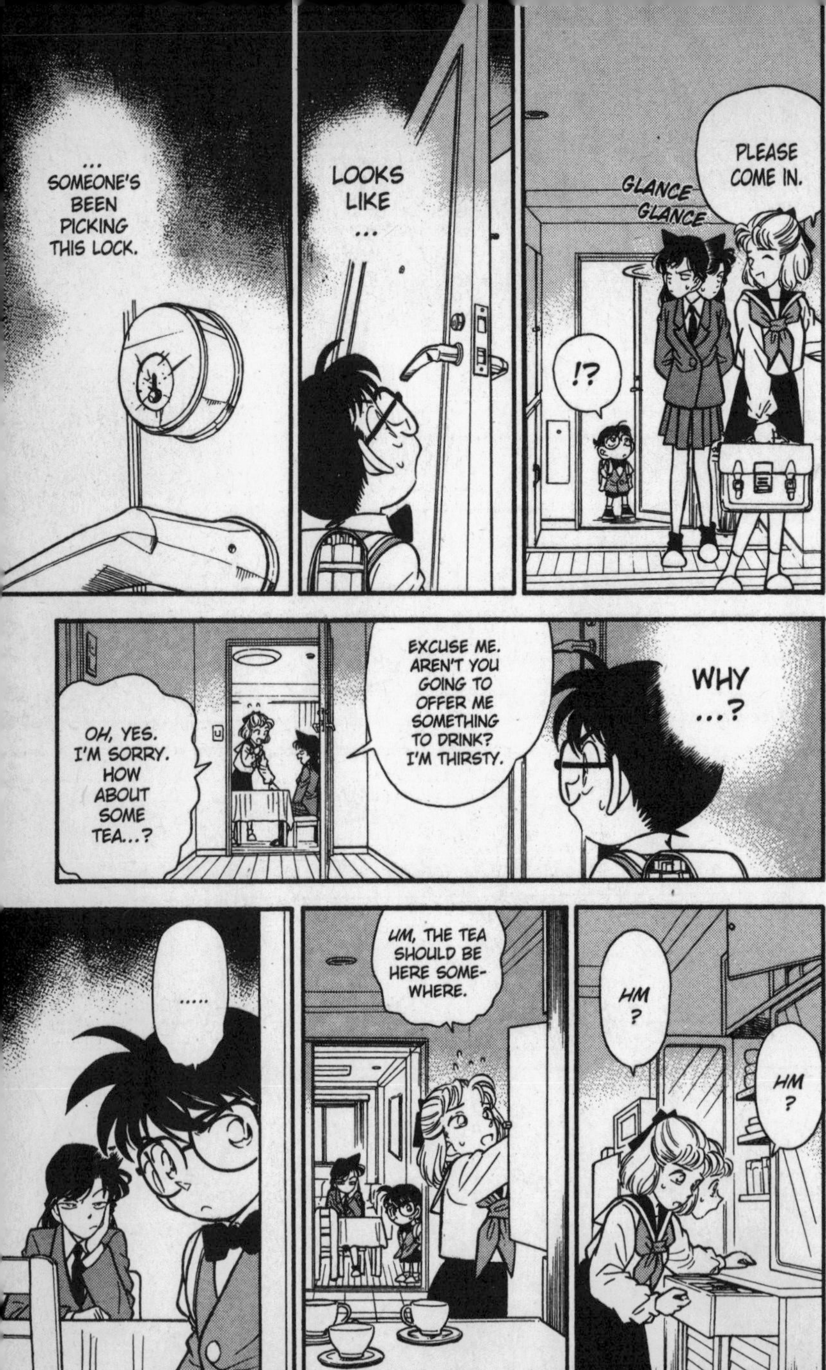
PLEASE COME IN.
GLANCE GLANCE
!?
LOOKS LIKE ...
... SOMEONE'S BEEN PICKING THIS LOCK.
WHY ...?
EXCUSE ME. AREN'T YOU GOING TO OFFER ME SOMETHING TO DRINK? I'M THIRSTY.
OH, YES. I'M SORRY. HOW ABOUT SOME TEA...?
HM ?
HM ?
UM, THE TEA SHOULD BE HERE SOME-WHERE.
.....

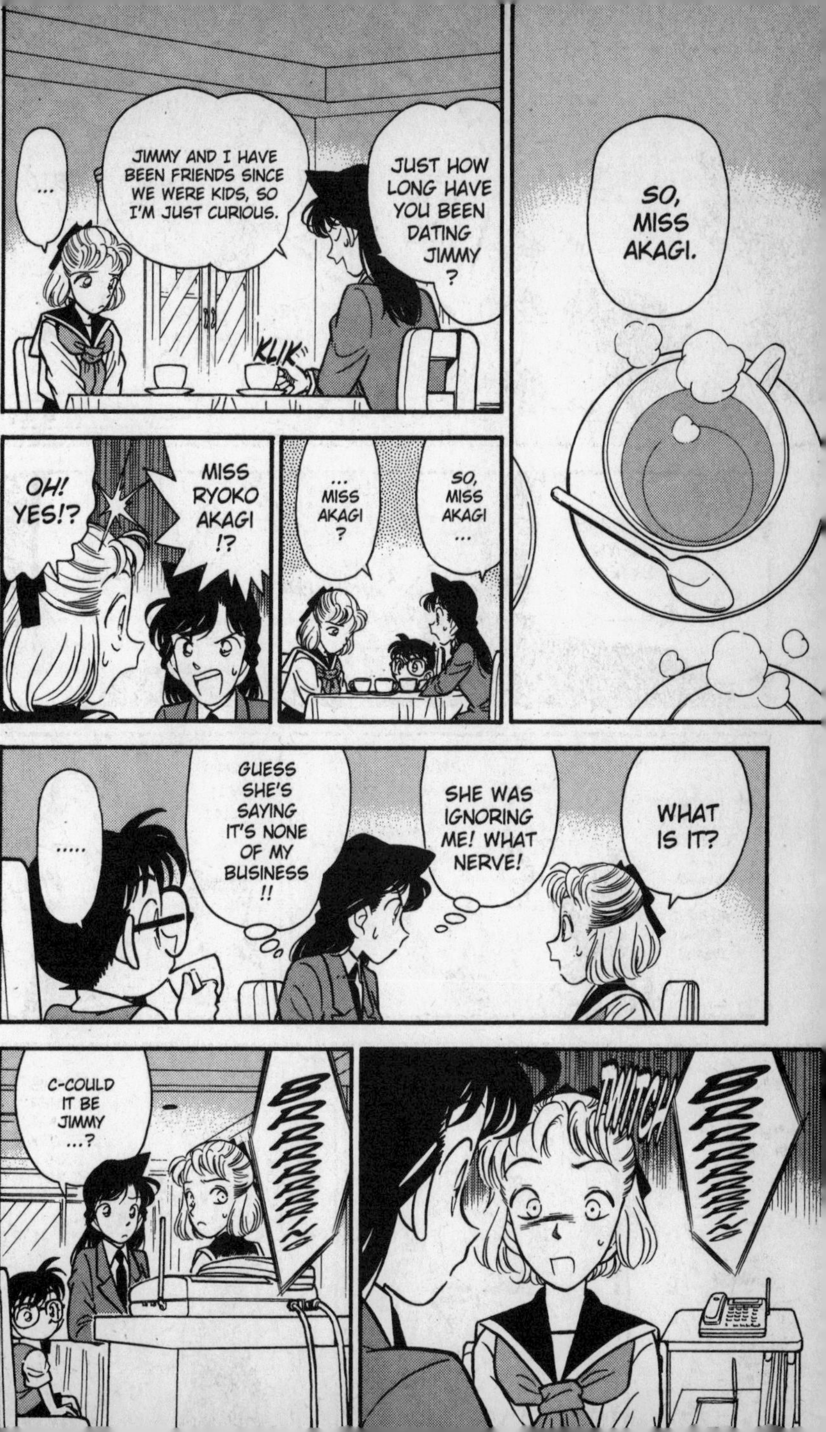
SO, MISS AKAGI.
JUST HOW LONG HAVE YOU BEEN DATING JIMMY ?
JIMMY AND I HAVE BEEN FRIENDS SINCE WE WERE KIDS, SO I'M JUST CURIOUS.
...
KLIK
SO, MISS AKAGI ...
... MISS AKAGI ?
MISS RYOKO AKAGI !?
OH! YES!?
WHAT IS IT?
SHE WAS IGNORING ME! WHAT NERVE!
GUESS SHE'S SAYING IT'S NONE OF MY BUSINESS !!
.....
TWITCH!
C-COULD IT BE JIMMY ...?

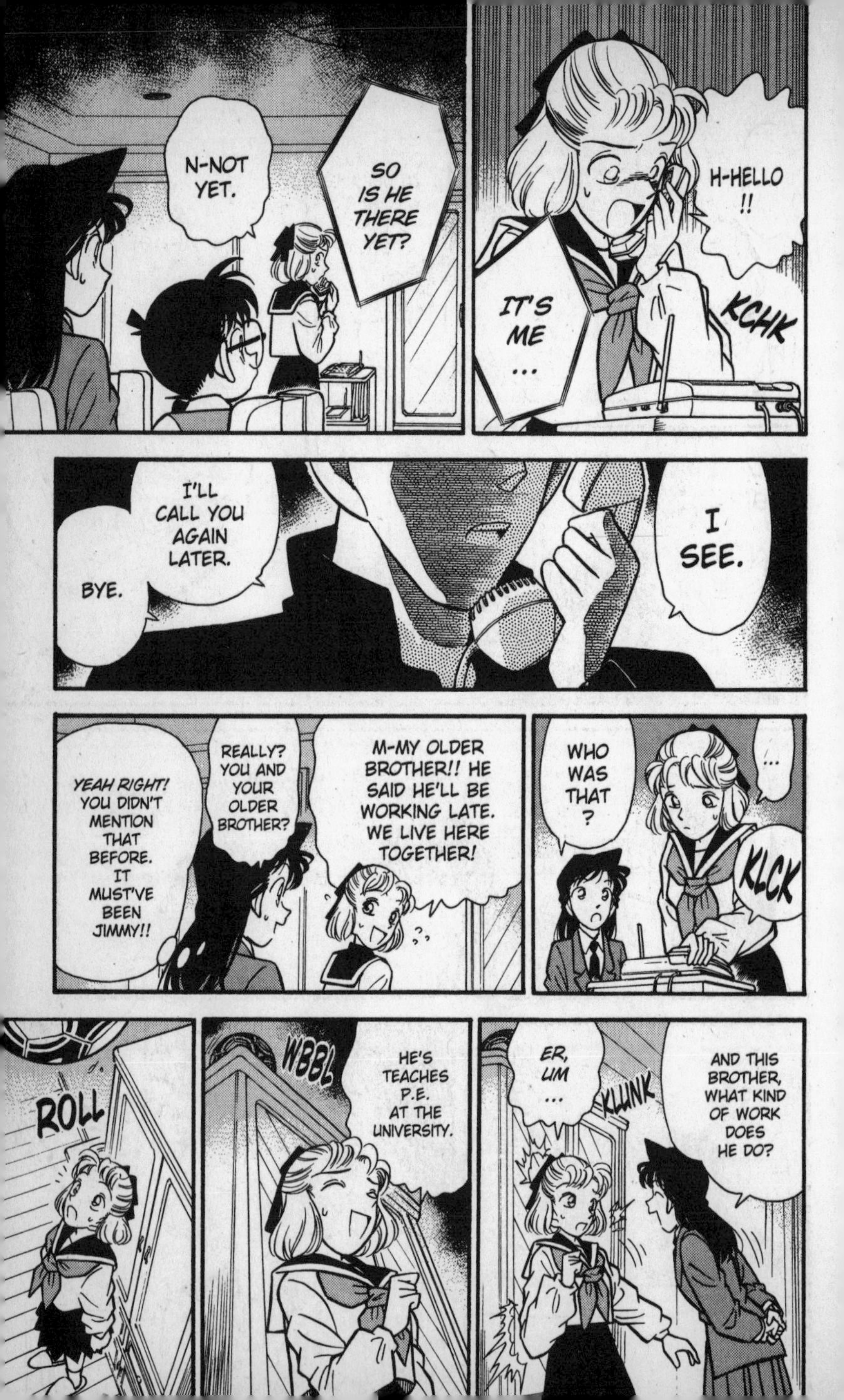
H-HELLO !!
KCHK
IT'S ME ...
SO IS HE THERE YET?
N-NOT YET.
I SEE.
I'LL CALL YOU AGAIN LATER.
BYE.
...
KLCK
WHO WAS THAT ?
M-MY OLDER BROTHER!! HE SAID HE'LL BE WORKING LATE. WE LIVE HERE TOGETHER!
REALLY? YOU AND YOUR OLDER BROTHER?
YEAH RIGHT! YOU DIDN'T MENTION THAT BEFORE. IT MUST'VE BEEN JIMMY!!
AND THIS BROTHER, WHAT KIND OF WORK DOES HE DO?
KLUNK
ER, UM ...
HE'S TEACHES P.E. AT THE UNIVERSITY.
WBBL
ROLL

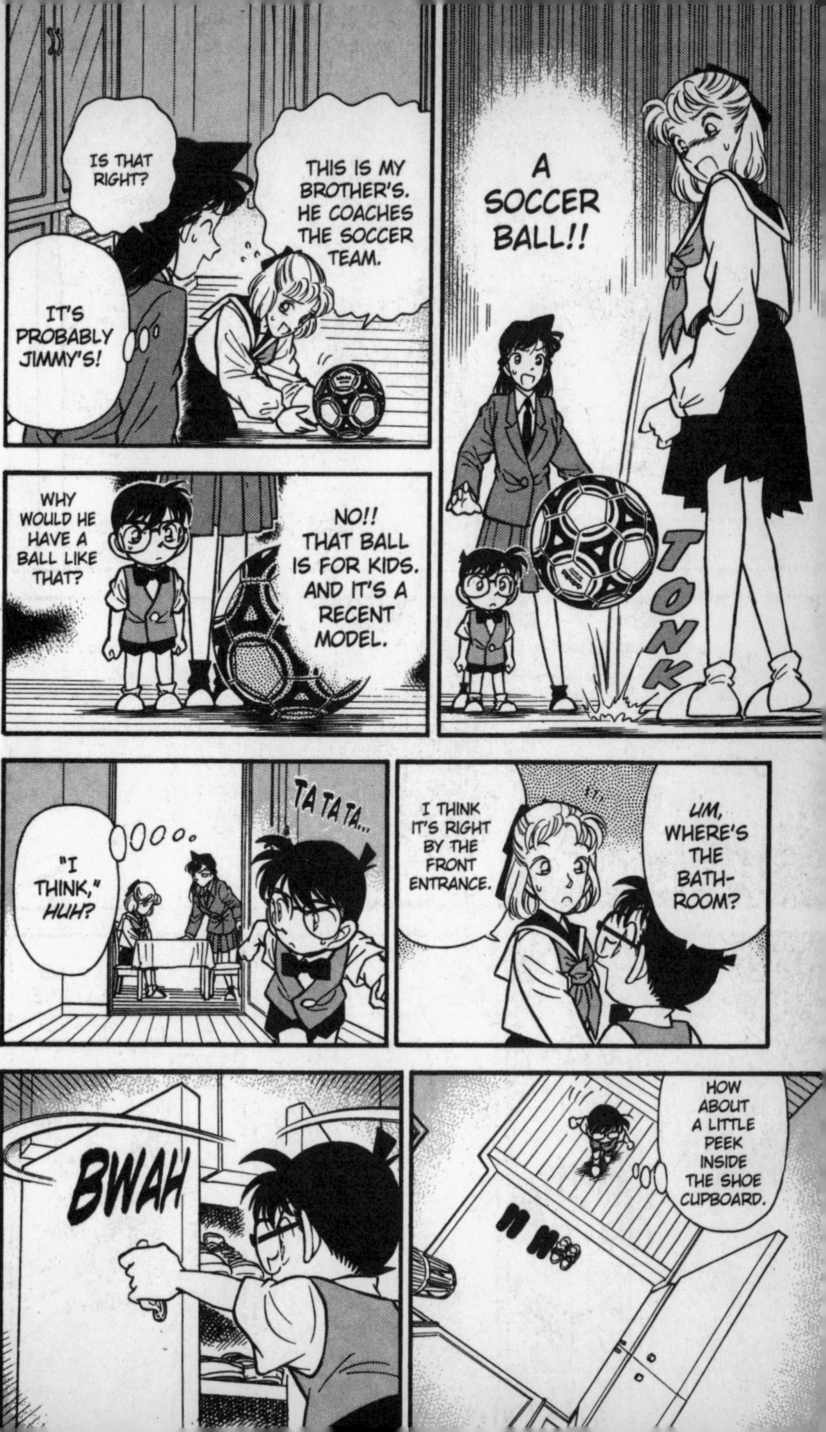
A SOCCER BALL!!
TONK
THIS IS MY BROTHER'S. HE COACHES THE SOCCER TEAM.
IS THAT RIGHT?
IT'S PROBABLY JIMMY'S!
NO!! THAT BALL IS FOR KIDS. AND IT'S A RECENT MODEL.
WHY WOULD HE HAVE A BALL LIKE THAT?
UM, WHERE'S THE BATH-ROOM?
I THINK IT'S RIGHT BY THE FRONT ENTRANCE.
TA TA TA...
"I THINK," HUH?
HOW ABOUT A LITTLE PEEK INSIDE THE SHOE CUPBOARD.
BWAH

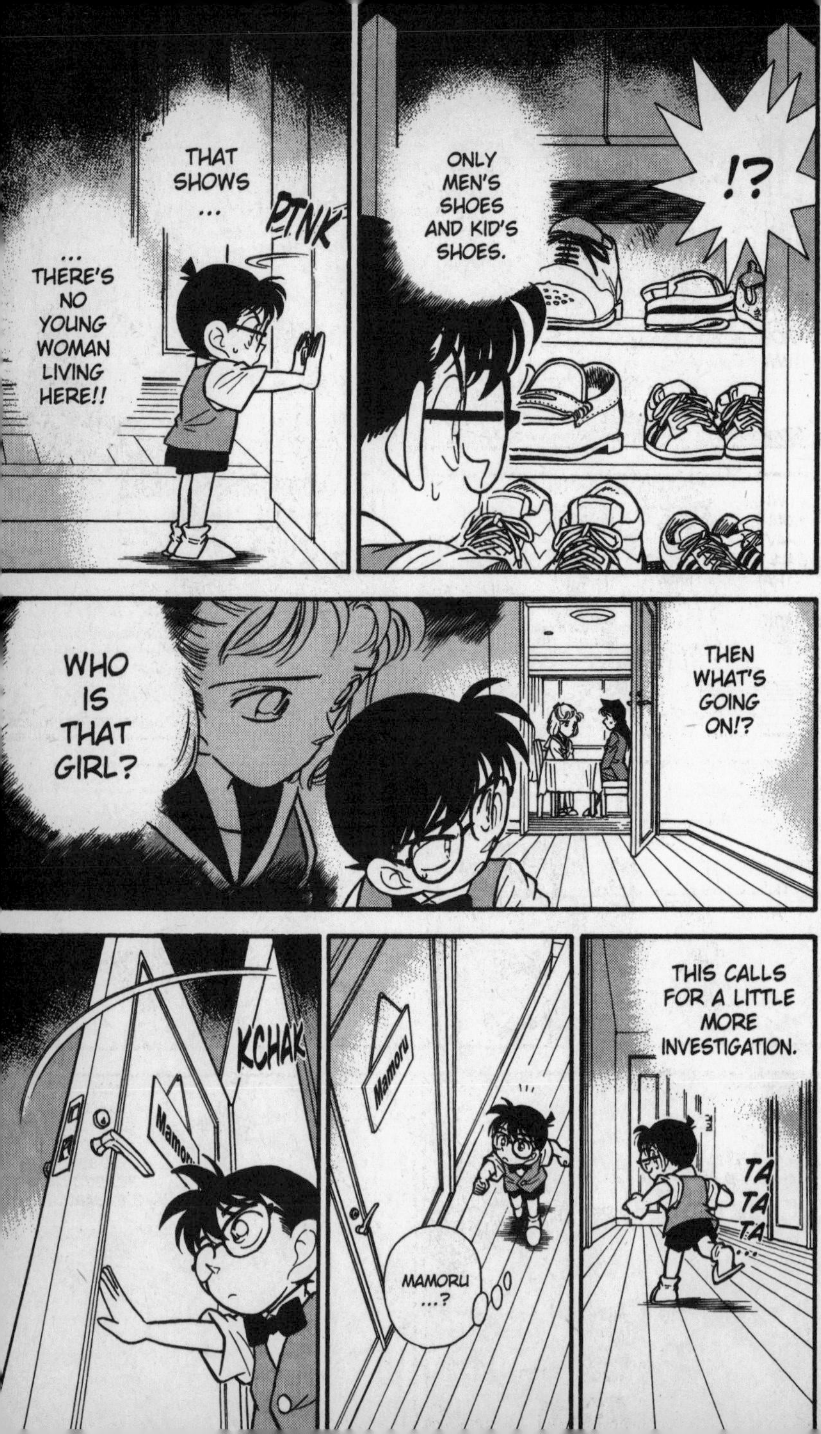
!?
ONLY MEN'S SHOES AND KID'S SHOES.
PTNK
THAT SHOWS ...
... THERE'S NO YOUNG WOMAN LIVING HERE!!
THEN WHAT'S GOING ON!?
WHO IS THAT GIRL?
THIS CALLS FOR A LITTLE MORE INVESTIGATION.
TA TA TA...
Mamoru
MAMORU ...?
KCHAK
Mamoru

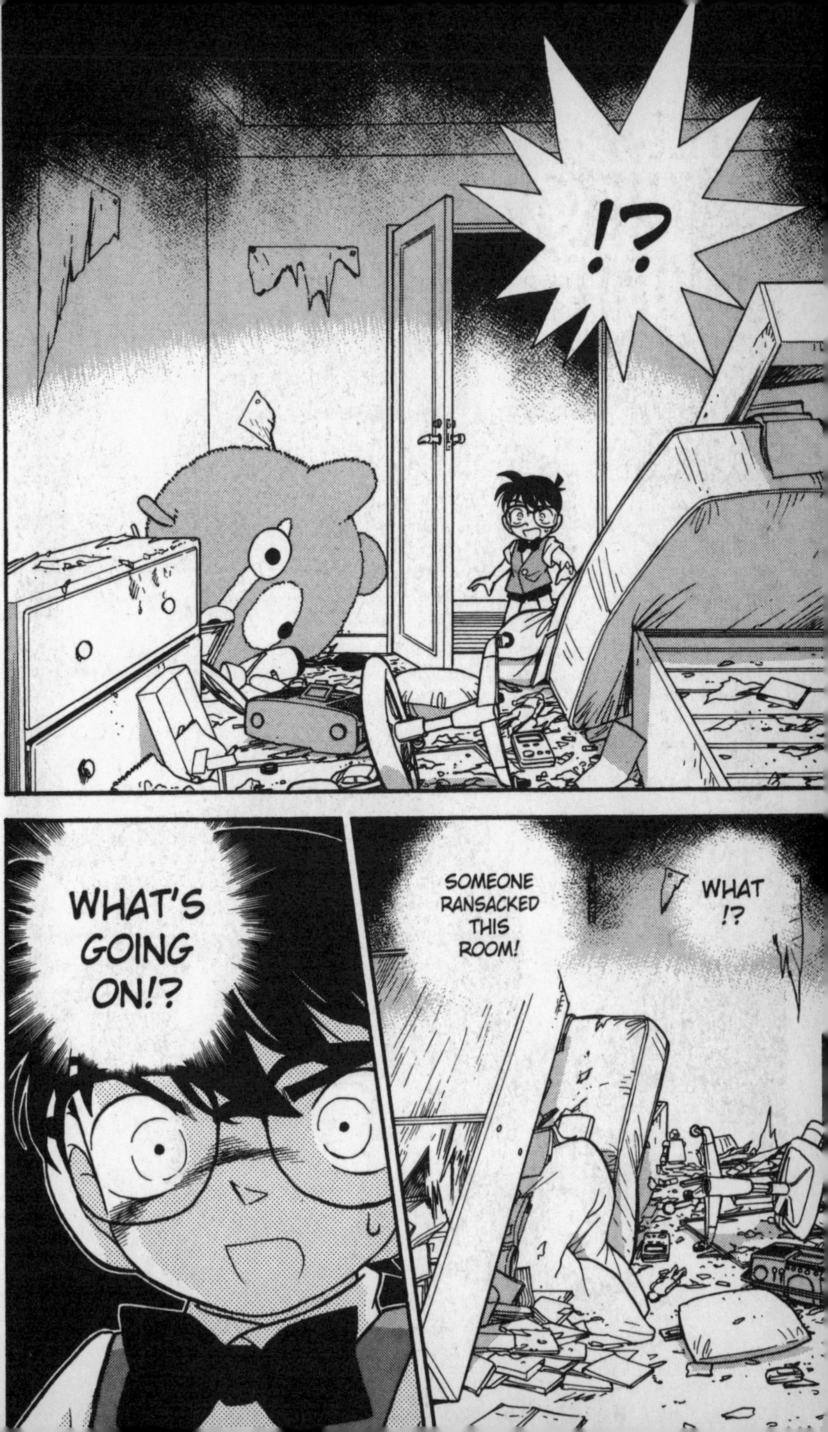
!?
WHAT !?
SOMEONE RANSACKED THIS ROOM!
WHAT'S GOING ON!?

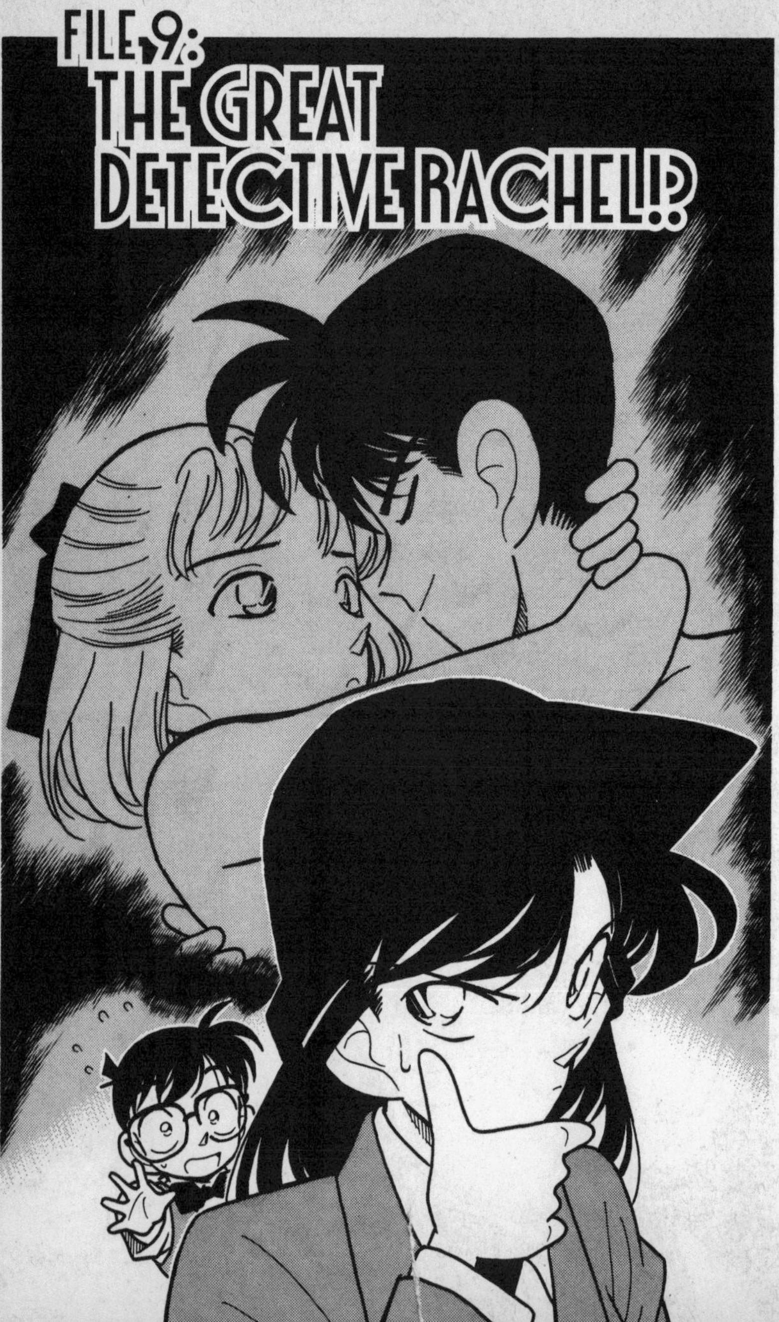
FILE 9:
THE GREAT DETECTIVE RACHEL!?

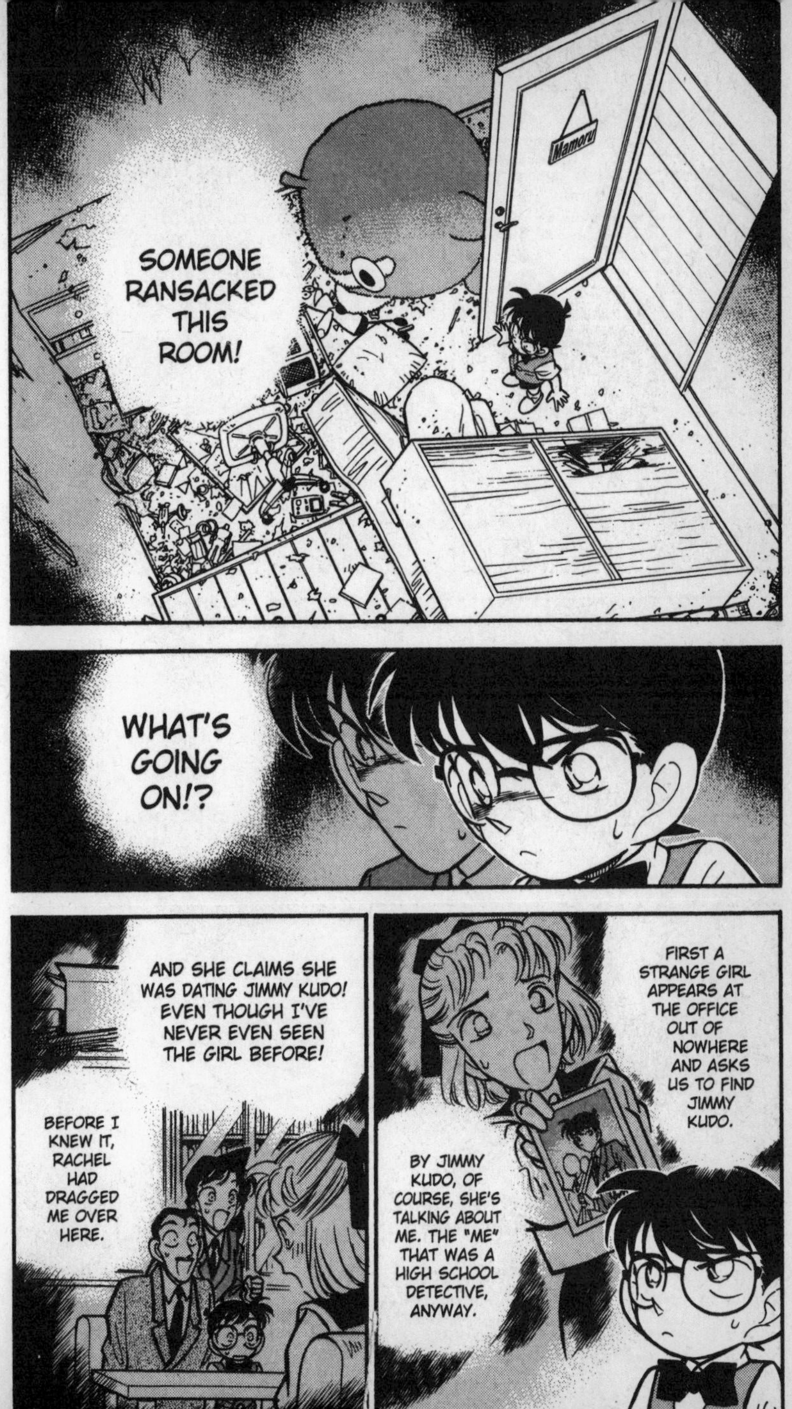
Mamoru
SOMEONE RANSACKED THIS ROOM!
WHAT'S GOING ON!?
FIRST A STRANGE GIRL APPEARS AT THE OFFICE OUT OF NOWHERE AND ASKS US TO FIND JIMMY KUDO.
BY JIMMY KUDO, OF COURSE, SHE'S TALKING ABOUT ME. THE "ME" THAT WAS A HIGH SCHOOL DETECTIVE, ANYWAY.
AND SHE CLAIMS SHE WAS DATING JIMMY KUDO! EVEN THOUGH I'VE NEVER EVEN SEEN THE GIRL BEFORE!
BEFORE I KNEW IT, RACHEL HAD DRAGGED ME OVER HERE.

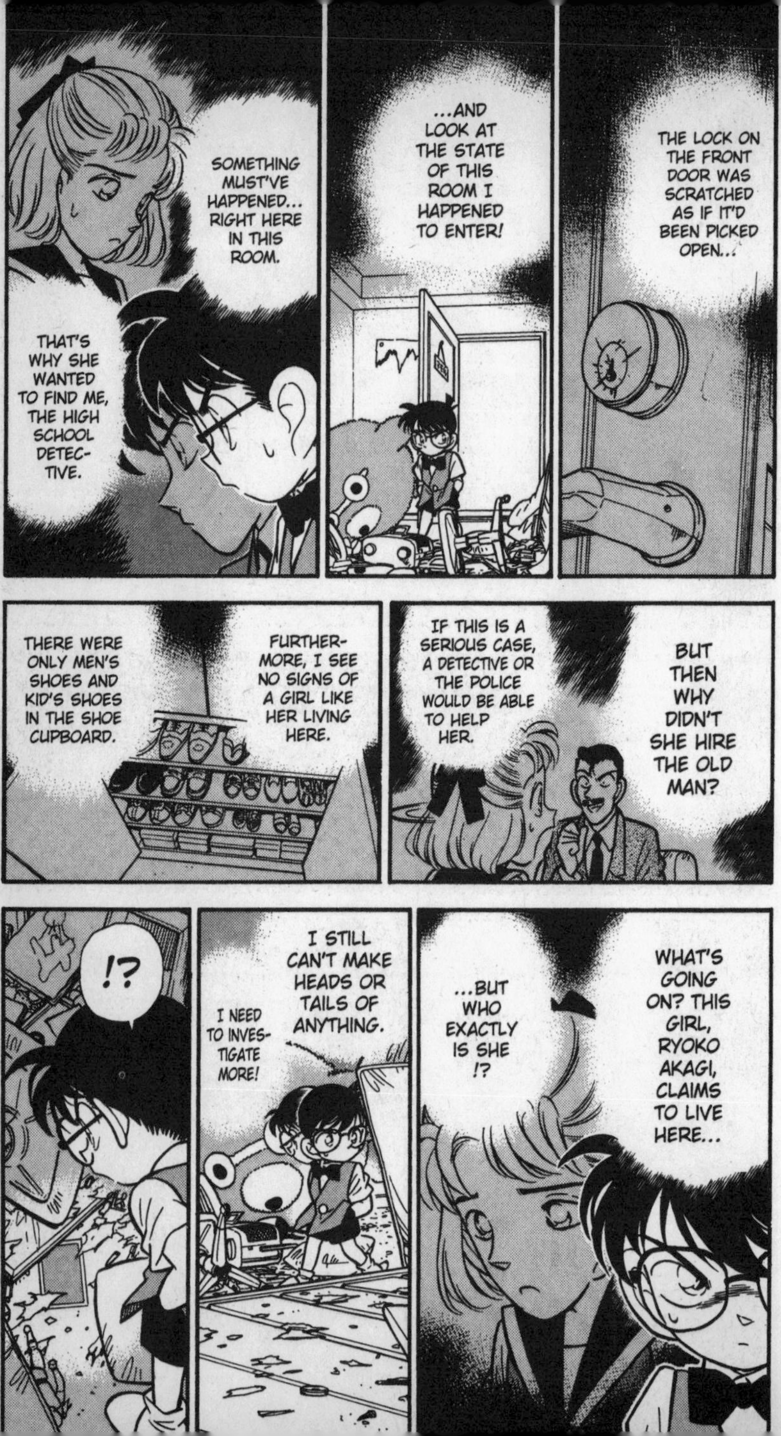
THE LOCK ON THE FRONT DOOR WAS SCRATCHED AS IF IT'D BEEN PICKED OPEN...
...AND LOOK AT THE STATE OF THIS ROOM I HAPPENED TO ENTER!
SOMETHING MUST'VE HAPPENED... RIGHT HERE IN THIS ROOM.
THAT'S WHY SHE WANTED TO FIND ME, THE HIGH SCHOOL DETEC-TIVE.
IF THIS IS A SERIOUS CASE, A DETECTIVE OR THE POLICE WOULD BE ABLE TO HELP HER.
BUT THEN WHY DIDN'T SHE HIRE THE OLD MAN?
THERE WERE ONLY MEN'S SHOES AND KID'S SHOES IN THE SHOE CUPBOARD.
FURTHER-MORE, I SEE NO SIGNS OF A GIRL LIKE HER LIVING HERE.
WHAT'S GOING ON? THIS GIRL, RYOKO AKAGI, CLAIMS TO LIVE HERE...
...BUT WHO EXACTLY IS SHE !?
I STILL CAN'T MAKE HEADS OR TAILS OF ANYTHING.
I NEED TO INVES-TIGATE MORE!
!?

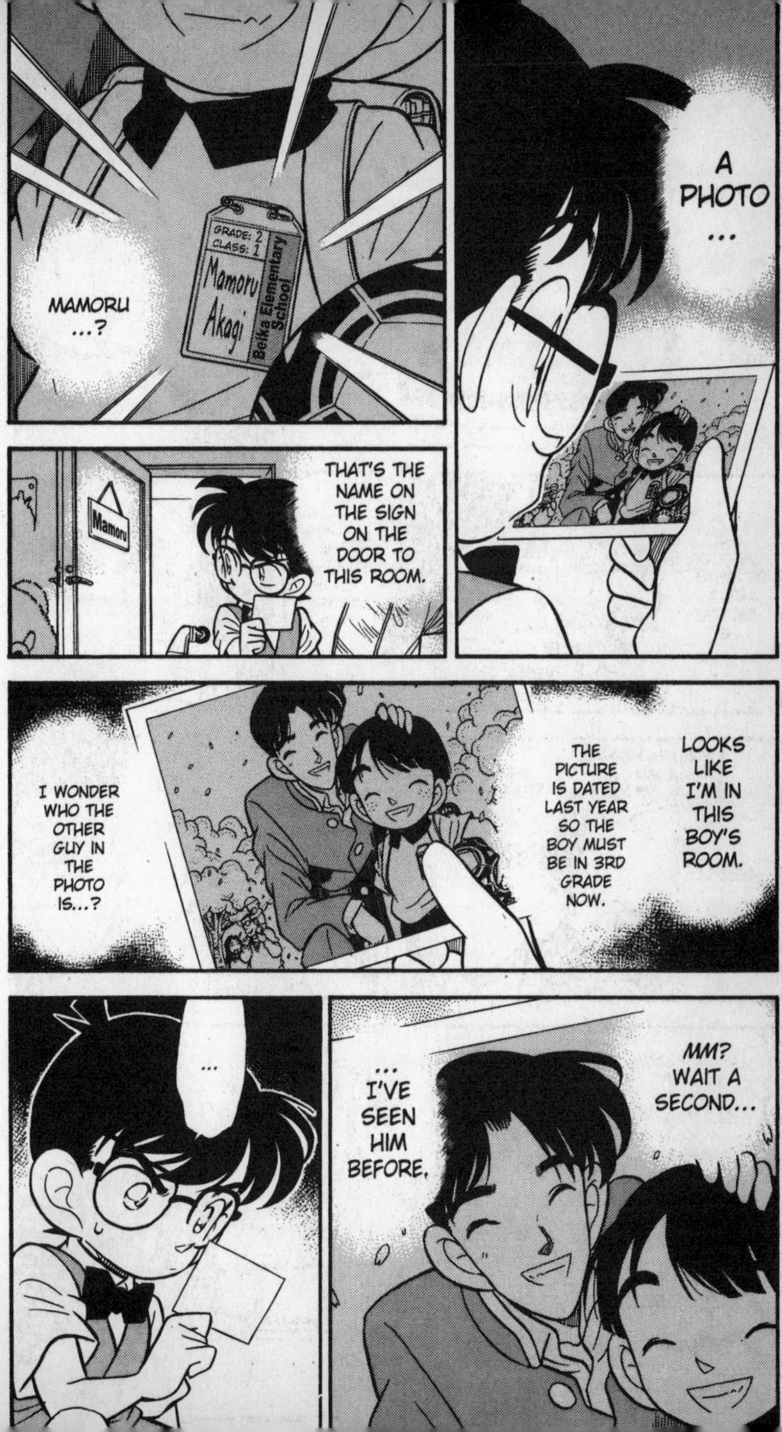
A PHOTO ...
GRADE: 2 CLASS: 1
Mamoru Akagi
Beika Elementary School
MAMORU ...?
Mamoru
THAT'S THE NAME ON THE SIGN ON THE DOOR TO THIS ROOM.
LOOKS LIKE I'M IN THIS BOY'S ROOM.
THE PICTURE IS DATED LAST YEAR SO THE BOY MUST BE IN 3RD GRADE NOW.
I WONDER WHO THE OTHER GUY IN THE PHOTO IS...?
MM? WAIT A SECOND...
... I'VE SEEN HIM BEFORE.
...

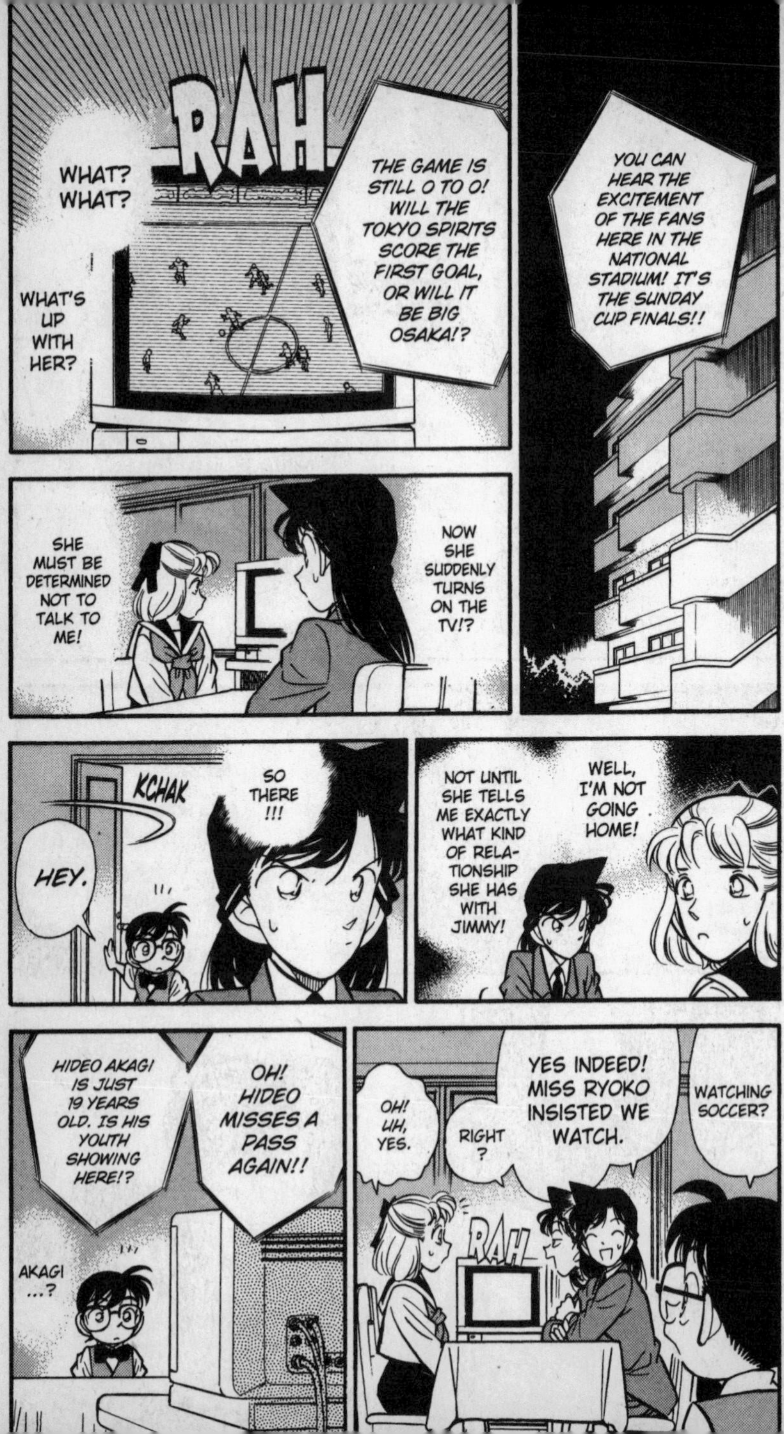
YOU CAN HEAR THE EXCITEMENT OF THE FANS HERE IN THE NATIONAL STADIUM! IT'S THE SUNDAY CUP FINALS!!
RAH
THE GAME IS STILL 0 TO 0! WILL THE TOKYO SPIRITS SCORE THE FIRST GOAL, OR WILL IT BE BIG OSAKA!?
WHAT? WHAT?
WHAT'S UP WITH HER?
NOW SHE SUDDENLY TURNS ON THE TV!?
SHE MUST BE DETERMINED NOT TO TALK TO ME!
WELL, I'M NOT GOING HOME!
NOT UNTIL SHE TELLS ME EXACTLY WHAT KIND OF RELA-TIONSHIP SHE HAS WITH JIMMY!
SO THERE!!!
KCHAK
HEY.
WATCHING SOCCER?
YES INDEED! MISS RYOKO INSISTED WE WATCH.
RIGHT?
OH! UH, YES.
RAH
OH! HIDEO MISSES A PASS AGAIN!!
HIDEO AKAGI IS JUST 19 YEARS OLD. IS HIS YOUTH SHOWING HERE!?
AKAGI ...?

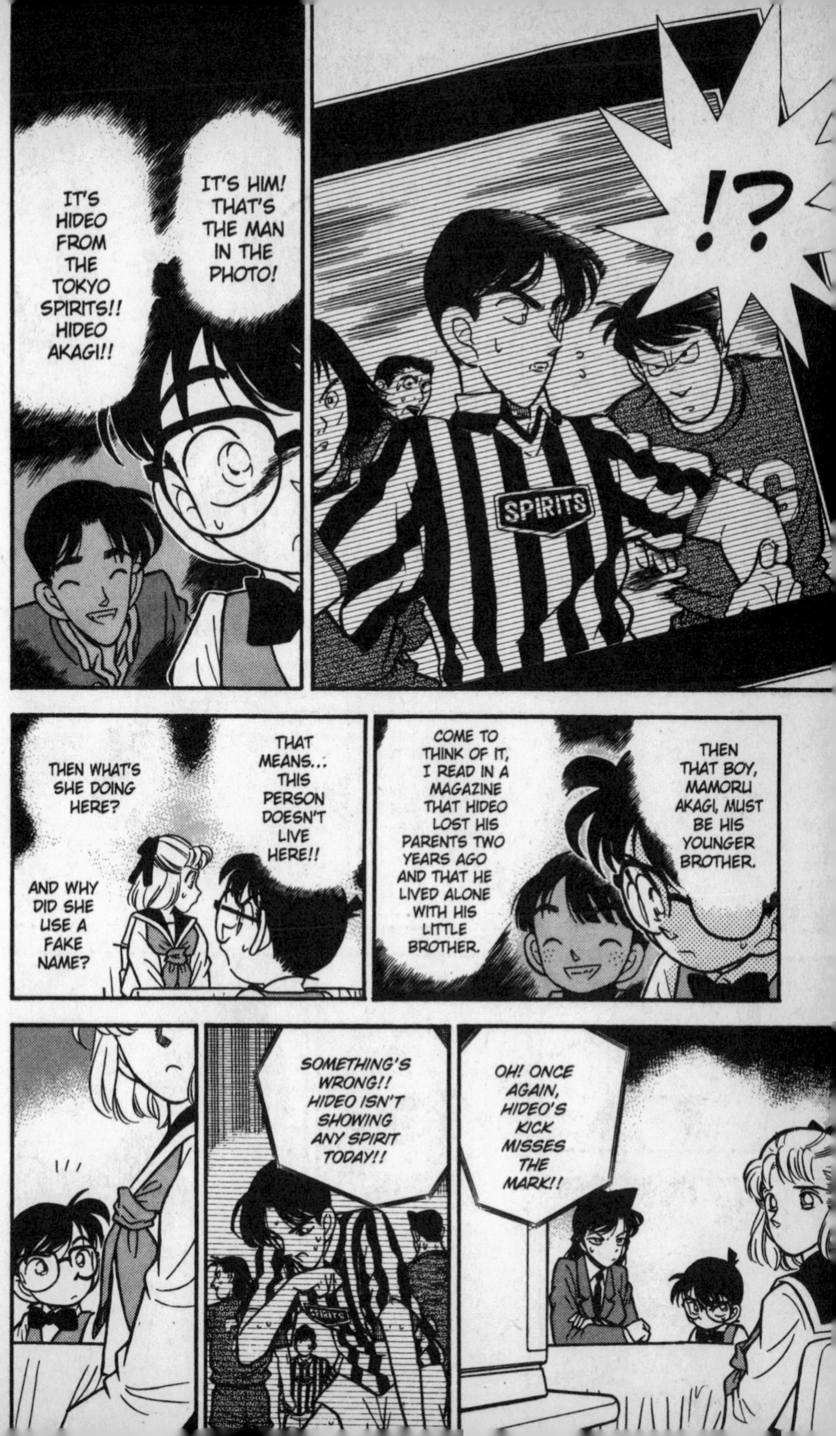

!?
SPIRITS
IT'S HIM! THAT'S THE MAN IN THE PHOTO!
IT'S HIDEO FROM THE TOKYO SPIRITS!! HIDEO AKAGI!!
THEN THAT BOY, MAMORU AKAGI, MUST BE HIS YOUNGER BROTHER.
COME TO THINK OF IT, I READ IN A MAGAZINE THAT HIDEO LOST HIS PARENTS TWO YEARS AGO AND THAT HE LIVED ALONE WITH HIS LITTLE BROTHER.
THAT MEANS... THIS PERSON DOESN'T LIVE HERE!!
THEN WHAT'S SHE DOING HERE?
AND WHY DID SHE USE A FAKE NAME?
OH! ONCE AGAIN, HIDEO'S KICK MISSES THE MARK!!
SOMETHING'S WRONG!! HIDEO ISN'T SHOWING ANY SPIRIT TODAY!!

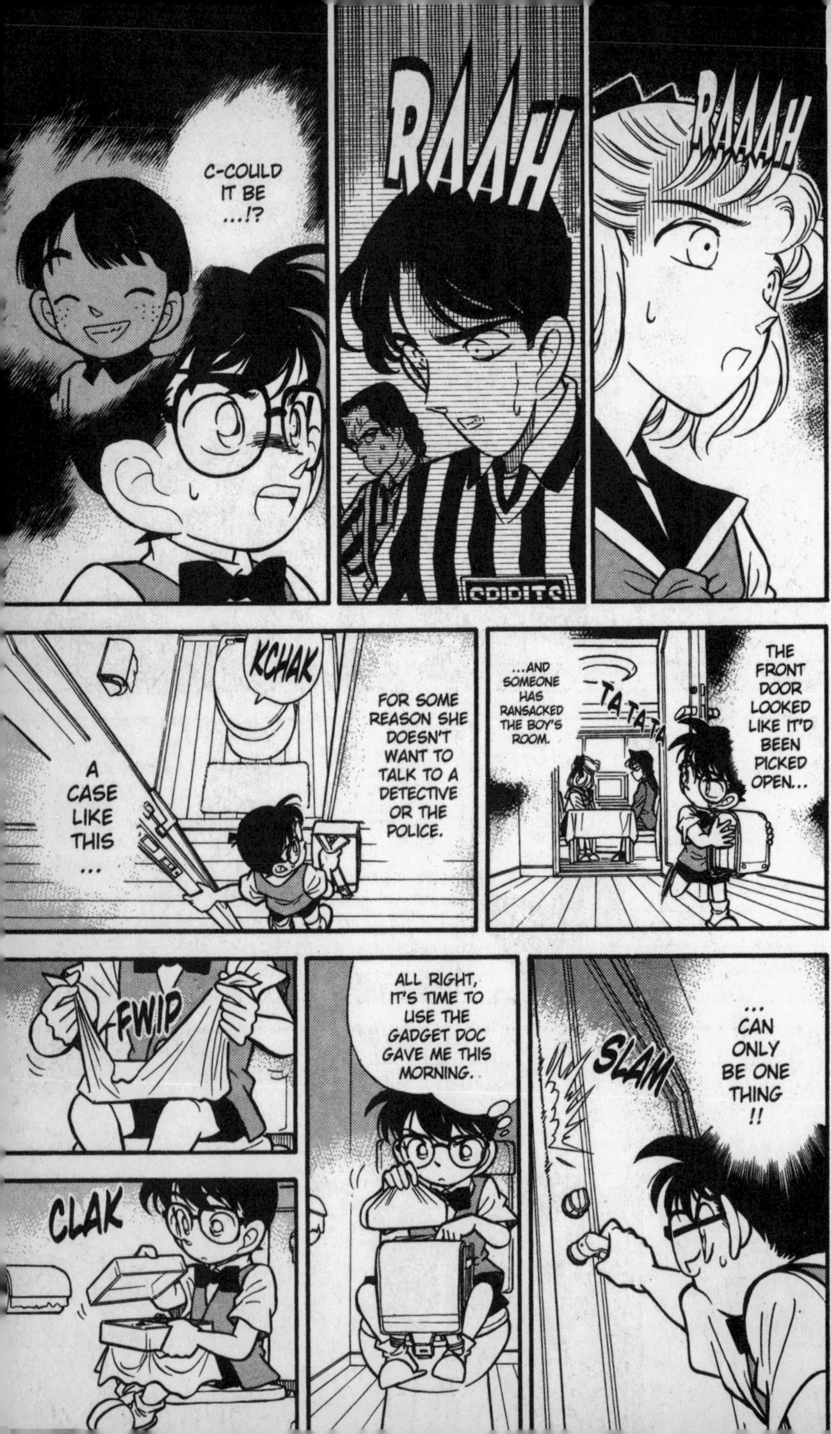
RAAAH
RAAH
C-COULD IT BE ...!?
THE FRONT DOOR LOOKED LIKE IT'D BEEN PICKED OPEN...
...AND SOMEONE HAS RANSACKED THE BOY'S ROOM.
TATATA
FOR SOME REASON SHE DOESN'T WANT TO TALK TO A DETECTIVE OR THE POLICE.
KCHAK
A CASE LIKE THIS ...
SLAM
... CAN ONLY BE ONE THING !!
ALL RIGHT, IT'S TIME TO USE THE GADGET DOC GAVE ME THIS MORNING.
FWIP
CLAK

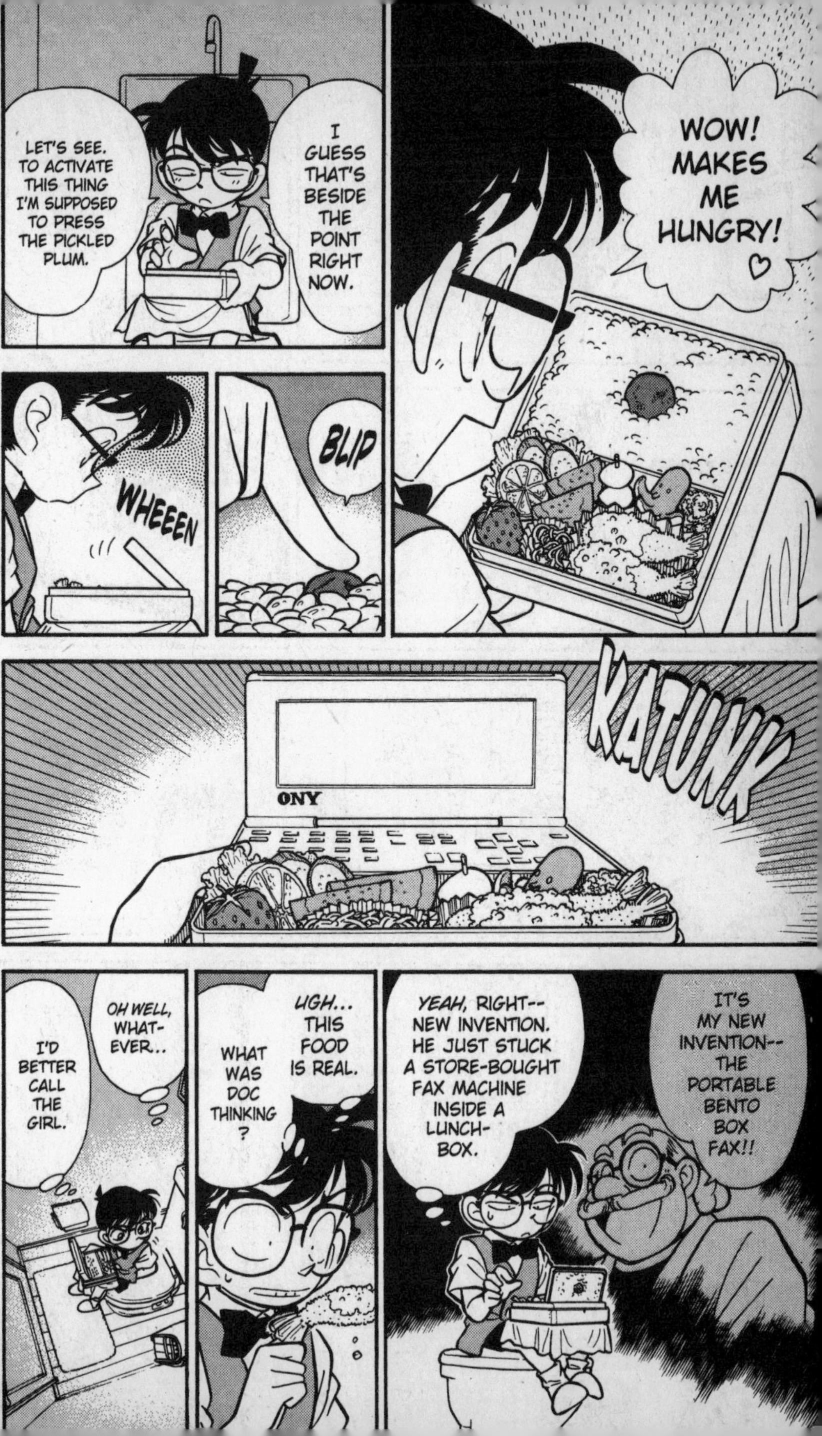
WOW! MAKES ME HUNGRY! ♡
I GUESS THAT'S BESIDE THE POINT RIGHT NOW.
LET'S SEE. TO ACTIVATE THIS THING I'M SUPPOSED TO PRESS THE PICKLED PLUM.
BLIP
WHEEEN
KATUNK
ONY
IT'S MY NEW INVENTION--THE PORTABLE BENTO BOX FAX!!
YEAH, RIGHT--NEW INVENTION. HE JUST STUCK A STORE-BOUGHT FAX MACHINE INSIDE A LUNCH-BOX.
UGH... THIS FOOD IS REAL.
WHAT WAS DOC THINKING?
OH WELL, WHATEVER...
I'D BETTER CALL THE GIRL.

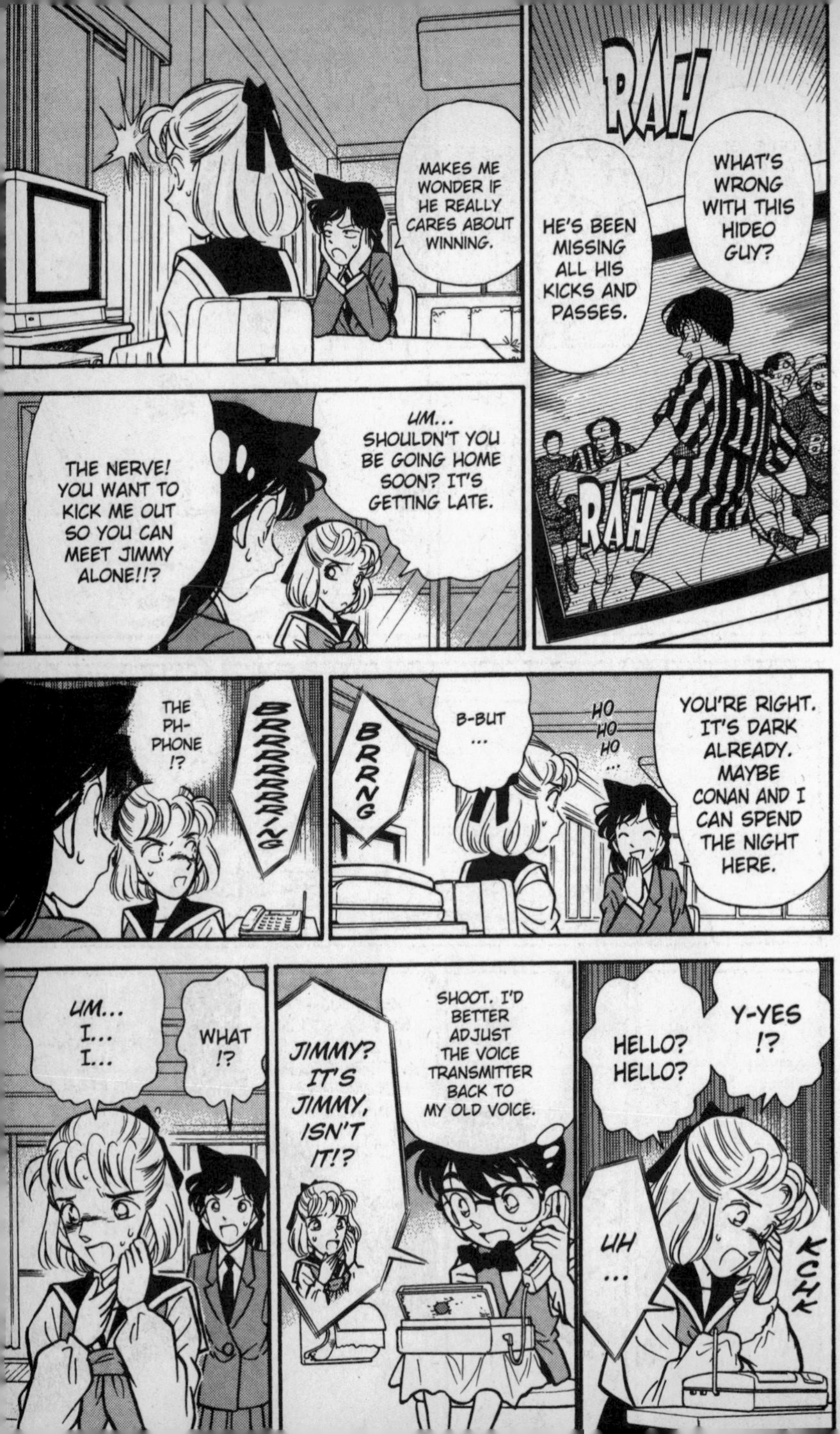
RAH
WHAT'S WRONG WITH THIS HIDEO GUY?
HE'S BEEN MISSING ALL HIS KICKS AND PASSES.
RAH
MAKES ME WONDER IF HE REALLY CARES ABOUT WINNING.
UM... SHOULDN'T YOU BE GOING HOME SOON? IT'S GETTING LATE.
THE NERVE! YOU WANT TO KICK ME OUT SO YOU CAN MEET JIMMY ALONE!!?
YOU'RE RIGHT. IT'S DARK ALREADY. MAYBE CONAN AND I CAN SPEND THE NIGHT HERE.
HO HO HO ...
B-BUT ...
BRRNG
BRRRRRRRING
THE PH-PHONE !?
Y-YES !?
HELLO? HELLO?
UH ...
KCHK
SHOOT. I'D BETTER ADJUST THE VOICE TRANSMITTER BACK TO MY OLD VOICE.
JIMMY? IT'S JIMMY, ISN'T IT!?
WHAT !?
UM... I... I...

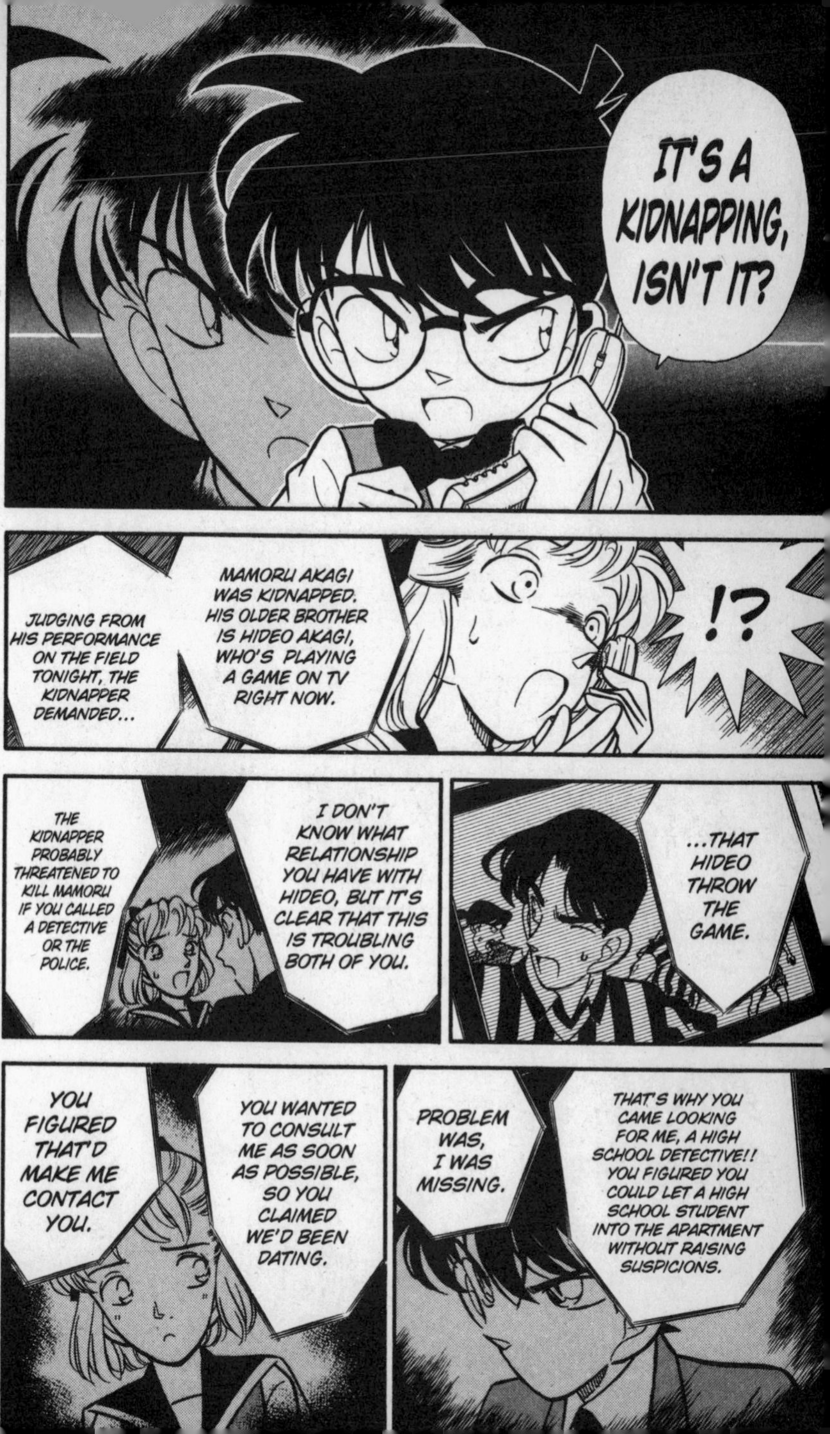
IT'S A KIDNAPPING, ISN'T IT?
!?
MAMORU AKAGI WAS KIDNAPPED. HIS OLDER BROTHER IS HIDEO AKAGI, WHO'S PLAYING A GAME ON TV RIGHT NOW.
JUDGING FROM HIS PERFORMANCE ON THE FIELD TONIGHT, THE KIDNAPPER DEMANDED...
...THAT HIDEO THROW THE GAME.
I DON'T KNOW WHAT RELATIONSHIP YOU HAVE WITH HIDEO, BUT IT'S CLEAR THAT THIS IS TROUBLING BOTH OF YOU.
THE KIDNAPPER PROBABLY THREATENED TO KILL MAMORU IF YOU CALLED A DETECTIVE OR THE POLICE.
THAT'S WHY YOU CAME LOOKING FOR ME, A HIGH SCHOOL DETECTIVE!! YOU FIGURED YOU COULD LET A HIGH SCHOOL STUDENT INTO THE APARTMENT WITHOUT RAISING SUSPICIONS.
PROBLEM WAS, I WAS MISSING.
YOU WANTED TO CONSULT ME AS SOON AS POSSIBLE, SO YOU CLAIMED WE'D BEEN DATING.
YOU FIGURED THAT'D MAKE ME CONTACT YOU.

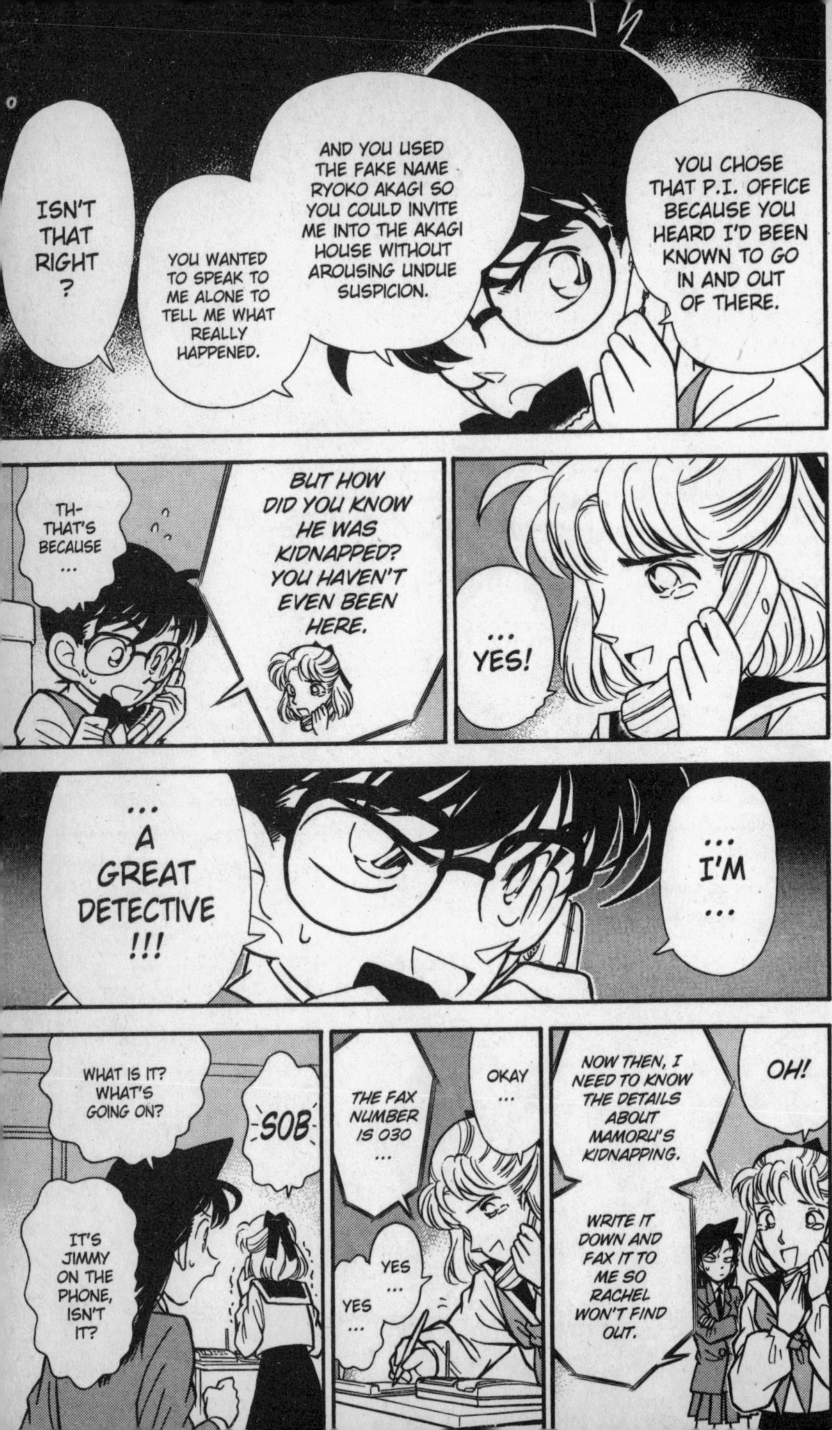
YOU CHOSE THAT P.I. OFFICE BECAUSE YOU HEARD I'D BEEN KNOWN TO GO IN AND OUT OF THERE.
AND YOU USED THE FAKE NAME RYOKO AKAGI SO YOU COULD INVITE ME INTO THE AKAGI HOUSE WITHOUT AROUSING UNDUE SUSPICION.
YOU WANTED TO SPEAK TO ME ALONE TO TELL ME WHAT REALLY HAPPENED.
ISN'T THAT RIGHT ?
... YES!
BUT HOW DID YOU KNOW HE WAS KIDNAPPED? YOU HAVEN'T EVEN BEEN HERE.
TH- THAT'S BECAUSE ...
... I'M ...
... A GREAT DETECTIVE !!!
OH!
NOW THEN, I NEED TO KNOW THE DETAILS ABOUT MAMORU'S KIDNAPPING.
WRITE IT DOWN AND FAX IT TO ME SO RACHEL WON'T FIND OUT.
OKAY ...
THE FAX NUMBER IS 030 ...
YES ...
YES ...
SOB
WHAT IS IT? WHAT'S GOING ON?
IT'S JIMMY ON THE PHONE, ISN'T IT?

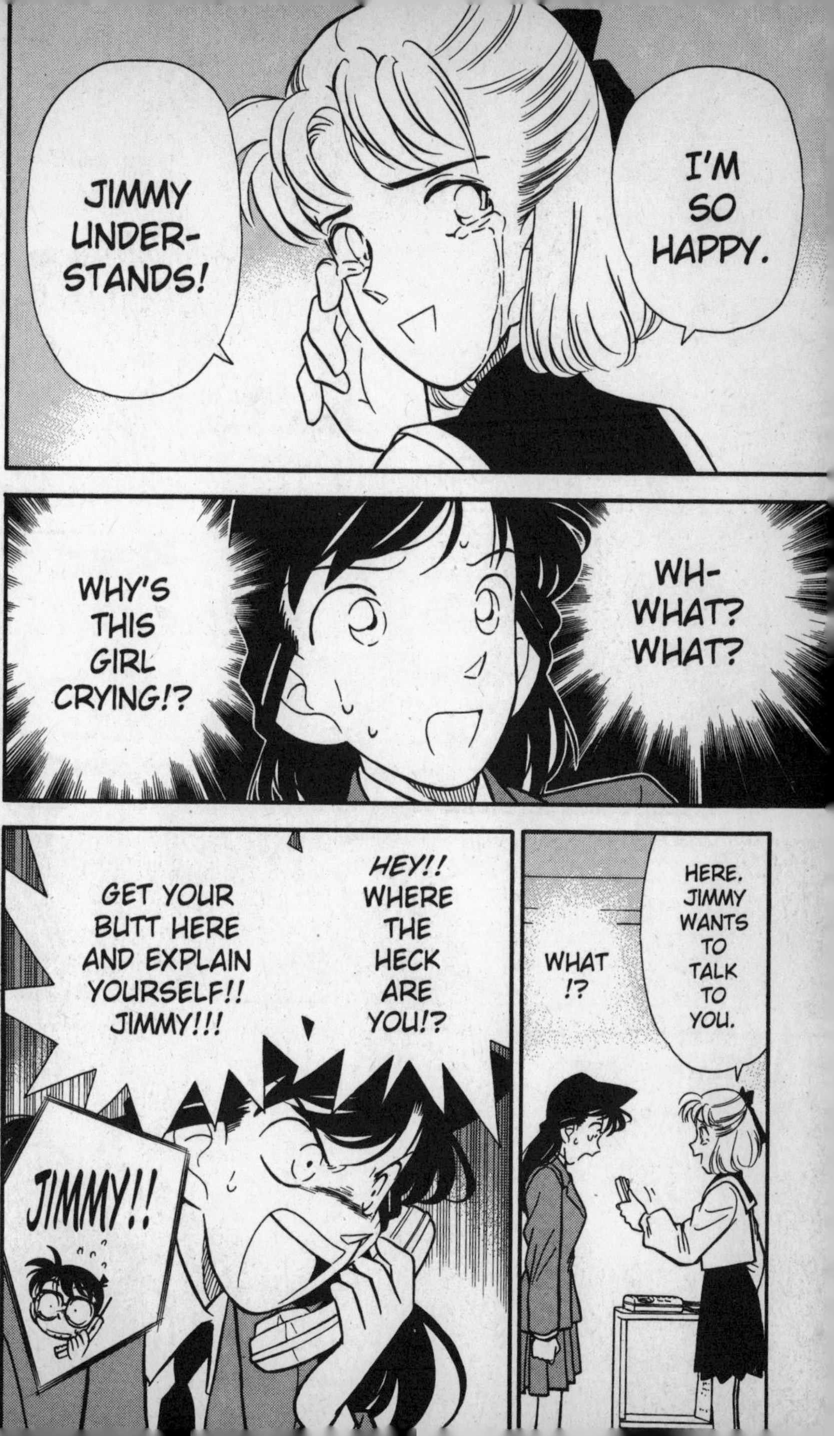
I'M SO HAPPY.
JIMMY UNDER-STANDS!
WH-WHAT? WHAT?
WHY'S THIS GIRL CRYING!?
HERE. JIMMY WANTS TO TALK TO YOU.
WHAT!?
HEY!! WHERE THE HECK ARE YOU!?
GET YOUR BUTT HERE AND EXPLAIN YOURSELF!! JIMMY!!!
JIMMY!!

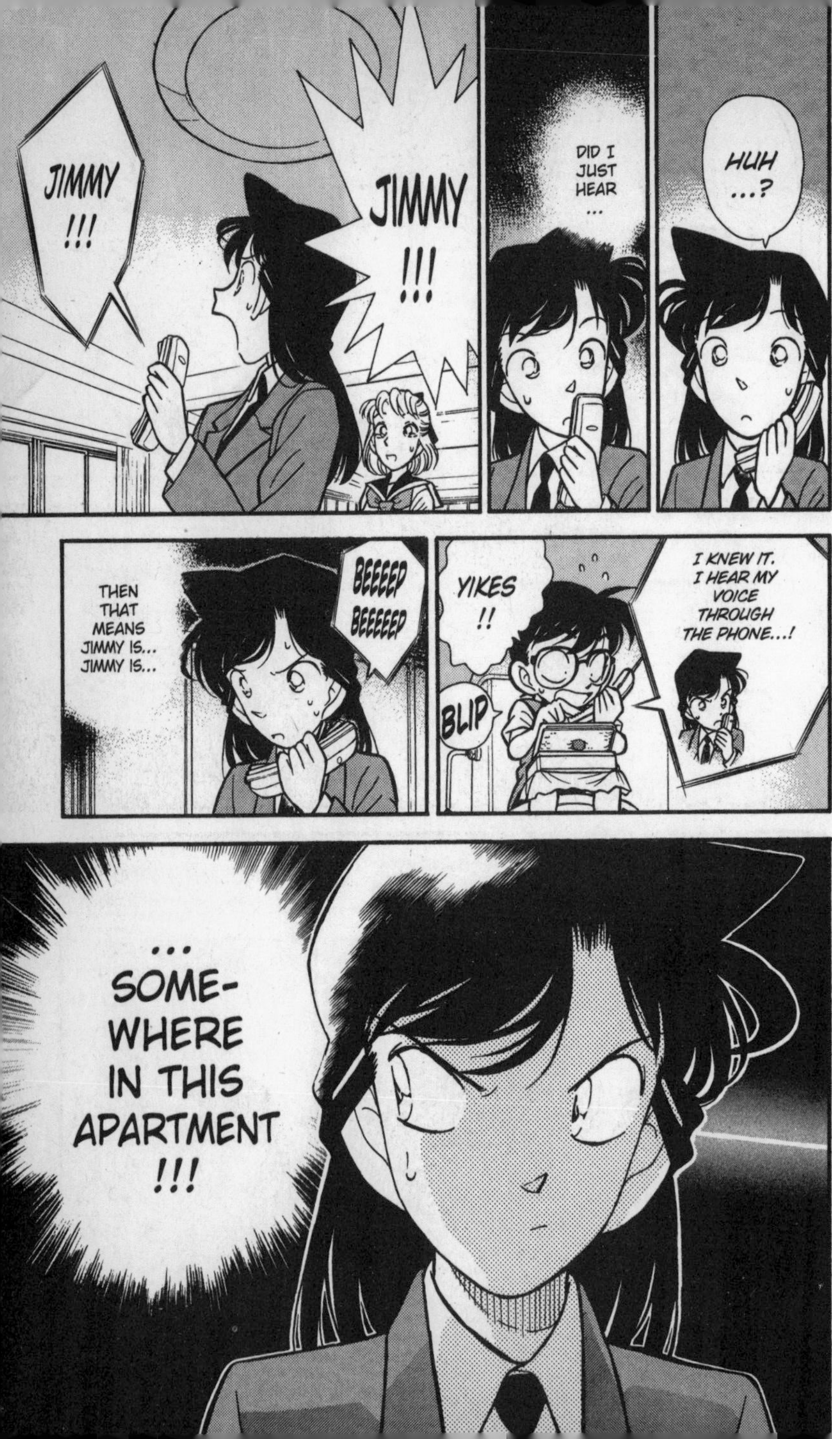
HUH ...?
DID I JUST HEAR ...
JIMMY !!!
JIMMY !!!
I KNEW IT. I HEAR MY VOICE THROUGH THE PHONE...!
YIKES !!
BLIP
BEEEEEP BEEEEEP
THEN THAT MEANS JIMMY IS... JIMMY IS...
... SOME-WHERE IN THIS APARTMENT !!!

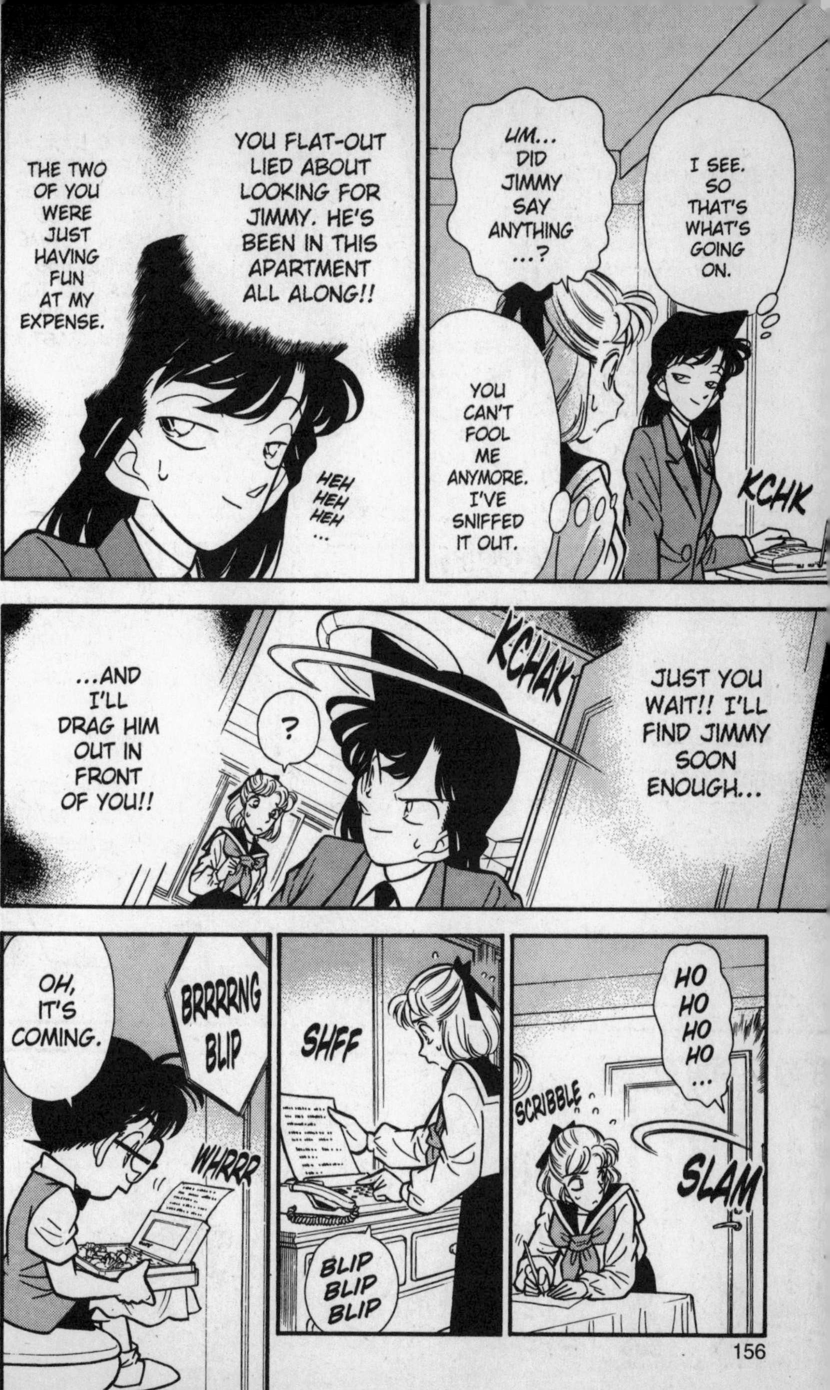
I SEE. SO THAT'S WHAT'S GOING ON.
UM... DID JIMMY SAY ANYTHING ...?
YOU CAN'T FOOL ME ANYMORE. I'VE SNIFFED IT OUT.
KCHK
YOU FLAT-OUT LIED ABOUT LOOKING FOR JIMMY. HE'S BEEN IN THIS APARTMENT ALL ALONG!!
THE TWO OF YOU WERE JUST HAVING FUN AT MY EXPENSE.
HEH HEH HEH ...
JUST YOU WAIT!! I'LL FIND JIMMY SOON ENOUGH...
KCHAK
?
...AND I'LL DRAG HIM OUT IN FRONT OF YOU!!
HO HO HO HO ...
SLAM
SCRIBBLE
SHFF
BLIP BLIP BLIP
BRRRRNG BLIP
OH, IT'S COMING.
WHRRR

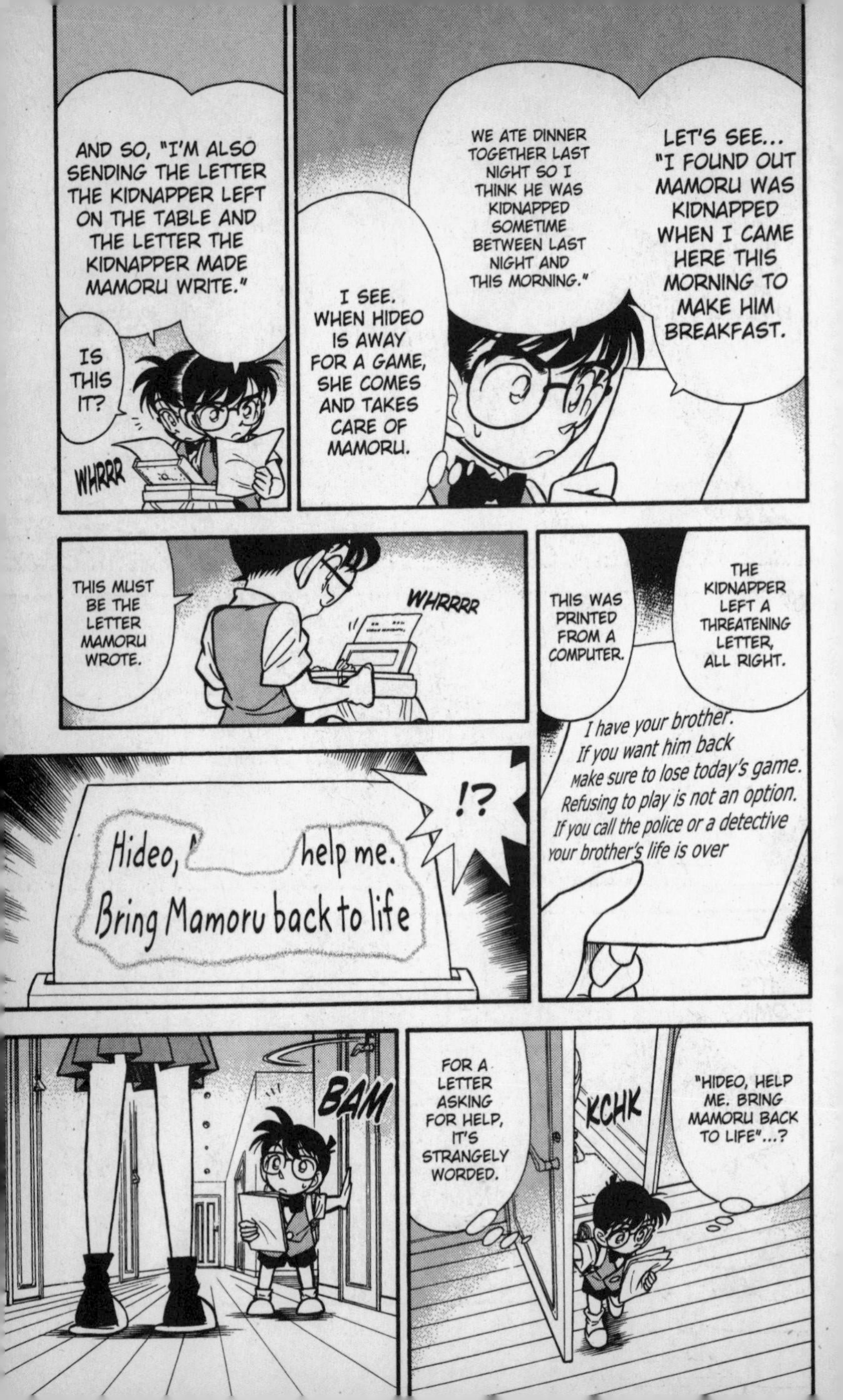
LET'S SEE... "I FOUND OUT MAMORU WAS KIDNAPPED WHEN I CAME HERE THIS MORNING TO MAKE HIM BREAKFAST.
WE ATE DINNER TOGETHER LAST NIGHT SO I THINK HE WAS KIDNAPPED SOMETIME BETWEEN LAST NIGHT AND THIS MORNING."
I SEE. WHEN HIDEO IS AWAY FOR A GAME, SHE COMES AND TAKES CARE OF MAMORU.
AND SO, "I'M ALSO SENDING THE LETTER THE KIDNAPPER LEFT ON THE TABLE AND THE LETTER THE KIDNAPPER MADE MAMORU WRITE."
IS THIS IT?
WHRRR
THE KIDNAPPER LEFT A THREATENING LETTER, ALL RIGHT.
THIS WAS PRINTED FROM A COMPUTER.
I have your brother.
If you want him back
Make sure to lose today's game.
Refusing to play is not an option.
If you call the police or a detective
your brother's life is over
THIS MUST BE THE LETTER MAMORU WROTE.
WHRRRR
!?
Hideo, help me.
Bring Mamoru back to life
"HIDEO, HELP ME. BRING MAMORU BACK TO LIFE"...?
KCHK
FOR A LETTER ASKING FOR HELP, IT'S STRANGELY WORDED.
BAM

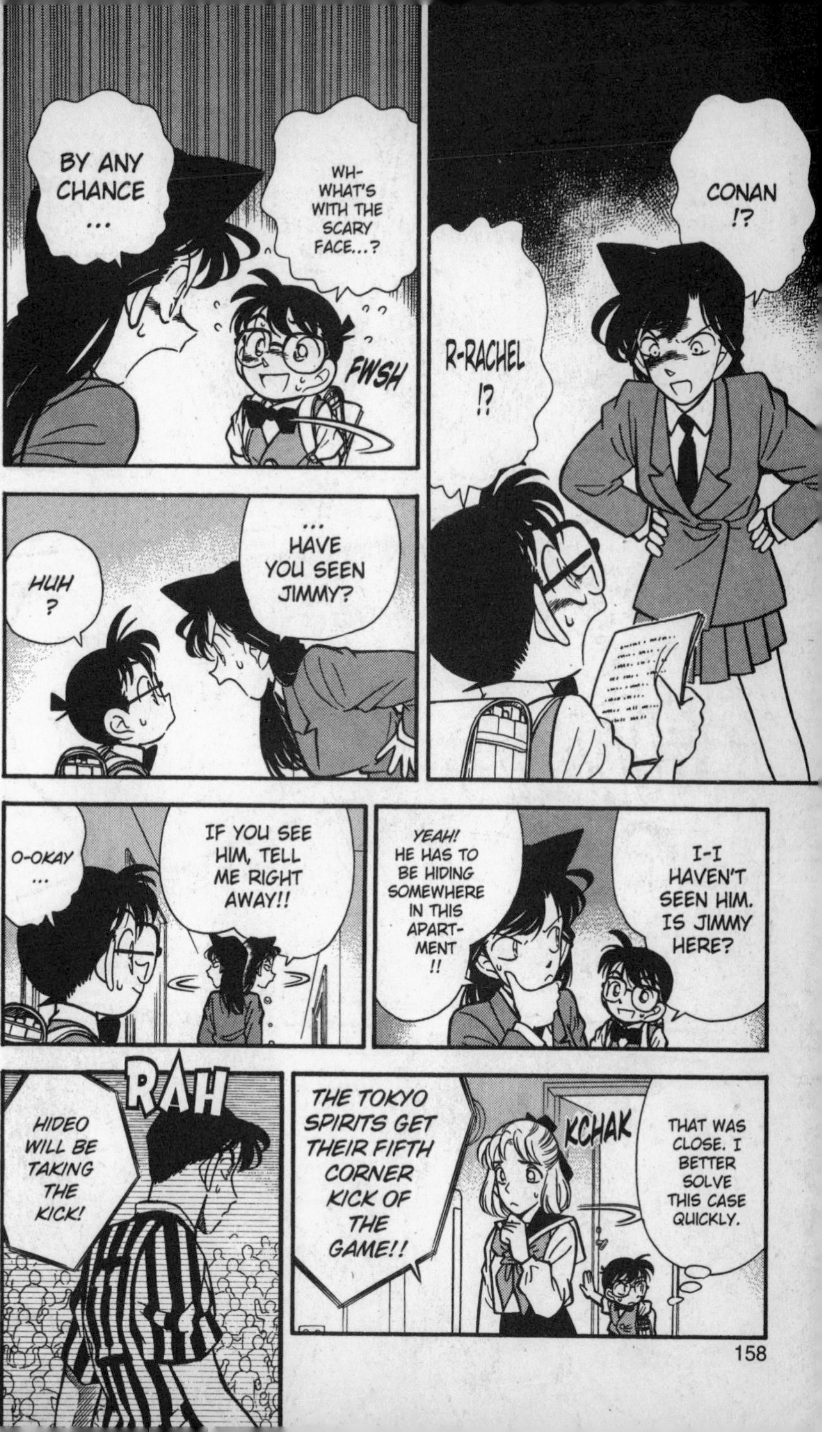
CONAN !?
R-RACHEL !?
WH- WHAT'S WITH THE SCARY FACE...?
BY ANY CHANCE ...
... HAVE YOU SEEN JIMMY?
HUH ?
I-I HAVEN'T SEEN HIM. IS JIMMY HERE?
YEAH! HE HAS TO BE HIDING SOMEWHERE IN THIS APART- MENT !!
IF YOU SEE HIM, TELL ME RIGHT AWAY!!
O-OKAY ...
THAT WAS CLOSE. I BETTER SOLVE THIS CASE QUICKLY.
KCHAK
THE TOKYO SPIRITS GET THEIR FIFTH CORNER KICK OF THE GAME!!
RAH
HIDEO WILL BE TAKING THE KICK!
FWSH

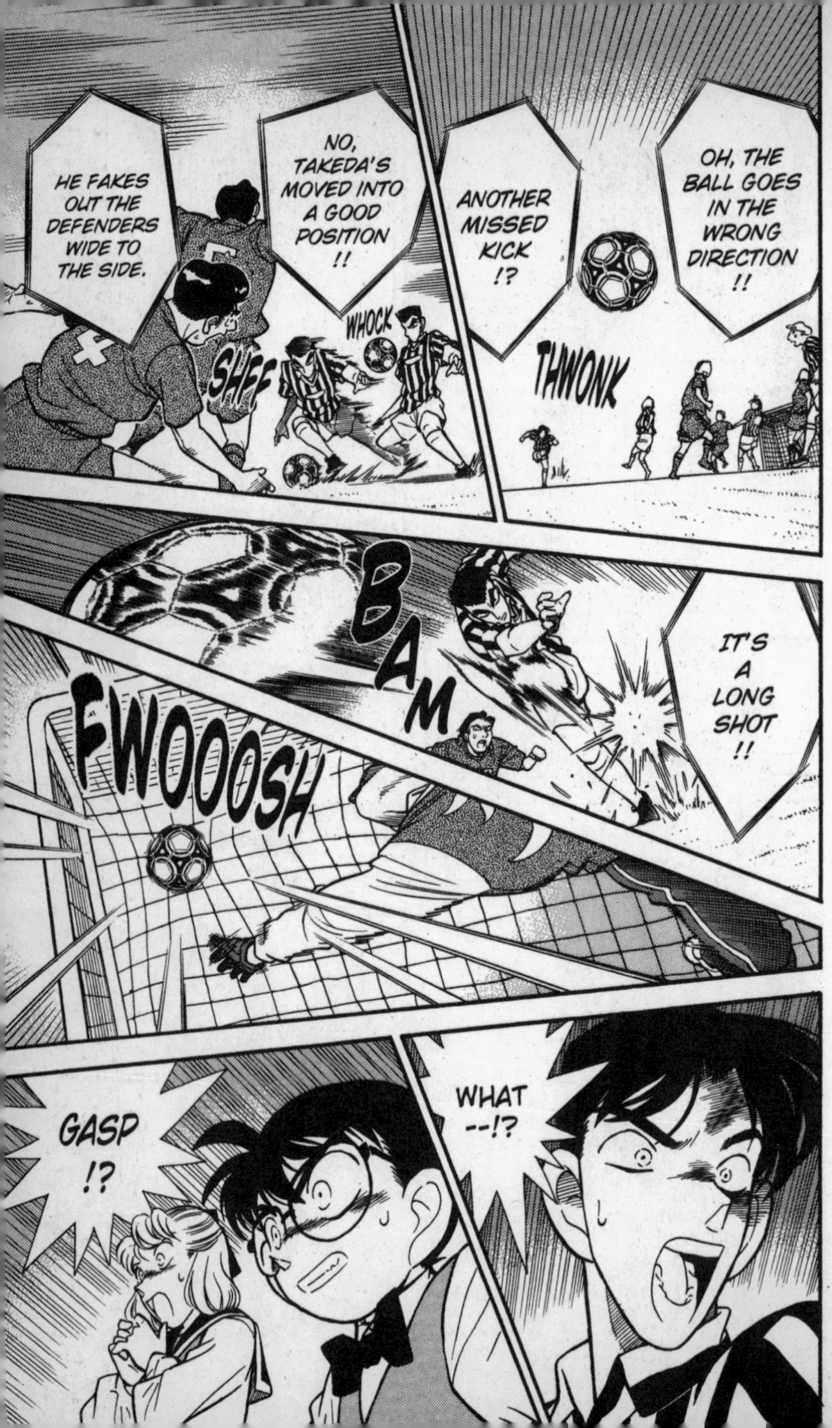
OH, THE BALL GOES IN THE WRONG DIRECTION !!
ANOTHER MISSED KICK !?
THWONK
NO, TAKEDA'S MOVED INTO A GOOD POSITION !!
HE FAKES OUT THE DEFENDERS WIDE TO THE SIDE.
WHOCK
SHFF
IT'S A LONG SHOT !!
BAM
FWOOOSH
WHAT --!?
GASP !?

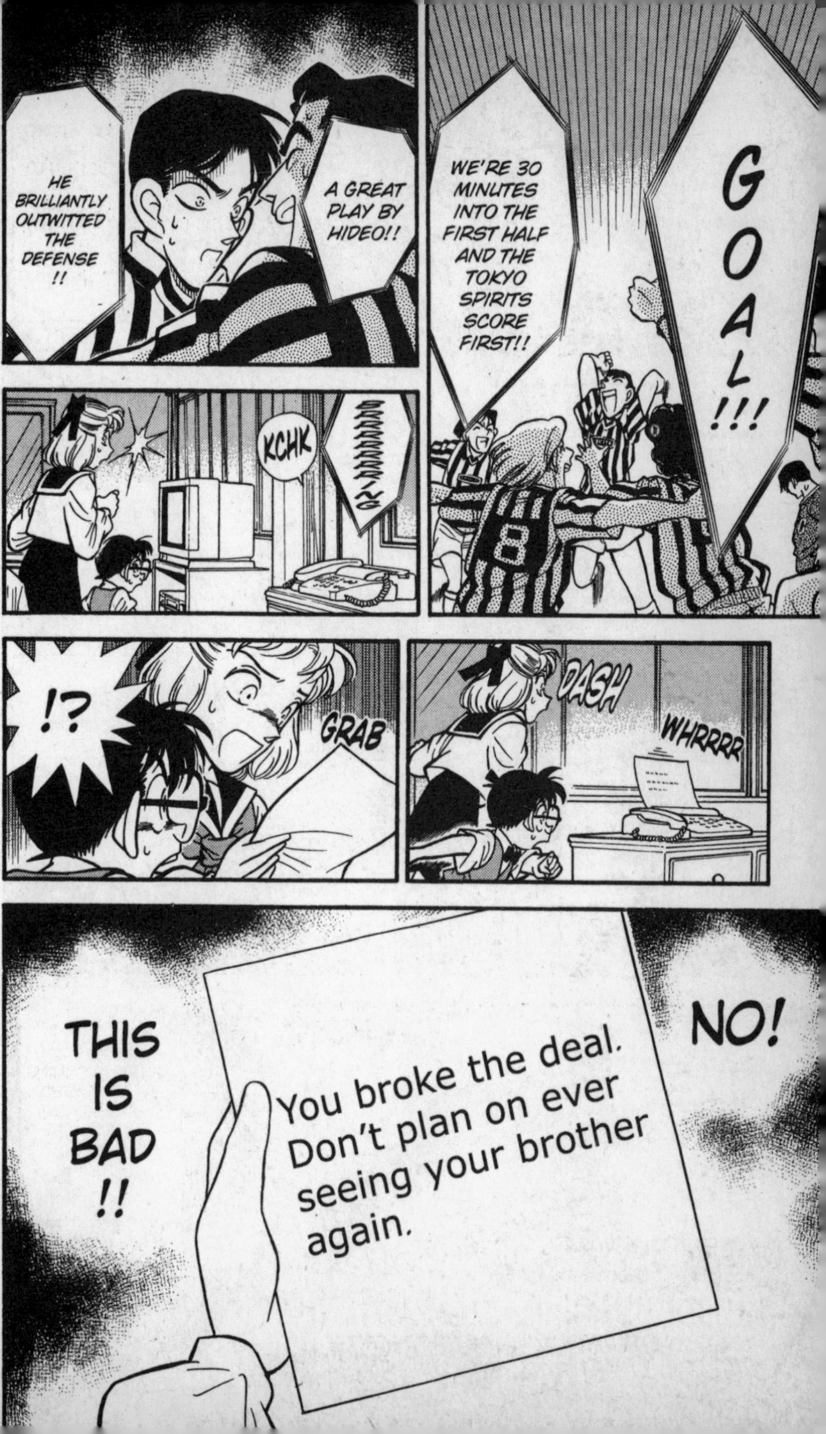
GOAL!!!
WE'RE 30 MINUTES INTO THE FIRST HALF AND THE TOKYO SPIRITS SCORE FIRST!!
A GREAT PLAY BY HIDEO!!
HE BRILLIANTLY OUTWITTED THE DEFENSE!!
BRRRRRRRING
KCHK
DASH
WHRRRR
GRAB
!?
NO!
You broke the deal. Don't plan on ever seeing your brother again.
THIS IS BAD!!

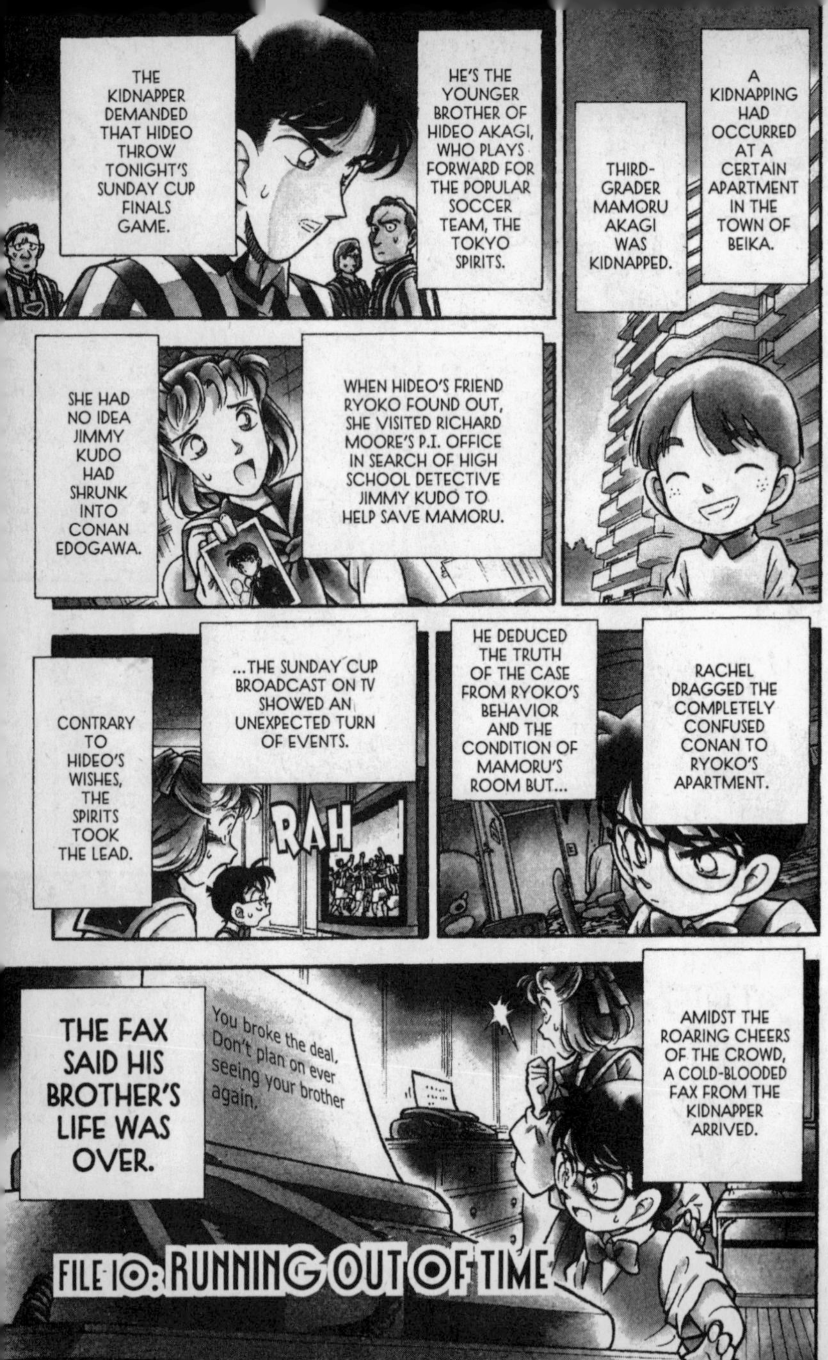
A KIDNAPPING HAD OCCURRED AT A CERTAIN APARTMENT IN THE TOWN OF BEIKA.
THIRD-GRADER MAMORU AKAGI WAS KIDNAPPED.
HE'S THE YOUNGER BROTHER OF HIDEO AKAGI, WHO PLAYS FORWARD FOR THE POPULAR SOCCER TEAM, THE TOKYO SPIRITS.
THE KIDNAPPER DEMANDED THAT HIDEO THROW TONIGHT'S SUNDAY CUP FINALS GAME.
WHEN HIDEO'S FRIEND RYOKO FOUND OUT, SHE VISITED RICHARD MOORE'S P.I. OFFICE IN SEARCH OF HIGH SCHOOL DETECTIVE JIMMY KUDO TO HELP SAVE MAMORU.
SHE HAD NO IDEA JIMMY KUDO HAD SHRUNK INTO CONAN EDOGAWA.
RACHEL DRAGGED THE COMPLETELY CONFUSED CONAN TO RYOKO'S APARTMENT.
HE DEDUCED THE TRUTH OF THE CASE FROM RYOKO'S BEHAVIOR AND THE CONDITION OF MAMORU'S ROOM BUT...
...THE SUNDAY CUP BROADCAST ON TV SHOWED AN UNEXPECTED TURN OF EVENTS.
CONTRARY TO HIDEO'S WISHES, THE SPIRITS TOOK THE LEAD.
RAH
AMIDST THE ROARING CHEERS OF THE CROWD, A COLD-BLOODED FAX FROM THE KIDNAPPER ARRIVED.
You broke the deal. Don't plan on ever seeing your brother again.
THE FAX SAID HIS BROTHER'S LIFE WAS OVER.
FILE 10: RUNNING OUT OF TIME

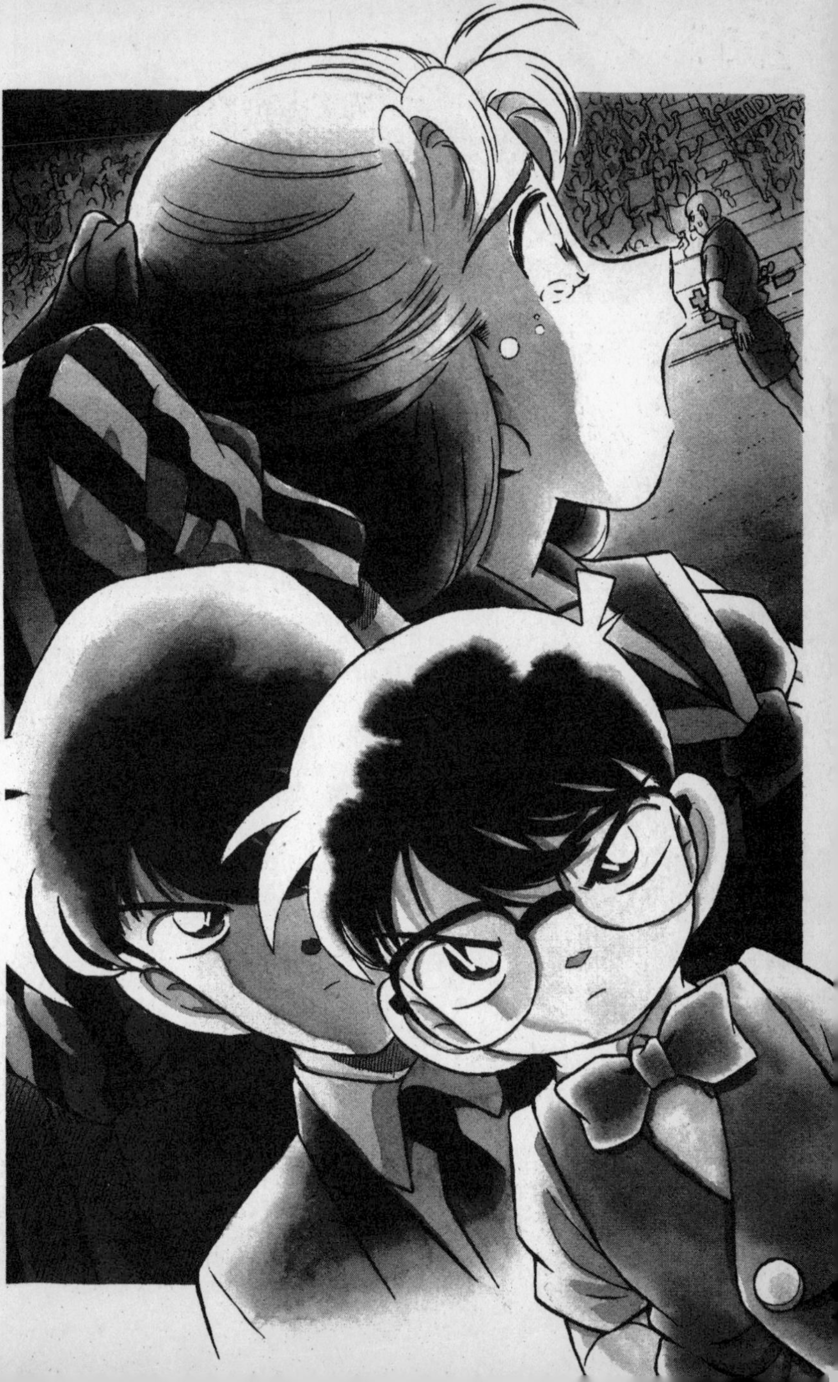

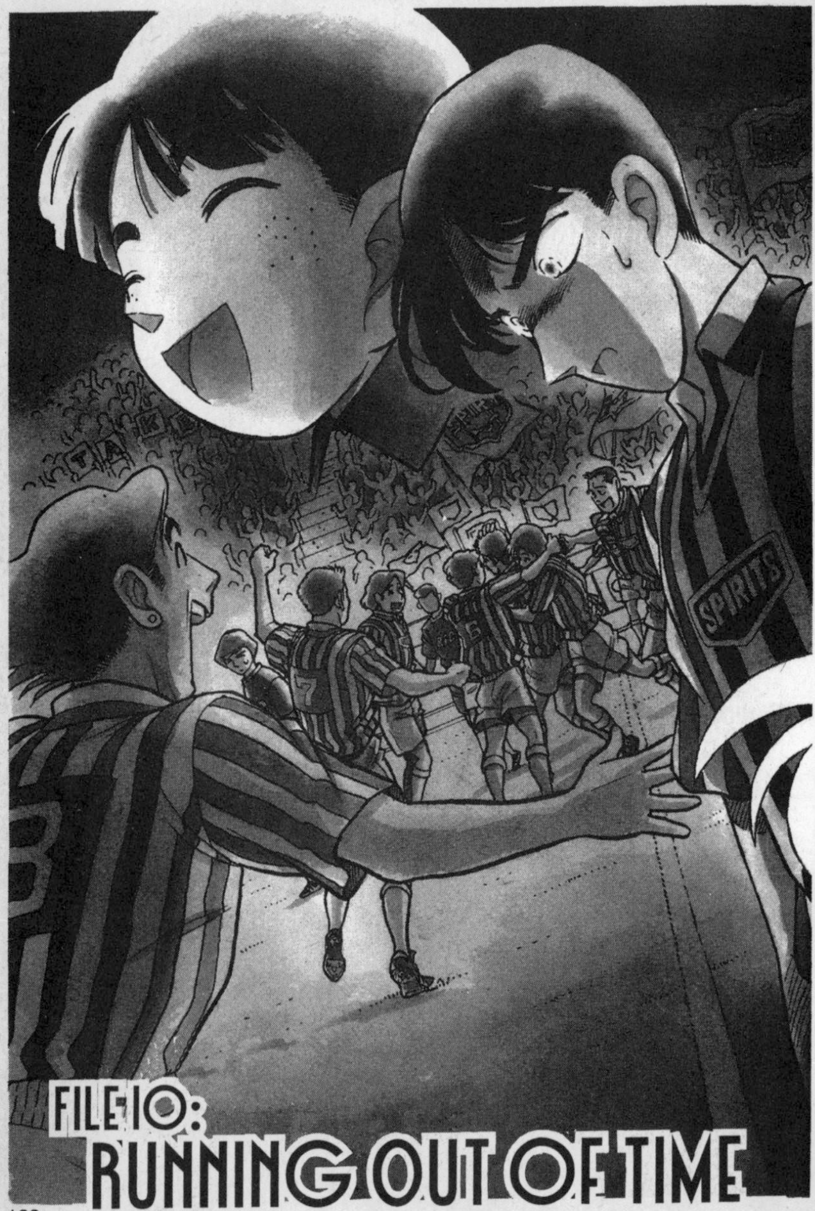
SPIRITS

FILE 10: RUNNING OUT OF TIME

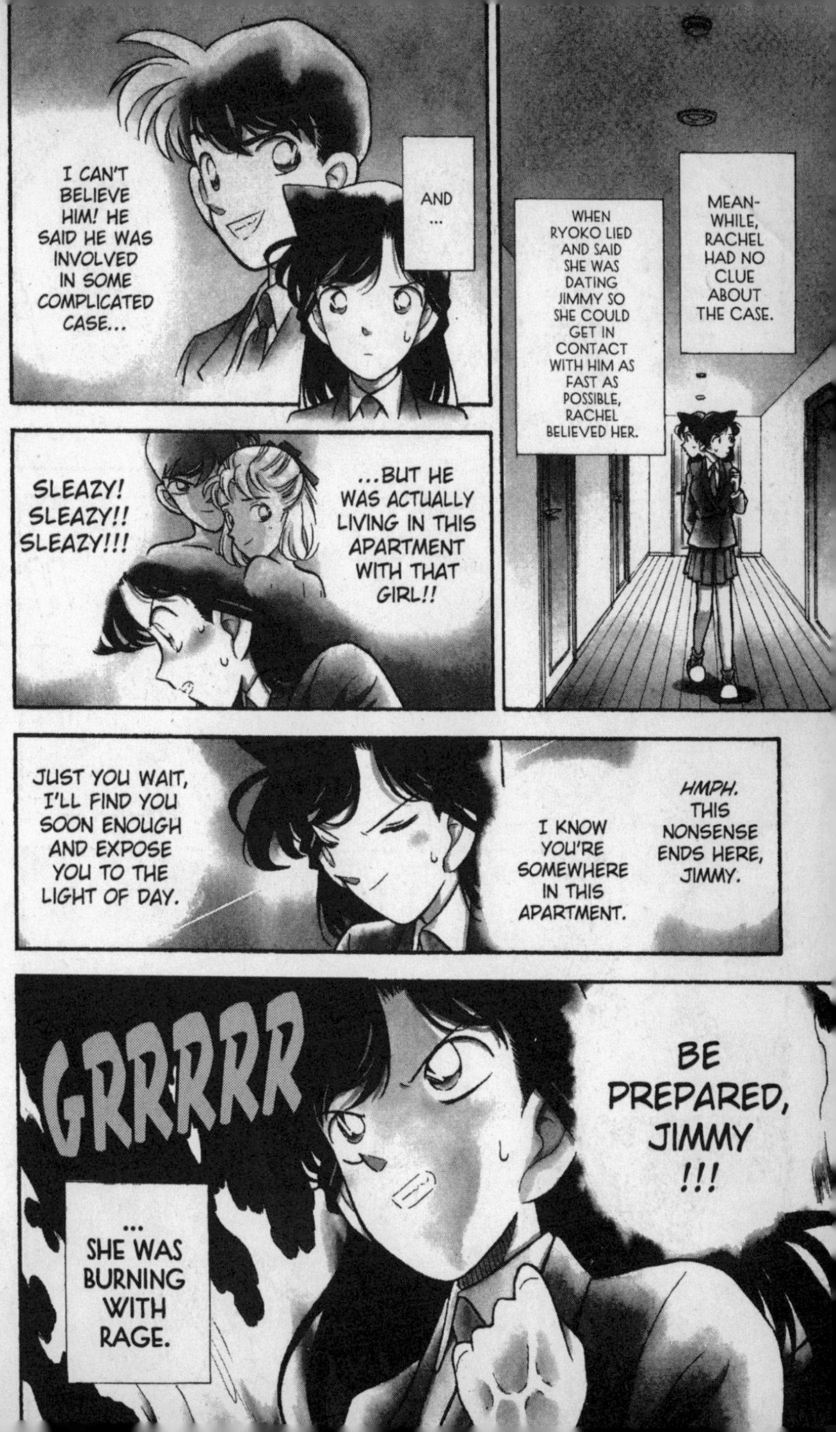
MEAN-
WHILE,
RACHEL
HAD NO
CLUE
ABOUT
THE CASE.
WHEN RYOKO LIED AND SAID SHE WAS DATING JIMMY SO SHE COULD GET IN CONTACT WITH HIM AS FAST AS POSSIBLE, RACHEL BELIEVED HER.
AND ...
I CAN'T BELIEVE HIM! HE SAID HE WAS INVOLVED IN SOME COMPLICATED CASE...
...BUT HE WAS ACTUALLY LIVING IN THIS APARTMENT WITH THAT GIRL!!
SLEAZY! SLEAZY!! SLEAZY!!!
HMPH. THIS NONSENSE ENDS HERE, JIMMY.
I KNOW YOU'RE SOMEWHERE IN THIS APARTMENT.
JUST YOU WAIT, I'LL FIND YOU SOON ENOUGH AND EXPOSE YOU TO THE LIGHT OF DAY.
BE PREPARED, JIMMY !!!
GRRRRR
... SHE WAS BURNING WITH RAGE.

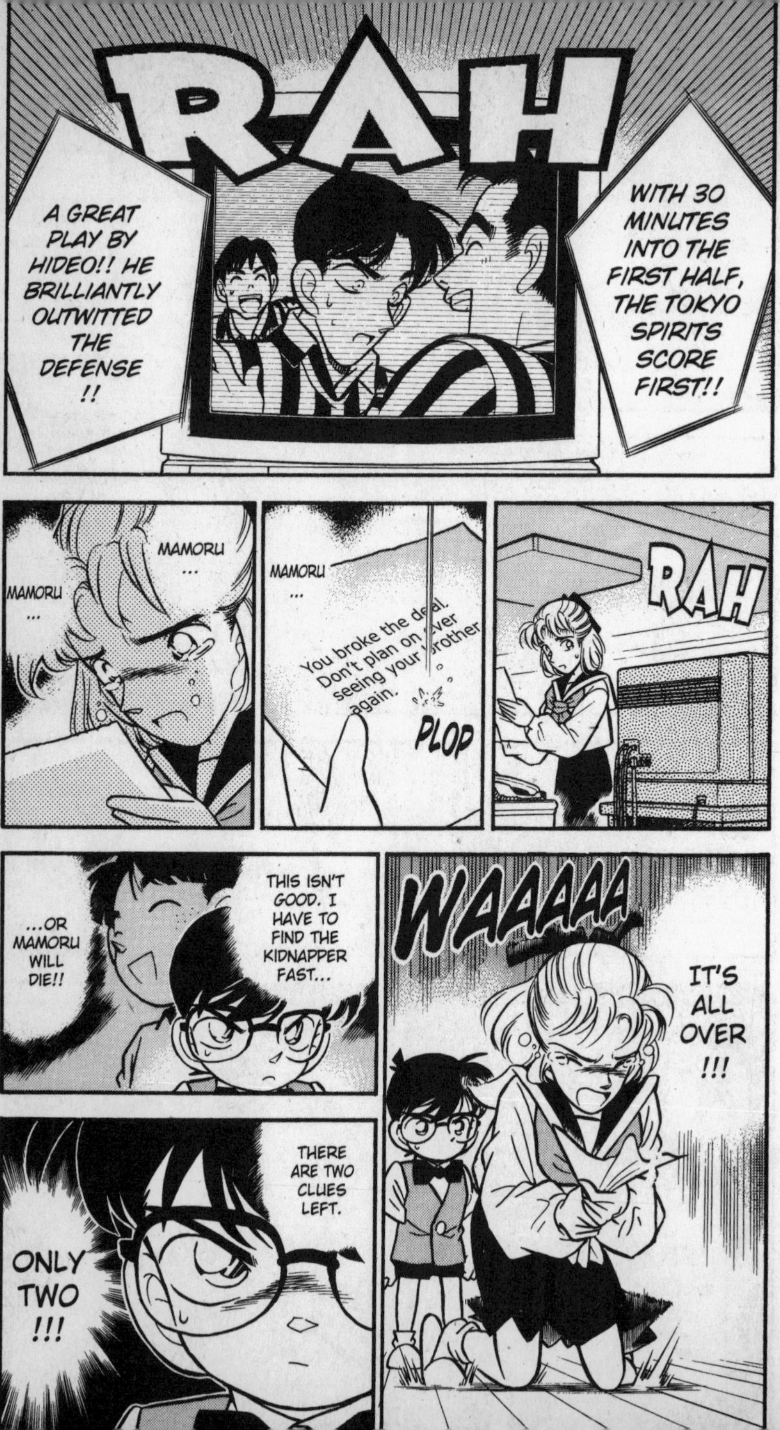
RAH
WITH 30 MINUTES INTO THE FIRST HALF, THE TOKYO SPIRITS SCORE FIRST!!
A GREAT PLAY BY HIDEO!! HE BRILLIANTLY OUTWITTED THE DEFENSE !!
RAH
MAMORU ...
You broke the deal. Don't plan on ever seeing your brother again.
PLOP
MAMORU ...
MAMORU ...
WAAAAA
IT'S ALL OVER !!!
THIS ISN'T GOOD. I HAVE TO FIND THE KIDNAPPER FAST...
...OR MAMORU WILL DIE!!
THERE ARE TWO CLUES LEFT.
ONLY TWO !!!

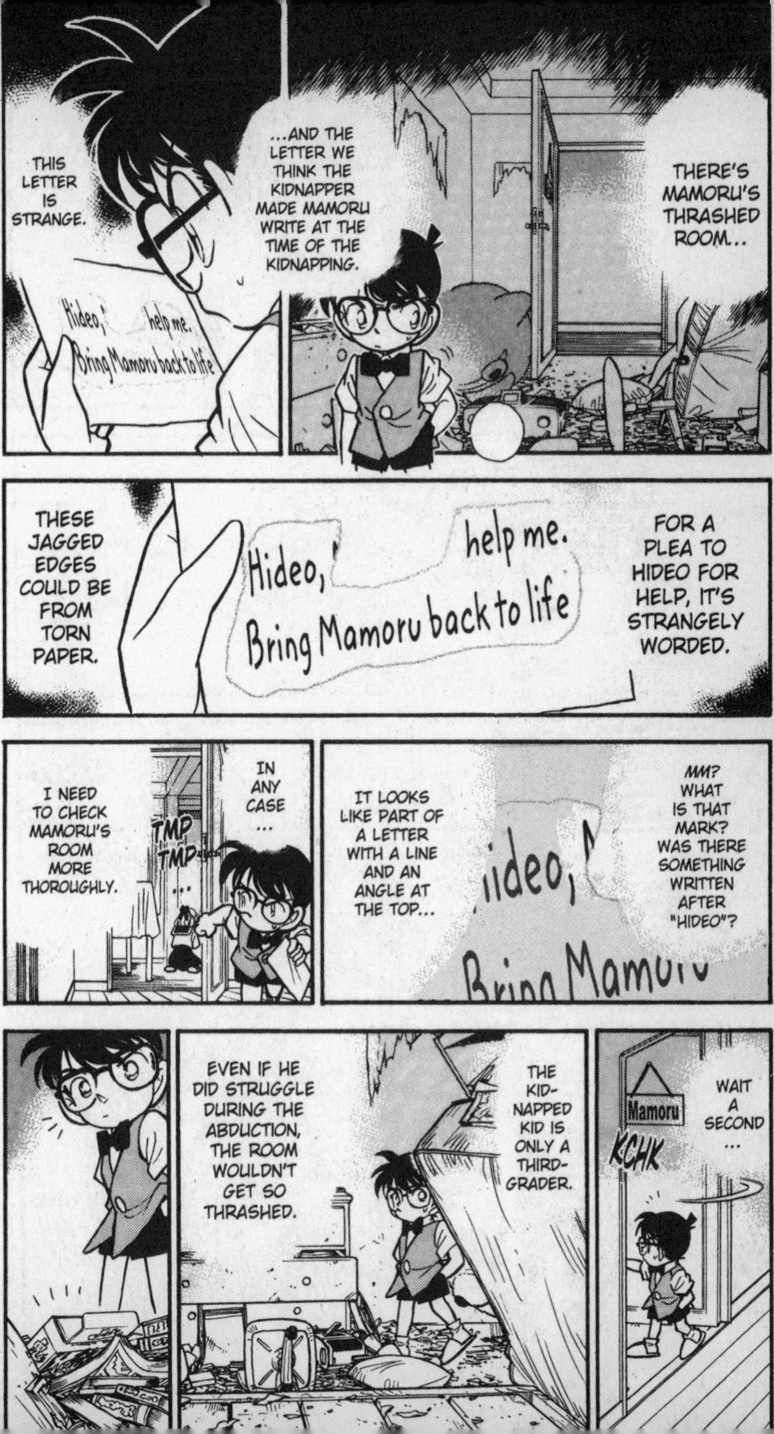
THERE'S MAMORU'S THRASHED ROOM...
...AND THE LETTER WE THINK THE KIDNAPPER MADE MAMORU WRITE AT THE TIME OF THE KIDNAPPING.
THIS LETTER IS STRANGE.
Hideo, help me.
Bring Mamoru back to life
FOR A PLEA TO HIDEO FOR HELP, IT'S STRANGELY WORDED.
Hideo, help me.
Bring Mamoru back to life
THESE JAGGED EDGES COULD BE FROM TORN PAPER.
MM? WHAT IS THAT MARK? WAS THERE SOMETHING WRITTEN AFTER "HIDEO"?
IT LOOKS LIKE PART OF A LETTER WITH A LINE AND AN ANGLE AT THE TOP...
IN ANY CASE...
TMP TMP
...
I NEED TO CHECK MAMORU'S ROOM MORE THOROUGHLY.
WAIT A SECOND...
Mamoru
KCHK
THE KID-NAPPED KID IS ONLY A THIRD-GRADER.
EVEN IF HE DID STRUGGLE DURING THE ABDUCTION, THE ROOM WOULDN'T GET SO THRASHED.

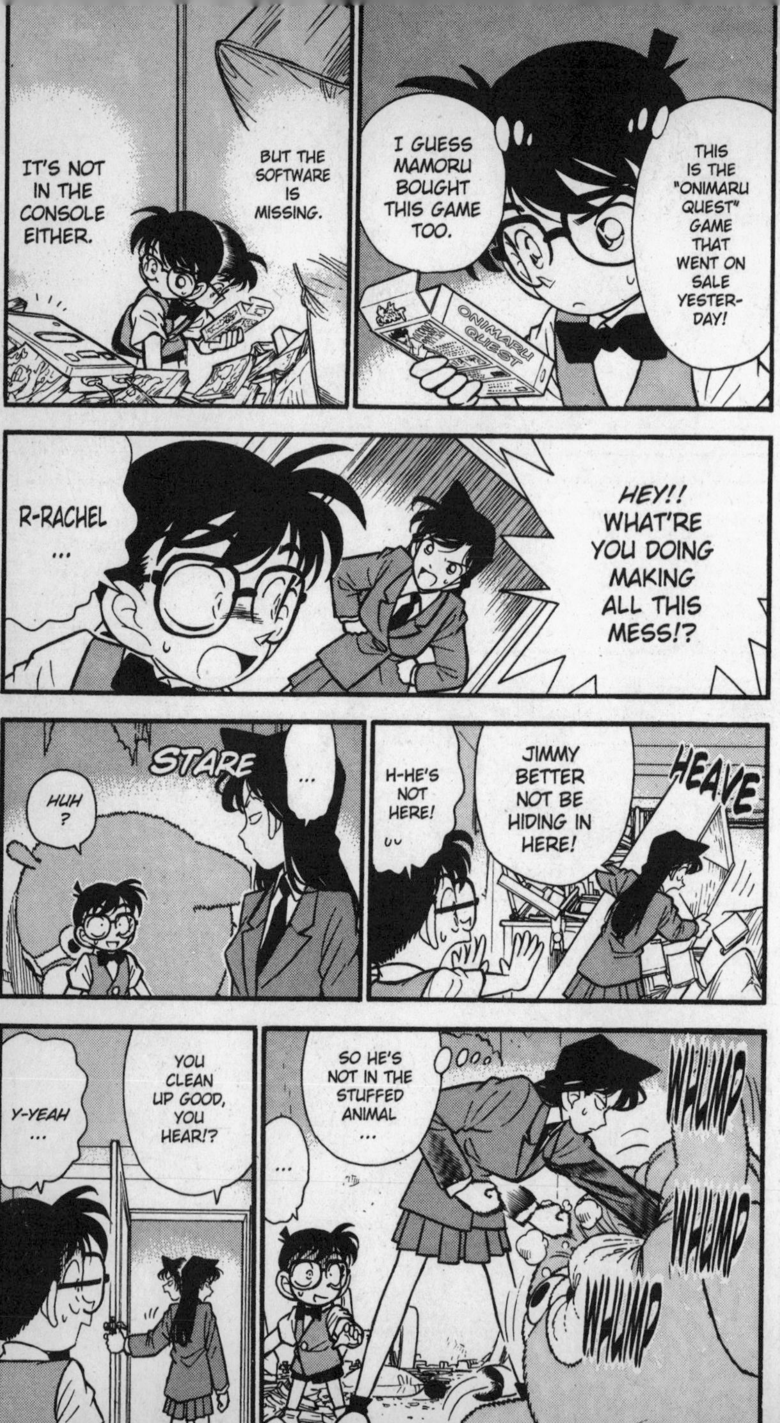
THIS IS THE "ONIMARU QUEST" GAME THAT WENT ON SALE YESTER-DAY!
I GUESS MAMORU BOUGHT THIS GAME TOO.
ONIMARU QUEST
BUT THE SOFTWARE IS MISSING.
IT'S NOT IN THE CONSOLE EITHER.
HEY!! WHAT'RE YOU DOING MAKING ALL THIS MESS!?
R-RACHEL ...
HEAVE
JIMMY BETTER NOT BE HIDING IN HERE!
H-HE'S NOT HERE!
...
STARE
HUH ?
WHUMP
WHUMP
WHUMP
SO HE'S NOT IN THE STUFFED ANIMAL ...
...
YOU CLEAN UP GOOD, YOU HEAR!?
Y-YEAH ...

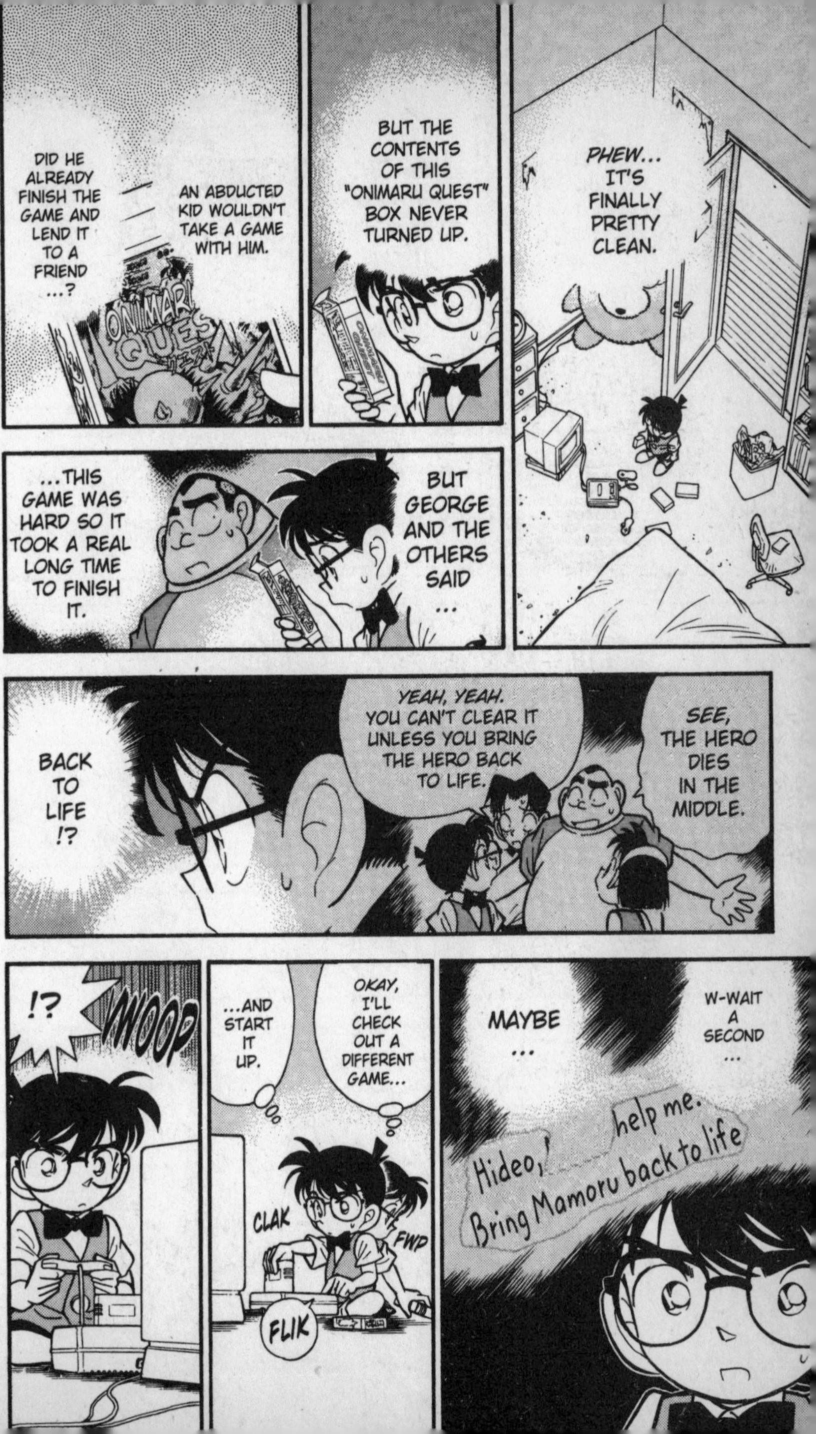
PHEW... IT'S FINALLY PRETTY CLEAN.
BUT THE CONTENTS OF THIS "ONIMARU QUEST" BOX NEVER TURNED UP.
AN ABDUCTED KID WOULDN'T TAKE A GAME WITH HIM.
DID HE ALREADY FINISH THE GAME AND LEND IT TO A FRIEND ...?
BUT GEORGE AND THE OTHERS SAID ...
...THIS GAME WAS HARD SO IT TOOK A REAL LONG TIME TO FINISH IT.
SEE, THE HERO DIES IN THE MIDDLE.
YEAH, YEAH. YOU CAN'T CLEAR IT UNLESS YOU BRING THE HERO BACK TO LIFE.
BACK TO LIFE !?
W-WAIT A SECOND ...
MAYBE ...
Hideo, help me.
Bring Mamoru back to life
OKAY, I'LL CHECK OUT A DIFFERENT GAME...
...AND START IT UP.
FWP
CLAK
FLIK
VWOOP
!?

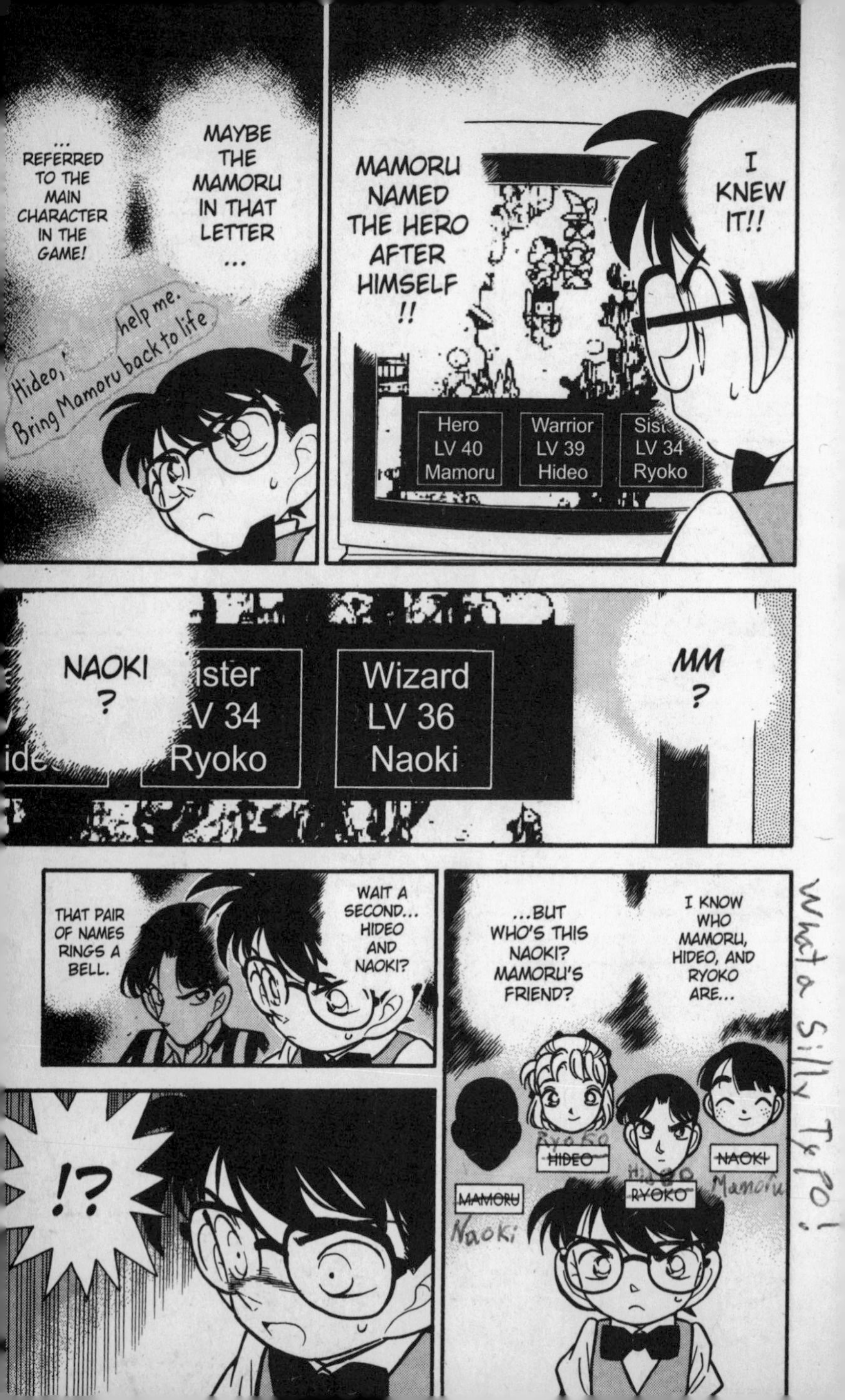
I KNEW IT!!
MAMORU NAMED THE HERO AFTER HIMSELF!!
Hero LV 40 Mamoru
Warrior LV 39 Hideo
LV 34 Ryoko
MAYBE THE MAMORU IN THAT LETTER...
...REFERRED TO THE MAIN CHARACTER IN THE GAME!
Hideo, help me.
Bring Mamoru back to life
MM?
NAOKI?
LV 34 Ryoko
Wizard LV 36 Naoki
I KNOW WHO MAMORU, HIDEO, AND RYOKO ARE...
...BUT WHO'S THIS NAOKI? MAMORU'S FRIEND?
NAOKI
Mamoru
HIDEO
Ryoko
RYOKO
Hideo
MAMORU
Naoki
WAIT A SECOND... HIDEO AND NAOKI?
THAT PAIR OF NAMES RINGS A BELL.
!?
What a Silly TyPo!

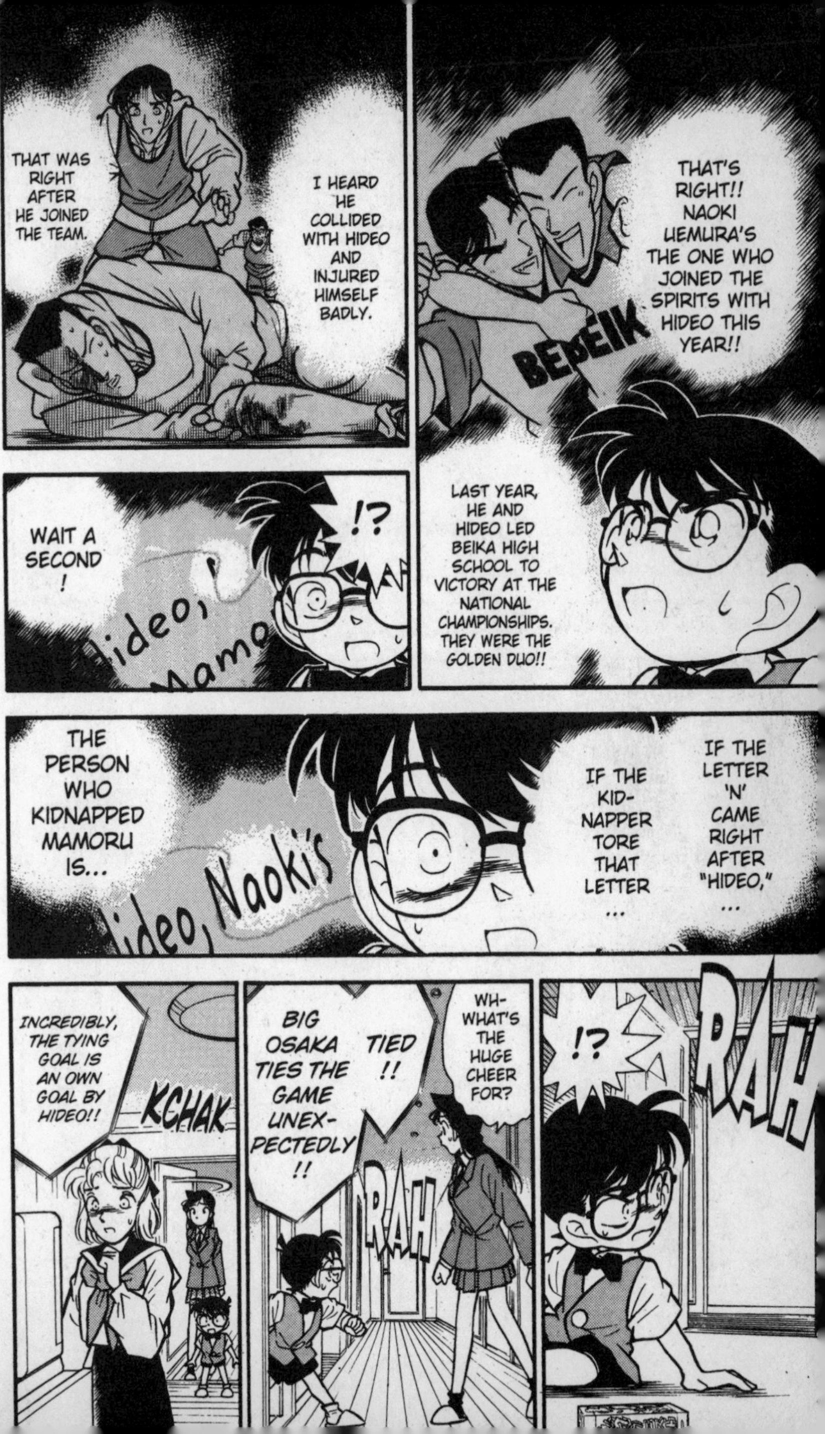
THAT'S RIGHT!! NAOKI UEMURA'S THE ONE WHO JOINED THE SPIRITS WITH HIDEO THIS YEAR!!
I HEARD HE COLLIDED WITH HIDEO AND INJURED HIMSELF BADLY.
THAT WAS RIGHT AFTER HE JOINED THE TEAM.
LAST YEAR, HE AND HIDEO LED BEIKA HIGH SCHOOL TO VICTORY AT THE NATIONAL CHAMPIONSHIPS. THEY WERE THE GOLDEN DUO!!
!?
WAIT A SECOND!
IF THE LETTER 'N' CAME RIGHT AFTER "HIDEO,"...
IF THE KID-NAPPER TORE THAT LETTER...
THE PERSON WHO KIDNAPPED MAMORU IS...
RAH
!?
WH-WHAT'S THE HUGE CHEER FOR?
TIED!!
BIG OSAKA TIES THE GAME UNEXPECTEDLY!!
RAH
INCREDIBLY, THE TYING GOAL IS AN OWN GOAL BY HIDEO!!
KCHAK

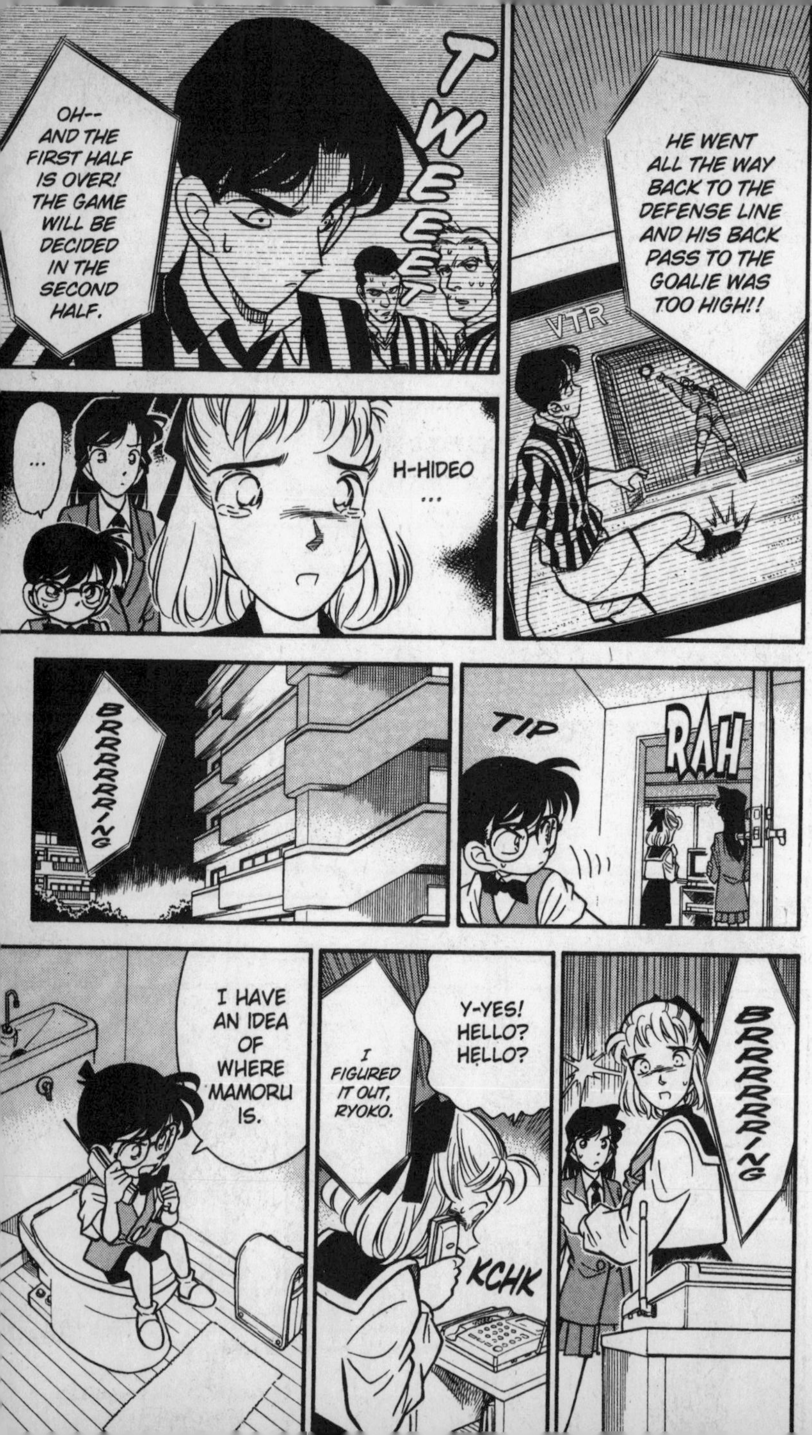
HE WENT ALL THE WAY BACK TO THE DEFENSE LINE AND HIS BACK PASS TO THE GOALIE WAS TOO HIGH!!
VTR
TWEEEET
OH-- AND THE FIRST HALF IS OVER! THE GAME WILL BE DECIDED IN THE SECOND HALF.
...
H-HIDEO ...
RAH
TIP
BRRRRRRING
BRRRRRRING
Y-YES! HELLO? HELLO?
I FIGURED IT OUT, RYOKO.
KCHK
I HAVE AN IDEA OF WHERE MAMORU IS.

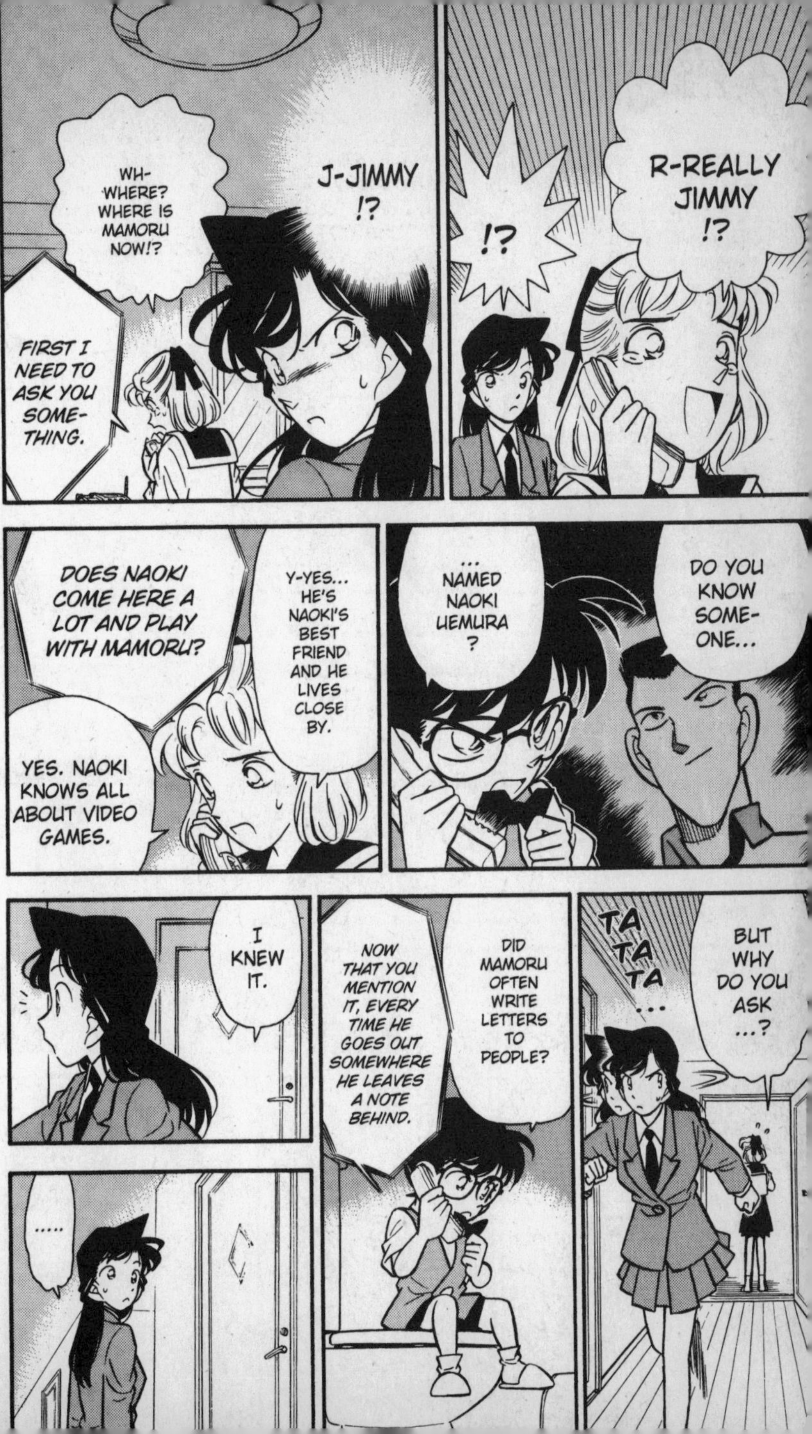
R-REALLY JIMMY !?
!?
J-JIMMY !?
WH- WHERE? WHERE IS MAMORU NOW!?
FIRST I NEED TO ASK YOU SOME- THING.
DO YOU KNOW SOME- ONE...
... NAMED NAOKI UEMURA ?
Y-YES... HE'S NAOKI'S BEST FRIEND AND HE LIVES CLOSE BY.
DOES NAOKI COME HERE A LOT AND PLAY WITH MAMORU?
YES. NAOKI KNOWS ALL ABOUT VIDEO GAMES.
BUT WHY DO YOU ASK ...?
TA TA TA TA...
DID MAMORU OFTEN WRITE LETTERS TO PEOPLE?
NOW THAT YOU MENTION IT, EVERY TIME HE GOES OUT SOMEWHERE HE LEAVES A NOTE BEHIND.
I KNEW IT.
.....

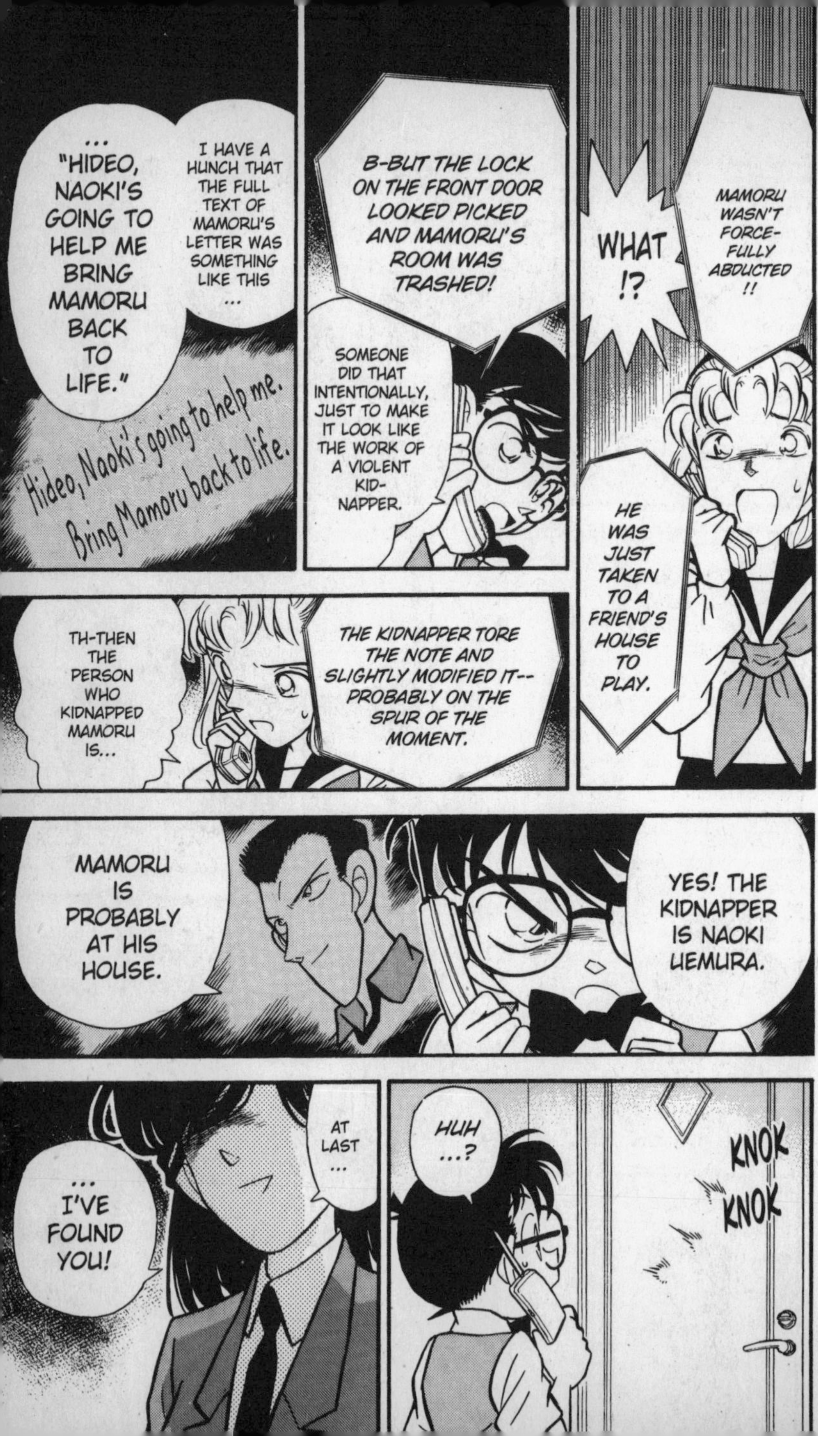
MAMORU WASN'T FORCE-FULLY ABDUCTED!!
WHAT!?
HE WAS JUST TAKEN TO A FRIEND'S HOUSE TO PLAY.
B-BUT THE LOCK ON THE FRONT DOOR LOOKED PICKED AND MAMORU'S ROOM WAS TRASHED!
SOMEONE DID THAT INTENTIONALLY, JUST TO MAKE IT LOOK LIKE THE WORK OF A VIOLENT KID-NAPPER.
I HAVE A HUNCH THAT THE FULL TEXT OF MAMORU'S LETTER WAS SOMETHING LIKE THIS...
... "HIDEO, NAOKI'S GOING TO HELP ME BRING MAMORU BACK TO LIFE."
Hideo, Naoki's going to help me. Bring Mamoru back to life.
THE KIDNAPPER TORE THE NOTE AND SLIGHTLY MODIFIED IT-- PROBABLY ON THE SPUR OF THE MOMENT.
TH-THEN THE PERSON WHO KIDNAPPED MAMORU IS...
YES! THE KIDNAPPER IS NAOKI UEMURA.
MAMORU IS PROBABLY AT HIS HOUSE.
KNOK KNOK
HUH...?
AT LAST...
... I'VE FOUND YOU!

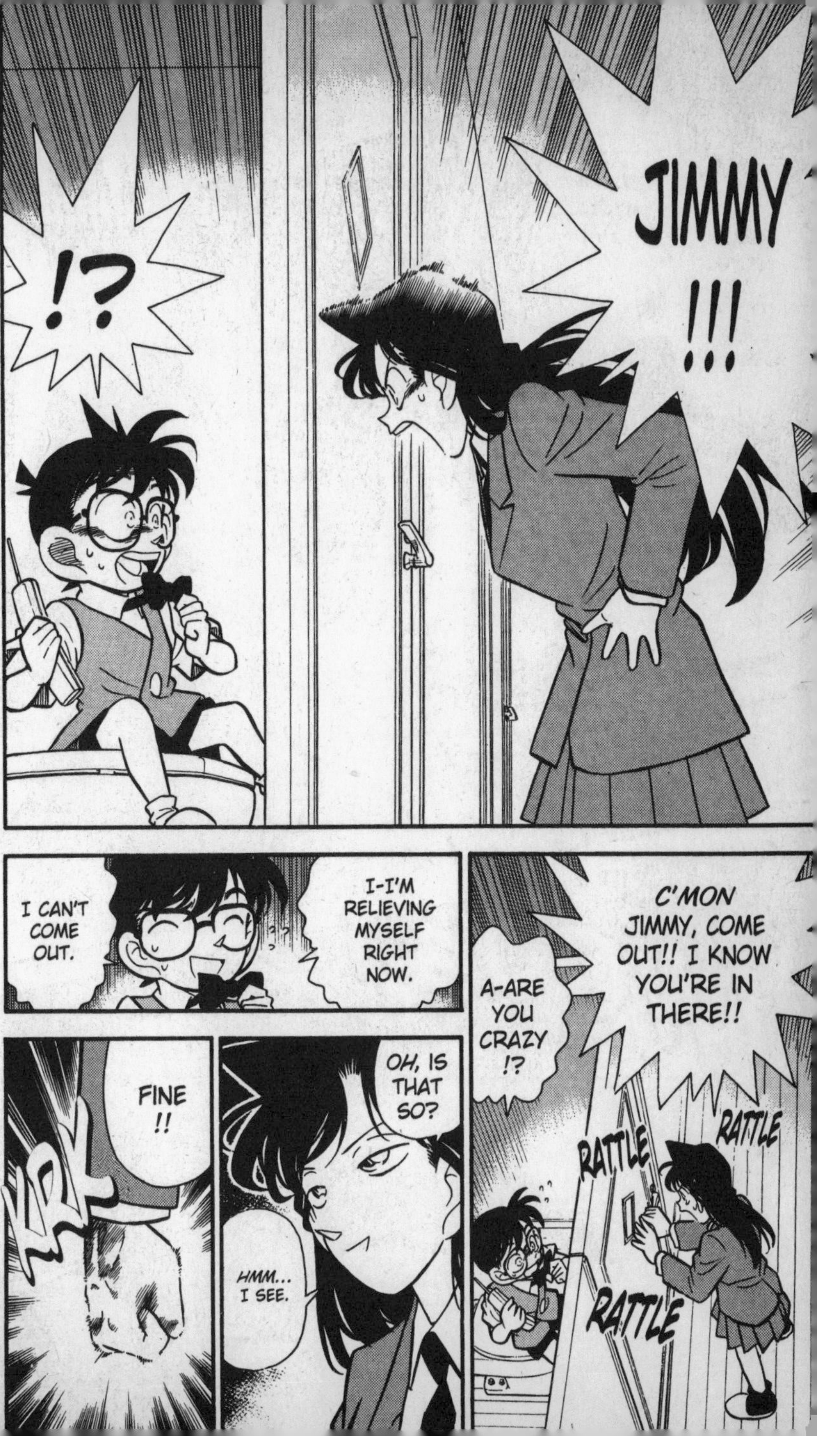
JIMMY !!!
!?
C'MON JIMMY, COME OUT!! I KNOW YOU'RE IN THERE!!
A-ARE YOU CRAZY !?
RATTLE
RATTLE
RATTLE
I-I'M RELIEVING MYSELF RIGHT NOW.
I CAN'T COME OUT.
OH, IS THAT SO?
HMM... I SEE.
FINE !!

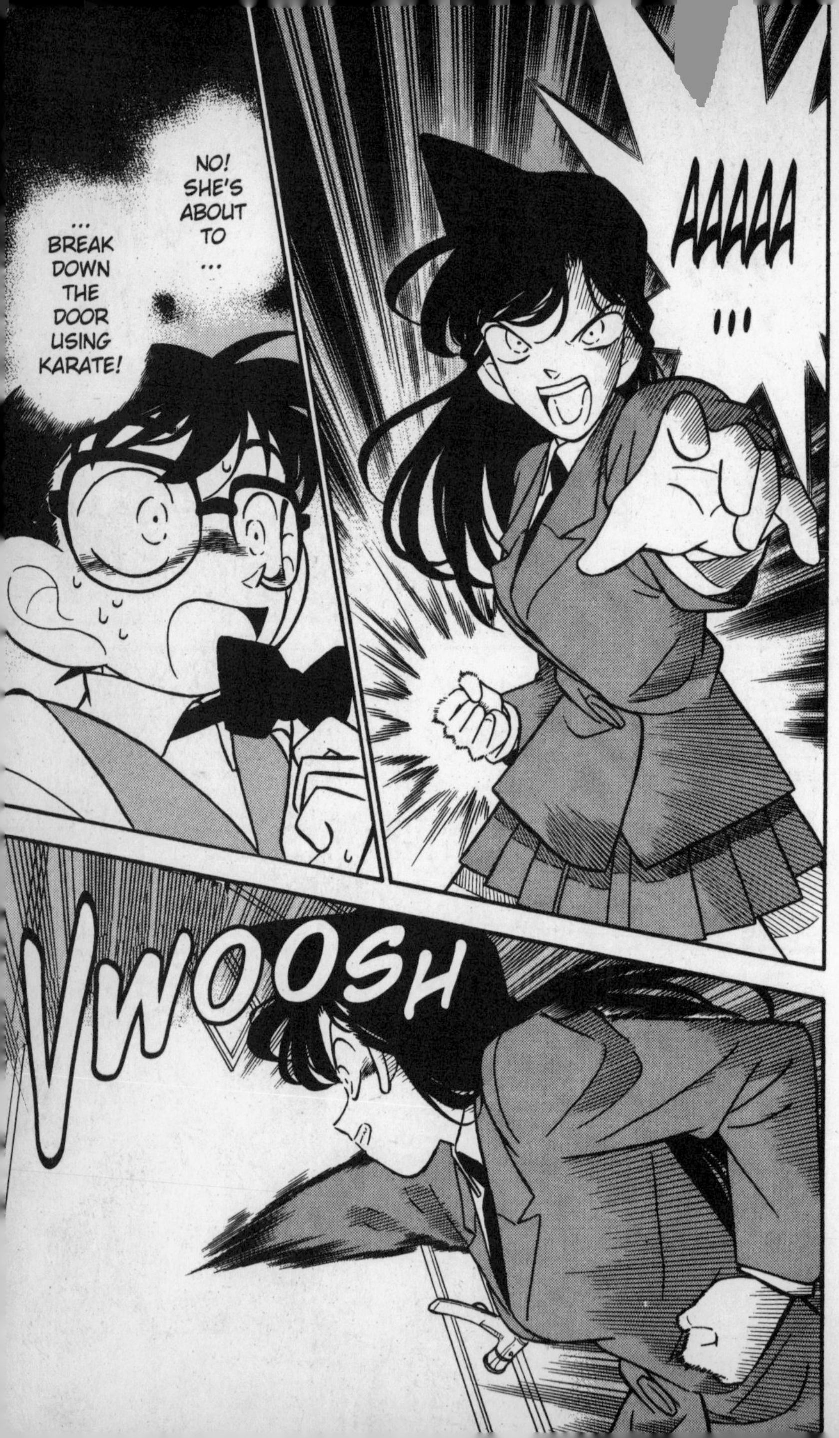
AAAAA !!!
NO! SHE'S ABOUT TO ...
... BREAK DOWN THE DOOR USING KARATE!
VWOOSH

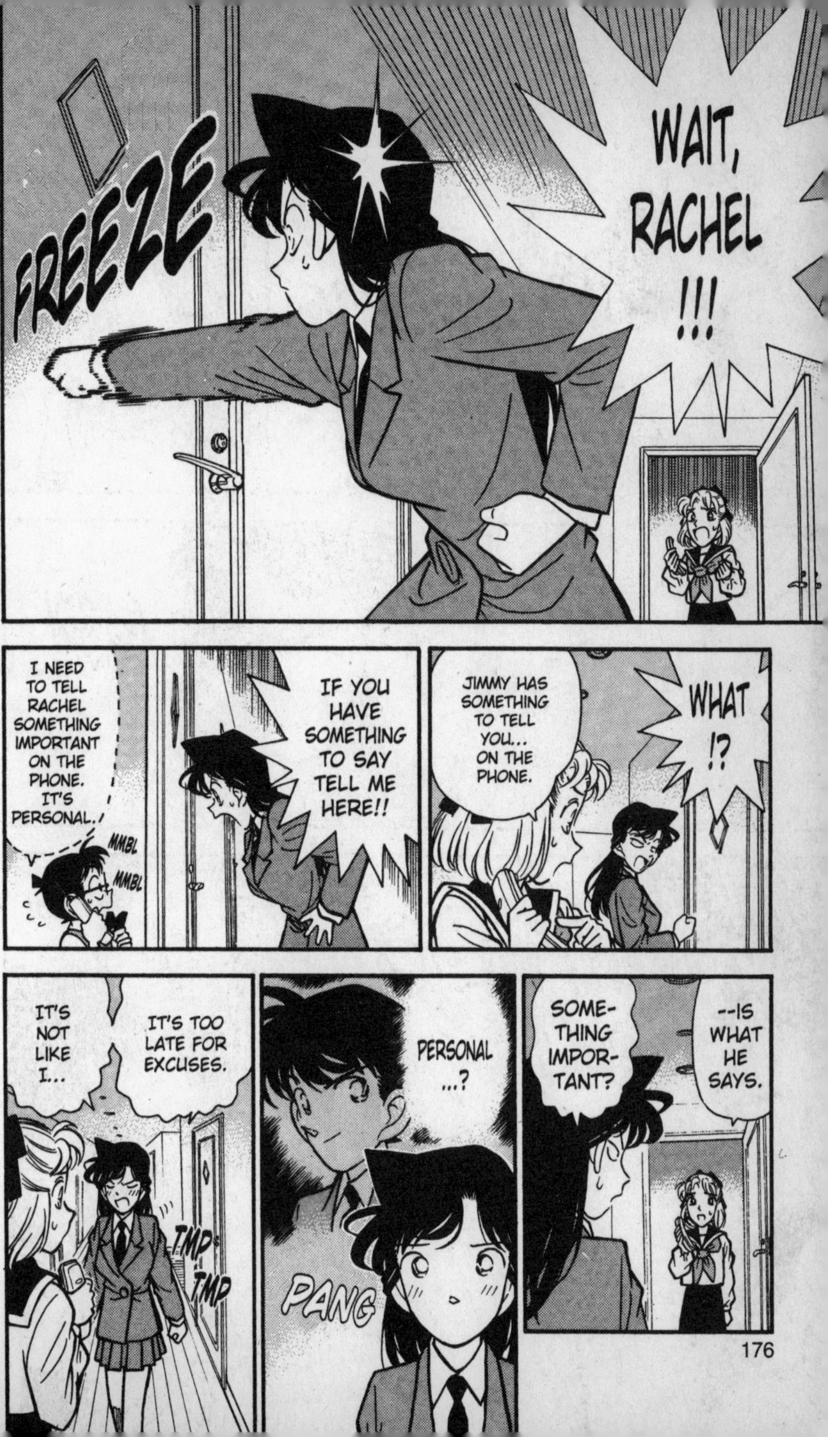
WAIT, RACHEL !!!
FREEZE
WHAT !?
JIMMY HAS SOMETHING TO TELL YOU... ON THE PHONE.
IF YOU HAVE SOMETHING TO SAY TELL ME HERE!!
I NEED TO TELL RACHEL SOMETHING IMPORTANT ON THE PHONE. IT'S PERSONAL.
MMBL
MMBL
--IS WHAT HE SAYS.
SOME-THING IMPOR-TANT?
PERSONAL ...?
PANG
IT'S TOO LATE FOR EXCUSES.
IT'S NOT LIKE I...
TMP
TMP

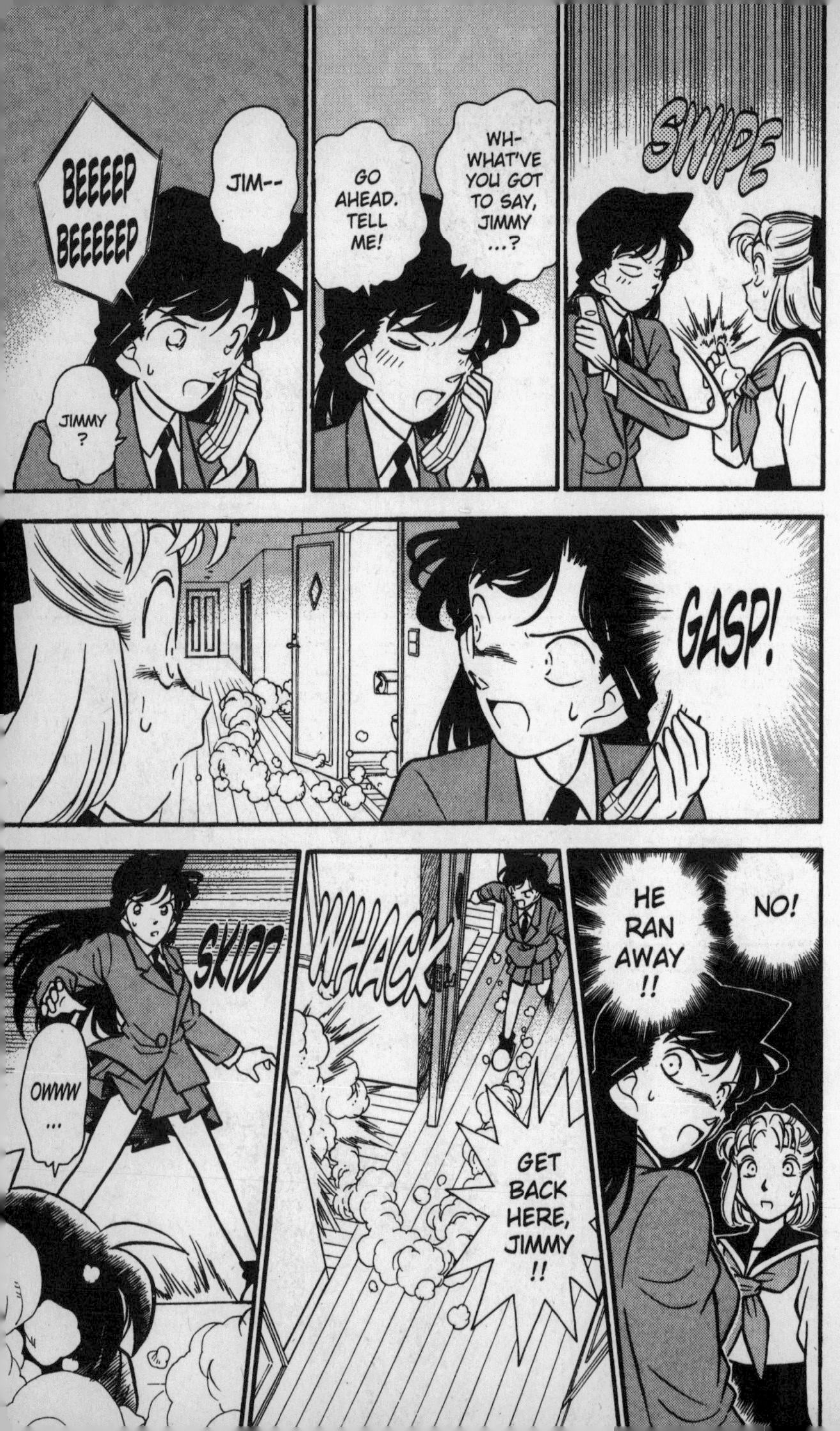
SWIPE
WH-WHAT'VE YOU GOT TO SAY, JIMMY ...?
GO AHEAD. TELL ME!
JIM--
BEEEEP BEEEEEP
JIMMY ?
GASP!
NO!
HE RAN AWAY !!
WHACK
GET BACK HERE, JIMMY !!
SKIDD
OWWW ...

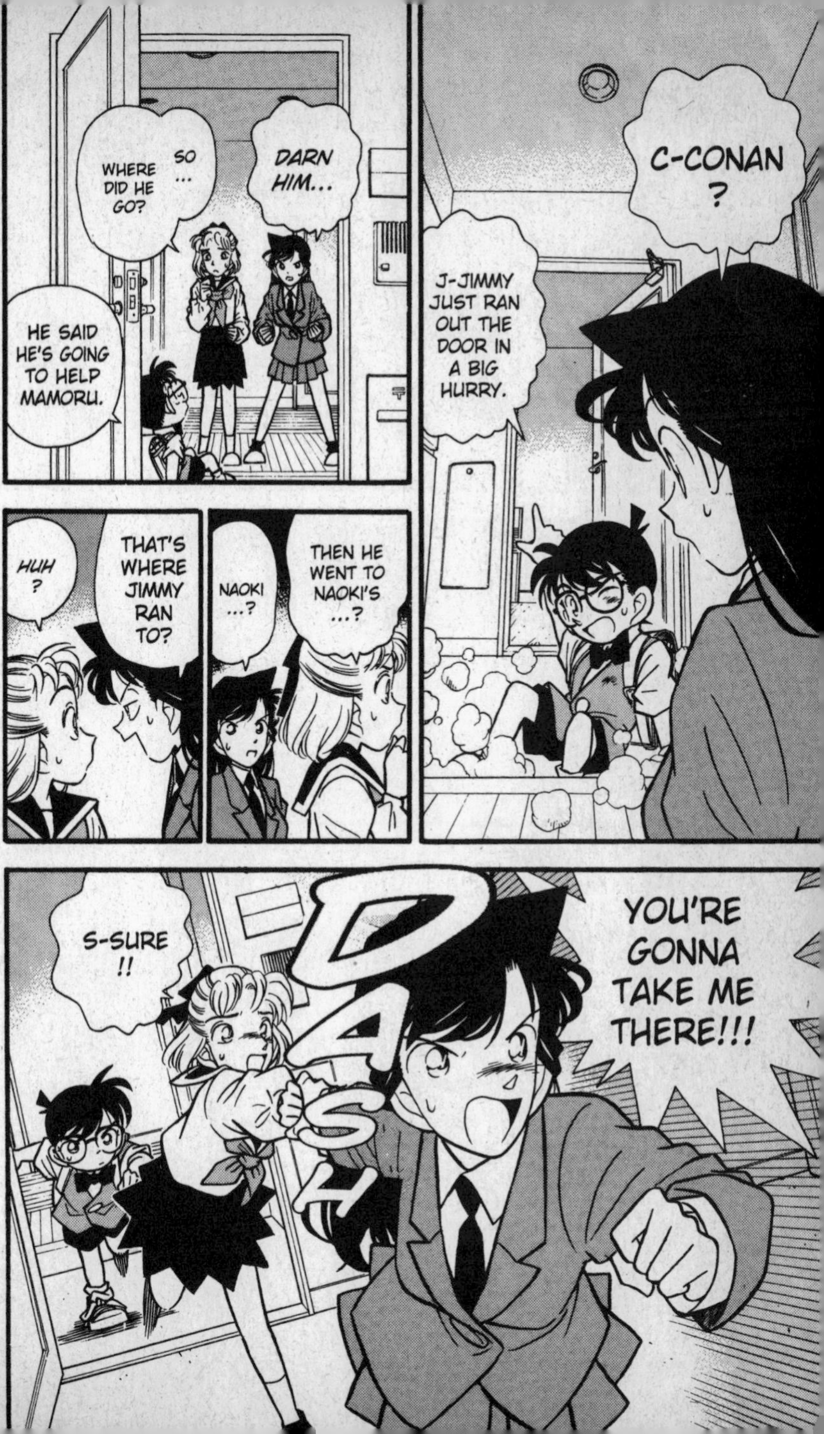
C-CONAN ?
J-JIMMY JUST RAN OUT THE DOOR IN A BIG HURRY.
DARN HIM...
SO ... WHERE DID HE GO?
HE SAID HE'S GOING TO HELP MAMORU.
THEN HE WENT TO NAOKI'S ...?
NAOKI ...?
THAT'S WHERE JIMMY RAN TO?
HUH ?
YOU'RE GONNA TAKE ME THERE!!!
DASH
S-SURE !!

Hello, Aoyama here.

Yay! We're being animated! On Yomiuri TV! By Tokyo Movie Shinsha! A national broadcast!! But now I've got way more work to do and I don't have time to play... But that's fine! (No it's not!)

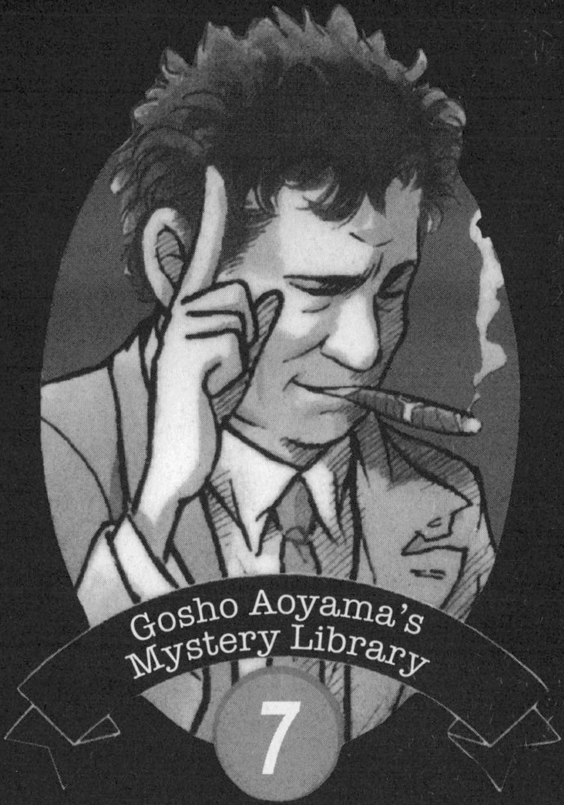
Gosho Aoyama's
Mystery Library
7

DETECTIVE COLUMBO

"My wife says..." he begins, and right away you know this detective with the Los Angeles Police Department's Homicide unit has got to be Lieutenant Columbo!! With a shabby raincoat and shaggy bed head, he drives around in a beat-up old car and drops ashes from cheap cigars. He's the perfect picture of a dull middle-aged man. You would never imagine him to be the great Lieutenant who solves one impregnable perfect crime after another with his superb deductive powers!! When questioning a suspect he is always humble, chatting away about unrelated matters and boring the listener. In fact the conversation is laced with clever traps that make criminals dig their own graves, so don't be caught off guard!! He is just so persistent! Once he's sussed out his suspects, he hounds them daily. He pursues them psychologically and sometimes even traps them into confessing their crimes. If I were a criminal, I think I would lay bare my crimes the instant I met him. I recommend "Any Old Port in a Storm."

EDITOR'S RECOMMENDATIONS

If you enjoyed this volume of **CASE CLOSED** then here's some more manga you might be interested in.

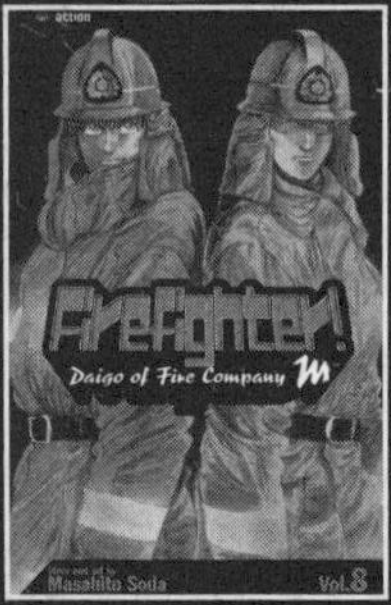

action
Firefighter!
Daigo of Fire Company M
Masahito Soda
Vol.8

Firefighter! Daigo of Company M
Story-driven manga about ordinary people doing extraordinary things. Meet Daigo Asahina—straight out of firefighting school, he's cocky and over-confident...until he goes out on his first call. He's got a lot to learn before he can call himself a true firefighter.

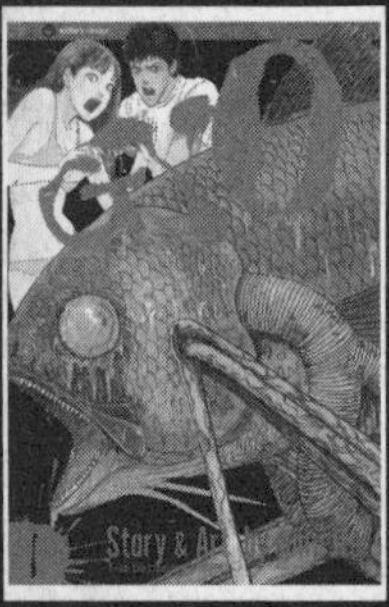

GYO
With hits like *UZUMAKI* and *TOMIE*, Junji Ito is Japan's manga master of horror. In *GYO*, something fishy is going down in Okinawa...something very fishy. With rich and detailed artwork and a creepy suspense filled storyline, this one is a real page-turner!

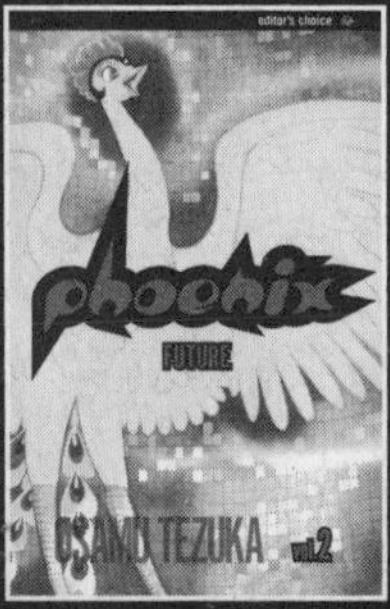

editor's choice
phoenix
FUTURE
OSAMU TEZUKA
vol.2

PHOENIX: A TALE OF THE FUTURE
A seminal work in the history of manga, the epic Phoenix series by "God of Manga" Osamu Tezuka is one of the classics and is a must read for all manga fans everywhere. *A TALE OF THE FUTURE* is a sci-fi apocalyptic tale of the future that starts off being part *BLADE RUNNER* and part *LOGAN'S RUN*, but ends up being much, much more.

action

VIZ MEDIA
www.viz.com

Starting at $7.99!

Vol. 8   Hiroyuki Nishimori

The latest volumes now available at store.viz.com:

Case Closed, Vol. 7
Cheeky Angel, Vol. 8
Firefighter! Vol. 12
Fullmetal Alchemist, Vol. 3
Inuyasha, Vol. 23*
Inuyasha Ani-Manga™, Vol. 11*
MÄR, Vol. 3
MegaMan NT Warrior, Vol. 8*

LOVE MANGA? LET US KNOW!

☐ Please do NOT send me information about VIZ Media products, news and events, special offers, or other information.

☐ Please do NOT send me information from VIZ Media's trusted business partners.

Name: _____

Address: _____

City: _____ **State:** _____ **Zip:** _____

E-mail: _____

☐ Male ☐ Female   Date of Birth (mm/dd/yyyy): ___ / ___ / ___   (Under 13? Parental consent required)

What race/ethnicity do you consider yourself? (check all that apply)

☐ White/Caucasian   ☐ Black/African American   ☐ Hispanic/Latino

☐ Asian/Pacific Islander   ☐ Native American/Alaskan Native   ☐ Other: _____

What VIZ title(s) did you purchase? (indicate title(s) purchased) _____

_____

What other VIZ titles do you own? _____

_____

Reason for purchase: (check all that apply)

☐ Special offer   ☐ Favorite title / author / artist / genre

☐ Gift   ☐ Recommendation   ☐ Collection

☐ Read excerpt in VIZ manga sampler   ☐ Other _____

Where did you make your purchase? (please check one)

☐ Comic store   ☐ Bookstore   ☐ Grocery Store

☐ Convention   ☐ Newsstand   ☐ Video Game Store

☐ Online (site:_____)   ☐ Other _____

How many man

(please check one f

titles?

MANGA

- ☐ None
- ☐ 1 – 4
- ☐ 5 – 10
- ☐ 11+

How much influence do special pr... the titles you buy?

(please circle, with 5 being great influence and 1 being none)

1 2 3 4 5

Do you purchase every volume of your favorite series?

☐ Yes! Gotta have 'em as my own ☐ No. Please explain: ______________________

What kind of manga storylines do you most enjoy? (check all that apply)

☐ Action / Adventure	☐ Science Fiction	☐ Horror
☐ Comedy	☐ Romance (shojo)	☐ Fantasy (shojo)
☐ Fighting	☐ Sports	☐ Historical
☐ Artistic / Alternative	☐ Other ______________	

If you watch the anime or play a video or TCG game from a series, how likely are you to buy the manga? (please circle, with 5 being very likely and 1 being unlikely)

1 2 3 4 5

If unlikely, please explain: ______________________

Who are your favorite authors / artists? ______________________

____

What titles would like you translated and sold in English? ______________________

____

THANK YOU! Please send the completed form to:

VIZ media

NJW Research
42 Catharine Street
Poughkeepsie, NY 12601

Your privacy is very important to us. All information provided will be used for internal purposes only and will not be sold or otherwise divulged.